The Sports

SCHOLARSHIPS
Insider's Guide

GETTING MONEY FOR
COLLEGE AT ANY DIVISION

2ND EDITION

DION WHEELER

SOURCEBOOKS, INC.®
NAPERVILLE, ILLINOIS

Published by Sourcebooks, Inc.
P.O. Box 4410, Naperville, Illinois 60567-4410
(630) 961-3900
FAX: (630) 961-2168
www.sourcebooks.com

Originally published in 2000.

Library of Congress Cataloging-in-Publication Data

Wheeler, Dion.
The sports scholarships insider's guide : getting money for college at any division / by Dion Wheeler.
        p. cm.
(alk. paper)
1. Sports--Scholarships, fellowships, etc.--United States. 2. Universities and colleges--United States--Admission--Planning. I. Title.

GV351.W475 2005
796'.079'73--dc22

2005003152

To all the track animals I ever coached.
You gave me infinitely more than I ever gave you.

Acknowledgments

With Special Thanks To:

Peter Lynch, my editor, who believed in this project and required that it be complete.

Betsy Lancefield Lane—my light at the end of the rejections.

My wife and best friend, Dianne, without whose publishing wisdom and insight and remarkable patience, this book would never exist.

Contents

Introduction

The confluence of two seemingly unconnected and important aspects of collegiate culture combine to create an interesting phenomenon: the distribution of financial aid for athletic ability by a huge majority of America's colleges. Soon after athletic competitions between schools began, it became clear that the student bodies of the schools took the contests quite seriously and they preferred winning as opposed to losing, no matter how much sportsmanship the athletes on the fields of competition exhibited. And they didn't want to win occasionally; they wanted victories on a consistent basis. The winning formula became obvious: when your team has better players, your team dramatically increases its chances to win these important contests. The obvious question followed, "How can the best players on the field wear our school's colors?" Athletic Scholarships (having little to do with scholarship) were created and the rest is Recruiting History.

Is your dream to exploit this situation so you can continue your athletic career and simultaneously have your athletic ability be rewarded with a reduced financial burden while competing and earning your college education? Is that why you are here, to leverage your athletic ability to create educational and other amazing opportunities for your future? If so, you've come to the right place.

This book is designed to help your son or daughter become a successfully recruited high-school student athlete. It is constructed to provide you with the tools, devices, and strategies to give you the best opportunity to continue an athletic career in college and to receive financial aid based upon your athletic ability. For the purposes of this book, the term *financial aid* will include scholarships, grants, low-interest loans, or any combination of the above. In short, *The Sports Scholarships Insider's Guide* is intended to give you an advantage over other equally qualified student athletes who dream your educational, athletic, and financial aid dream.

I am uniquely qualified to lead you through the tangled web of recruiting confusion, duplicity, and unfairness. For twelve years I coached at a NCAA member university. One of the primary responsibilities in my position was recruiting high-school student athletes.

I coached at three high schools in two Midwestern states over a fourteen-year period. Much of this time was spent working with college recruiters, as well as the parents and prospects of those who were being recruited. I have two grown children who were both successfully recruited: one by a Division I state university and the other by a private Division III college. One was an All-American and the other's career was cut short by injury.

I empathize with the positions that all the parties involved find themselves in. I know intimately what each one is going through during all phases of the recruiting process, especially the crucial and fragile negotiating prior to an offer of athletic or other financial aid and a roster position. I owned a college prospect recruiting service. My clients were academically and athletically qualified student athletes wanting expert help in becoming professionally exposed to college coaches. I contacted and often negotiated with coaches and recruiters on behalf of my clients. I am a member of the Recruiting Education Speaker's Bureau of the National Collegiate Scouting Association: www.ncsasports.org. You are about to use the inside knowledge I have accumulated, sometimes painfully, over many years of experience as the parent of recruited student athletes, a high-school coach, a recruiting service owner, and as a college coach and recruiter.

Today, there exists a nearly uncountable number of opportunities for qualified athletic prospects to leverage their ability to play and to learn. More than 1,700 colleges and universities offer athletic programs. That's good news! There's more good news, however there's some not so good news, too. Only 7 percent of those 1,700 institutions offer full grant-in-aid Division I athletic scholarships. That covers less than *1 percent* of student athletes! So it should be obvious that a colossal majority of the opportunities to play your sport and receive financial aid for your athletic ability are located outside Division I. And the coaches of those colleges want to put uniforms with their school's colors on the best players available. *But how will they find them? They need your help!* Although you may be an outstanding prospect, you may well be overlooked and not offered financial aid for your athletic ability, especially in non-revenue sports. *How will those coaches find you? They need your help!* This book will help you help them and create opportunity for yourself, as well. Need more proof of athletic financial aid opportunity? According to an NCAA Executive Summary, since 1981, the number of college women athletes has increased by nearly 98,500 and men athletes by nearly 61,500.

And the NCAA has raised the minimum number of Division I varsity teams from fourteen to sixteen, which means that fifteen to thirty new prospects must be recruited.

Effectively using the information in this book requires that you have discipline, courage, and persistence (fundamental traits of successful athletes). If you studiously follow its suggestions and techniques and are in fact qualified to compete in college (either a four- or a two-year school), both in the classroom and in your sport, you can look forward to being successfully recruited and receiving significant financial aid for your athletic ability.

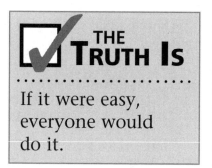

THE TRUTH Is

If it were easy, everyone would do it.

Throughout, you will find statements, which give you the facts: the truth. As is so often the case, the truth has a hard edge. Usually the truisms located in this book are hard-edged. Often you will not want to hear them. Why? Because they will force you to clearly recognize that a journey toward your athletic and academic dreams will not be convenient or easy.

Many college coaches/recruiters aren't going to like that you will know their recruiting secrets. Their vested interest in recruiting as many good athletes as they can for the least amount of money is jeopardized. Because they know the secrets, they can keep you confused. Your confusion benefits them. You are about to slash through the confusion so you can get what you want and deserve. So a word of caution: when communicating with coaches or the NCAA, be very discreet.

Recruiting Myths

1. Division III schools don't offer financial aid for athletic ability.

   This myth is shattered on page 129.

2. If a prospect is good, the coaches will find him or her.

   This myth is shattered on page 7.

3. If a coach wants a prospect, a coach can get him/her enrolled even if he/she has poor grades.

   This myth is shattered on page 35.

4. A prospect can trust everything the coach says and promises.

   This myth is shattered on page 7.

5. A prospect can wait until his/her senior year to find financial aid based on athletic ability.

   This myth is shattered on page 161.

6. Most athletic scholarships are "full-rides."

   This myth is shattered on page 3.

Chapter 1

Understanding the Recruiting Process

This chapter shatters Myth #2 and Myth #4 (see page 5 for a list of myths). The recruiting process is fundamentally unfair. It is unfair for many reasons, but the primary ones are money and winning. This unfairness impacts college coaches, prospects and their families, and high-school coaches. College coaches have to win to keep their jobs. No matter how this fact is shaded, colored, coated, nuanced, veiled, or denied—it is fundamental.

It is the wellspring of the unfairness in the recruiting process. College coaches coach for a reason; they do it because they love it. There may be a few exceptions, but not many. Very, very, very few coaches make the big money of the highly visible basketball and football coaches you hear about.

No matter what sport they coach, when their team competes against another team, the score of the contest is kept. The winner and loser are easily identified. If the coach's team loses too often, the coach will be dismissed (fired). If a coach is fired, it usually means he/she will no longer have the opportunity to enjoy the experience of coaching. He/she will no longer get paid (usually for much less than what they are worth) for doing what he/she loves to do. The pressure on coaches to win is as intense today as it has ever been in college athletics. (Note the scandals that continuously rock colleges from all three divisions. To see the extent of prohibited activity, log on to the NCAA website and access the violations link.) *U.S.News & World Report* has done admirable reporting on NCAA violations as well as other college financial aid issues. I encourage you to investigate its website at www.usnews.com/college. It is continuously updated with unusually pertinent information concerning choosing colleges and strategies for enrolling and receiving financial aid. That pressure may be better disguised than in the past as the NCAA trumpets its laudable attempts to raise the academic standards for college prospects. Recently, the *NCAA News* has been running small strips declaring that winning isn't everything. Look at the facts. You decide.

To its credit, the NCAA is demanding academic integrity from the nation's colleges, along with raised academic entrance standards in an effort to coerce them to pay greater attention to their student athletes' education. The NCAA has successfully reduced the influence of supporters of athletic programs from participating in the recruiting process (although the recent Ohio State football scandal makes one wonder). The penalties can be very severe. Just ask Indiana University's basketball program or Lewis University's volleyball and track & field programs. Yet most administrators would agree that they are under some pressure from the supporters of athletic interests (usually alumni and local businesses that benefit from game attendance) to develop and maintain winning programs. While many administrators try to resist overt pressure from boosters, it's difficult to resist the influence of donations (money) to the institution by boosters. When sports programs don't meet the expectation of contributing boosters, something gives—usually the coach's job or a reduction in the amount of donations. It doesn't take a rocket scientist to figure out which one gives first. In the article "College Sports" published by *U.S.News & World Report*, the authors, Gordon Witken and Jodi Schneider, state that the system's toughest problems arise from commercialization. In the same article, Maureen Devlin of the Knight Commission says, "The analogy is that money is an arms race that nobody will win and that we need multilateral disarmament." In other words, every institution has to give up the money and play by the same rules or violations will continue. How likely is that to happen? You decide.

At the opening business session on January 8 of the 2005 NCAA Convention in Dallas, Myles Brand delivered a wide-ranging speech in which he forthrightly discussed the status of money and winning on institutions' and coaches' motivations for recruiting. He revealed his disappointment after he repeated a quote from a coach, "I was hired to win; I wasn't hired to graduate student athletes." He went on to say, "in fact the security of his future employment is based on winning..."

Why is winning so important? Because, as Brand went on to explain, the money that is used to fund invest-

> **THE TRUTH IS**
>
> A significant minority of college coaches violate the NCAA recruiting rules and regulations in order to stay competitive—and in order to keep their jobs.

ments for new building on campus is "paid by projected future athletics-generated revenues." This means that the more they win, the more money should pour in, which "has resulted in an inflated need to increase wins." Do you suppose this pressure might influence a coach's recruiting motivations?

When coaches get fired, it is painful. It hurts. To avoid losing their jobs, they try to find ways to ensure that they win. Coaches who win usually don't get fired. One of the best ways to ensure a winning program is to have athletes on their team that are better than the athletes on opposing teams. Because most coaches don't want to be fired, they try to find ways to enroll superior athletes. You can decide what this fact means: in 2007-08 there were thirty-one coaching changes in Division I football programs. That's ten percent of the programs.

How do coaches get better athletes? They recruit them. They know that other coaches are recruiting for the best athletes, too. They also know that competing coaches are recruiting for their financial and professional lives. They know that the competition is vicious. If they are to be successful in the recruiting battle, they must be prepared to do everything possible to recruit the best athletes.

We hear of violations primarily in the highly visible, Division I, revenue-producing sports, but coaches in other sports and other divisions violate and/or stretch the limits of the NCAA rules, regulations, and bylaws, as well. Remember the value (and therefore the importance) of booster donations to

Green Influence

The December 20, 2004, *NCAA News* quotes Doug Williams, former NFL quarterback with the Washington Redskins and current college coach, "We may say it's about black and white, but in the end it's green. The big-time boosters and alumni are out there and the [college] presidents and athletic directors are afraid to make a decision that might irk some of their big-time boosters."

college athletic programs and the influence on college administrators that those donations create. Booster donors can be found influencing institutions at every division level. Some may say the foregoing is an exaggeration. The truth is, it's not. Because recruiting is so intense, vicious, and unfair, many people get hurt along the way. It is unlikely that any coach intentionally hurts a prospect, yet because of the mechanics of the recruiting process and the high stakes involved, prospects and their families get hurt.

As an example, if a coach follows the three to four prospects for every position recommendation of Dave Kaplan's *Ultimate Recruiting Seminar*, a multi-day seminar designed to train college recruiters of high-school prospects, three of four prospects for every recruited position are being strung along. I confess that during the recruiting year 1998–1999, I strung along four athletes while my number one choice considered which of many offers she would accept. She accepted our program's offer late into the recruiting season. I then had to call the others to tell them the bad news. You can imagine the response to my apology and my offer that the prospect could walk on and that I'd try to get them athletic aid the next year. Although she and one of the other prospects that did walk on became great friends, my ears continue to ring.

The Truth Is: You Are Entering a High-Stakes Contest Where Only the Opposition Knows the Rules

You need to learn and effectively use the rules to provide yourself a chance to win the recruiting contest. Can you imagine participating in a game (infinitely more important than any state championship) with unknown, non-understandable rules and that when you violate those secret rules you are severely penalized? This is the quintessential picture and definition of a tilted playing field. So, despite my best efforts, it is likely that you will experience some pain. It goes with the territory. However, this book provides you with recruiting rules knowledge along with the strategies, devices, and tools required to be successfully recruited by a college with an academic program, an athletic program, and a coach that is best for you.

First, by following *The Sports Scholarship Insider's Guide,* you will be found. Why? Because every college coach your profile is sent to will know who you are, where you are, what you can do, and what they can expect from you when you begin competing in college. Many qualified prospects are overlooked because coaches can't be everywhere or see everything. *You cannot be overlooked.*

Second, very few colleges have the budgets or the scouts to be able to locate all the prospects who would be qualified to compete in their program. It's that simple. No college coach can possibly know where every potential prospect for his or her program is located.

The number of qualified prospects a coach learns about depends on the size of the college, the program, interested alumni, number of assistants, and the coach's recruiting budget. Coaches of small- and medium-sized colleges and programs want to locate qualified prospects just as desperately as coaches in larger institutions. Unfortunately, smaller schools don't have adequate budgets or personnel to compete. They need help locating prospects. You, a qualified prospect, need help being exposed to those coaches. By sending your credentials, you provide them with the help they need and, ultimately, you help yourself locate the right school, the right program, and the right coach.

Other than the largest Division I revenue-producing programs, very few programs have a sufficient level of funding to make full-ride athletic financial aid offers to the prospects they are recruiting. This is especially true for Division II and III colleges (the bogus assertions concerning no financial aid based on athletic ability at Division III colleges require a separate section, which follows).

Consequently, these restrictions cause the coach to be very careful about which prospects are offered athletic scholarships or financial aid awards. It is essential to remember, for these divisions and for NAIA, that the less money spent to recruit any one prospect (which could be you) means there are more funds available to recruit other prospects. The cheaper a coach can recruit higher-quality prospects, the more funds are available to recruit additional good prospects. This means coaches increase their chances to have better athletes than their competition and ultimately, they can produce a winning program and keep their jobs.

Essential Companion Guide

To be able to follow the suggestions and learn the recruiting rules in this guide, you must obtain an essential companion guide, the *NCAA Guide for the College-Bound Student-Athlete.* You can get a free copy from your guidance counselor or athletic director. If a copy is not obtainable, call the NCAA and request a copy. The NCAA number is (800) 638-3731. The Internet address is www.ncaa.org.

Get prepared. Get moving. Get recruited.

Chapter 2

Recruiting and Financial Aid

While it is not my intention to provide you with a course on comparative recruiting philosophies of different colleges, some discussion of why colleges recruit is necessary. You need some information about the basics of recruiting philosophy in order to understand why and how the suggestions made in this guide can help you achieve your athletic and academic goals.

Colleges offer athletic financial aid and other types of financial aid for many reasons, some more obvious than others. Many big-time Division I programs offer "full-ride" athletic scholarships for the most obvious reason: money. These programs sign and enroll "blue-chip" student athletes so that they can have powerful, winning programs.

Generally, powerful, winning programs in Division I football and basketball generate substantial revenue for their institutions. Very few other programs generate enough revenue to even be self-sustaining and are subsidized by the institution itself. However, most other colleges want to have winning programs, too, but they have additional reasons for recruiting student athletes and offering financial aid based on athletic ability.

Even though coaches may be from programs that are not as powerful, they too must recruit as hard and as smart as they can. But often these coaches are forced to recruit with three additional burdens placed on them:

- The institution's financial aid award packaging formula,
- The recruiting objectives of the coach, and
- The combined recruiting and enrollment philosophy of the institution for which they coach.

Colleges Operate Like Businesses

Most institutions use the awarding of financial aid as a tool to encourage potential students to enroll at their college. Financial aid is a powerful marketing tool used to remain or become competitive in the bidding war among colleges for worthy students. Fundamentally, here's how it works: each institution creates a budget (very few colleges publish theirs) that is required to deliver the level of educational services desired by the institution's administrators. The institution's administration calculates how much money is required to deliver the desired educational services while keeping the college solvent. Generally, college administrators fashion tuition policies to accomplish those two interwoven objectives.

The money required to keep the college operating on a sound financial basis comes from a number of different sources. In addition to other sources of funding, the most important source of funds related to the mission of this guide: tuition, fees, room, board, and other expenses charged to students enrolled in any college.

Most institutions calculate non-student funding resources (*i.e.*, endowment, state funds, if applicable, billable use of facilities, donations, etc.) available to the institution in the fiscal year. The amount of non-student funding is subtracted from the budget. The remainder of the budget must be generated from the tuition, fees, and other related charges from the college's student body.

Generally, figures are calculated that define the number of students required to enroll and what enrollment will cost the students. The calculation of the number of students multiplied by the cost per student is structured to allow the institution to remain financially stable. For a number of reasons, some understandable, others not so understandable, many colleges announce inflated costs for attending the college for that year. The final, inflated cost published by the institution is called the "sticker price," which is somewhat analogous to a new car sticker price. In other words: sticker price = pretend price.

The largest groups of colleges that discount the sticker price are private colleges with substantial sticker prices. Less expensive private colleges provide less financial aid/discounted tuition. Often state colleges and universities have their tuition levels written into law. This type of restriction fundamentally disallows the college from using the flexibility accorded to the director of financial aid to use professional judgment, which means that in the judgment of the financial aid director a financial aid package can be adjusted based upon factors regarded as important by the director. And that judgment is not necessarily bound by the parameters of the institutions recruiting or financial aid regulations, in order to discount the "sticker price." Most financial aid directors have remarkable flexibility in deciding what's important and how and why to discount tuition and fees for any particular student. However, state taxes help keep state college's tuition lower than most private schools and therefore constitute invisible tuition discounts.

According to a College Board survey done during the

2007–2008 school year, students attending four-year colleges paid just $6,185 on average for tuition for the school year. So don't allow yourself to be intimidated by the "sticker prices." There is more than $130 billion, yes BILLION, in student aid available. And over $1 billion of that aid is financial aid for athletic ability. Is it possible that you don't qualify for some of that combined colossal amount of aid?

A *U.S.News & World Report* article, "America's Best Colleges," which recommended methods for cutting the costs of college education stated, "And 'pretend' is the operative word. There just aren't enough people with enough money. Nowadays, after acceptance letters go out, a season of souk-like haggling and price-cutting begins. The actual cost of a private college education is at least 30 percent less than the 'sticker price.'" That is to say: $19,700 × 70 percent = $13,790.

When colleges talk about money, need can mean many things.

Apparently, the institution's administrators hope to attract as many students who will pay the full tuition (known as "full-freight" students) and other costs as possible. Those students will then not only be paying for the cost of their education, they also provide funds to help cushion the cost of enrolling students who the administrators decide shouldn't have to pay or can't afford to pay the full tuition and fees. The more "full-freight" students a college can enroll, the more financial aid flexibility the institution has, thus enabling it to provide financial aid relief to those "can't pay" and/or "shouldn't have to pay."

How to Get Financial Aid

It would take three chapters to explain the convoluted and tortured reasons why some students, especially the "shouldn't-have-to-pay" category of students, are provided relief from paying full tuition and fees. Generally though, discounts are provided because of: merit (pretend and real), academic potential or achievement, athletic ability, special circumstances (to be determined by the financial aid director's "professional judgment"), ethnicity, family and legacy relationships, and need. The concept of "need" is virtually impossible to define. When discussing need as it pertains to financial aid, it can mean virtually anything the college administration wants it to mean. Fortunately for you, the athletic prospect, it can mean you need financial assistance. Or just as conveniently—in the professional judgment of the financial aid director for the recruiting institution—it can mean "we need rebounds." Or "we need pass completions or sacks or pole-vaulters or base hits." You get the picture: the recruiting institution is solely responsible for defining what its needs are and can therefore decide what it can do to accommodate its needs.

Each college can, and normally does, create a financial aid awarding formula which uses its own unique mix of available federal, state, as well as its own institutional funds. This formula is calculated to meet the dual and concurrent needs and requirements of delivering the institution's intended level of educational services to its students while maintaining financial solvency.

A very important component in receiving sufficient funds necessary to accomplish the two interwoven service and solvency goals is financial aid provided by government programs, both state and federal, to students with proven financial need according to the Department of Education's computers. Usually financial need is determined by applying a formula to the financial information that a student provides on the *Free Application for Federal Student Aid* (FAFSA) form. Based on the formula, needy students can be awarded financial aid in the form of grants, work-study payments, and loans. All states provide financial aid to needy students, usually in addition to the federal aid. And if the financial aid director wants you to have a larger discount because the college wants/needs you (in your case, for your athletic ability), in his/her professional judgment you just might be needier than first evaluated.

It's important to remember that all federal and state need based financial aid is based on the formula used in the FAFSA. *Need does not mean poverty status.* The best advice for a FAFSA applicant is to assume nothing. The FAFSA forms are available after January 1. You can get the form from your high-school guidance counselor, or you can download a form or complete the form online at www.fafsa.org.

Generally, state and federal funds are awarded to the enrolling student, but paid directly to the college. Some colleges offer their own grants or awards to students. Institutional grants are based on a college's own unique formula, called institutional methodology, for awarding financial aid. This money comes directly from the institution's own financial aid budget and not from the state or federal government. According to the College Board, $130 billion in financial aid was available for students in the school year 2007–2008. That's a record. New numbers from the Department of Education project that overall financial aid to students will be more than $83 billion in 2008. That will equal about 60 percent of all awarded financial aid. But, the 2008 Annual Report on College

Get Paid 378.3025 N485

SS Inside's 796.075 J562

Getting Recruited 796.071173 B879

Put Me In 796.07173 R635

How to Win... 796.079 H358

Your Kios... 796.083 K77

Intro 615.85156 M818

Resource Book ✓

Navigating 616.8916056 N

(right now it is all or nothing)

ɔm the rest of the screen

:ample is a publication which is
ear.

g the township of the patron.
:tfinder does not acknowledge

Affordability states that college tuition and fees rose by a staggering 439 percent while, during the same period, median family income rose 147 percent. It's all too clear: the burden of college tuition continues to exact a very heavy toll on family finances. Financial aid for athletic ability is a realistic method for reducing that burden.

A Word about Student Loans

If you are a prospect for a Division II or III program, it is highly likely that your financial aid package will include a subsidized student loan. There are two different types of subsidized loans: Stafford and Perkins. Whether one agrees or not, student loans are considered financial aid. You borrow money that you don't plan to begin repaying for at least four years. When anyone borrows money, they have to at least pay interest on the amount they've borrowed. But with student loans, you (the borrower) don't have to pay interest on the money as long as you are a student in good standing.

But someone is paying the interest. That someone is the federal

---

Credits and Deductions

A helpful reduction of the financial burden of a college education is the Hope Tax Credit. It can be used during a student's freshman and sophomore year to a maximum of $1,500. One dollar in tax credit means a one-dollar savings in federal tax. Another available credit is the Lifelong Learning Credit. It is calculated on the first $10,000 and awards 20 percent of that total to a maximum of $2,000. It is means-tested with a maximum income for families of $83,000 for full credit and $103,000 the disqualifying income level. Certain politicians have decided that those who earn these levels of income are wealthy. The politicians decided those earners should be penalized for their earning power and are disqualified. Income limits on singles is $41,000 and $51,000; again such income levels designate wealthy taxpayers who are evidently worthy of the disqualification penalty. So there. That will teach you to own an alarm clock.

(continued)

> You can claim up to $3,000 of tuition as a tax deduction. But you can't claim both a credit and a deduction. Remember that a deduction only reduces income that is eventually taxed. The average taxpayer can anticipate a savings of about $800.

government. They are willing to risk paying interest on $4,731 (the freshman year maximum) for the next four years to give you an opportunity to attend college and play your chosen sport. They also risk nonpayment by the student athlete because they guarantee the loan. When you begin repayment, the government continues to subsidize the interest rate on your loan, keeping it well below market rates. Most students who accept loans subsidized by the Department of Education are also required to participate in the federal work-study program. Students usually work at on-campus jobs, are usually paid minimum wage, and normally work 10 to 15 hours per week.

Many states offer education loans at below-market rates. Check with your state's treasurer's office to see if a state loan is available.

It doesn't require a brain surgeon to recognize that a grant (money given to you that you don't have to repay) is a better deal than a loan. But it is quite probable that a loan will be part of a financial aid package. Loans are pretty good deals. That's why last year students borrowed over $32 billion in subsidized loans.

Loan Update

In 2001, Congress decided that you can deduct $2,500 of college educational costs from federal income taxes. And still more good news: if you choose to work for a charitable organization or some type of governmental body, you could have your loan forgiven with no tax consequences.

Many student athletes competing in all three NCAA divisions are receiving some federal and/or state financial aid. In addition, many students are awarded institutional financial aid on top of the federal and state aid that is loaded into a student athlete's total financial aid package.

Another Financial Aid Consideration

You may win a scholarship from an organization outside the college's regular financial aid sources, such as your church or booster club. If you do, most colleges ask that you report or even send the award to the school's financial aid office. Typically, the financial aid office will reduce your financial aid package by the amount of the award. This saves the school money, but won't improve your overall financial aid package. Ask the organization to give the award directly to you so the school won't reduce your financial aid package by the outside entity's award amount.

Pell Grants

After you have completed the FAFSA form and sent it in to the Department of Education, its computers will decide if you are in need of a federal financial aid grant. If so, it awards the grant based on a sliding scale. The maximum award is $4,731 and is renewable each year that you are in good academic standing. The award is made directly to the institution and credited to your total financial aid package.

Awarding Financial Aid

There exist a number of methods and means for institutions to award financial aid for athletic ability. Institutions attempt to fashion financial aid packages in such a manner that the recruited student is satisfied with the package and that the institution's objectives are met while recruiting and providing financial aid to that student.

The awarding of financial aid to students with proven athletic ability is generally awarded in four ways:

1. "Full-ride" athletic scholarships—Division I and II
2. Partial athletic scholarships—Division I and II and NAIA
3. Combination financial aid awards, including partial athletic scholarship—Division I and II and NAIA
4. Combination financial aid, not to include scholarships related to athletic ability—Division III and NAIA

Please note that NCAA rule #15 requires that Division III colleges are obliged to tell you that they do not offer athletic scholarships. (Chapters 17, 18, and 19 reveal the truth about this bogus assertion.)

Chapter 3

Preparing for College and the Future

The future is where you will spend the rest of your life. Do you wish to be in control of your future so that you get from it what you want and deserve? Is your answer yes? If it is, you must grasp this fact: it is highly unlikely that you will get what you want from the future unless you know what it is that you want. Before reading another word, close the book and take at least five minutes to consider what kind of future you want for yourself.

The more specific you are as to what you want to own, what experiences you would like to enjoy, what accomplishments you wish to achieve, what career and/or occupational goals you have, the more valuable this imaging activity is. As you discover each element, item, or aspect of your desired future, write it down. Do that now.

_____

_____

_____

_____

_____

_____

_____

_____
_____
_____
_____
_____
_____
_____
_____
_____
_____
_____
_____
_____
_____
_____
_____
_____
_____
_____
_____
_____
_____

Welcome back. If you have completed discovering your future—great; if you chose not to consider your future, you have made a colossal error. If you were traveling to a destination to which you had never been, you certainly must know you'd be a fool to try to get there without a map or directions, right? The most important place you are going is into your future.

Is it smart to journey somewhere without a clue about how to get there or how you'll know when you've actually arrived at your destination? You know the answer.

If you haven't done the imaging activity, demonstrate some discipline, go back, and do it now.

You have one more activity to accomplish before we move on to the issue that caused you to purchase this book. You have identified the fundamental elements of a future you wish for yourself. For each element, you must identify in writing what you know you must achieve, acquire, and do and are prepared to do, acquire, and achieve to secure the future you have described.

THE TRUTH Is

If you don't know where you're going, you'll probably end up somewhere else.

Review the elements of your desired future. Now focus on the goal of becoming successfully recruited. You are about to begin the process of turning this most important goal from a fantasy—a dream—into reality.

Complete the following steps:

1. **State your exact goal.** (State your goal clearly and precisely. Do this in order to visualize your exact goal.)

_____

_____

_____

_____

_____

_____

_____

2. **State the date.** (Indicate the future date by which the goal will be accomplished. Use the month and year. Specifically

targeting the exact date for the accomplishment of your goal helps you avoid procrastination.)

_____

_____

_____

_____

_____

_____

THE
TRUTH Is

There is no worthwhile goal that can be achieved without effort, discipline, and sacrifice.

3. **Determine what you will sacrifice.** (What will you personally sacrifice to achieve your goal?

Be sure you understand what it is that must be sacrificed and what you will sacrifice. If what you intend to sacrifice is less than what you know is required to achieve your goal, it is highly unlikely you will achieve it.)

_____

_____

_____

_____

4. **State your plan of action.** (The great Olympic sprinter, Michael Johnson, tells of his father always asking him, "How do you plan to do that?" whenever he told his dad that he wanted to get something or achieve something important. He credits the discipline of planning as essential to his determination to sacrifice as he prepared for achieving Olympic immortality.)

_____

_____

_____

_____

_____

Is your plan worth the discipline and sacrifice it takes to commit it to paper? By writing down the plan, you have created something tangible upon which your thoughts and ideas are recorded. You can then refer to the plan on a regular basis.

THE TRUTH IS

The more you want, the more you must be willing to sacrifice.

Writing your action plan organizes your goal-oriented direction and activities, makes them more understandable, more real, and therefore more doable. Referring to the plan as you move toward your goal provides you the information you need to make any mid-course corrections that may be required.

You must constantly reinforce your visual image; if not, your desire, your belief, or your plan will wither and die. You will experience almost immediate results if you read your plan daily.

This goal-planning strategy works not only for achieving successful recruitment; it works for achieving any important goal you might have.

Sample Goal

1. I want to be on a college swim team at a school where I can receive a great education, compete, and receive a large financial aid award.
2. I will be successfully recruited by April 2010.

THE TRUTH Is

If something is easy, everyone will be doing it.

Easy Button

- It's easy to be lazy.

- It's easy to let others take care of you.

- It's easy to whine about how tough life is.

- It's easy to not try something challenging, and therefore avoid disappointment.

- It's easy to blame your disappointment on others.

- It's easy to blame others for your lack of accomplishment.

- It's easy to blame circumstances for a lack of achievement.

It's important to remember, as you proceed toward the future, the only place that cheese is free is in a mousetrap.

3. I will make successful recruitment my priority. If I must miss time with friends or must choose between other things or activities and pursuing my goal, I will pursue my goal. I will devote 100 percent of the time and effort necessary to achieve my goal.

4. I will:
- Create an irresistible profile.
- Send profiles and cover letters to 50 college swimming coaches in Division II and III.
- Organize a communications log and file folder holder.
- Respond immediately to every request for information from any coach until I know I don't want to attend that college.
- Visit at least three colleges.
- Gain acceptance into at least two colleges.
- Negotiate with the coach for the best financial aid package at the school of my choice.
- Use *The Sports Scholarships Insider's Guide* suggestions and processes.

I know it won't be easy, but I can and I will discipline myself and make sacrifices to accomplish my goal.

Chapter 4

Your Education and Athletics

Hopefully, acquiring a good education is one of the goals you listed in the previous activity. While the goal of this book is to help you be successfully recruited by a college coach and receive financial aid for your athletic ability, its mission is to help you obtain the best possible education you can.

THE TRUTH Is

You will do much more important things in your life than compete in athletic contests.

That means the academic portion of your high-school work is more important to your preparation for future success and fulfillment than your athletic activities.

You may be one of the many young athletes who dream of a career in professional sports. You may have been told by others that nature has wired you up well enough that if you work hard you could in fact become a professional athlete.

While many young American athletes dream of careers in professional tennis, golf, softball, soccer, and track and field, most student-athlete dreamers wish to be professional baseball, football, or basketball players. The truth is:

- On average, fewer than 225 rookies earn a position on a professional football team in any one year.

- Over 280,000 seniors will play high-school football in that same year. 225 ÷ 280,000 = .00080
- A professional football player can expect an average pro career of about 3.5 years.
- Professional football players sometimes end their careers financially broke, live on average less than 60 years, and have many more personal problems than the general public.

Basketball has equally disturbing statistics:
- Over 150,000 high-school seniors play boy's basketball each year.
- Approximately 1 in 30 high-school seniors playing basketball will play in the NCAA. 1 ÷ 30 = .0333
- About 50 rookies make pro teams each year. 50 ÷ 150,000 = .00033
- While basketball players appear to live longer, their personal problems seem to be even greater than football players.

And baseball:
- Approximately 1 in 20 high-school baseball players will play in the NCAA.
- Approximately 1 in 200 high-school baseball players will be drafted by (notice that no one said "play on") a major league team.
- Baseball players seem to enjoy lives more similar to normal Americans.

I'm not advocating that young athletes not aspire to be professional athletes, it's a worthy goal. But the following chart of sobering statistics concerning opportunities to compete in athletics after high school is worth very serious study.

Table 1: Estimated Probability of Competing in Athletics Beyond the High School Level

Student-Athletes	Men's Basketball	Women's Basketball	Football	Baseball	Men's Ice Hockey	Men's Soccer
High School Student-Athletes	549,500	456,900	983,600	455,300	29,900	321,400
High School Senior Student-Athletes	157,000	130,500	281,000	130,100	8,500	91,800
NCAA Student-Athletes	15,700	14,400	56,500	25,700	3,700	18,200
NCAA Freshman Roster Positions	4,500	4,100	16,200	7,300	1,100	5,200
NCAA Senior Student-Athletes	3,500	3,200	12,600	5,700	800	4,100
NCAA Student-Athletes Drafted	44	32	250	600	33	76
Percent High School to NCAA	2.9	3.1	5.8	5.6	12.9	5.7
Percent NCAA to Professional	1.3	1.0	2.0	10.5	4.1	1.9
Percent High School to Professional	0.03	0.02	0.09	0.5	0.4	0.08

Note: These percentages are based on estimated data and should be considered approximations of the actual percentages.

Certainly, your athletic preparation and performance are very important. You will not be recruited unless the recruiter/coach feels that you can contribute to the success of his/her program. So, for the rest of your high-school career, you must seriously and with the greatest amount of discipline prepare yourself for college competition: both in the classroom and in your sport. Your academic credentials will be just as important to your successful recruitment as your athletic credentials.

So this can't be stated forcefully enough: *the authentic value of a college athletic scholarship is the opportunity it provides its recipient to prepare for a future of success and fulfillment by acquiring a college education.*

Reality Check

The hope, even the expectation, that a high-school athlete has of becoming a professional athlete must be tempered by the foregoing statistics. Too many prospects regard athletics as the only path to achievement, wealth, and fame. This is particularly true of minority prospects, as Harry Edwards, author and a famous counselor to minority student athletes, notes as he writes about this issue in the *Lexington Herald Leader*, "Big-name athletes who tell black kids to 'practice and work hard and one day you can be just like me' are playing games with the future of black society... [African Americans] have a principal responsibility to understand that sports must be pursued intelligently and the [African American's] involvement in sports is no game."

Chapter 5

Academic Requirements

This chapter shatters Myth #3. The academic requirements to be eligible as a freshman continue to become tougher. To be eligible at a Division I institution you must complete, with a 2.0 average in the core (required) curriculum, at least 16 academic units, or full-year courses, which must include the following units:

- 4 English;
- 2 social sciences;
- 3 math, including Algebra I or higher;
- 2 science (at least one lab course, if a lab course is offered at your high school);
- 4 or more units in any of the above or in foreign language, computer science, philosophy, or nondoctrinal religion; and
- 1 more unit from among English, math, and natural or physical science.

To be eligible for Division I competition, you must also accomplish the following:

- Graduate from high school;
- Successfully complete the 16 core courses listed above; and
- Have a core course GPA combined with an SAT score or an ACT sum score based on the 16 core GPA/Test score index.

The NCAA has developed a sliding scale in order to accommodate variations in GPA in combination with either the SAT or ACT scores you achieve. The sliding scale can be located in your *NCAA Guide for the College-Bound Student-Athlete*. To be current with any academic eligibility rule, log on to www.ncaa.com/NCAA/student/index/student.html and check out the list.

Division II schools have no sliding scale. To be eligible at D-II institutions:

- You must earn a 2.0 GPA on a 4.0 scale in 14 courses in the core curriculum; and
- You must earn a combined score of 820 on the reading and math portions of the SAT or a composite score of 68 on the ACT.

Division III has no eligibility requirements.

THE TRUTH Is

Your future success will be determined more by what you achieve in the classroom than in any sport.

NCAA Early Certification

If, by the end of your sixth semester (end of your junior year), you meet the following academic criteria, you can be awarded early certification by the NCAA Initial Eligibility Center.

- 1000 SAT score (composite of reading and math sections)
- 86 ACT score
- 3.0 average in the NCAA Core Curriculum referenced on page 35.

If you have met these academic standards, contact the NCAA Initial Eligibility Center to inquire about early certification. Owning this certification removes a significant obstacle to successful recruitment because any coach recruiting you need not concern him- or herself with your academic credentials.

Because of NCAA regulations, Division III schools must claim they don't award financial aid based on athletic ability, and therefore aren't bound by the constraints of Bylaw 14.3. The institution, conference, and other NCAA regulations govern eligibility for financial aid and roster positions. Chapters 19-23 expose the truth about the Division III bogus claim of no financial aid for athletic ability.

Check all eligibility information against your *NCAA Guide for College-Bound Student-Athletes*. It is absolutely essential to discuss your transcript and core courses with your high-school counselor to be certain that you meet all the NCAA Bylaw 14.3 requirements. The NCAA Eligibility Center is demonstrating a very tough attitude about student athletes meeting the core-curriculum requirements.

NCAA General Recruiting Rules

Contacts

You become a prospect when you enter ninth grade. You become a recruited athlete if a college coach contacts you or a member of your family about either attending the school or participating in an athletic program. Other than men's basketball, coaches are not allowed to contact* you until September 1 of your junior year, then by letter only. Other than football and basketball, you may not be contacted by telephone by a college coach until after July 1 prior to your senior year of

---

*Be sure to consult with your *NCAA Guide for the College-Bound Student-Athlete* for the precise definition of the contact rules. You can examine the *Guide* by going online at www.ncaa.org/eligibility/cbsa/index1.html.

competition. Consult your *NCAA Guide for the College-Bound Student-Athlete* for telephone football and basketball contact rules. You or your parents may contact a coach by phone at any time. After the aforementioned July 1 date, if available, you may contact a coach via a provided toll-free number. No student or athlete from the school may make a recruiting call to you, but you can call them after the July 1 date.

Evaluations

An evaluation is "any off-campus activity used to assess your academic qualifications or your athletic ability, including a visit to your high school (during which no contact occurs) or watching you practice or compete at any site." Sound confusing? It can be. That's why it's important to own an *NCAA Guide for the College-Bound Student-Athlete* so that you can refer to it on an as-needed basis.

Contacts and evaluations are both considered by the NCAA as "recruiting opportunities." All sports other than football and basketball must limit recruiting opportunities to seven. Basketball has a limit of five and football three. And with many sports contacts and evaluations are limited to certain calendar dates. Other times are designated as "dead time." Again the need to consult your *NCAA Guide for the College-Bound Student-Athlete* becomes essential to be successfully recruited.

There are many other Byzantine restrictions and regulations explained in the *Guide*. Each school can require even more robust standards than the NCAA, if they choose—but very few do.

Table 2: NCAA Recruiting Chart

	DIVISION I MEN'S BASKETBALL	DIVISION I WOMEN'S BASKETBALL
Sophomore	Recruiting Materials • June 15 following sophomore year Telephone Calls • Once per month beginning June 15 following sophomore year	
Junior	Telephone Calls • Once per month through July 31	Recruiting Materials • September 1 Telephone Calls • April calls permissible on or after Thursday following Women's Final Four • One call in May • One call June 1–20 • One call June 21–30 • Three during month of July following junior year
Senior	Telephone Calls • Twice per week Off-Campus Contact • September 9 Official Visit • Opening day of classes	Telephone Calls • Once per week Off-Campus Contact • September 16 Official Visit • Opening day of classes
Evaluation and Contacts	130 recruiting-person days during academic year Not more than seven recruiting opportunities (contacts and evaluations combined) during the academic year per prospect Not more than three off-campus contacts during prospect's senior year No off-campus contacts during junior year Practice/competition site restrictions	100 recruiting-person days during academic year Not more than five recruiting opportunities (contacts and evaluations combined) during the academic year per prospect and not more than three of the five opportunities may be contacts Practice/competition site restrictions

	DIVISION I FOOTBALL	DIVISION I OTHER SPORTS
Sophomore		**Women's Ice Hockey:** Telephone Calls • One call to international prospect during the month of July following her sophomore year **Men's Ice Hockey:** Recruiting Materials • June 15 following sophomore year Telephone Calls • Once per month beginning June 15 following his sophomore year
Junior	Recruiting Materials • September 1 Telephone Calls • One between April 15 and May 31	Recruiting Materials • September 1 Telephone Calls • Once per week July 1 following junior year for all sports except men's ice hockey Off-Campus Contact • July 1 following junior year **Men's Ice Hockey:** Telephone Calls • One per month through July 31 **Gymnastics:** Off-Campus Contact • July 15 following junior year
Senior	Telephone Calls • Once per week beginning September 1 (unlimited during contact period) Off-Campus Contact • Last Sunday following the last Saturday in November Official Visit • Opening day of classes	Telephone Calls • Once per week Off-Campus Contact • No more than three Official Visit • Opening day of classes **Men's Ice Hockey:** Telephone Calls • Once per week beginning August 1

Evaluation and Contacts	6 selected evaluation days during September, October, and through the last Saturday in November (I-A)	**Softball:** 50 evaluation days between August 1 and July 31
	42 evaluation days during fall evaluation period (I-AA)	**Women's Volleyball:** 80 evaluation days between August 1 and July 31
	Limit of 3 evaluations during academic year • One evaluation during fall • Two evaluations April 15 through May 31 (one evaluation to assess athletics ability and one to assess academic qualifications)	Seven recruiting opportunities (contacts and evaluations combined) per prospect and not more than three of the seven opportunities may be contacts
	Not more than 6 off-campus contacts per prospect at any site	
	Practice/competition site restrictions	Practice/competition site restrictions

	DIVISION II	DIVISION III
Sophomore		Recruiting Materials • Permissible Telephone Calls • No limitations • Permissible freshman and sophomore years
Junior	Recruiting Materials • September 1 Off-Campus Contact • No more than three off-campus contacts beginning June 15	Recruiting Materials • Permissible Telephone Calls • No limitations Off-Campus Contact • Conclusion of junior year
Senior	Telephone Calls • Once per week beginning June 15 Official Visit • Opening day of classes	Recruiting Materials • Permissible Telephone Calls • No limitations Off-Campus Contact • Permissible Official Visit • Opening day of classes
Evaluation and Contacts	No restrictions on the number of evaluations Contacts restricted at the prospect's practice/competition site until such time as the competition has concluded and the prospect has been released by the appropriate authority	No restrictions on the number of contacts and evaluations Contacts restricted at the prospect's practice/competition site until such time as the competition has concluded and the prospect has been released by the appropriate authority

NAIA Eligibility Rules

The number of scholarships available for any sport at an NAIA college is unlimited. The school alone decides how many to award and the amounts per award. Rarely does an NAIA institution award a full grant-in-aid, also known as a "full ride."

To be eligible you must qualify in two of three standards:
- Graduate in the top half of your graduating class;
- Score a minimum of 18 on the ACT or 860 on the SAT; or
- Achieve a high-school GPA of 2.0 on a 4.0 scale.

Once accepted and competing you must:
- Be in good academic standing according to school standards;
- Make normal progress toward graduation according to school standards;
- Be enrolled in 12 credits during your season of competition;
- Accumulate a minimum of 24 credits the two previous terms (repeated courses don't apply to that 24);
- As a junior, you must have achieved a GPA of 2.0 on a 4.0 scale; and
- In your second competitive season, you must have accumulated a minimum of 24 semester hours of credit (that number is factorial for years three and four).

There is no eligibility center in the NAIA. Also, you may transfer among NAIA colleges with no "sit out" penalty. You may have a campus tryout for a team and not be penalized.

Why Are You Here?

By purchasing this book, you have shown the desire and possess the dream of continuing your athletic career in college; you want to compete in your chosen sport. The foregoing information should make it

THE TRUTH Is

You will have a large, even unfair advantage over the many, many other qualified prospects who have the same dream as you.

very clear that if you don't take your academic preparation as seriously as your athletic preparation, you are most certainly jeopardizing your dream.

As was discussed previously, if your dream is to only tolerate college athletics as a short, unwanted stopover before becoming a professional athlete, you are making a colossal error. Research indicates that high-school athletes who harbor this dream-poisoning attitude very often don't even graduate from high school, much less become either college athletes or (what a joke) professional athletes.

THE TRUTH Is

The future is never inherited; it is created. Create your future now. Your future is where you will spend the rest of your life.

By using the exposure strategies and techniques in this book, you will generate massive, national exposure or regional exposure—whichever you want.

The advantage will mean nothing if you don't demonstrate to the college coaches that you are constantly developing and improving, both academically and athletically. If you delude yourself into thinking that the exposure you receive will be all that is required for you to be successfully recruited, you are in for a huge disappointment.

While exposure is the only strategy that accomplishes successful recruitment, coaches won't recruit student athletes who may have a difficult time staying eligible or who fail to demonstrate continuing improvement in their sport. The best way to avoid problems is to be the finest student and dedicated athlete you know how to be. *You must: study, hustle, think, practice, believe in and discipline yourself, and compete as hard as possible.*

Another valuable exposure technique is enrolling in top-level summer camps in your sport. Be sure college coaches are either running the camp or are teaching at the camp. Camps provide instant exposure. However, the truth is that most college coaches that observe athletes at these camps are there not to discover athletes for their programs. They are usually in attendance to observe prospects that they are already recruiting. I strongly recommend that you attend sports camps that teach skills as their primary objective. If you wish to attend a camp that teaches skills and development, I further recommend attending a camp run by an area high-school coach who has developed a reputation as a great teacher in the sport. These high-profile high-school coaches often alert college coaches about developing athletes participating in their camps. The truth is that high-school coaches are generally interested in helping you improve and develop; college coaches are interested in helping themselves. By making these commitments, you can reach the dream of playing your sport at the collegiate level and receive financial aid from the college for which you compete.

Unfortunately, there are many prospects that want the recruiting process to be easy. They are uncomfortable with, some even hostile to, the expectation that they must perform in the classroom, sacrifice during practices, and execute on the field of competition. They don't want to

THE TRUTH Is

You will spend the rest of your life as an adult.

make disciplined choices for themselves that may interfere with having fun and hanging out with friends or ingesting illegal substances. Arrests and dumb stunts on YouTube or Facebook are championship stupid! They can destroy your future. Others refuse to let their sport or their education interfere with their social life. If this describes you, you will fail. You must reorder your priorities!

Doesn't it make sense to be well prepared for the rest of your life? If it was easy, everyone would be recruited. It's not easy. And too few are. So be prepared to be tough on yourself. Almost everyone has a will to win. As a track coach, I noticed that every competitor has heart during the last ten meters of the race. Too many athletes call upon their will to win only at the instant of competition. Winners have the will to prepare to compete. Vince Lombardi, the legendary coach of the Green Bay Packers, said that the will to prepare was more valuable to individual success than the will to win.

If anyone tells you the recruiting process will be easy, they are mistaken. As you will discover, it is fundamentally unfair. The truth is that *you're entering a high stakes contest where only the competition knows the rules.* You'll also learn that every effort you make will generate substantial benefits.

You now have an opportunity to do what very few young people do: take control of your future. If you hold tightly to your goals and use the suggestions to follow, you can obtain what you want.

Chapter 6

Constructing the Profile

To be successfully recruited you must create maximum exposure for yourself and your ability. You must make yourself known to the greatest number of coaches that might be interested in recruiting you as possible. You need a device that creates specific, usable information for a coach to evaluate you and you need that device in the hands of at least 50 coaches; I urge you to place that device in the hands of 100 coaches. The most useful exposure device is the personal profile.

A profile is a structured compiling of data about you and your athletic and academic record of accomplishments. It is organized in an arrangement that allows an interested coach the opportunity to quickly evaluate your potential to contribute to the coach's athletic program. A properly created profile can generate tremendous interest in you as a prospect. As you will learn, a thoughtful, well-designed profile will create many benefits for you. A sloppy profile filled with hot air and information that is useless to recruiters or coaches will be promptly discarded.

The guiding principle to building an effective profile is simple to understand, yet often difficult to execute. You must be truthful!

You and your parents have a lot at stake concerning your college education. The emotional intensity generated by the considerations of money and pride can (and too often does) cause people to inflate the accomplishments of the prospect. Student athletes, parents, and high-school coaches must overcome the understandable urge to oversell the potential, achievements, statistics, and coachability of a prospect. However, some "selling" should take place in your cover letter, which will be covered in the next chapter.

THE TRUTH Is

Lying on the profile will most certainly destroy your chances to be successfully recruited.

Recruiters and coaches have experienced many snow jobs and are alert for them. Most coaches will check the accuracy of the information you have provided if they sense that you are trying to deceive them.

Your profile should contain the following information:
- Name
- Address
- Phone number (include area code)
- Email address
- High school
- Enrollment
- Conference
- High-school phone number
- Date of birth
- Height/weight
- 40-meter-dash time (depending on sport)
- Bench press (depending on sport)
- Squat (depending on sport)
- Vertical jump (depending on sport)

- NCAA Initial Eligibility Center PIN number (to be covered later)
- FAFSA/SAR report and EFC number (to be covered later)
- Academic statistics: graduation date, SAT/ACT score(s), intended major or undecided, NCAA core-course GPA, class rank, current courses, significant academic honors (honor roll; National Honor Society; school, local, regional or national awards; but avoid listing *Who's Who*)
- Athletic statistics: all customary statistics (see following list) for the most recent season related to the sport for which you wish to be recruited and other significant athletic awards and honors.
- Coach's evaluation

Personal Profile

Joe Smith
1370 Deforest Rd.
Anywhere, OH 53111
(216) 555-5467

Sport: Track
Position: 800M/CC
Birth Date: 7/25/94
Height: 6′ 1″
Weight: 165 lbs.
Speed: 40 Yds. 4.9
Strength: Bench: 160 lbs. Squat: 300 lbs.
Other sports: Cross-country
Anywhere High School
Coach: Jack Simpson (216) 555-1234

Academic Statistics: Graduation Year 2012
149/322 ACT: 19 GPA: 2.76
Intended Major: Education
Current courses: Geometry, English 3, US History, Zoology, Intro. to Computers

Athletic Statistics: 800M 1.57.9, 400M 49.8, 200M 23.6, 100M 11.7, 1600M 4.35.1, 3000M (CC) 16.51

Honors/Awards (Athletic): Conference Champion 2011–800M, Regional Qualifier, 2010-11–800M, Sectional Champion 2010-11–800M, MVP (CC) 2010-11 State Qualifier (CC) 2010, 2011, Placed 31st.

Honors/Awards (Academic/Extracurricular): B Honors, Key Club

Coach's scouting evaluation: Joe's greatest strength is an ability to concentrate on relaxing when he is in pain at the end of a race. While other runners are tying up, he is able to maintain good running mechanics, often edging out competitors who are stronger than him. He has learned to run very tactical, smart races, often deceiving his opponents and then surging past them and breaking their will at critical points in the race. "Joe is an athlete who knows what he wants to do in track, does whatever it takes to prepare to accomplish his goals, and leaves nothing of himself at the end of a race. His determination to win is inspiring." He needs to continue increasing his distance base and weight lifting to get even stronger, especially in the upper body.

His coach and your recruiter project him to be a Division II 800M & cross-country prospect.

Videotape available.

Customary Athletic Statistics and Guidelines by Sport

Your profile should include the following statistical and skill information pertaining to your sport.

Basketball:
- assists
- field-goal percentage—2-point/3-point
- free-throw percentage
- rebounds
- steals
- minutes-per-game average

Division I Women's Guidelines:

Position	Height	Skills
Center	6'2"+	aggressive/powerful rebounder, 8'6" jump/touch, quick first step, set solid pick, accurate shooting with shots beginning with back to basket and face up, maintain post position under pressure, fearless, 60 percent free throws
Power Forward	6'0"+	good rebounder, accurate shooter (both perimeter and inside), aggressive defender, creative/accurate passer, 70 percent free throws
Small Forward	5'10"+	high shooting percentage (both perimeter and inside), aggressive defender, creative/accurate passer, good penetration ability, 70 percent free throws
Point Guard	5'4"+	exceptional ball handler/passer, leader, good speed, great court sense, creative/accurate passer, good penetration ability, 70 percent free throws
Shooting Guard	5'6"+	excellent perimeter shot, excellent ball handler, creative/accurate passer, quick off pick, excellent catch and release shooter, 75 percent free throws

Division I Men's Guidelines

Position	Height	Skills
Center	6'9"+	aggressive/powerful rebounder, 10'6'" jump/touch, quick first step, set solid pick, accurate shooting with shots beginning with back to basket and face up, maintain post position under pressure, fearless, 60 percent free throws
Power Forward	6'7"+	good rebounder, accurate shooter (both perimeter and inside), aggressive defender, creative/active passer, 65 percent free throws
Small Forward	6'5"+	high shooting percentage (both perimeter and inside), aggressive defender, creative/active passer, good penetration ability, 70 percent free throws
Point Guard	6'0"+	exceptional ball handler/passer, leader, good speed, great court sense, creative/accurate passer, good penetration ability, 75 percent free throws
Shooting Guard	6'2"+	excellent perimeter shot, excellent ball handler, creative/accurate passer, quick off pick, excellent catch and release shooter, 75 percent free throws

Baseball
- batting average: .350+
- earned run average (ERA): pitchers–2.1+
- extra base hits
- fielding average
- throwing speed (pitchers): 87–92+/D–I, 84–87+/D–II
- pitches–fastball, curve/slider, change up
- speed–60 yard: 6.7–7.2
- runs batted in (RBI)
- stolen bases
- win/loss record (pitchers)

Cross-Country
- distance and times
- places: conference, invitational, regional, state
- 3200 meters D–I men: 8:30–9:10; women: 10:10–11:00
- 5000 meters D–I men: 15:15–16:00; women: 16:50–17:30

Diving
- dives, degree of difficulty, best score
- places: conference, invitational, regional, state

Football
- attempts and completions
- assists and tackles
- field goals: attempts and goals, longest, average
- fumbles recovered
- interceptions

- kickoffs: attempts, longest, average
- receptions: number, total yards, average yards, touchdowns
- sacks
- tackles: solo
- yards rushing: attempts, average, total yards

Position	Acceptable	Preferred	Speed
QB	6'2"/200'	6'4"/225'	4.7/40
RB	5'11"/205'	6'0"/215'	4.4/40
FB	6'0"/215'	6'2"/230'	4.8/40
WR	6'0"/175'	6'2"/185'	4.5/40
OL	6'2"/250'	6'4"/265'	5.0/40
DL	6'1"/250'	6'5"/275'	5.1/40
LB	6'2"/215'	6'3"/245'	4.7/40
DB	5'9"/170'	6'0'/185'	4.5/40
FS/SS	5'10"/180'	6'2"/200'	4.5/40

Golf

- handicap D-I men: 0–3 women: 0–7; D-II men: 3–7 women: 5–9; D-III men 8–12 women: 8–13
- average 18-hole score: D-I men: 70–74 women: 71–80; D-II men: 74–82 women: 78–84; D-III men: 79–84 women: 82–90
- medalist number
- places: conference, invitational, regional, state

Gymnastics

- event scores: average and best
- places: conference, invitational, regional, state

Soccer
- assists
- blocked shots
- goals

Softball
- batting average
- ERA (pitchers)
- extra base hits
- fielding average
- throwing speed (pitchers)
- RBI
- stolen bases
- win/loss record (pitchers)

Swimming
- event: distance and best time
- places: conference, invitational, regional, state
- 100-Free men: 50.5–54.3; women: 55.6–62.3
- 100-Back men: 59.4–64.0; women: 61.6–70.8
- 100-Breast men: 1:08.8–1:16.6; women: 1:10–1:20
- 100-Fly men: 59–68.5; women: 60.4–70
- 200-IM men: 1:53.5–2:04.8; women: 2:05–2:17

Tennis
- position: singles and doubles
- handedness
- record
- places: conference, invitational, regional, state

Track and Field: Division I

- 100-meters men: 10.2–10.9; women: 12.0–13.0
- 200-meters men: 20.5–22.5; women: 23.5–24.7
- 400-meters men: 44.5–48.0; women: 52.0–57.2
- 800-meters men: 1:51–1:55; women: 1:58–2:03.5
- 100-meter hurdles men: 13.0–14.3; women: 13.5–14.8
- 300-meter hurdles men: 37.5–41.0; women: 41.5–47.0
- high jump men: 6'6"+; women: 5'8"+
- long jump men: 23'4"+; women: 18'+
- shot put men: 52'+; women: 37'+
- discus men: 150'+; women: 130'+
- pole vault men: 15'+; women: 10'5"+
- event and personal best
- places: conference, invitational, regional, state

Volleyball

- aces: number and average
- assists
- blocks
- digs
- kills

Division I
Middle/Outside
- height: 5'10"+
- jump touch 10'0"+
- strong shoulders
- good arm speed
- pass and defend
- handle ball skillfully

Setter
- height 5'8"+
- jump touch 9'0"+
- strong hands and fingers
- quick and agile
- team leader

Wrestling
- record and weight
- escapes
- near falls: 2-point and 3-point
- reversals
- pins and falls
- takedowns
- places: conference, invitational, regional, state

Speak to your high-school coach about your goals and your exposure action plan. Unfortunately, some high-school coaches do little or nothing to help their athletes with the recruiting process. While their support isn't essential for you to be successfully recruited, it can be very helpful.

If your coach is willing to make a comment for your profile, be sure it is short and hard-hitting. It should be about attitude, practice habits, coachability, etc. Keep the comments to one short paragraph. The paragraph should be the last item on your profile.

Also, you should affix a picture to the top right hand corner of the profile. A high-school graduation or similar picture is the best. One in uniform is okay, but it should be close enough for your face to be easily seen. A picture often creates a subtle, psychological familiarity between the coach and you. You are no longer just a name or a list of statistics.

Your profile must be clean and neat, grammatically correct, all words spelled correctly, and computer generated. Ask someone who is qualified (an English teacher is a good choice) to check and edit the components of your profile.

Sending profiles that don't follow these rules greatly reduces your chances to be successfully recruited.

Chapter 7

The Cover Letter

You will have opportunities to meet and communicate with those who can help you realize your goal of being successfully recruited: college coaches. You must present yourself so that a coach will not only be interested in your abilities as an athlete, but your character as a mature person.

Below are important factors for a good presentation:

1. **Confidence.** Have confidence in the skills and abilities you have developed in your sport. Present those skills and abilities demonstrating your confidence that they are equal to the task of positively contributing to the team's success.

2. **Respect.** Demonstrate your respect for the coach/recruiter and the institution he/she represents. Few things destroy a prospect's chances to be offered an athletic tender or a financial aid award letter more quickly than a prospect who appears verbally or mentally undisciplined. These prospects are regarded as not coachable. The consequences are obvious.

3. **Humility.** You must be proud of your accomplishments and achievements; you have worked hard and persistently to reach the level of skill you have achieved. While many people are ignorant of the price you have paid, you and the recruiter know that the level of ability you possess is no accident. Remember, the recruiter knows, so there's no need to brag— demonstrate humble pride.

Even though your home phone number is included in the profile, you should provide it in the cover letter as well. Tell coaches when the best time is to call either you or your parents. If your high-school coach is willing to have coaches call him or her at home, mention the coach's number (including area code), as well as the best contact times.

The same editing, grammar, and spelling rules apply to your cover letter as those recommended for your profile. Keep your cover letter to one page.

If your cover letter appears to be mass-produced, it is likely that it will receive less serious attention. The following devices will ensure that the coach knows the letter is written specifically to him or her:

- Use the college name.
- Use the college address.
- Use the team name.
- Use the coach's name.
- Keep it to one page.

By using the first four suggestions, it quickly reveals that you have done research on the school and athletic program that you are making contact with. Comments about a team or athlete success gleaned from the school's website can make a valuable first impression. Use a small item like that in your cover letter.

A sample cover letter follows.

Sample Cover Letter

May 28, 2011

Mr. Clyde Wienerschnots
Head Track Coach
Vogelheimer University
6676 West Benchbottom Street
Athletica, NH 04111

Dear Coach Wienerschnots,

I would like to introduce myself to you. I am currently a junior sprinter and long jumper at Einars High School. I have spoken to a number of coaches and other qualified people concerning the Laser Track Program. They all say it's a good track program.

Last year I qualified for the state meet in each event. While I didn't make it to finals, I have already improved on the performances this season. I am determined to win state meet medals in June. My personal best in the 100 meters is 10.64 achieved at the Spring Valley Invitational. My 200 meters personal best is 22.12, achieved during a home dual meet on May 4, 2010. I jumped 22' 9" at the Porker Relays. I expect my performances to continue to improve.

I scored a 23 on the ACT, have a 2.9 GPA in 13 NCAA core courses, I'm enrolled in three more this year, I have a 3.1 cumulative GPA, and I rank 61 in a class of 233. I plan to take the ACT again.

I believe my performance and my continued development demonstrate that I could contribute to your program. I would like to continue my track career at Vogelheimer, as well as pursue my educational and career goals.

I have enclosed my profile and results of some of my recent competitions. I've also included next season's meet schedule so that you can evaluate me, if time permits. Please send me whatever materials are required for me to be further considered as a prospect for Laser Track and Field.

My home phone number is (502) 555-2573. I should be available on weekdays after 6:00 p.m. My coach, Bobo Otendoten, invites you to call him at school (502) 555-2200. I look forward to hearing from you in the near future.

Sincerely,

Horace T. Bunkerschnives

Enclosures

Chapter 8

The Videotape

If interested, team sport coaches almost universally ask for videotape. It is a quick and effective way to evaluate your skill, ability, intelligence, and intensity. Even some individual-event coaches request videotape (*e.g.*, track, wrestling, swimming). A well-produced videotape can generate great benefits for you. A poorly produced one, while not a kiss of death, does not help you accomplish your objective.

The best videotapes include five sections:

1. **Video profile.** An opening 30-to-40-second still shot of the top section of your profile (but don't include the picture).

2. **Personal introduction.** You, on camera, introducing yourself, giving a few personal statistics (name, age, high school, height, weight, graduation date, position/event, high school coach's name, ACT/SAT score, NCAA core-course GPA, etc.), and a short statement similar to the following. Practice the statement—out loud.

"Hi, I'm Morsly Horsefeather. I play defensive tackle and fullback for Homefield High School. I weigh 207 pounds and am 6'1" tall. I graduate in June of 2011. My ACT score is 21 and my core-course GPA is 2.6. My coach is Bobo Otendoten. I want to be considered as a prospect for Rumbler football. I hope you will agree that this tape shows that my level of play qualifies me to make a solid contribution to your program. Thanks for your time and consideration."

    3. **Competition.** You—competing in games, matches, or meets.

      a. **Team sport competitors.** Two complete quarters (or periods), one each from two of your best games, start to finish. Don't be tempted to cut or splice out poor performances. The coaches will detect it and wonder what it is that you're trying to hide. The consequences of creating suspicion should be obvious. Remember, coaches know that nobody plays a perfect game.

      b. **Event competitors.** Two to ten performances, depending on the event length (500 meter free style, 1600 meter run) and technical requirements (hurdles, diving, parallel bars).

    4. **Highlights.** Five to ten of your season's highlight plays or performances. These plays should demonstrate athletic ability, effort, versatility, and intensity, and not just dramatic episodes (ten slam dunks or five goals scored against an inferior goalkeeper won't help you). Highlights always follow game/performance sections.

    5. **Final profile.** End your tape with no more than a minute of demonstrating the required skill at your position in a non-competitive presentation (passes, receptions, shooting, ball handling, dribbling, hurdle mechanics, etc.) followed by another 15/20-second segment of your profile.

Try to get help in editing, splicing, dubbing, and special effects for your videotape. You may even want to use a professional or experienced videographer. Sometimes, all the help you need may be found in your high-school media department. However, if you can't find help or can't afford it, still send the best video you can if a coach requests one. Don't send unsolicited tapes or discs; they end up in the recycle bin.

Chapter 9

Sending Credentials

Where should I send my credentials? Before you can answer this question, you must ask and answer a few preliminary planning questions:

1. Am I willing to attend a college far from home or am I willing only to attend local or regional institutions? And are my parents/guardians willing to let me attend a college far from home or would they prefer me to stay close to home?

2. Do I want to attend small/large or public/private schools?

3. At what level of competition do I realistically believe I can successfully compete? (Division I, II, III, NAIA I, II, or 2-year junior college?)

4. Is my choice of a major course of study more important than where I compete?

THE **Truth Is**

If you are a senior currently competing in your sport season and you haven't been recruited by Division I schools, it is highly unlikely that you will be offered an athletic scholarship by a Division I coach.

The answers to these questions can provide a frame of reference for you as you decide which coaches to send your profile to. That's right—you send your profile to a specific coach of your sport at the college receiving your profile.

Use the list in the last section of the book to locate the information you need. If you use the foregoing suggestions, you should receive an excellent response; that is, unless you send profiles to only Division I programs. Then you can anticipate only limited responses.

The truth is that unless you are one of the elite "blue chip" prospects in your sport, virtually all Division I programs will ignore you because less than 1 percent of high school prospects are recognized as "blue chip" athletes. Rarely does a non-"blue chip" athlete get to choose which school he will attend, unless as a walk-on. Division I programs pick which students will be attending that school. It's likely that you purchased this book because you recognize that you need help realizing your athletic dreams, so I'm confident that you've decided that, while you're qualified athletically and academically to participate and contribute to a college program, you're not in that 1 percent that gets to choose the school they'll attend. Like I warned, the truth often has a hard edge.

"Walk-On" Harsh Reality

You may, however, be offered an invited or preferred—meaning the coach *prefers* to give the "athletic grant" to another prospect—"walk-on" status, perhaps with an inducement that if you do well your freshman year that you might get a scholarship the following year.

In most cases the reality is that "walk-on" status in Division I usually means you will get to *practice* your sport for four years.

You will rarely, if ever, compete in an intercollegiate contest. The unique pride of a National Letter of Intent signing—ain't happening! Most scholarship athletes receive preferential class schedules so that practice and travel is convenient—not you!

But if you're satisfied with being a practice opponent (often known as a "scout," "gray," or "hamburger squad") for the team's regular players, then go for it. What you are as a walk-on is a necessary team burden to assist the real players' practice and not taken seriously by your teammates or the coaches. Not an inspiring achievement. But maybe that's OK for you. That is, unless your parents need your help in reducing the financial burden they will bear (or the debt load you'll inherit upon graduation) helping you get a college education and an opportunity to continue your athletic career. The Department of Education calculated that the average student loan debt of college seniors was over $19,000 in 2004. It's more now: according to the Center for American Progress, 42 percent of college students have more than $25,000 in debt. A gray squad walk-on saddled with colossal debt or a Division III campus hero with little or no debt; you choose. But before you do, I urge you to log onto www.sportsjungle.com/USCwalkontryouts.

Sometimes a degree from a certain institution (Stanford, Notre Dame, Northwestern, etc.) is sufficient motivation to walk on. And some walk-ons do receive scholarships in later years. A painfully small percentage of walk-ons do receive scholarships and create for themselves an opportunity to play regularly. I suggest that having a substantial part of your college education paid for is no small accomplishment for you and no minor detail for your parents. If significant financial aid is a priority, you should strongly consider NCAA Division II and III and NAIA colleges.

How Many Colleges Should Receive My Credentials?

The greater your exposure to college coaches, the greater your chances to be successfully recruited. Depending on your sport and your realistic appraisal of your ability, you should be exposed to a minimum of 50 colleges; 100 is better. Even if your realistic appraisal causes you to conclude that you are a D-I prospect, you should send many profiles to D-II and D-III institutions. Thirty to each is good.

"But I want to compete in a glamorous or prestigious program," you say, meaning of course—Division I. You truly may be qualified to compete at Division I, but the truth is, if you were a solid Division-I prospect, a Division-I program probably would have recruited you by now and it's likely that you wouldn't be studying this book.

Fifty or more colleges? Absolutely. Here's why: coaches recruit prospects that fit their coaching philosophy, system, and style of play. Your abilities and objectives may not fit the coach's requirements. Also, coaches just aren't recruiting for every position or event every year, so there may be no need for a prospect in your position or event.

Even if you interest coaches with your credentials and they make contact with you, you may be low on the recruiting depth chart. You may not move up high enough on the chart to be recruited. Conversely, the more depth charts you are on, the better your chances to move up and eventually be recruited.

If you follow the suggestions in this guide, your credentials will be in the hands of 50 or more coaches in the various divisions. This will produce the results you want and deserve. Very often, this part of the recruiting process is a numbers game. So you must generate sufficient numbers to overwhelm the odds.

Credential Evaluation

When college coaches and recruiters receive your profile, cover letter, and video, they will look at them in a manner similar to the way prospective employers look at resumes. Once the profile has been evaluated, coaches then consider their individual needs to determine their interest in you. Factors such as the number of

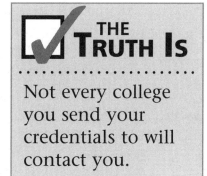

THE TRUTH Is

Not every college you send your credentials to will contact you.

graduating seniors on their roster, the players playing your position and competing in your event, and available financial aid, in addition to the previously mentioned academic and athletic criteria, all contribute to the degree of interest coaches will have in you as a prospect.

Interested Coach?

If they are interested, most colleges will send you an introductory letter and/or questionnaire. The questionnaire is an important first step. You must understand, however, that its function is more of an elimination process as compared to the selection process. Remember, the only time you are technically offered a scholarship is by an athletic tender or a financial aid award letter.

The questionnaire sent by colleges serves several purposes; but, very importantly, it is a tool with which the coach determines your interest in the college and in his or her program. An important factor considered by the coaches is how quickly you respond to any contact, be it a letter/questionnaire/phone call. (If you have any interest in a college, send the information requested immediately.)

Do whatever is requested quickly and accurately. Often, when a coach must choose between student athletes who are similar academically and athletically, they most often choose the one who has demonstrated discipline and maturity in his/her communications with the coach.

Some recruiting services recommend that a prospect staple a copy of a personally created questionnaire. That is a colossal error. When a coach receives a stapled questionnaire returned from a prospect that has made the first contact by sending a profile, it demonstrates that the prospect is fishing for scholarships and has no special interest in the coach's program. Some coaches may not care if they receive mass-produced and stapled questionnaires to their questionnaire, but most feel exploited and don't pursue that prospect.

Chapter 10

Organize, Organize, Organize

As you can appreciate, if you are contacted by each college you send your profile to, you will be receiving a lot of information. In the early stages of recruiting there will be a process of elimination both by you and by a number of the coaches you are communicating with. For you to make a wise decision you need to have as much information about each school, program, and coach as you can find. It is essential that you record the content of each of your conversations with all coaches as you begin your personal elimination process. It is so easy to forget what was discussed and equally easy to confuse one discussion with another.

If you choose not to organize all information, you will eventually confuse programs and coaches and/or lose important information from phone calls, letters, or documents. Demonstrate some discipline. Get organized.

You must have a filing system for each college to which you send information. Manila file folders are a good beginning. On the tab place the name of the college. On the left inside cover place the address and each coach's name and phone number. A very detailed review of the initial contact between you and the coach/recruiter is very helpful. All contacts should be recorded on a communications log.

Record each contact from the institution: letter, document, visit (college coach at your high school, your college visit(s), or college coach that comes to your home), or phone call. Each phone call or visit must be recorded. The discipline you demonstrate doing this important task will be a powerful tool in your successful recruitment. The recording should include date, time, coach/recruiter name, and the content of the conversation and any planned next step in the process. Be prepared to be a great listener and a great note taker. Keep your logs clipped in chronological order. The communications log that follows can and should be photocopied.

It is very important to send a thank-you note to each coach expressing your gratitude to him/her for taking the time to speak with you and to consider you for the program. Making an impression as a mature and intelligent prospect is always in your best interest.

Communications Log

1. Date: _____   Time: _____
2. Type of contact: ☐ letter   ☐ personal note
   ☐ questionnaire   ☐ phone call
   ☐ face-to-face visit at home
   ☐ face-to-face visit at high school
   ☐ face-to-face visit at a college campus
   ☐ sent newspaper clippings
3. Initiated by whom? ☐ me   ☐ coach
4. Recruiter/coach and college: _____
5. Content of discussion: _____
6. Next step: ☐ by coach   ☐ by me
7. Thank-you note sent? ☐ yes   ☐ no
8. Date sent: _____

Organizing your recruiting communications intelligently and efficiently is crucial to your success. Truly, you are creating your first major business deal. This deal could be worth $100,000 or more over four or five years. The earning power of a college graduate as compared to a person with a high-school education has recently been pegged at $1,700,000 over a lifetime. (Yes, that's more than one million dollars.)

THE TRUTH Is

Most student athletes do not appreciate the value of their college education.

Chapter 11

Critical Documents

Because of NCAA Eligibility Center regulations, Department of Education regulations, and institutional requirements, you can anticipate a request for a number of documents to be sent to the:

1. Coach/recruiter: athletic information
2. The institution's Admissions Department: academic transcripts and special requirements
3. The institution's Financial Aid Department: financial aid information
4. The NCAA: eligibility information

Many shattered dreams lie strewn on the road to successful recruitment because prospects decide to wait until tomorrow to act on requests to send documents.

The documents requested are normally required for admittance to the college, required by the financial aid office to begin awarding financial aid or required to certify your eligibility to practice and/or participate in NCAA competition.

THE TRUTH Is

Coaches are looking for prospects with inner motivation and mature responsibility; prospects who are self-starters. Procrastination is championship stupid.

Document List

This list may not include all the documents required by the institutions you are considering. Any additional documents requested by the coach, admissions office, financial aid office, or the NCAA must be responded to immediately.

1. **Application form.** No financial aid will be awarded to you unless this form is completed and received by the admissions office. Financial aid offices are forbidden to generate awards until the admissions department has accepted the prospect. It is likely that the admissions form will request that you send an application fee.

   Call the coach and tell him/her that you can't handle the admission fee right now. Ask if he/she can help you get the fee deferred until you enroll. In many cases, they can. Often they will suggest you send the application directly to them. The coach will then deliver the form to the admissions office. As you will appreciate, if you follow the suggestions of this book and seek acceptance at a number of colleges, sending a check of between $25 to $85 along with each application can become quite expensive. Your goal should be to pay an application fee only to the college in which you ultimately enroll. If you are fortunate enough to receive a scholarship, usually the application fee is waived.

2. **Free Application for Federal Student Aid (FAFSA).** This form can be found in your high-school guidance office. Ask your counselor for it. When you receive it, immediately complete it with the help of your parent(s) or guardian(s). Be certain to complete all sections of the form. If it is incomplete, you will be asked to complete it by the U.S. Department of Education and the enrolling

college before any financial aid other than an athletic scholarship can be awarded to you. Mail it in the enclosed envelope.

Some parents don't complete the FAFSA. They may believe they will not qualify for any type of aid because their income is too high. As stated earlier: assume nothing. Others may determine that they won't divulge the personal and tax return information requested on the FAFSA.

While I appreciate a desire for privacy, it is probably foolish to be stubborn in this circumstance. The requested information is very similar to that on your tax return. It is a mistake not to complete and mail the FAFSA. Unlike the IRS, which wants to loot your money, colleges use the information on the FAFSA to award you money.

THE TRUTH Is

Many families with incomes in the six-figure range are receiving need-based financial aid. No kidding. And no cheating.

Factors other than income influence eligibility for federal or state financial aid. And state financial aid is almost always calculated based on the formula (called Federal Methodology) the Department of Education's computers use to evaluate the information provided on the FAFSA. And state financial aid is more easily awarded because state standards are often less demanding than the federal financial aid standards. Your financial aid forms are sent to a central processing unit in Illinois. Computers crunch the data and determine how much you can afford to pay. Personal, family, financial, or employ-ment issues are not part of the calculation executed by the computer program. Many families miss opportunities to reduce the financial burden of a college education because they choose not to complete and mail the FAFSA.

Many colleges award institutional grants (discounts from the announced tuition, room, and board) and other financial aid based on the information generated by the FAFSA. When information from the FAFSA is used as a baseline for awarding financial aid, it is called Federal Methodology. While this aid is from the col-lege's financial aid budget, it was calculated with Federal Methodology. And often a college's need-based financial aid awarding standards are less rigid than either the state or federal standards. Often, an institution uses its own unique financial aid awarding formula for calculating stu-dent need and consequently determining which students will receive tuition and/or room and board discounts; when an institution uses its own formula, it's called Institutional Methodology.

If there is no baseline data like that generated from the FAFSA available for the college, very often the conclusion drawn by the financial aid office is that you should be a "full-freight" student. You didn't buy this book in order to become a "full-freight" student, did you?

3. **CSS profile.** Over 800 colleges require incoming freshmen to complete a form called a profile. The profile questions provide the institution information that the FAFSA doesn't ask. These colleges use the information on the profile to help the director of financial aid determine how much of a discount (Institutional Methodology) from the sticker price

you should receive. Like all other requests for documents from a college, complete it and send it immediately.

4. **Student Aid Report (SAR)**. This report is generated by the Department of Education's computers. The SAR is based on the information you provide on the FAFSA. Your parent(s) or guardian(s) will receive a copy of this report. A number of the colleges you are interested in will receive a copy of the SAR. You will have directed, by naming them in section G of the FAFSA, which colleges will receive a copy of the SAR on the FAFSA form completed by you and your parent(s). When you receive your SAR, examine it—there may be mistakes on it that could cost you plenty. Also, call immediately to request another free copy of the SAR at (319) 337-5665.

> **Student Aid Report (SAR) To Do List**
>
> • Keep your copy in a place where it will remain neat and clean. You may have to make a number of photocopies of the SAR.
>
> • Take an SAR with you on each visit you make to a college, even if you think the college has already received a copy.
>
> • Give a copy of your SAR to any coach/recruiter or admissions counselor who visits you at school or at your home.

You will discover a number called the Expected Family Contribution or EFC. The college's financial aid office will calculate (Federal Methodology) the federal and state financial aid available to you from the EFC# and other information found in the SAR.

5. **High-school transcript**. The process of sending your transcript to a college and the NCAA Eligibility Center is the responsibility of your high-school guidance counselor. Even if you haven't finished high school, you should

request that transcripts be sent to the admissions department of the colleges that interest you. Final transcripts will be sent to both colleges and the Eligibility Center upon your graduation. Your grade point average (GPA) in the core course requirements, as identified by the NCAA in the *College Bound Student Athlete Guide* and presented earlier in the book, plays an important role in your eligibility to practice and compete.

Many types of financial aid are awarded based on your high-school GPA. Doesn't it make sense to be a good high-school student and focus on achieving as high a GPA as possible?

6. **ACT/SAT scores.** To be NCAA eligible, you must sit for the ACT/SAT on one or more of the National Testing Dates. Your counselor can give you the dates and locations of these tests. You can take the ACT/SAT as often as you want (on a National Testing Date) to achieve a better score, which will help you to be NCAA eligible. (Refer to the academic eligibility section in your *NCAA Guide for the College-Bound Student-Athlete.*)

As with your high-school transcript, your high-school counselor sends your ACT/SAT scores to the college admissions department. Like your GPA, your ACT/SAT scores play an important role in your eligibility to practice and compete. (Refer to the academic eligibility section of your *NCAA Guide for the College-Bound Student-Athlete.*) Also, like your GPA, many financial aid awards are based on the scores of these tests. Some colleges will allow you to retake the ACT or SAT test on the college campus to give you an opportunity to improve your score in order to increase your academic financial aid award. Ask the college admissions office if they offer this opportunity.

Remember, sitting for an ACT/SAT test on the college campus can't change an ACT/SAT score for the purposes of NCAA eligibility because it isn't given at a National Testing Date location. The ACT/SAT scores that the NCAA recognizes for the purpose of determining your eligibility are those scores earned on the National Testing Dates only.

If you follow the advice of this guide, it is likely that you'll take the SAT/ACT more than once as you try to improve your score. If you are concerned that a college will notice that your initial test scores might be low and wish for them to see only your best score (most likely a later one), the following strategy can be quite helpful. Each test has a section that offers you the opportunity to have the score sent to different entities. The selection of the entities to which you want your score sent is accomplished by the test taker filling in a number of four letter boxes. These numbers correspond to a college. The number 9999 tells the testing company to send the score to the Initial Eligibility Center. Each score received by the center is included in the information sent to any college asking for Initial Eligibility Center Credentials of an athlete. So if you have four ACT scores of 17, 19, 20, and 24, it's likely that you'd prefer any college interested in you to see only the 24 score and not the sequence of scores. If you don't include 9999 in your "send to" box, only you or the colleges you select will see the other scores. When the 24 score arrives at your home, you can contact the College Board or ACT, and for a small fee, usually around $15, they will send the best score to the Initial Eligibility Center for inclusion in your credentials.

7. **Financial Aid Estimator.** Many Division II and III colleges use an FAE to provide preliminary information from which they can estimate the amount of financial aid you might need to be able to attend that institution. A coach/recruiter or admissions counselor may send you an FAE. This document helps the coach make preliminary recruiting decisions based on the results of yours and other prospects' FAEs. As you can appreciate, if the coach receives a requested FAE from a prospect who has similar academic and athletic qualifications as you and doesn't receive your FAE, guess who's going to be offered a scholarship. This isn't brain surgery, is it?

8. **Institutional Financial Aid Application Form.** An institution may ask you to complete a Financial Aid Application Form even though you also have completed a FAFSA and a CSS Profile. Private schools often have financial aid available for special circumstances. Having a "Special Circumstances" category adds to the flexibility of a director of financial aid to award discounts. Examples are: alumni-sponsored scholarships and major field of study scholarships (*i.e.*, nursing, engineering, elementary education, or a religious institution that awards members of its faith).

9. **NCAA Eligibility Center Form—"Making Sure You Are Eligible to Participate in College Sports."** This form must be completed and sent to the NCAA Center in Indianapolis, IN. There is an $18 registration fee. The Eligibility Center certifies your eligibility to participate in practices and competition. You're not eligible in Divisions I or II without Eligibility Center Certification, even if you meet the eligibility standards.

Coaches rarely offer any kind of financial aid to students who haven't been certified eligible by the NCAA Eligibility Center. You can get the form free from your guidance counselor, athletic director, or coach. If it's not available, call the NCAA Eligibility Center at (800) 638-3731 or www.ncaa.org for a free form.

You and the college coach will receive notice of your eligibility certification from the NCAA. You will be given a Personal Identification Number (PIN). On the NCAA Eligibility Form, you will be asked which colleges you wish to be notified. The NCAA will notify those colleges you identify of your eligibility status.

Chapter 12

Communication Activities

If a college coach/recruiter that you are interested in calls or sends you an email, you should immediately write or email a short letter thanking him/her for "your interest in me as a recruit for your program." Tell him/her of your interest in both the college and the athletic program. If there is additional information (awards won, recent performances, etc.) about yourself you want to share, do it at this time. This is also a good time to include your upcoming competition schedule. Be prepared with some questions, too. Some of the questions located in the chapter "The Visit" can be asked over the phone. Another source of good questions is the NAIA's *Guide for the College-Bound Athlete*. A coach to whom you sent nothing might contact you. Don't be shocked; word of good prospects can travel quickly.

As indicated previously, you may receive more than one phone call or email from the same person or other people related to a program. This is no accident. Additional calls or emails are very good signals, but you haven't been recruited yet. You must continue to do your part. After a few contacts by the coach/recruiter, you will detect a pattern of questions that indicate an increasing level of interest and/or concerns:

- Asking for videotape of last game or performance.
- Asking for your coach's home phone number.
- Asking if you plan to retake the ACT/SAT.
- Asking if you have applied for admission.
- Asking if you have sent transcripts and ACT/SAT scores to Admissions.
- Asking about recent injury.
- Asking if you'd be willing to change playing positions in college.
- Asking you to send an SAR to him/her.
- Asking if they may visit you at home.
- Asking you to visit their institution.
- Asking if you would be willing to walk on.
- Asking if you would commit to their program if you get a partial scholarship.
- Asking how much financial aid it will take for you to enroll.

Try to anticipate questions. Write down what you feel are the kind of answers you want to give and practice them—out loud. As the recruiting season progresses, you'll discover that the questions will begin to change. Some coaches will stop calling or returning your calls or emails (in this case, you've probably been strung along). Others may begin sending you handwritten notes or emails (a very positive sign). By following the suggestions in the "Organize" section, you will be prepared for the changes and be ready to answer critical questions.

Communications That You Initiate

Some Internet-savvy and enterprising prospects have actually created their own recruiting websites. If you own the capability to create this valuable tool, I urge you to make one and get it on the Internet. You'll find many outstanding examples on YouTube and Facebook. If you don't currently have website capability—get it! Whenever you are cited in the newspaper or other media, enter it on your website or send another note to the coach ("Coach, I thought you might be interested in this article," etc.) that includes a photocopy (or referencing that he/she should visit your profile or website and add it to your personal information) of the article that presents you favorably. Or send it as an email attachment.

Be certain to have an answering device on your telephone. If you aren't home when a coach calls, it is wise to return the coach's call as soon as possible. You may telephone (at your expense) and email a college coach as often as you wish. Keep communicating. A coach may conclude that you've lost interest if he/she doesn't hear from you. You may visit a college campus (unofficial visit) as often as you wish. However, you must avoid creating the impression that you can be recruited with little or no financial aid or that you will accept loan-type aid only or that the financial aid office can GAP you (offer you less financial aid than your certified need as indicated by the Estimated Family Contribution # on the SAR Student Aid Report). You should never pay more than EFC# amount.

Chapter 13

The Visit

If a coach is really serious about recruiting you, he/she will ask to make a home visit or ask you to visit the campus. Once, the parent of a prospect on my recruiting service asked me this question: "Is there any way to cut to the chase and eliminate all this foolishness?" I didn't know the answer then, but I know it now. The answer is: ask the coach, "Are you going to make a home visit?" or, "Are you going to ask my kid to come to your school for an official visit?" The answer to these questions slashes through all the "foolishness" and provides profound insight into the honest interest of a coach in a prospect. I now refer to these questions as the "killer questions." Always ask if they will be "handling" (don't say "paying") the expenses for the visit. Remember, there are certain restrictions concerning official—that is to say, paid—visits. Refer to your *NCAA Guide for the College-Bound Student-Athlete.*

Remember, you can make as many unofficial visits to a campus as you wish. That means you handle (pay) your expenses. Be sure you contact the coach; tell the coach of your plans to visit the college and that you'd like to meet the coach while you're there. Often the coach will arrange for you to be escorted by a team member. If you're visiting on a game day, the coach may even reserve some tickets for you. In football some coaches even offer to let you attend the games on the sidelines. If the program pays little attention to you on the unofficial visit, the least you have is some very valuable information about the potential of receiving financial aid for your athletic ability.

You may take one "official visit" per school and five total official visits. Be sure you visit only colleges in which you are interested. It's unfair to waste other people's time, but more importantly, don't waste your own time. An official visit must always be followed by a sincere thank-you note, no matter if you're recruited by that college or not. After all, the program has invested time, financial, and personnel resources in you.

On any visit you must try to speak with faculty and staff in many different departments of the college, in particular:
• Admissions Office
• Financial Aid Office
• Housing
• Athletic Department
• Department head of your intended major field of study

Be certain to examine all the facilities that will directly impact your life on that campus:
• dorms
• athletic facilities
• dining facilities
• laboratories
• classrooms
• student union
• library

Get a feel for the campus ambiance, as well.

Recruiting Is Too Often Unfair!

While being asked to visit is a very positive step toward being successfully recruited, a cold dousing of reality is needed here. As you now know, the coach is almost surely recruiting more than one prospect for any one position. You should be aware that it is highly unlikely that the coach will successfully recruit each prospect that is his/her first choice for a position or event. In order to protect themselves, most coaches have back-up recruit lists. These lists are usually referred to as "depth charts."

The problem you are likely to encounter is that you may be a back-up recruit, one that is low on the depth chart, and never know it. You may very well experience the same kind of reception and may be told the same things as the recruit who is #1 on the coach's depth chart. This is known as being *strung along.*

At a recent *Ultimate Recruiting Seminar* designed for college coaches and recruiters, the following suggestion was part of the seminar content: "For every scholarship you have, you should be recruiting four prospective student athletes." In other words, effective recruiting requires that the recruiter/coach string along three prospects. This is the harsh reality. To ignore this reality is championship stupid. *You are entering a high stakes contest where only the opposition knows the rules.*

That's why it is so important for you to never, never ever place your college future in one coach or college. You must have some options available to you until you receive the "letter of intent" from the college. Coaches are shopping for prospects and keeping their options (their rules) open; so you must shop for coaches and programs keeping your options open, too. Remember, the recruiting process is often a numbers game—you must play the game, too. Overwhelm the odds with massive numbers. College coaches commonly have five hundred or more potential recruits on their initial mailing lists.

Chapter 14

Visit Questions

The wise prospect seeks answers to many important questions. While the coach/recruiter of the college will be your primary source for answers, be aware that other sources are also available. These include: other athletes (usually met while visiting the campus and not necessarily the guide assigned to you by the coach), college-produced introductory reading material, catalogs, college websites, and observations made on the campus. Arm yourself with this book by keeping it conveniently located at your telephone and with you (but out of sight) at all times when visiting a campus.

A word of caution: be careful not to appear that you are investigating the coach. However, be sure to get the answers as they can provide you with the information from which you can make an informed and therefore, good decision. While a coach may string you along, it is quite rare that a coach will lie when asked a direct question.

It is very important that you get satisfactory answers to each of the following questions before you commit to a coach or college. Some of these questions will be better asked in-person while on a visit. As your conversation proceeds with the coach, you will get an idea what questions you should ask while on the phone and which questions to ask when you visit the college.

Go over the questions with your parent(s)/guardian(s) and highlight a few of the questions which you determine are most important to get answers to so you can generate a level of interest in the coach, his/her program, and the school.

Most of your conversation will be spent listening. The coach will spend a lot of time telling you about his/her program and selling you on his/her school. Be patient and be a good listener. There will be time to ask your questions.

The following four topics encompass most of the experiences you will have as a student athlete at any school. You should know which school appears to be the best fit for you in all four areas.

Put your questions on 3 × 5 cards. It is not a good idea to let any school official see you using this book.

Athletic

1. How much time is spent in practice?
2. When does the season begin? End?
3. Are there additional training periods?
4. What are practice hours?
5. What are my off-season responsibilities?
6. Can I compete in other sports?
7. What is the team's past record?
8. What conference and division does the team compete in?
9. How many games/meets per season?
10. How often does the team travel?
11. Can he/she describe the athletic facilities? (If not, wait and observe during the visit.)
12. What is the coach's philosophy?
13. What are my chances of regularly competing and when?
14. What position/event/class am I being considered for?

15. How many freshmen at your position are being recruited?
16. What position am I on the recruiting depth chart?
17. Will I be redshirted?
18. What are the housing arrangements for athletes?
19. Have you seen me play or compete?
20. Do my skills fit into your program?

Academic

1. Are my career goals compatible with the college's majors and programs?
2. Am I allowed time to make up classes and tests missed because of the competition schedule?
3. Am I qualified to meet admission standards?
4. Are tutors provided for athletes?
5. What percent of freshmen graduate? Graduate with their class?
6. What is the college's policy toward student athletes during summer session?
7. Will I have an academic advisor?
8. Will the coaches provide any guidance if I have academic problems?
9. How many hours of studying per day is average for my major?
10. Do professors teach?

Legal

1. Do I receive a written contract/tender?
2. If I get injured or become sick, will I lose my financial aid?
3. What medical expenses does the college cover?

4. a. How many credits are required for me to be eligible to compete?

   b. How many credits are required for me to keep my financial aid?

5. What is the status of the college's relationship with the NCAA?

Financial

1. Is there academic or need-based financial aid available?
2. What is the amount of financial aid being offered?
3. How many years is it being offered?
4. What criteria is used to determine renewal of aid?
5. What portion of the total (yearly/semester) cost is covered by the financial aid I will receive?
6. What expenses does the financial aid cover (tuition, room, board, books, special assessments, supplies, etc.)?
7. What sources and types of financial aid will be included in the total financial aid package? (state, Pell, USEOG, institutional, special awards, grants, loans, etc.)
8. Am I eligible for additional financial aid now? In future years?
9. If I need five years to graduate, will I continue to receive the same amount of financial aid as the other four years?

After the Visit

After your visit, you should review the visit by asking yourself the following questions:

1. Did the coach/recruiter say negative things about other schools in an attempt to persuade me to attend his/her college?

2. Were the coaches interested in my academic success?
3. What was the attitude of the players toward their coaches?
4. Does the institution satisfy my requirements?
5. Would I attend this college if I weren't going to be an athlete?
6. Can I play in games here or will I be a member of the "gray" squad?
7. Was I offered benefits or enticements that I realize were sleazy?

Chapter 15

Why Prospects and Families Get Hurt

Prospects and families get hurt because they are entering a contest where only the opposition knows the rules. They don't understand their value in the recruiting marketplace. They don't know how to interpret the meaning (both obvious and hidden) of all the calls, letters, promises, and other communications from college recruiters. They don't know when they are being strung along or when they are being told the truth.

You can be intensely recruited with letters, personal notes, and phone calls for months and suddenly hear nothing because you were being strung along. It goes with the territory.

Protect yourself with the following counterforce of knowledge and strategies to level the playing field:

1. Until you have an offer in writing (award letter, contract, or tender) and until you make a commitment to a coach; you must always create the impression that you are considering other colleges' offers. In fact, you should always have at least one backup in case of an unpleasant surprise.

   Why? Sometimes, if a coach believes that you are being recruited by other coaches and you are at or near the top of another coach's recruiting depth chart, the coach (or some other official at the college) may offer additional incentives (financial aid) for you to choose his/her program. If a coach believes you have no other options, often he/she will try to recruit you for as little as possible. That way, he or she can use the unused resources that you didn't receive for some other recruit who is bargaining more effectively than you are.

2. Remember, ask if the coach is recruiting other athletes for the same position. Why? This question signals the coach that you have a grasp of a fact basic to recruiting: that most coaches are recruiting (and usually saying the same things to) more than one prospect. (In cases like this, the coach is stringing someone along. Is it you?) If the coach really wants you, he/she will know that you understand the foregoing facts and may be eager to make you an offer that is satisfactory to you.

3. Gain admittance to several colleges that you have visited that have the right ingredients for you to be a successful student athlete. Why? If you are admitted to a number of institutions that are recruiting you, you have two very important benefits:

   • The coach can begin working early with other departments (admissions, financial aid, athletic, housing, etc.) in order to insure that you receive all the financial aid and other benefits to which you are entitled.

   • You can honestly tell any coach that you have been accepted at other colleges that are recruiting you. With this weapon you can bargain from a position of strength.

Sleazy Recruiting Tactics

While the majority of college coaches are people who wish to be a positive influence on the student athletes they coach and are fundamentally honest, a minority of them have little interest in you beyond your helping them have a winning program and thus keeping their jobs. These are harsh comments about some in the coaching ranks, but it is sadly the truth. Be alert for them.

The following points can help you recognize sleazy recruiting tactics and therefore, the coaches to avoid:

1. A coach who has a "booster" contact you or tells you that a "fan" will contact you about the program. The NCAA is making a concerted effort to eliminate from the recruiting process those persons who have "an interest" in the program. Even if they offer you nothing, which is highly unlikely, you are in violation of the NCAA guidelines.

   Even though the NCAA often looks the other way on many violations, to its credit it severely punishes those who violate the "booster" rules. Even if you just talk to a "booster," you jeopardize your future with the NCAA. Refer to the *NCAA Guide for College-Bound Student-Athletes.*

2. A coach who promises that your "best friend" can walk on. This coach has no interest in you or your friend. He is manipulating you by dangling a false hope in front of your friend.

3. A coach who promises you a starting position your freshman year. Or one who guarantees that you will be an All-American, national champion, or have a professional career in sports primarily because you compete for him/her. (Remember, there is a difference between a guarantee and a statement about your potential.)

4. Coaches who "trash, slam, or bum raps" other colleges, programs, or coaches. If coaches can't persuade you to join their program because of its qualities and their coaching abilities, you'd be a fool to enroll. Be especially alert for this sleazy tactic.

5. Some coaches may tell you that the academic program in the field of study you plan to pursue is the "best in the nation" at their college or some similar hyperbole. Consult with your high-school counselor, or there are a number of publications, easily accessed on the Internet, to check the accuracy of that statement. It is usually a sleazy recruiting tactic.

6. Some coaches may promise you easy courses, easy professors, and no academic pressure. These coaches have little concern about your future beyond helping their program. By making your academic requirements easy, the coaches have done you no favors. After all, you are going to do more important things in your life than compete in athletic contests. You'll need a good education that requires you to rise to high standards if you are to be successful in those more important things.

7. Student guides that invite prospects to parties where alcohol, drugs, or sexually provocative activities are, unfortunately, not uncommon. There are many reports of these sleazy recruiting tactics in Division I football and basketball, but there is anecdotal evidence of this sleazy tactic being employed at other divisions and other sports. If you experience this on a visit, you know that the coach has sunk to odious recruiting depths and has no interest in your success or welfare as a student athlete.

8. There is substantial evidence that some (usually Division I football/basketball) coaches have offered substantial inducements to prospects to enroll in their school and compete for their team. Some have even offered money to high-school coaches if they would "steer" a blue-chip athlete to a certain school. Recently, a credible allegation has

been made of a high-school coach being paid $200,000 to "steer" one of his athletes. Any inducement by a college coach or program to a prospect or his coach is an NCAA violation. When discovered, the NCAA deals very harshly with the violators. Prospects are banned for life from the NCAA.

An Important Word of Caution

If you or your parents accept money or any kind of gift from a school representative, you will be declared ineligible to compete in the NCAA.

Chapter 16

Awarding of Athletic Financial Aid

Virtually all colleges that sponsor a sport that competes on the intercollegiate level want that sport program to be successful (to be a winning program). To enjoy the benefits of a winning program, some level of recruiting is required. The level, intensity, directness, and operation of collegiate recruiting by any particular school is affected by a number of factors.

As you have learned, NCAA Division I and II offer designated athletic scholarships of some monetary value applied toward the cost of the tuition and/or fees of the institution awarding the financial aid. Division I schools often offer full rides, although they sometimes split some athletic scholarships up and offer partial rides. Division II programs offer full rides much less often than does Division I. They split up their athletic scholarships more often than Division I. As you now know, NCAA rules restrict the number of athletic scholarships in each sport for both Division I and II. And Division II is allowed fewer athletic scholarships in nearly every sport than Division I.

When you are being recruited by a Division I or II college, the recruiters and coaches will discuss financial aid in terms of athletic scholarships. Usually Division II coaches will discuss additional financial aid opportunities in other terms, as well, like: need-based, academic, special-talent, minority, merit, leadership, institutional grants, or loans (Stafford, Perkins, PLUS, etc.).

Division II institutions (more often than Division I institutions) try to combine one of the foregoing types of financial aid with a partial athletic scholarship in order to increase the total amount of financial aid to a prospect. The larger the non-athletic financial aid package, the greater the chance of recruiting the prospect. However, unlike Division III institutions, Division I and II colleges usually don't negotiate an increase in the non-athletic categories of financial aid. The category left open for negotiations is usually the athletic financial aid award.

As you discuss/negotiate financial aid, paying very, very close attention to your financial aid arithmetic, be sure you are combining all types of financial aid in order to calculate the total financial aid package. When you and the coach agree upon the athletic scholarship, he/she and the athletic director will notify the college financial aid office of the amount offered. This is accomplished by sending an initial Athletic Tender (that must be signed by you, the athletic director, and the coach) to the institution's financial aid office. The NCAA requires this so that the total amount of financial aid being offered in that sport can be monitored. It's required so that all athletic tenders offered are compatible within the institution's and the NCAA's allowable limits of total athletic financial aid for that particular program.

The financial aid office then combines the athletic scholarship with the financial aid you will be awarded in the other categories previously noted. You will receive two documents indicating the awarding of financial aid:

1. **Award Letter.** This document itemizes each financial aid

award (in every category *i.e.*, athletic, academic, work-study, loan, institutional, grant, etc.) you will receive if you choose to attend that college. You will be asked to confirm your decision to attend by accepting the award letter or signing a letter of intent or both. You may receive competing and similar offers from two or more schools. I suggest using the worksheets from www.collegeboard.com in order to carefully compare the offers.

Financial Aid Award Letter

Bunkerschnives University
Financial Aid Award

March 21, 2012
ACCEPT/DECLINE (Circle One)

Morsly Horsefeather
1 Prospect Street
Athletica, PA 12345

Dear Morsly,
Bunkerschnives University is pleased to offer you financial assistance for the academic year 2012–2013.

This award is not official until this form is completed and returned to the Office of Financial Planning.

Please read the enclosed Information for Financial Aid Recipients before accepting any part of this award.

Congratulations,

Financial Aid Director
Bunkerschnives University

Information for Financial Aid Recipients

Bunkerschnives University Grant $7,500	☐ Accept	☐ Decline
Founders Grant $1,000	☐ Accept	☐ Decline
Leadership Award. $500	☐ Accept	☐ Decline
Religious Service Award $500	☐ Accept	☐ Decline
Alumni Grant. $500	☐ Accept	☐ Decline
Diversity Grant. $1,000	☐ Accept	☐ Decline
Pell Grant $2,000	☐ Accept	☐ Decline
Federal Work-Study (potential earnings). . .$1,500	☐ Accept	☐ Decline
Federal Stafford Student Loan–if needed . .$2,500	Please Apply	

The white copy of this form must be signed and returned to the Office of Financial Planning by April 16, 2012.

After this date, Bunkerschnives University cannot guarantee the receipt of any funds offered in this award. Deadline extensions may be granted upon written request until May 1.

For more information, please contact the Bunkerschnives University Office of Financial Planning.

Statement of Educational Purpose

I understand my rights and responsibilities. I declare that I will use any funds I receive under the Pell Grant, SEOG, College Work-Study, Perkins Loan, Stafford Student Loan, PLUS Loan, or any funds administered by the Bunkerschnives University Financial Planning Office solely for the expenses contacted with attendance at Bunkerschnives University. I further understand that I am responsible for repayment of the prorated amount of any portion of payments made which cannot be attributed to meeting educational expenses related to attendance at Bunkerschnives University.

You will not receive Title IV financial aid unless you complete the following statement:
☐ I certify that I am not required to register with the Selective Service, because (check one):
   ☐ I am a female.
   ☐ I am in the armed services on active duty (Note: members of the National Guard are not considered on active duty).
   ☐ I have not reached my eighteenth birthday.
   ☐ I was born before 1960.
   ☐ I am a permanent resident of the Trust Territory of the Pacific Islands or the Northern Mariana Islands.
☐ I certify that I am registered with Selective Service.

I accept the awards above, and hereby authorize Bunkerschnives University to directly credit my account with the applicable state, federal, college, and/or outside agency funds, as, and when appropriate, in accordance with current regulations. I further certify that I am not in default on any educational loan and that I do not owe a refund on any grant funds previously received to attend Bunkerschnives University. I certify that if I receive a Pell Grant, as condition of my Pell Grant, I will not engage in unlawful manufacture, distribution, dispensation, possession, or use of a controlled substance during the period covered by my Pell Grant.

I further understand I must maintain full-time enrollment (12 hours or more) each semester to receive the Bunkerschnives Grant, Recognition Award, Sibling Grant, Alumni Grant, Diversity Grant, and International Award. I will refer to the Bunkerschnives Undergraduate Bulletin for refund policies pertaining to state, federal, and institutional financial aid, should I withdraw or go less than full-time.

Signature: _____ Date: _____

2. **Athletic Tender.** This document has two purposes:
   a. To describe the type and amount of athletic financial aid (and only the amount of athletic financial aid) you will receive if you choose to attend that college.
   b. To secure your attendance at the institution and to bar you from competing at any other NCAA institution.

You can sign the Award Letter, and even though it is unethical, you could still decide to attend a different institution. However, if you sign the Athletic Tender, you can compete only at that NCAA institution. Do not sign one without knowing the contents of the other. If you do sign one without knowing the contents of the other, you lose virtually all your negotiating leverage. The best insurance is to only sign the two of them at the same time.

Athletic Tender of Financial Assistance

Bunkerschnives University
Athletic Tender of Financial Assistance

_____	_____
Name of Applicant	Date
_____	
Street Address	
_____	☐ Initial ☐ Renewal
City	
_____	_____ Academic Year
State, Zip	
_____	
Date of Entrance	
_____	_____
Sport	In University

1. This Tender represents all commitments to you by Bunkerschnives University and is subject to:
   a. Fulfillment of the admissions requirements of Bunkerschnives University;
   b. Fulfillment of NCAA academic eligibility requirements; and
   c. Fulfillment of financial aid requirements set forth by the NCAA and Bunkerschnives University.

2. This Tender covers the following as checked:
   ☐ a. Full Grant: Includes tuition and all fees, standard room (double occupancy), and board (meal plan 1).
   ☐ b. Partial Grant of _____

3. You will be eligible for a year-to-year renewal of the Tender according to this University's renewal policies at the end of the academic year. Should you fall below the academic eligibility GPA requirement, you will be allowed a one-semester probation period to increase your GPA to the required status.

4. If you wish to accept this Tender, please return four (4) signed copies of this form to the Athletic Office no later than _____

Signed

_____	_____
Director of Athletics	Financial Aid Director

ACCEPTANCE

THIS TENDER IS CONTINGENT UPON THE SUBMISSION OF THE FINANCIAL
AID FORM (FAF)

I accept this Tender of Financial Assistance. In doing so, I certify that I have not
accepted any other Tender of Financial Assistance from another school.

I understand that:
a. The value of this Tender shall not exceed the value of the permissible Bunkerschnives University and NCAA expenses applicable to ISSC and Pell Grant
   awards.
b. The aid provided in this Tender will be canceled if I sign a professional sports
   contract or accept money for playing in an athletic contest.

Signed

_____   _____   _____
            Student   Date   Social Security Number

Signed

_____   _____
      Parent or Legal Guardian   Date

A Letter of Intent is a contract that binds you to compete for the institution and binds them, for one year, to the level of financial aid stated on it as long as the prospect fulfills the obligations cited in the contingency section. Sign the Letter of Intent at the same time that you sign the Athletic Tender, otherwise you lose all negotiating leverage.

Letter of Intent

Fighting Prospects
Bunkerschnives University
123 Main Street
Anywhere, FL 12345

National Soccer Letter of Intent

Athletic Aid Agreement: Expected Behavior; Practices and Games

This is to say that Joe S. Athlete will be awarded as much as $2000.00 in athletic aid for the year of 2012–2013 ***

Awards are contingent of the following:
1. Attendance at all practices.
2. Attendance at all games.
3. Maintaining academic eligibility and full-time student status.
4. Appropriate conduct to avoid being dismissed from the athletic team.
5. Completion of all required financial aid applications on a timely basis.
6. Official acceptance by the College of Admissions Department.
7. Other: Exceptions to numbers 1 and 2 will be determined by the coach: for example, illness or extenuating circumstances. Also, do not sign this contract unless you have received acceptance by the College of Admissions Department. Please notify the Athletic Department if you have not yet been accepted.

Pledge: I understand that I must fulfill the above obligation and any infraction could lead to a loss of my athletic aid for one or all semesters.

_____	_____
Signature of Athletic Director	Date
_____	_____
Signature of Student Athlete	Date

*** Athletic aid cannot be awarded over and above the total bill of your education for the year and, if you are awarded full government aid, athletic aid may have to be reduced.

On the previous pages are examples of what you will receive from a college offering you athletic financial aid: A National Letter of Intent and an Athletic Tender of Financial Assistance. Please note that both of these samples include a line item with a $ sign. This is the amount (or value) you will receive in athletic financial aid. Some Division III institutions also issue a National Letter of Intent, even though NCAA regulations require that Division III colleges claim they offer no athletically related financial aid. This is normally done to "lock in" the prospect so that he/she can only compete at that institution. (More on this bogus claim later.)

Chapter 17

Negotiating Guidelines

In order for a prospect to receive the maximum amount of financial aid for athletic ability, he/she must be prepared to negotiate for that maximum. If you have examined any college's "sticker price," you know the enormous cost, other than most junior colleges, of a college education. The more you attempt to reduce the cost of a college education from the sticker price, the more you increase the pressure on the institution's financial aid officer to resist further reductions. Because of the flexibility of "professional judgment" by the financial aid director, combined with the desire of an institution to enroll a prospect, one rarely knows how much of a reduction can be secured. The only strategy that delivers the reductions you want and deserve is negotiation. If negotiating is a dialogue that makes you so tense that you choose not to do it, you must be ready to accept the inevitable financial consequences. Many uncomfortable, timid parents have left thousands of dollars on the table because they failed to deal with their anxiety about negotiations and potential confrontation. Don't you be one of those timid parents! The money you didn't negotiate for will go to someone who did. Practice using the following strategies, tools, and devices, and you will dramatically increase the chances of getting what you want and deserve.

Negotiations (never use this term with financial aid officers—they hate it!) require some careful balancing and delicate control. Use the following guidelines to ensure that you are in control:

- Be sure the coach always knows that the amount of the financial aid award will be a critical factor in choosing a college. A parent might say, *Coach, I don't mean to be audacious, but it's important to me that you know I need/expect financial aid for my son/daughter.*

- Be sure the coach knows that no commitment will be made until an award letter, tender, or contract is forthcoming. *Coach, I mean no offense, and I'm confident you understand when I say that we can't make a final commitment to you until we receive the award letter [Division III] or athletic tender [Division I or II]. Is that fair?*

The importance of asking "Is that fair?" Are you kidding? You've been telling me that the recruiting process is unfair. Guess what: it is.

This seemingly innocuous sales technique has a powerful effect on the receiver of its message. (If the recipient of that question says no, then that person is unfair.) This subtle psychological device is very powerful because the receiver usually perceives him/herself as a fair person and instinctively wishes to maintain that perception with a "yes" answer. (Meaning: I am a fair person.) Also, the question is unexpected in an emotionally intense situation giving the recipient less psychological room to gather his/her thoughts and respond in his/her best interests and not respond to the psychological protection of their

THE TRUTH Is

Very few people, including coaches, enjoy being perceived as unfair.

image of being fair. (I know it's tough, but you need to be tough. Be tough on yourself and your opponent.) You may wish to use synonyms for the word fair. Try: reasonable, decent, square, evenhanded, principled, above-board, straight, appropriate, all right, okay, equitable, satisfactory, etc. to reduce the ferocity of the question.

- Always tell the coach that his/her institution is your number one choice. *Coach, as you know, you are our number-one choice, but it's very important to us that all the issues, including financial aid, get satisfactorily resolved.*

If you must have more aid, or feel you can negotiate for more, do it with the coach/recruiter. The basis for further negotiation should be the athletic tender. The objective is to increase the amount of the athletic tender. *Coach, I apologize, but after carefully calculating the total financial aid package offered in the award letter, I'm going to need a little more help. I need another $500/$1,000/$2,000. Can you handle that additional amount?* Then be quiet. The first negotiator who talks after a question is asked, loses.

Negotiating Is Selling

Because you are now engaged in a contest where only the opposition knows the rules, the coach and the institution are generally in a position to put psychological pressure on you. They recognize (utilizing rules that they know and that you may not know) that they are in a position of power and control and are usually quick to take advantage of the psychological stress you feel. You need a psychological counter-force (using their rules to compete against them) to level the playing field.

Successful salespeople know what devices to employ when they want to put the ball into the customer's court: that is to say, make them buy the product or service they are selling. A simple counter-force device is one of the most powerful psychological stressors known to man: silence.

A salesperson will ask a closing question like, "Would you like to take the shoes home?" When the customer doesn't answer right away, say fifteen seconds, the timid salesperson can't stand the pressure of no one talking and breaks the silence. The moment he or she starts talking, the sale is lost.

The wise and courageous salesperson remains silent and forces the customer to talk first. When the customer talks, often he or she says yes.

Sometimes the coach will ask a question. This is a good sign.

- It demonstrates the coach's interest in you.
- It provides you the opportunity to ask another closing question.

A coach may ask a question similar to "I can't go $2,000. If I could increase the award letter by $1,000 would that be okay?" Now the coach has asked a closing question. That is to say, he wants you to say yes. That's in his/her best interest.

Only you know the answer to this or a similar question. If your answer is no; say no. Now the ball is back in the coach's court. If you sense the coach is bluffing with that type of question, be quiet.

Colleges give away close to $12 billion of their own funds for financial aid each year. If you want more money (a discount on tuition) than what you are initially offered, you must ask for it. Otherwise your financial aid package will not be increased. And if there is additional financial aid available, it will go to someone else who did ask for it.

If the coach suggests that you sign either of the documents (Athletic Tender or Financial Aid Award Letter) you must decline. "Well, go ahead and sign the award letter and I'll see what I can do."

Your answer should be, *Coach, I don't mean to be offensive, but it's important to me to see if you can secure the increase with a new Financial Aid Award Letter. If you can, I'll sign both the award letter and the athletic tender at the same time. Is that fair?* OR *Coach, I mean no disrespect, but I'd rather sign an Award Letter and the Athletic Tender that both show the additional amount as awarded. Is that fair?* Then be quiet.

If the coach refuses to budge, you've lost nothing. Don't be afraid that the coach will become angry or withdraw the offer. (You have the documents in your hands. Signing them legally compels the institution.) Most coaches expect people to negotiate and usually respect those that negotiate aggressively, yet fairly.

Belligerence and threatening will accomplish nothing. Many parents don't realize that it's important to a financial aid counselor whether you attend the institution as it may affect him or her keeping his or her job. (Another rule they know and you may not know.) Some admission counselors have to generate certain predetermined numbers. If they don't, jobs can be lost.

Sometimes you may have to appeal the financial aid package with a financial aid officer. If you feel that you've not been offered an amount that the institution should reasonably handle or if you can cite new or changed financial circumstances that change your ability to pay, usually a financial aid officer will hear an appeal. If the appeal is for the former, normally, the coach recruiting you will prepare you for the appeal interview. If it is the latter, normally you would handle this yourself.

Remember that the awarding of financial aid is a marketing

tool used to increase or sustain enrollment. If a small- to medium-sized private college is recruiting you, the following bold question often provokes outstanding results. *Isn't it better for the college to have a student enrolled who is receiving enhanced financial aid rather than having an empty seat or an empty bed?* Then be quiet. Pleading and groveling are counterproductive.

You must always be reasonable and calm, yet in control. As you can appreciate, there will be certain schools where negotiations will be less productive than at others. There is a waiting list at many prestigious schools so they don't need to give discounts to attract students.

Chapter 18

Financial Aid Limits

The NCAA limits financial aid for each sport in both Division I and Division II. The NCAA counts athletic financial aid in two categories:

1. **Head-Count Sports.** Used for some Division I sports. Any athlete who receives institutional financial aid, no matter the amount of aid, is counted as one. Head count limit sports are only in Division I. Most, but not all, head count awards are full grant-in-aid (full-rides). All NCAA Division I institutions offer athletic scholarships. All awarded scholarships are on a one-year basis, but can be renewed yearly up to five years over a six-year time period.
   - I-A Football: 85
   - I-AA Football: 63
   - Men's Basketball: 13
   - Ice Hockey: 30 counters/18 equivalencies
   - Women's Basketball: 15
   - Women's Gymnastics: 12
   - Women's Tennis: 8
   - Women's Volleyball: 12

2. **Equivalency Sports.** Any sports not listed above are considered equivalency sports. Generally, this means that one full grant-in-aid (full-ride) can be divided among more than one

student athlete. Each college publishes the cost for a student to enroll in that institution. That cost is used as the benchmark for one full grant-in-aid athletic scholarship. That benchmark scholarship number multiplies the equivalency number assigned to a sport. The product of that multiple determines the actual dollar amount available to award to athletes in the sport being considered. The number of athletes receiving athletic financial aid is irrelevant; only the total amount of dollars in aid given matters in equivalency sports.

Equivalency Limits for Division I Sports

Men's Sports	Women's Sports
Baseball 11.7	Archery 5.0
Cross-Country/Track 12.6	Badminton 6.0
Fencing 4.5	Bowling 5.0
Golf 4.5	Cross-Country/Track 18.0
Gymnastics 6.3	Fencing 5.0
Ice Hockey 18.0	Field Hockey 12.0
Lacrosse 12.6	Golf 6.0
Rifle 3.6	Ice Hockey 18.0
Skiing 6.3	Lacrosse 12.0
Soccer 9.9	Rowing 20.0
Swimming 9.9	Skiing 7.0
Tennis 4.5	Soccer 12.0
Volleyball 4.5	Softball 12.0
Water Polo 4.5	Squash 5.0
Wrestling 9.9	Swimming 14.0
	Synchronized Swimming 5.0
	Team Handball 10.0
	Water Polo 8.0

Some Division I institutions offer cross-country but not track and field.

These institutions may offer 5.0 equivalencies for men and 6.0 equivalences for women in cross-country.

Equivalency Limits For Division II Sports

Men's Sports	Women's Sports
Baseball 9.0	Archery 5.0
Basketball 10.0	Badminton 8.0
Cross-Country/Track 12.6	Basketball 10.0
Fencing 4.5	Bowling 5.0
Football 36.0	Cross-Country/Track 12.6
Golf 3.6	Fencing 4.5
Gymnastics 5.4	Field Hockey 6.3
Ice Hockey 13.5	Golf 5.4
Lacrosse 10.8	Gymnastics 6.0
Rifle 3.6	Ice Hockey 18.0
Skiing 6.3	Lacrosse 9.9
Soccer 9.0	Rowing 20.0
Swimming 8.1	Soccer 9.9
Tennis 4.5	Softball 7.2
Volleyball 4.5	Squash 9.0
Water Polo 4.5	Swimming 8.1
Wrestling 9.0	Synchronized Swimming 5.0
	Team Handball 2.0
	Tennis 6.0
	Volleyball 8.0
	Water Polo 8.0

All Division II sports are considered equivalency sports.

Football, Basketball, and Baseball Special Considerations

Football, basketball, and baseball are the three sports that dominate the American media's attention. These sports all originated in America and each has a rich history of great players, great plays, great games, and zealous fans. Because of their traditions and histories, each of the games is experiencing intense media coverage that in no small part motivates young people with athletic interest to aim for participation, if not glory, by competing in one of the sports.

Not long ago, basketball and football players aspiring to the professional leagues learned and perfected their craft while in college. Aspiring baseball players developed their major-league skills at the minor-league level. Few college baseball players went on to become major-league stars.

While professional football leagues have wisely maintained (except in a few highly publicized instances) their policy of drafting players from college, professional basketball leagues have begun drafting high-school players who are college-basketball prospects. Both sports allow college underclassmen to announce their availability for their sport's draft. More baseball players are emerging from the college ranks, although the best prospects are inundated with offers of money to forego their college education and continue their development in the minor leagues.

Football, basketball, and baseball are securely woven into the sports culture of America and are the goals for most aspiring American athletes. Because of this, special attention must be paid to the necessary preparation required to become a prospect and to the recruiting circumstances unique to each.

Football

Many high-school football players who are college prospects get strung along as they seek roster positions and financial aid. Remember, coaches aren't trying to harm any prospect; their priority is fielding a winning team.

Good college football coaches create a prospect depth chart for the positions for which they are recruiting (computer software is available that helps coaches organize both a depth chart and a prospect chart). If you watched the movie *We Are Marshall*, you saw a wall board sample of a Recruiting Depth Chart. A coach's preference would be to recruit the prospect that is their first choice (number one on the position depth chart). They know, however, that often they will lose their first choice to another college, so they need to have a second and third choice, perhaps even more.

To be certain that coaches keep all the prospects on the depth chart strongly considering their programs, they usually treat all prospects as if they were their first choice. If you happen to be the coach's third or fourth choice, you may think you're as good as successfully recruited because of the way the coach talks to you. But more likely than not, the phone calls and promises will abruptly stop because the coach has successfully recruited a prospect higher on the position depth chart. Some coaches will call to tell you that you are no longer be considered for athletic financial aid, but unfortunately, too many don't and families get hurt. (A rule they know and one you may not know.)

You must never allow yourself to be strung along. You must ask early in the recruiting process where you are listed on the recruiting depth chart for your position. Coaches rarely deceive a prospect when asked a direct question. If you are listed as number three, for example, but you really want to join that program, tell the coach that you want him or her to continue considering you for the roster position. You also want to increase your leverage in the process. *Coach, I appreciate that you think there might be another player that can play my position better than me. Your program is my first choice, and I look forward to demonstrating that I'm the type of player you're looking for. I'm talking to (two, three) other coaches about their programs, so if you choose not to include me in your plans, would you please let me know so I can sign with another college?* Then, be quiet.

While your profile is important, football coaches rarely recruit players without first seeing videotape of them playing. That is why the creation of a video is so vital to your being successfully recruited. Refer back to the section concerning creating an effective videotape.

Many football coaches sponsor or attend football camps or combines. Be sure you know which coaches will be working or attending the combine or camp you attend. Combines are usually organized around a number of activities that allow attending coaches to evaluate speed, power, courage, and strength of prospects. Camps are designed with football skill evaluation and development as the primary objective. Many coaches attend the best camps in order to evaluate prospects they are recruiting. Rarely do college coaches attend camps searching for prospects. However, the wise football prospect will be certain to attend at least one combine.

Basketball

Basketball is the toughest recruiting challenge for a prospect. Why? There are fewer roster positions and scholarships available than in most other major sports.

If it is important to you to play intercollegiate basketball (as opposed to practicing as the "scout squad" against your school's real team), you will want to maintain a higher level of flexibility in your negotiations with the coach. Because of the number of scholarships available, wise prospects have three to four potential programs they are negotiating with in order to ensure a roster position and a solid financial aid package.

As with football, videotape is an essential ingredient to your successful recruitment. Create yours carefully, using the suggestions provided in the videotape section.

Include in your video episodes of ball-handling drills; demonstrate your shooting ability, using every shot you have developed. This is especially important to centers and power forwards as they need to demonstrate they can face the basket and score as well as possess shots that begin with their backs to the basket like turnaround jumpers and hook-shots. Players in these positions must also demonstrate that they can and will score in the face of an opponent.

As with football, participation at prestigious or elite camps is good for creating exposure. Shoot-outs are also the best venues for basketball exposure. Many coaches attend prestigious high-school shoot-outs. However, it's important to remember, they are usually in attendance to evaluate prospects they are already recruiting. If your coach doesn't enter your team in a summer shoot-out, ask him or her to enter one in your area.

Coaches like shoot-outs for scouting purposes as it gives them the opportunity to observe their prospect really playing basketball with all its intensity and skill, demanding the best of the players. Try to learn which coaches will be scouting the shoot-outs you attend.

Baseball

No matter how accomplished you are in the field, no matter your speed from home to first or in the outfield, no matter how strong or accurate your throwing arm (unless you are a pitcher), if you can't hit the baseball, you won't be recruited. Learn to hit. If you can hit, learn to hit better. Batting cages, baseball camps that emphasize hitting, hitting coaches, hitting instructional videos and books, batting tees, and wiffle balls should be a part of your preparation to be a successfully recruited baseball prospect.

Baseball camps and summer leagues are a must for the aspiring intercollegiate baseball prospect. Your video must emphasize your hitting ability. If you are a pitcher, you must emphasize the speed of your fastball as well as its location.

Chapter 19

Solving the Division III Athletic Financial Aid Mystery

This chapter shatters Myth #1: NCAA Regulations and Bylaws disallow Division III institutions from awarding financial aid based on athletic ability. However, it is important to recognize that the vast majority of students participating in sports at the Division III level are receiving substantial financial aid packages. The fact is, NCAA Division III colleges very often provide financial aid for athletic ability. Here is how some timid recruiting education publications and sites deal with the reality of Division III financial aid for athletic ability: Recruiting 101 states that, "While you hear some rumors that some (Division III) do, it is not true. What the coaches can do is find creative ways to give their most sought after prospects money in different areas." That's not financial aid for athletic ability? Likewise, college-athletic-scholarship. com states that, "Division III schools do not offer athletic scholarships, however, the coaches at these schools often know of handsome academic scholarships and grants you might be eligible for." And that statement, too, does not describe financial aid for athletic ability? Give me a break! Supercollege.com, slightly more forthcoming, says, "Division III schools do not offer athletic scholarships. These schools do also consider athletic achievement when deciding to offer grants, financial aid packages, and academic scholarships." Very many of the financial aid awards that these and other recruiting education sites and publications are referencing are often at or near full-ride levels. Plainly stated, Division III colleges are funding the education of student athletes, while publicly pretending that the financial aid that their students receive is for some merit other than athletic ability. How this funding is accomplished is the focus of this chapter.

The NCAA Regulations impacting the types and amounts of financial aid that Division III colleges can award student athletes, by rule, must also be available to all students. The regulations of NCAA rule 15.4.9 states: "The composition of the financial aid package offered to a student athlete *shall be consistent with the established policy* of the institution's financial aid office for all students..." [italics mine]

Rule 15.4.9(c) states: "The financial aid package for a particular student athlete cannot be *clearly distinguishable from the general pattern* of all financial aid for all recipients (of financial aid) at the institution..." [italics mine]

Rule 15.4.9(a) states: "A member institution *shall not consider athletics ability* as a criterion in the formulation of the financial aid package..." [italics mine] (Rules 15.49, 15.49(c), and 15.49(a) are from *NCAA Manual*).

After receiving a profile from one of my clients, a Midwest Division III private college basketball coach contacted her and said she was interested in having her play basketball for the school and asked if she would come to campus for a visit. Prior to the visit, all the pertinent documents were sent to the admissions and financial aid offices. She and her father visited the school, which was not too far from their home. They met the coach, who they liked, and explored the campus with a student guide who was also a basketball player. My client was able to ask questions of the guide, the coach, the athletic director, and others at the admissions office. The tour ended at the financial aid office. The officer presented a financial aid package that I felt was quite generous, filled with impressive grants, awards, and loans, but no athletic scholarship. Her father knew not to expect any, but did some negotiating using the college's grants as a basis. He knew from our discussions that he should negotiate if he felt that she should receive more aid. They both knew that this college was their first choice even though there were two others that they were in serious discussions with.

He reviewed the award letter in front of the officer and declared that it was close to what he had hoped but that he "needed a little more help to get the package to match another college's offer that interested his daughter, as well." The officer asked which college, and found that it happened to be in the same conference. "How much more have you been offered?" It was approximately $1,000. The officer said that she would review the package with the financial aid director and get back to them the following day, which she did. "We can give you an additional $500 in your academic award." As I suggested, he replied, "I'm sorry, but that is $500 that will be very difficult for me to pay, isn't there anything else that can be done?" He then shut up. The officer said that she didn't have the authority to offer any more and suggested that he call the women's basketball coach. He did and explained what had transpired with the financial aid office and that even though her school was their first choice she would be attending the other school and playing basketball for them. The coach asked him to give her another day before a commitment to the other school was made so she could have time to "modify the offer." The athletic director called an hour later and explained to the father that if his daughter would send a short essay on why she wanted to attend and would discuss the essay with him, he might be able to award her an "Interview Scholarship" of $500. She received a great education at that school and played basketball there for four years.

NCAA Division III coaches or recruiters are obliged to tell you that they can't/don't (rule 15.4) offer scholarships for athletic ability (*i.e.*, athletic scholarships). Still, substantial financial aid will very often be awarded to a prospective student athlete. A potential financial aid award for a prospective student athlete by an NCAA Division III school will never, never, never be discussed with you in terms of athletic scholarships or athletic ability. Many of these institutions have learned how to use the scholarship "name game." You *must* play along.

Financial aid will likely be discussed in terms of merit awards, leadership awards, diversity awards, academic and honors awards, loans, employment, "awards of circumstance," and institutional awards. Institutional awards have many names, some of the more common names are: presidential award, founders grant, trustees award, leadership scholarship, etc.

Most colleges offer an institutional grant. Some offer more than one, each grant being given a different name. This institutional grant, no matter what inventive name the college chooses to give it, is a discount on the "sticker price" of that college. The grant often has the college's name as part of the grant title, but some colleges use very creative names.

The meaning is clear. Many NCAA Division III institutions award financial aid to prospects because of athletic ability; but

ILLICIT FINANCIAL AID
CASTS SHADOW ON
DIVISION III
from the *NCAA News*

The Division III subcommittee of the NCAA President's Commission is presently considering restructuring in the areas of governance, membership, and championships, in addition to strengthening Division III transfer-eligibility legislation.

After reading the August 2, 1996, memorandum from the chair of the subcommittee, it is apparent that a sizeable part of its agenda deals with providing fair competition within the Division III membership. Though the committee's structural proposal for governance does include a "committee on eligibility and infraction," there was no mention of any emphasis on eliminating a major cause of our tilted playing field, that cause being illegal financial aid given to Division III student athletes.

Whether it is because there are no television contracts or no large amounts of money involved, there seems to be either a naïve assumption that financial aid violations do not occur at the Division III level or a lack of desire to resolve or even acknowledge the problem.

Well, there is a problem. It is of significant dimensions and not much is being done about it.

The regulations concerning financial aid for student athletes are defined clearly in the NCAA Manual. Bylaw 15.01.10 states that Division III institutions shall award financial aid to student athletes only on the basis of financial need shown by the recipient. Bylaw 15.4 delineates the situations in which athletic ability is not allowed to be a criterion for awarding financial aid.

Yet, in the name of winning, some Division III coaches and administrations are sacrificing their personal and professional integrity, as well as putting the reputation of their schools at risk, by awarding excessive financial aid to student athletes under the guise of leadership, merit, or presidential (or other inventive titles) scholarships.

No matter what the competitive level or reward for winning, these violations of the financial aid rules have no justification. The present Division III administrative restructuring process provides the NCAA with a great and timely opportunity to increase the emphasis on dealing with these violations and those who commit them.

It is also our responsibility as coaches and administrators to deal with the rule breakers. We are supposed to be builders of character, examples of commitment, and role models for the acceptance of responsibility.

We know violations are occurring. Many of us know some who are guilty. Yet, for some reason closely akin to the misguided principle of "honor among thieves," we have allowed and abetted behavior we would not accept from our players or children.

Chris Murphy,
Head Basketball Coach
Maine Maritime Academy

invent an award name so that it appears that the award is for some other criteria.

Very simply, that's the method used by NCAA Division III institutions that decide to circumvent Rule 15.4 and thereby make scholarship money available to students with athletic ability.

If a college offers institutional grants, they are often described in the scholarship description section of the college catalog. The description of the grants may be similar to the following statement: "The Presidential Grant—is given to students to meet their gift eligibility as determined by their financial need and the [name of the college/university's] Assistance Packaging Formula." That formula is usually known only by the financial aid director. Or "Institutionally funded financial aid offered to students to help defer their cost of an education." (Both use Institutional Methodology.) Or as the *U.S.News & World Report* article cited previously states, "Aid officials look at their own school's 'need' (that is to say, how badly they want you to attend based on your academic accomplishments or other talents) [good grief, could they possibly mean athletic ability?] before deciding how much...financial aid...they'll actually award." It goes on to further illuminate the issue, "the first lesson in college economics: financial need is in the eye of the beholder." Fortunately, the foregoing dissembling and hyperbole can be simply distilled into this truth: the financial aid package you receive at most Division III colleges will be based on how badly the school *needs* you!

Often financial aid is awarded based on need. Where financial aid money is concerned, need can mean almost anything. Technically though, this type of award is meant to be based on the financial need of the student. But it has become quite obvious that many Division III institutions have used their unique Assistance Packaging Formula (review the preceding examples of these formulas) to broaden the meaning of need to mean nearly anything that accommodates any perceived needs that are designated and defined, openly or secretly, by the institution and arbitrarily protected by the formula.

Hey! Have you noticed? We need rebounds.

This formula, while usually having financial aid award elements consistent with other institutions is uniquely designed to meet the needs—we need pass receptions—of the particular institution and its students. The institution alone decides what its needs—we need strikeouts—are. The institution alone decides how it will structure its assistance packaging formula. If the college's need—we need sprinters—happens to be powerful or improved athletic teams...well, this isn't brain surgery, is it?

In other words, the institutions are free to structure their assistance packaging formulas so they have considerable flexibility. The institution is also free to name the financial aid grants they award any student or student athlete for the purpose of either enhancing or concealing the real purpose of the financial aid award. The director of financial aid is the staff member responsible for accomplishing

THE TRUTH Is

A great minority of Division III institutions use institutional needs, professional judgment, assistance packaging formulas, and other devices, gimmicks, and methods to circumvent or bend NCAA recruiting rules and regulations.

the institution's enrollment goal. He or she normally has great latitude to be flexible in deciding which prospective student gets what level of assistance and from what category according to the "Assistance Packaging Formula." This latitude, literally written into the enabling federal legislation, is called "professional judgment." A financial aid director using "professional judgment" can change the rules whenever it suits his/her purpose. (We need Iron Crosses.)

College administrators, usually directors of financial aid, decide which prospects "meet" (qualify) the "established criteria" of the financial aid assistance packaging formula. Just as importantly, these administrators also get to decide the meaning for defining and measuring the qualifying terms such as, "consideration, clearly distinguishable, consistent, and general pattern" in designing the institution's award packaging formula. They are also given the freedom, enabled by federal legislation, to use their professional judgment.

The coach of a powerful Division III athletic program stated in an alumni newsletter "If private schools choose to be marginal in their ethics when it comes to awarding scholarships and grants, they can have a pretty good financial aid package." And Fredrick Starr, former president of Oberlin College, stated, "There are many gray areas in the aid formulas. And increasingly, colleges are using aid to shape their classes to ensure that they include students with all the backgrounds and talents the schools are seeking." I'll let you decide what the backgrounds and talents might be for any particular school. The fact is an ever-increasing number of colleges are luring talented freshmen with special inducements like grants and loans based on academic merit, leadership ability (you, like college admission officers, can interpret that term to fit certain needs), and special skills. Hey! We need takedowns.

A confidential study by the National Association of College and University Business Officers Director of Research Robin Jenkins says, "The price warfare is beginning to resemble the frequent-flier programs in the airline industry."

As recently as August 2004, the NCAA's Executive Committee has approved a rule requiring institutions to file, by December 2004, with the NCAA their individual and conference recruiting regulations in an additional attempt to force colleges to comply with the recruiting rules. Violators would face NCAA sanctions.

* * *

After receiving a profile from one of my clients, a Division III state university contacted him to ask if he would come in for a visit to discuss playing football at the school. As it was a relatively small college with an unremarkable football program, I encouraged visiting because he might be able to start as a freshman, which was important to him. He had mediocre grades and a 17 on the ACT and would have been unable to attend any Division I or II institution, yet was told by the coach that that wouldn't be a problem. I called the school and had a catalog sent to him. We met before he and his mom went on the visit, that was to a neighboring state. It was no surprise to me, although it was a shock to his mother and him, that according to the catalog he would be required to pay out-of-state tuition to the tune of $1,965 per semester. They knew they couldn't afford that amount; as a matter of fact, the prospect could only afford to go to a school where a financial aid package equaled nearly a full ride. The mom was reluctant to spend the money to go on a two-day college visit with little hope of her son being accepted. I called the coach, who of course knew that the prospect was on my service, and shared with him the prospect's mother's reluctance and asked him if he would "handle" the trip. He agreed to make it an official visit. I never spoke to him again.

I prepared the mother for the visit in the same manner the book prepares you for a college visit. We especially focused on the out-of-state tuition. During the interview with the coach, the mother expressed her inability to handle the costs of the prospect's education at that institution. The coach replied by asking her not to make any decision until he had talked with the people in admissions and financial aid. He explained to them that he couldn't accompany them to either office because of recruiting rules, but he was confident that her son would be offered a good package. When they were finished being presented with the financial aid package, he told them to ask the officer to call him and he would come to get them to take them to lunch. To their astonishment, they found that they were eligible for a full Pell Grant, a hefty academic award, a Stafford Loan, a minority/diversity grant (the prospect was Hispanic), a Leadership Award, and a waiver of the out-of-state tuition. Their out-of-pocket expenses were $785 per semester, which they could cover.

Even though my client struggled academically for the first year, he not only snagged the roster position, he was a starter after the second game of the season. He accepted the academic challenge his sophomore year, became a small college football hero, and graduated with honors.

Chapter 20

Interdepartmental Communications

NCAA rule 15.4.2 states: "All forms of financial assistance for student athletes shall be handled through the regular college agency or committee that administers financial aid for all students" (*NCAA Manual*, NCAA, p. 217).

Division III recruiting regulations forbid a coach, an athletic director, or for that matter, any person who as an interest in a particular athletic program or from the athletic department to have communications with the college's Financial Aid Department concerning financial aid for any prospective student athlete. This restriction is created to prevent athletic department representatives (coaches) from influencing or manipulating acceptance, enrollment, or a financial aid package on behalf of any prospect. Is that a great concept or what?

Coaches recruit top prospects knowing full well that they can designate to the financial aid director those prospects who should be granted large financial aid packages that are sometimes nearly "full-rides."

THE TRUTH Is

A majority of Division III institutions tolerate this type of communication.

THE TRUTH IS

Some schools in fact encourage these types of communications or give permission to certain coaches within an athletic department to recruit top high-school prospects.

Many metaphorical terms are given to the recruiting practice whereby Division III coaches can recruit top prospects, promise them excellent financial aid packages, and know that the financial aid director will use his or her professional judgment to award that prospect what the coach has already promised. The most common term is called "chipping." This chipping has nothing to do with golf or potatoes. This is chipping as in "blue chip."

Some football coaches have been known to "move the goalpost" for a highly prized prospect. Some softball coaches have recognized the benefits of "shading the pole" for a pitcher who will take her team to the next level. Be alert the next time you watch a professional athletic contest. Listen for the athlete's names and colleges being announced prior to the battle. From time to time you'll hear the name of a college that may be unfamiliar to you. Find that college's home page on the Internet and visit the athletics link. Very often you will learn the NCAA Division of that college is Division III or an NAIA institution.

Division III, as well as NAIA (National Association of Inter-collegiate Athletics) schools are often very competitive with many Division II and even some Division I programs. It is no accident that some of the nation's finest athletes can be found at these schools. Large financial aid packages (usually based on need, the prospect's financial need, or—we need home runs—

often play a crucial role in a student athlete's enrollment in an NCAA Division III or NAIA institution.

So if you are convinced you are a Division I prospect, but you feel you are being overlooked or are being strung along, your best choice for continuing your education and your athletic career, as well as receiving financial aid for your athletic ability, may well be at Division III or NAIA.

Recently, an Indiana high-school football prospect was contacted and pursued by Purdue. Evidently, he fell so low on the depth chart that the calls from the Purdue coaches stopped. No explanation—just stopped! Then Ball State, another Division I college, albeit I-AA, began calling and discussed potential financial aid for the prospect's football ability. Wow—he was excited! He'd still get to compete in Division I. He discovered he wasn't #1 on the depth chart when Ball State signed a prospect from Michigan. He was then contacted by Division III Franklin College. With his opportunities rapidly disappearing, he visited the college and talked with the football coach. "Our high school is bigger than Franklin," he told his high-school coach. He decided that Division III was beneath his Division I ability. But as signing day approached and he realized he wouldn't be sitting with his teammates, his coach beaming behind him, signing a letter of intent on signing day, he swallowed his Division I pride and asked his high school coach to call the Franklin coach to tell him he'd play for Franklin. After a few days of practice, the high school prospect that had convinced himself that he was a Division I prospect called his high school coach to tell him he was going to leave Franklin and come home. The coach incorrectly concluded that his former player just didn't like playing at the Division III level. "Coach, I'm the worst player on the team!" He remained at

Franklin, received a terrific education, and enjoyed competing and contributing to its football program. Division III sports are tough, intense, and the athletes compete as fiercely as any Division I athlete.

Sports Success Matters at Small Colleges, Too

When I started my own recruiting service, Midwest Scouting Reports, I received many surprises, even though I'd persuaded myself that I knew everything; I didn't then and I don't know everything now. A few of my Division III prospects' parents returned visit reports that stated that Division III and NAIA coaches told them that it wasn't important to the school if their teams were successful on the fields of competition. "Our president doesn't care if we win or lose," was one of the comments I heard.

It didn't take long to recognize the duplicity of that statement. Consider being a non-athletic, prospective student being interviewed by an admissions counselor at a small Division III college. Remember the "souk-like haggling" after letters of acceptance go out? Those students that were rejected at Stanford, Texas, Maryland, and MIT are now prospects of the smaller colleges. Often, these schools have too many vacancies to generate the income necessary to remain solvent and deliver the educational services that they promise. The fact is that there aren't enough academically-qualified students to go around (note the increasing size and frequency of so-called "Bridge Programs"; *i.e.*, summer school for at-risk freshmen) for many of the smaller Division II and III colleges; they are anxious to persuade qualified students that attending their college would be a great choice. So there you and your parents sit as an admissions counselor encourages you to recognize the attributes of her school and the wisdom of your choice to attend it. She gushes, in her enthusiasm for the college, "Our president doesn't care if our teams are successful. One of the delightful experiences you can look forward to here at Bunkerschnives University is, on Saturday afternoons in the fall, going to the stadium and watching our losing football team. It's absolutely inspiring. And, if that isn't exciting enough, during the winters months you can watch our losing basketball team as well. Now isn't that another great reason to attend Bunkerschnives?" Not so much. The president *does* care, because she knows the student body wants winning athletic programs. Most incoming students investigate the quality of the school's athletic programs; from what I'm told, athletics is usually the first link clicked from the home landing page.

Little-known and almost-tiny Davidson University marched through larger, popular Division I programs in the 2008 NCAA basketball championships. That team and that coach were inspiring, and I'm not the only one that noticed them. In the two months following the school's unlikely NCAA basketball success, the number of inquiries for enrollment at Davidson increased by more than 45 percent. Winning sports programs attract students to colleges. So coaches, no matter how much money they can or can't offer qualified prospects, must still field competitive and usually winning teams. They know the consequences if they don't!

Twins were cut from a cheerleading squad as seniors in high school, even though they had been members since they were freshmen. Rather than spend a lot of emotional energy on feeling sorry for themselves, they decided that they wanted to do something at school to replace the busy lives they led as cheerleaders. The school had a nascent swimming program so the sisters decided that they would try swimming, as it was a long winter season that was similar to the cheer season. With no prior competitive experience, the two of them quickly became the best team swimmers and team leaders, and they were rewarded with a trip to the state swim meet. However, they were barely recruited.

The Division III school closest to their home (although just across the state border) that showed the most interest in them invited the twins and their parents for a visit. The twins loved the coach, the school, and the swim-team guides they met. In the interview with the coach after the campus tour and before their visit to admissions, the coach told them plainly that she wanted both girls on the team. The family discussed with the coach the cost of sending the twins to the private college. Even though the family had been frugal and owned a modicum of assets, the father made it clear that he couldn't afford to send them without considerable help. The twins were not his only children. The coach encouraged the family to join (an NCAA rules violation) her in a trip to the admissions and financial aid offices (their admission and financial documents had already been received by the school). During the meeting at the financial aid office, the coach explained (this type of meeting and discussion is an NCAA recruiting rules violation) to the combined admissions and financial aid officers that she would be pleased if both girls could join the swimming program, but that the costs for both of them to attend would be prohibitive. The financial aid officer asked the father what it would take for both girls to come to the college. "Two for one," was his answer and, as I taught him, he then remained quiet. After a long, tense silence, the admissions officer finally replied, "We can do that."

The twins have graduated and are both successful teachers.

Other Benefits for Student Athletes

As a former public school teacher and retired School of Education college faculty member, there are few stronger advocates for strong academic attitudes and performance by student athletes. However, I'm realistic enough to recognize that some prospects simply don't have the academic credentials to enter the nation's top ranked colleges. That said, athletes often receive preferential treatment regarding admissions, even at the snootiest of institutions. If a college determines that a prospect can help a team win, generate

THE
TRUTH IS

The NCAA hasn't yet perfected the resources and it appears to have little desire to monitor Division III intensely enough to discover and punish the institutions that are intentionally violating the rules.

substantial and positive public relations, increase the school's brand recognition, and help sell tickets, some admissions legerdemain may well be applied for that athlete. (Remember, institutional methodology.) Recently, it was determined that an athlete had better than a 50 percent admissions advantage over a student with the same SAT/ACT score, even better than the highly publicized admission advantages enjoyed by minority and legacy admissions.

You may not be quite as competitive academically as other students applying for admission and still be admitted to many Division II, III, or NAIA colleges. Your status as an athletic prospect (we need goals) may cause you to receive a "waiver" of the academic entrance standards (SAT/ACT scores, GPA, class rank, etc.) required of other entering students. Because Division III offers no athletic scholarships, the NCAA allows Division III institutions to set their own admission standards. If a Division III college determines that a certain needy student—Hey! We need stuck dismounts—requires a loosening of the admissions requirements, the magic of professional judgment solves the problem.

Some athletic departments conform a little more closely to the regulations, yet still make their wishes known concerning financial aid awards and waivers for good prospects. They inform the admissions department or a counselor concerning what the financial aid requirements are for enrolling a hot or blue-chip prospect. Then Admissions passes the information on to Financial Aid (an NCAA rules violation) so that it can work the magic of financial aid flexibility based on institutional methodology.

Sometimes a list of desirable prospects mysteriously appears on the desk of the appropriate financial aid officer. Then the assistance packaging formula can, with the proper professional judgment flexibility, be fortuitously applied to those prospects' total financial aid packages. If an institution is found to be significantly violating recruiting rules and regulations, to its credit, the NCAA will deal with the violating institution in a severe manner. The NCAA requests that violations be "self-reported," to the NCAA. Most often these self-reported violations are minor in nature and are usually followed by perfunctory NCAA action or no action taken.

Are there any Division III institutions that obey the recruiting regulations? Yes. Of course. You can find them—they are consistently at the bottom of their conference's standings.

Some coaches of these obedient institutions write guest editorials in the *NCAA News*, an online newspaper sent to all NCAA members, pleading that the violations stop, asking that the playing field be level for all Division III institutions. The violations continue.

THE TRUTH Is

Most major violations are reported to the NCAA from outside the athletic program or by student athletes within the program.

As you have learned, many Division III programs do violate the spirit, if not the actual bylaws of the NCAA. You are now aware of this tendency to violate. And you also know how to use the strategies I've created to exploit the systemic violations of NCAA rules and regulations by Division III institutions.

You learned earlier from a letter from a Division III coach to the *NCAA News* that financial aid violations regularly take place. In the past, it appeared that the NCAA either couldn't or didn't want to enforce its own Division III recruiting regulations. Some coaches had accused the NCAA of simply denying that any infractions were occurring. But a long train of complaints and highly publicized violations combined with the potential of new technology has evidently brought the apologists and deniers out of their delusions.

On January 12, 2004, the NCAA Division III President's Council decided to consider a number of proposals. Some were agreed to and are to be implemented. Three of the proposals the council agreed to have a direct bearing on Division III recruiting and awarding of financial aid to Division III student athletes as reported in the *NCAA News*. The most important recommendation made (and consequently implemented) was to begin a process of electronically monitoring the financial aid packages of student athletes and comparing the average value of an enrolled athlete's package with those of regular students. After a pilot program was adopted, the Division III Financial Aid Reporting Program was implemented. Any Division III institution beyond a 4 percent variance between the two groups would be designated for review. (A 4 percent variance can equal as much as $2,500 for a Division III prospect's financial aid package.) An enforcement committee was created to alert and recommend changes to violators. Violators can be sanctioned or otherwise penalized. While a number of Division III institutions generally agree with the objectives of the Financial Aid Reporting Program, many have made their disagreement quite clear. The disagreements identified in a Division III membership survey include: the athletics program's impact on student enrollment, impact on remaining competitive, the unique character of each Division III institution's individual enrollment needs, institutional culture protection, wild cost disparities between Division III institutions, and conference prerogatives in structuring competitive parity. As you have learned, leadership grants provide substantial reductions for many enrolled students, both athletes and regular. Many Division III colleges are asking the NCAA to use sports/athletic leadership grants for certain (probably exceptional) athletes to help reduce their financial burden. At this writing, that exception is being denied. Stayed tuned; the pressure to allow the foregoing grants is substantial. Many schools that feel burdened by the Financial Aid Reporting Program have already been creating ways to circumvent its intent.

One strategy being employed is to invite regular students that might have an interest in an athletic program to "walk-on." These "walk-on" students are then listed on the team rosters and their names, as well as their financial aid packages, are included in the rosters sent to the NCAA. Often, the "walk-on" financial aid package is smaller than the recruited athletes. A significant portion of those "walk-ons" leave the team after a time, yet their financial aid packages remain in the NCAA files. Other rule circumventions continue to be quietly discussed and tried. But the most successful strategy, as described by a Division III lacrosse coach in the *NCAA News*, "Colleges just buy athletes for their programs. It's become especially true for athletes with good academic credentials..." (Being a good student evidently has its rewards.)

The Division III Management Council also recommended to the Division III President's Council that institutions reporting no Level II (minor infractions) violations at the end of an academic year be required to certify that no violation occurred. This appears to be a thinly veiled attempt to force Division III institutions to improve their self-monitoring and self-reporting obligations to the NCAA.

It should be clear that the NCAA is attempting to regulate financial aid awards to student athletes enrolling in Division III institutions. It should be equally as clear that student athletes enrolling in those colleges can and do receive significant financial aid, in addition to other benefits. The NCAA creates the parameters within which Division III colleges are supposed to operate. Within those parameters, each institution makes its own individual, unique financial aid award decisions. Very often, decisions to award financial aid dramatically stretch and often break the recruiting rules and regulations.

So there's good news and bad news. The bad news is that violations are very common. The good news is that if you know the system, you can exploit Division III financial aid flexibility to get what you want and deserve.

Chapter 21

Division III's
Pleasant Surprise

As the foregoing has noted, Division III institutions claim that they don't offer financial aid based on athletic ability. You have learned that all divisions (including Division III) have great flexibility in packaging financial aid awards.

You have also learned that many students attending Division III colleges are playing sports and receiving substantial financial aid. Athletic scholarships awarded by Division II and I are usually awarded on a year-to-year basis. The coach is very often the person who decides if your athletic financial aid is renewed.

Usually, the only way you can lose your financial aid when enrolled in a Division III institution is because your academic performance doesn't meet the institution's publicly announced standards. That standard is normally related to a student's grade point average.

Poor performance during an athletic season isn't supposed to be used as a reason or excuse for reducing the amount of a financial aid package. In fact, you should be able to quit the team and maintain your financial aid package as though you were still on the team. After all, if you weren't awarded any financial aid because of your athletic ability, how can you lose financial aid because you choose to no longer participate in athletics? Your Division III financial aid had nothing to do with you being a recruited student athlete. Right?

Chapter 22

Negotiate, Negotiate, Negotiate

You can and should use the very same flexibility that Division III assistance-packaging formulas provide any college's financial aid director. Deciding to negotiate, but never, ever using that term, and knowing on what basis and what strategies to negotiate with can produce substantial benefits.

Remember, Division III coaches are obliged to tell you, and will always tell you, that the college doesn't offer athletic scholarships. After the coach has made his obligatory comment concerning no athletic scholarships, then you must listen carefully to the next comments.

If those comments indicate that the college "creates excellent financial aid packages," or "works very hard to be sure that our athletes get every dollar they're entitled to," or "we have lots of financial aid available," or "nobody can give you more financial aid than we can," or "we have a strong recruiting program," or "we'll match any financial aid package you're offered," (many financial aid departments will actually request that you send a copy of your financial aid award letter from another school for the purpose of matching it) or similar comments, let the negotiations begin. Each of the foregoing comments were made to my clients when they talked to Division III coaches that were interested in them.

Start your part of the initial negotiations with something like this: *Coach, you're our first choice, so I'm happy to hear that about financial aid, because the amount of financial aid my son/daughter gets will be crucial in the enrollment decision we make.*

Remember, when discussing financial aid with a Division III coach you must always avoid using the term "athletic scholarship" or any similar terms. Your use of this term creates real difficulties for the coach. He/she may feel that it's not in the program's best interest to recruit you.

As you negotiate a financial aid package with a coach, recruiter, or financial aid officer, be sure you are prepared for the discussion by reviewing the paragraphs and scripts from chapters 10, 11, 13, and 15. Have your questions ready.

Many parents make the unfortunate mistake of immediately asking, "How much financial aid is my son/daughter going to get?" This is a colossal error because it immediately puts the coach on the defensive. The coach probably has a good idea of what you can contribute to his/her program, but knows nothing about your EFC# or other pertinent factors used in determining your financial aid package.

Ask first about academics, housing, cost per credit hour, instructor-to-pupil ratio, major fields of study available, food plan, percentage of program athletes who graduate in four/five years, etc. Remember, the coach is interested in the quality of his/her program, not about the financial aid concerns of any one prospect. And it's likely that he/she is recruiting between two and four prospects for the position you want.

Most coaches and financial aid departments are in no position to tell you how much financial aid will be forthcoming on the occasion of your first contact with them. They need transcripts and ACT/SAT scores provided to the Admissions

Office and the Student Aid Report (SAR) made available to the Financial Aid Office.

Only after these documents are in the hands of both admissions and financial aid counselors can they begin to determine the financial aid implications for you and your parents. Only then do they have the data to create a financial aid package using federal and state government grants and loans (federal methodology) and institutional grants and scholarships (institutional methodology). Be persistent, but be patient.

Chapter 23

The Ultimate Negotiating Weapon

Your ultimate negotiating weapon is provided to you free of charge by the college's Financial Aid Office, sometimes called the Office of Financial Planning or Financial Planning Office. That weapon is the Financial Aid Award Letter. It is a letter or form from the college, which states by line item what financial aid awards, grants, loans, work study, etc. you are being offered. See sample Financial Aid Award Letter on page 107.

As you can see, the form is structured in such a way that you can indicate whether you accept or decline each item in the financial aid award package. The form identifies a date by which the completed form must be returned. If the financial aid offered on the Financial Aid Award Letter is not acceptable, or not what you agreed to with the coach, admissions counselor, or financial aid officer, you must return it.

But first send a photocopied form to the coach with a note indicating why you've returned the letter or form and ask him/her to help you get what you want and deserve. If the coach wants you on the team, it is highly likely that someone from the institution's Financial Aid Office will be contacting you shortly to review your financial aid package. Probably they will "modify" the financial aid award to better meet your needs.

This is typically the type of situation for serious negotiation.

You must be ready to use all your negotiation strategies and techniques presented to you in chapters 10, 11, 13, and 15. Generally, what you receive with the first Financial Aid Award Letter is your individual sticker price. It's the price that institution hopes you will settle for. The sticker price can often be changed through negotiations. Remember the "souk-like haggling" mentioned in chapter 1? This is when very serious haggling happens. Be prepared to negotiate.

Here are some suggestions for your negotiation opener:

I'd love for my son/daughter to come to your college, it's his/her first choice and ours, too. For him/her to go there, we need a little more help than what is in the award letter. Could you take a look at the package and see if my son/daughter can be awarded an additional $500/$1,000/$3,000 or more?

or

We've nearly got a deal here. We need an additional ($750) for my son/daughter to be able to attend the university. Can you review the package and see if in the financial aid director's professional judgment *the amount of the award could be increased?* [Using this description subtly informs the coach that you are aware of a rule that most parents and prospects don't know.]

or

I'm sorry, but I was under the impression that my son/daughter would qualify for ($12,500) in financial aid. The award letter only provides for an ($11,000) package. My son/daughter won't be able to attend unless he/she receives that level of help. That will be a shame because you are our first choice.

On the other hand, if the coach can't get additional financial aid or doesn't want to ask the Financial Aid Office for more aid, he/she will contact you. By his/her explanation you will know that you have been awarded all you will receive from that institution. Then it's time to decide to accept the package or move on to another program's offer. (You are negotiating with more than one college, aren't you?)

Once you have made your decision about which college you will attend, it's very important that you notify the other institutions that you've been negotiating with that you will be attending another school. This may well provide someone who is being strung along an opportunity to be recruited and receive financial aid based on his/her athletic ability.

Whether it is called a scholarship, grant, financial aid, or any other name (except a loan), this is an amount of money that you or your parents will not have to pay "out of pocket." Many student athletes receive financial aid that is called or titled everything from a Presidential Grant to a Room Grant to a Leadership Grant, or whatever. Don't get caught up in the semantics of what these funds are called. What's important is the money, not the name associated with it.

Remember this: Talk is cheap, if you don't have it in writing you have nothing. Get it in writing; it will come in the form of an award letter or a similar format.

☑ THE TRUTH Is

Few colleges refuse to reconsider award letters. A substantial majority of American colleges are under extreme pressure to enroll students. They discount tuition and accommodate other needs whenever possible.

Chapter 24

How Do I Contribute to My Future Success?

It's easy. Easier said than done. But you can ensure the kind of future you want for yourself by understanding that those who are the most successful in life recognize that there is no substitute for the will to prepare.

You first prepare by planning. As you know, very few high school athletes continue their athletic careers in college. Just to remind you, less than 10 percent of high-school football players will play in college. Less than 5 percent of high-school basketball players will play in college. Even if you receive a questionnaire from a college coach, the odds are better than 50 to 1 against you receiving a roster position on that college team. So you must prepare for more important things than competing in athletic contests. You must prepare academically to be successfully recruited, as well as being prepared for the more important things coming in your future. Here's how:

Freshman Year
- Get a physical examination from a doctor; present the results to your school's athletic department.
- Meet with your counselor; tell him/her of your goal of playing college sports.

- Ask for an academic course plan that prepares you to meet or exceed the core curriculum requirements that includes courses that can make you an attractive prospect.
- Meet again to discuss your sophomore schedule to be certain you are taking courses that meet the NCAA standards.

Sophomore Year

- Prepare for the ACT/SAT by taking the PACT/PSAT. Take the test at least twice, and more often if possible.
- Watch the NCAA video–*ABC's of Eligibility for College-Bound Student-Athletes*. Your counselor or athletic director should have a copy.
- Meet with your counselor at the end of the first semester to review your transcript and plan your junior courses.

Junior Year

- Tell your coach you want to continue your athletic career in college.
- Take PSAT/PACT again for a final practice before taking the test at the National Testing Site.
- Get a copy of *NCAA Guide for the College-Bound Student-Athlete*. Be certain you are complying with all the regulations. Discuss the *Guide* with your parents.
- Attend your school's college search day. Talk with all schools in which you have any interest.
- Send profiles to at least 50 colleges during the early part of your second semester.
- Sit for the SAT or ACT on the National Testing Date in the winter. Be sure to see your score as soon as possible. If you're not satisfied with the score, sit for the test on the spring National Testing Date.

- Begin recruiting activities as recommended in this book.
- Begin visiting colleges.

Senior Year

Contact Period Rules—For Seniors Only

Contact Period: Unofficial visits, official visits, home visits, off-campus visits, letters, email, coach-initiated phone calls, and high school or club evaluations allowed.

Evaluation Period: Coach-initiated phone calls, letters, email, official visits, unofficial visits, and athletic evaluations at your high school or club allowed. While a coach may watch you play during an evaluation, the coach is prohibited from meeting you off-campus during an evaluation. With that rule stated, some coaches find creative methods to circumvent the rule.

A few years ago, I attended a summer basketball shoot-out at a far western Chicago suburb. A Chicago public high school junior-class blue chipper (named a McDonald's All American after his senior year) was playing with his high school team at the shoot-out. The high-school's bleachers were filled with coaches from the powerful Division I basketball programs in the country. SEC, ACC, Big Ten, Pac Ten, and Big East conferences each had coaches in attendance. They were there to evaluate the players and were prohibited by NCAA rule to meet with any prospect. However, then as now, coach-initiated phone calls to prospects are permissible during the evaluation period. During a game break, I wandered toward the bathrooms. Having been to the high school on many occasions, I knew where seldom used bathrooms were located and made my way toward them. The hallway where these lavatories are located had a bank of eight phones for student use during school hours. As I approached the phone bank I recognized the colossal afro of the Chicago blue chipper in the first booth chatting animatedly on the phone and facing the phone booth on the far end of the phone bank. I slowed down so that I might hear some of his conversation and quickly realized he was talking not with his mother or another family member, but with a college coach. The college coach with whom he was talking was standing in the phone booth on the other end of the phone bank. The coach, now retired from an ACC institution, had and still has a remarkable reputation for winning and ethics. Despite them facing one another and discussing the prospect's recruitment, I guess he could deny that he'd met the blue chipper that day they spoke over the phone from separate phone booths. I know what I concluded; you can decide for yourself. The prospect ended up playing at the University of Illinois and had an unremarkable two years in the NBA.

Quiet Period: Unofficial visits, official visits, home visits, letters, and email allowed. This term and period can be quite confusing. Coaches can have off-campus meetings with you. Coaches can also evaluate you. And you can meet the coach on the college campus. Some might say that's not very quiet.

Dead Period: Only letters, email, and coach-initiated calls allowed. No coach/prospect personal contact anywhere.

Official Visits can begin on the first day of your senior classes.

Refer to your *NCAA Guide for the College-Bound Student Athlete* to be certain that you are complying with the NCAA Recruiting Guidelines.

Too many seniors believe that if they haven't been recruited early in their senior year that the opportunity for successful recruitment has passed them by. Drawing this conclusion is a colossal error! Remember the section on Recruiting Depth Charts? You may well have been on some depth charts. As coaches determine which prospects on their individual depth charts will (or can) be offered financial aid, it causes others on the depth chart to fall lower or even off the chart completely. If you know that you are on one or more depth charts (you did ask when you were speaking to coaches, "Where am I on your recruiting depth chart?" didn't you?) and have fallen too low to be offered athletic financial aid, ask the coach this question: "Coach, do you know of a lower level program that might be interested in me?" After signing day, Division I-AA, Division II, and Division III coaches inundate higher level programs in all sports, asking if they know of an athlete who would be a prospect for their program. Most Division II programs and some Division III programs are populated by athletes who were at one time on Division I depth charts. If you were holding out hope for a Division I offer that didn't come through, contact the Division II or III programs that appeared to be a good fit during your research. In most cases, you can anticipate positive results. While you should begin your personal exposure recruiting activities suggested in the previous chapters early in your high-school career, that certainly doesn't mean that you can't or won't be recruited during your senior year. The truth is that 80 percent of all college recruiting decisions are made after January 1 of your senior year. The wise prospect never gives up! Unless, of course, you make the unfortunate decision to "walk on."

- Meet with your counselor during the first month of school. Review your transcript to be certain you will meet the NCAA Initial Eligibility Center requirements.
- Meet with your coach. Ask his/her advice about improving your chances to continue your athletic career in college and recommendations for schools to consider.
- Begin mailing college applications.
- You have three more National Testing Days for the ACT/ SAT. Take the test until you are satisfied that you have attained your best score. And, if you haven't made a verbal commitment, don't despair. As I said before, 80 percent of college programs make their recruiting decisions after January 1 of a prospect's senior year.

THE TRUTH Is

Luck will have very, very little to do with your becoming successfully recruited. Luck will also have little to do with your success and fulfillment as an adult.

How do you continue to prepare? By committing to yourself, every day, that you will be the best student and the best athlete you can be. How can you accomplish that? You must think, hustle, study, practice, concentrate, persist, focus, and win. You must always believe in yourself. Remember: winners never quit and quitters never win.

Usually when a book of this type ends, the reader is wished good luck. Sorry.

Consider yourself lucky if you're not lazy. Consider yourself lucky if you don't quit. Consider yourself lucky if you believe in yourself.

Create your own luck. Follow the suggestions of *The Sports Scholarships Insider's Guide* so you can be successfully recruited, continue your athletic career, and receive financial aid for your athletic ability. Good courage, good skill, and good preparation.

Chapter 25

Professional Help Wanted

As you can now fully appreciate after reading this book, the trail you are about to begin will not be easy or painless. Engaging the recruiting process takes a commitment of time; of attention to sequence, documentation, and detail; of persistence; and of skill. By following this guide's suggestions carefully, and if you are academically and athletically qualified, you can look forward to receiving financial aid for your athletic ability.

But, as I've learned through many conversations, there are families who realize, because of a wide diversity of circumstances, that they are unable to give the time necessary to a successful recruiting outcome. These families need help. If your family is one of them, there is a solution to your problem: a scouting service with the experts, technological infrastructure, and impeccable reputation with collegiate coaches to match athletically and academically qualified prospects to the right college, right program, and right coach and then walk you through the twists, turns, and unpleasant surprises of the recruiting process until you have been awarded a roster position and financial aid for your athletic ability. That scouting service is *The National Collegiate Scouting Association*. The NCSA matches college coaches with athletically and academically qualified prospects using its state-of-the-art Recruit-Match Program. NCSA redefines collegiate recruiting, having pioneered the "College Recruiting 101" workshops that utilize speakers who are recruiting experts—each with a remarkable personal story, owning comprehensive knowledge of the recruiting process and possessing impressive backgrounds in sports media, collegiate coaching (of which I am one), or collegiate and professional football or basketball. At this writing, it has hosted over four thousand of these immensely valuable workshops at high schools, combines, clinics, tournaments, and camps. NCSA has developed the highly praised *Collegiate Power Rankings Chart*. Scores based on academics, athletics, and graduation rates are calculated and ranked, enabling prospects to evaluate each college and develop a comprehensive understanding of a sports scholarship opportunity at any school.

Over 35,000 college coaches access NCSA's streaming highlight videos and recruiting data via email. It is the largest reliable source for college coaches to locate, identify, and evaluate prospects. NCSA scouts for and recruits for more than 2,100—and the list grows monthly—colleges and universities in twenty-five sports. To learn more, log on to www.ncsasports. org/saef-insidersguide. You will be directed to a landing page available only to those who've read this book. If you can't undertake the exposure process described in this guide and you need help to secure the athletic financial aid you want and deserve, I'm confident you'll be satisfied with the expert assistance that you'll receive from NCSA.

Glossary of Recruiting Terms

athletic scholarship: A discount or grant-in-aid, based on athletic ability, subtracted from the announced tuition and fees of a college.

blue-chip prospect: A student athlete who has demonstrated during high-school competition that he/she has exceptional ability and will likely have an immediate impact on a top-level Division I program.

booster: Any person who demonstrates an interest in a specific sport or in the athletic program of any NCAA college. NCAA prospects or student athletes will lose all NCAA eligibility if found to respond to any direct contact of a booster, including phone calls, mail, or in person.

campus visit: *Official Visit*—A visit that is paid for by the recruiting institution, including: transportation, food, lodging, and entertainment for the prospect. *Unofficial Visit*—A visit that is paid for by the prospect. A prospect can have an unlimited number of unofficial visits to a campus.

combine: A series of tests, measures, and drills used by college coaches to determine the potential of many prospects at one time.

contact: Any face-to-face meeting among a prospect, his/her parents, and any representative (official or unofficial) of a recruiting institution.

core courses: Fourteen required courses in which a prospect must earn a C average. Generally, the courses include: 4 years of English, 3 years of math, 2 years of science, 2 years of social science, and an additional 4 courses drawn from any of the other categories.

division: The NCAA has three divisions: I, II, and III. The NAIA has two divisions: 1 and 3. Recruiting rules vary by division and association.

early signing period: A one-week period in November during which prospects other than football players may sign a National Letter of Intent that commits an athlete to a specific school.

financial aid: Discounts of tuition, fees, and other associated costs that are not based on athletic ability. Athletic ability is likely to be an important factor in the granting of financial aid. Conference and association rules vary, but many schools who claim that they don't offer athletic scholarships still provide substantial financial aid to students who are athletes too.

gender equity: Colleges are required to provide athletic opportunities for women in proportion to the school's population.

graduation rate: The number and percentage of student athletes who have graduated from a college within a six-year period.

JUCO: An acronym for the term "junior college." It identifies two-year junior and community colleges.

Letter of Intent: A document that binds a prospect to a particular institution when signed by the student athlete. The college is bound to provide an agreed-upon athletic scholarship.

NAIA: The National Association of Intercollegiate Athletics is an association of close to 400 small to medium colleges. They sponsor 26 sports for men and women.

23500 West 105th Street

Olate, KS 66051-1325

(913) 791-0044

www.naia.org

Member Institutions

www.naia.org/local/memberschools.html

NCAA: The National Collegiate Athletic Association is an organization consisting of member institutions that create rules and regulations governing eligibility, recruiting, and all aspects of competition for its over 800 members.

700 West Washington St.

P.O. Box 6222

Indianapolis, IN 46206-6222

(317) 917-6222

www.ncaa.org

NCAA Initial Eligibility Center: The Eligibility Center is a department of the NCAA that gathers prospects' test scores and transcripts. It provides eligibility information to both colleges and the prospect.

The NCAA provides a brochure, "Making Sure You Are Eligible to Participate in College Sports," that has a Student Release form. It can be obtained from either your high- school counselor or from the NCAA at their website, www.ncaa.org, or by calling and requesting a form at (319) 337-1492.

Proposition 48: The proposition that created the NCAA regulation that requires prospects to score at least minimum scores on standardized tests and achieve at least a C in the core courses as identified by the Eligibility Center.

prospect: A student athlete who has entered at least ninth grade and has drawn the interest of college recruiters.

qualifier: A prospect that has achieved the grade requirements in the core courses while achieving the minimum acceptable score on the ACT or SAT.

questionnaire: A document that asks a prospect for personal, academic, and athletic information.

recruiting: The process of identifying, contacting, evaluating, persuading, and signing prospects.

Recruiting Calendar: The annual sequence of periods during which coaches may contact prospects by mail or telephone and make home visits, and when prospects can officially visit a college and sign a Letter of Intent.

Recruiting Service: A company that offers to help a prospect by either locating schools that may match the prospect's interests or provide athletic and academic information about prospects to college coaches.

redshirting: The practice of holding a player out of competition for a year. The athlete may still practice with the team. Coaches typically redshirt student athletes so they can add size, strength, or skill, or be in a better depth-chart position for the next season. Injured athletes are sometimes redshirted.

representative of athletic interests: Anyone, whether or not they have an official connection with a school, who supports or assists the school in its recruiting efforts.

scholarship athlete: A student athlete who has been given some form of financial aid based on athletic ability.

signing day: The NCAA designates a day that starts the period when prospects can sign Letters of Intent. Most sports sign in April except for football, which signs in February or during the Early Signing Period in November.

sport camp/clinic: Fee-based sessions during which participants are to receive intensive and qualified coaching in their particular sport. Too often these sessions are used to attract college coaches to evaluate blue-chip talent, with the result that the other participants receive little coaching attention.

strung along: When a prospect is not the number-one choice of a recruiting coach but receives the same treatment as the prospect who is number one.

tape: A videotape that illustrates a prospect's athletic performance or skills.

test scores: An NCAA Division II prospect must score a 700 on the SAT or a 17 on the ACT. NCAA Division I prospects' tests must be combined with their GPAs to determine eligibility. There is a sliding scale, which can be found in your *NCAA Guide for College-Bound Student-Athletes*. For the NAIA, the requirements are 18 ACT or a 740 SAT + 2.00 GPA.

tryout: Practice episodes that demonstrate athletic potential by measuring, weighing, or timing a prospect. They may engage in practice-type games or scrimmages as a part of the tryout. In NCAA divisions, only Division II can hold tryouts. NAIA schools can also hold tryouts.

verbal commitment: The announced intention of a prospect to accept a scholarship from a particular school. Verbal commitments are not binding on prospects.

walk-on: A prospect who opts to try out for a roster position with a college team without receiving an athletic scholarship.

Appendix 1

Additional Resources

Statistical Inventory

Approximate Number of Student Athletes by Division

Division	Men	Women	Total
I	85,800	62,800	148,600
II	45,300	29,500	74,800
III	79,900	57,900	137,800
Total	211,000	150,200	361,200

NCAA Women's Sports Sponsorships

Division	I	II	III
archery	3	0	0
badminton	0	0	3
basketball	325	276	422
bowling	29	15	2
cross-country	321	252	367
equestrian	13	0	0
fencing	25	3	15
field hockey	76	26	153
golf	225	99	142
gymnastics	64	6	15
ice hockey	30	2	40
lacrosse	77	32	149
rifle	11	0	2
rowing	85	16	42

NCAA Women's Sports Sponsorships *(continued)*

Division	I	II	III
rugby	1	0	1
skiing	16	9	18
soccer	295	203	398
softball	265	254	389
swimming	187	68	232
synchronized swimming	3	1	3
tennis	312	210	357
track (indoor)	289	108	219
track (outdoor)	294	156	252
volleyball	312	260	407
water polo	30	10	18

NCAA Men's Sports Sponsorships

Division	I	II	III
baseball	286	227	352
basketball	327	278	390
cross-country	306	224	340
fencing	20	3	13
football	238	151	229
golf	290	192	263
gymnastics	17	1	2
ice hockey	58	7	69
lacrosse	54	29	129
rifle	4	0	4
skiing	14	8	17
soccer	199	157	373
swimming	143	52	191
tennis	269	166	307

track (indoor)	247	106	208
track (outdoor)	264	151	243
volleyball	23	15	43
water polo	21	9	16
wrestling	86	39	98

Financial Aid Information Resources

Websites

Finaid: Financial Aid Information Page at www.finaid.com

Worldwide College Scholarship Directory at www.800headstart.com

College Costs and Financial Aid at www.collegeboard.org

SallieMae Student Loans at www.salliemae.com

FAFSA Information at www.fafsa.ed.gov

Junior Achievement at www.ja.org

Merit Scholarships and Essay Contests at www.fastweb.monster.com

Essay Writing Tips at www.supercollege.com

Other Scholarships at www.wiredscholar.com

More information at www.CollegeSource4u.com

Federal Student Aid Programs at www.studentaid.ed.gov

Scholarship Announcements at www.scholarshipamerica.org

Other Scholarship Strategies at www.studentrewards.com

General Financial Aid Information at www.usnews.com and www.petersons.com and www.collegemoney.com

Financial Planning Calendar, Financial Aid Glossary, and a To Do List for Juniors at www.StudentLoanXpress.com

Connect to over 2,000 colleges and universities at www.collegeNet.com

Virtual College Visitation Day at www.collegeweeklive.com

One-Stop College Shopping at www.collegeparents.org
Help for Low-Income Students at www.collegeaccess.org
Learn the Right Steps at www.knowhow2go.org
More Help with Funding at www.efcagroup.org
Start Planning for College at www.nextstepmagazine.com

Books

Kaplan Scholarships 2009 (Kaplan, 2009)
College Free Board Scholarship Handbook 2008
1001 Ways to Pay for College (Supercollege, 2007)

Recommended Recruiting Service

National Recruiting Service at www.nationalrecruits.com

Appendix 2

Institution Contact Information

All colleges and universities have websites. Connect to the athletics link and you will be presented with the information you'll need to contact any person in the Athletic Department. You can also research any information you wish.

Abilene Christian University
Abilene, TX
www.acu.edu

Adams State College
Alamosa, CO
www.adams.edu

Adelphi University
Garden City, NY
www.adelphi.edu

Adrian College
Adrian, MI
www.adrian.edu

Agnes Scott College
Decatur, GA
www.agnesscott.edu

Alabama Agricultural and Mechanical University
Normal, AL
www.aamu.edu

Alabama State University
Montgomery, AL
www.alasu.edu

Alaska Pacific University
Anchorage, AK
www.alaskapacific.edu

Albany State University
Albany, GA
www.asurams.edu

Albertus Magnus College
New Haven, CT
www.albertus.edu

Albion College
Albion, MI
www.albion.edu

Albright College
Reading, PA
www.albright.edu

Alcorn State University
Alcorn State, MS
www.alcorn.edu

Alderson-Broaddus College
Philippi, WV
www.ab.edu

Alfred University
Alfred, NY
www.alfred.edu

Alice Lloyd College
Pippa Passes, KY
www.alc.edu

Allegheny College
Meadville, PA
www.allegheny.edu

Allen University
Columbia, SC
www.allenuniversity.edu

Alma College
Alma, MI
www.alma.edu

Alvernia College
Reading, PA
www.alvernia.edu

Alverno College
Milwaukee, WI
www.alverno.edu

American Indian College of the Assemblies of God
Phoenix, AZ
www.aicag.edu

American International College
Springfield, MA
www.aic.edu

American Jewish University
Bel Air, CA
www.ajula.edu

American University
Washington, DC
www.american.edu

Amherst College
Amherst, MA
www.amherst.edu

Anderson University
Anderson, IN
www.anderson.edu

Anderson University
Anderson, SC
www.andersonuniversity.edu

Andrews University
Berrien Springs, MI
www.andrews.edu

Angelo State University
San Angelo, TX
www.angelo.edu

Anna Maria College
Paxton, MA
www.annamaria.edu

Appalachian State University
Boone, NC
www.appstate.edu

Aquinas College
Grand Rapids, MI
www.aquinas.edu

Aquinas College
Nashville, TN
www.aquinas-tn.edu

Arcadia University
Glenside, PA
www.arcadia.edu

Arizona State University
Tempe, AZ
www.asu.edu

Arizona State University—West
Phoenix, AZ
www.west.asu.edu

Arkansas Baptist College
Little Rock, AR
www.arbaptcol.edu

Arkansas State University
State University, AR
www.astate.edu

Arkansas Tech University
Russellville, AR
www.atu.edu

Armstrong Atlantic State University
Savannah, GA
www.armstrong.edu

Art Academy of Cincinnati
Cincinnati, OH
www.artacademy.edu

Art Center College of Design
Pasadena, CA
www.artcenter.edu

Asbury College
Wilmore, KY
www.asbury.edu

Ashland University
Ashland, OH
www.ashland.edu

Assumption College
Worcester, MA
www.assumption.edu

Atlanta Christian College
East Point, GA
www.acc.edu

Atlantic Union College
South Lancaster, MA
www.auc.edu

Auburn University
Auburn University, AL
www.auburn.edu

Auburn University—Montgomery
Montgomery, AL
www.aum.edu

Augsburg College
Minneapolis, MN
www.augsburg.edu

Augusta State University
Augusta, GA
www.aug.edu

Augustana College
Rock Island, IL
www.augustana.edu

Augustana College
Sioux Falls, SD
www.augie.edu

Aurora University
Aurora, IL
www.aurora.edu

Austin College
Sherman, TX
www.austincollege.edu

Austin Peay State University
Clarksville, TN
www.apsu.edu

Averett University
Danville, VA
www.averett.edu

Avila University
Kansas City, MO
www.avila.edu

Azusa Pacific University
Azusa, CA
www.apu.edu

Babson College
Babson Park, MA
www.babson.edu

Bacone College
Muskogee, OK
www.bacone.edu

Baker College of Flint
Flint, MI
www.baker.edu

Baker University
Baldwin City, KS
www.bakeru.edu

Baldwin-Wallace College
Berea, OH
www.bw.edu

Ball State University
Muncie, IN
www.bsu.edu

Baptist Bible College
Springfield, MO
www.bbcnet.edu

Baptist Bible College and Seminary
Clarks Summit, PA
www.bbc.edu

Bard College
Annandale on Hudson, NY
www.bard.edu

Bard College at Simon's Rock
Great Barrington, MA
www.simons-rock.edu

Barnard College
New York, NY
www.barnard.edu

Barry University
Miami Shores, FL
www.barry.edu

Barton College
Wilson, NC
www.barton.edu

Bates College
Lewiston, ME
www.bates.edu

Bay Path College
Longmeadow, MA
www.baypath.edu

Baylor University
Waco, TX
www.baylor.edu

Beacon College
Leesburg, FL
www.beaconcollege.edu

Becker College
Worcester, MA
www.beckercollege.edu

Belhaven College
Jackson, MS
www.belhaven.edu

Bellarmine University
Louisville, KY
www.bellarmine.edu

Bellevue University
Bellevue, NE
www.bellevue.edu

Belmont Abbey College
Belmont, NC
www.belmontabbeycollege.edu

Belmont University
Nashville, TN
www.belmont.edu

Beloit College
Beloit, WI
www.beloit.edu

Bemidji State University
Bemidji, MN
www.bemidjistate.edu

Benedict College
Columbia, SC
www.benedict.edu

Benedictine College
Atchison, KS
www.benedictine.edu

Benedictine University
Lisle, IL
www.ben.edu

Bennett College
Greensboro, NC
www.bennett.edu

Bennington College
Bennington, VT
www.bennington.edu

Bentley College
Waltham, MA
www.bentley.edu

Berea College
Berea, KY
www.berea.edu

Berklee College of Music
Boston, MA
www.berklee.edu

Berry College
Mount Berry, GA
www.berry.edu

Bethany College
Scotts Valley, CA
www.bethany.edu

Bethany College
Lindsborg, KS
www.bethanylb.edu

Bethany College
Bethany, WV
www.bethanywv.edu

Bethany Lutheran College
Mankato, MN
www.blc.edu

Bethel College
Mishawaka, IN
www.bethelcollege.edu

Bethel College
North Newton, KS
www.bethelks.edu

Bethel College
McKenzie, TN
www.bethel-college.edu

Bethel University
St. Paul, MN
www.bethel.edu

Bethune-Cookman University
Daytona Beach, FL
www.bethune.cook-man.edu

Biola University
La Mirada, CA
www.biola.edu

Birmingham-Southern College
Birmingham, AL
www.bsc.edu

Black Hills State University
Spearfish, SD
www.bhsu.edu

Blackburn College
Carlinville, IL
www.blackburn.edu

Bloomfield College
Bloomfield, NJ
www.bloomfield.edu

Bloomsburg University of Pennsylvania
Bloomsburg, PA
www.bloomu.edu

Blue Mountain College
Blue Mountain, MS
www.bmc.edu

Bluefield College
Bluefield, VA
www.bluefield.edu

Bluefield State College
Bluefield, WV
www.bluefieldstate.edu

Bluffton University
Bluffton, OH
www.bluffton.edu

Boise State University
Boise, ID
www.boisestate.edu

Boricua College
New York, NY
www.boricuacollege.edu

Boston Architectural College
Boston, MA
www.the-bac.edu

Boston College
Chestnut Hill, MA
www.bc.edu

Boston Conservatory
Boston, MA
www.bostonconserva-tory.edu

Boston University
Boston, MA
www.bu.edu

Bowdoin College
Brunswick, ME
www.bowdoin.edu

Bowie State University
Bowie, MD
www.bowiestate.edu

Bowling Green State University
Bowling Green, OH
www.bgsu.edu

Bradley University
Peoria, IL
www.bradley.edu

Brandeis University
Waltham, MA
www.brandeis.edu

Brenau University
Gainesville, GA
www.brenau.edu

Brescia University
Owensboro, KY
www.brescia.edu

Brevard College
Brevard, NC
www.brevard.edu

Brewton-Parker College
Mount Vernon, GA
www.bpc.edu

Briar Cliff University
Sioux City, IA
www.briarcliff.edu

Bridgewater College
Bridgewater, VA
www.bridgewater.edu

Bridgewater State College
Bridgewater, MA
www.bridgew.edu

Brigham Young University—Hawaii
Laie Oahu, HI
www.byuh.edu

Brigham Young University—Idaho
Rexburg, ID
www.byui.edu

Brigham Young University—Provo
Provo, UT
www.byu.edu

Brown University
Providence, RI
www.brown.edu

Bryan College
Dayton, TN
www.bryan.edu

Bryant University
Smithfield, RI
www.bryant.edu

Bryn Athyn College of the New Church
Bryn Athyn, PA
www.brynathyn.edu

Bryn Mawr College
Bryn Mawr, PA
www.brynmawr.edu

Bucknell University
Lewisburg, PA
www.bucknell.edu

Buena Vista University
Storm Lake, IA
www.bvu.edu

Burlington College
Burlington, VT
www.burlington.edu

Butler University
Indianapolis, IN
www.butler.edu

Cabrini College
Radnor, PA
www.cabrini.edu

Cal Poly—San Luis Obispo
San Luis Obispo, CA
www.calpoly.edu

Caldwell College
Caldwell, NJ
www.caldwell.edu

California Baptist University
Riverside, CA
www.calbaptist.edu

California College of the Arts
San Francisco, CA
www.cca.edu

California Institute of Technology
Pasadena, CA
www.caltech.edu

California Institute of the Arts
Valencia, CA
www.calarts.edu

California Lutheran University
Thousand Oaks, CA
www.clunet.edu

California Maritime Academy
Vallejo, CA
www.csum.edu

California State Polytechnic University—Pomona
Pomona, CA
www.csupomona.edu

California State University—Bakersfield
Bakersfield, CA
www.csub.edu

California State University—Chico
Chico, CA
www.csuchico.edu

California State University—Dominguez Hills
Carson, CA
www.csudh.edu

California State University—East Bay
Hayward, CA
www.csueastbay.edu

California State University—Fresno
Fresno, CA
www.csufresno.edu

California State University—Fullerton
Fullerton, CA
www.fullerton.edu

California State University—Long Beach
Long Beach, CA
www.csulb.edu

California State University—Los Angeles
Los Angeles, CA
www.calstatela.edu

California State University—Monterey Bay
Seaside, CA
www.csumb.edu

California State University—Northridge
Northridge, CA
www.csun.edu

California State University—Sacramento
Sacramento, CA
www.csus.edu

California State University—San Bernardino
San Bernardino, CA
www.csusb.edu

California State University—San Marcos
San Marcos, CA
www.csusm.edu

California State University—Stanislaus
Turlock, CA
www.csustan.edu

California University of Pennsylvania
California, PA
www.cup.edu

Calumet College of St. Joseph
Whiting, IN
www.ccsj.edu

Calvin College
Grand Rapids, MI
www.calvin.edu

Cambridge College
Cambridge, MA
www.cambridgecollege.edu

Cameron University
Lawton, OK
www.cameron.edu

Campbell University
Buies Creek, NC
www.campbell.edu

Campbellsville University
Campbellsville, KY
www.campbellsville.edu

Canisius College
Buffalo, NY
www.canisius.edu

Capital University
Columbus, OH
www.capital.edu

Cardinal Stritch University
Milwaukee, WI
www.stritch.edu

Carleton College
Northfield, MN
www.carleton.edu

Carlow University
Pittsburgh, PA
www.carlow.edu

Carnegie Mellon University
Pittsburgh, PA
www.cmu.edu

Carroll College
Helena, MT
www.carroll.edu

Carroll College
Waukesha, WI
www.cc.edu

Carson-Newman College
Jefferson City, TN
www.cn.edu

Carthage College
Kenosha, WI
www.carthage.edu

Case Western Reserve University
Cleveland, OH
www.case.edu

Castleton State College
Castleton, VT
www.castleton.edu

Catawba College
Salisbury, NC
www.catawba.edu

Catholic University of America
Washington, DC
www.cua.edu

Cazenovia College
Cazenovia, NY
www.cazenovia.edu

Cedar Crest College
Allentown, PA
www.cedarcrest.edu

Cedarville University
Cedarville, OH
www.cedarville.edu

Centenary College
Hackettstown, NJ
www.centenarycollege.edu

Centenary College of Louisiana
Shreveport, LA
www.centenary.edu

Central Baptist College
Conway, AR
www.cbc.edu

Central Christian College
McPherson, KS
www.centralchristian.edu

Central College
Pella, IA
www.central.edu

Central Connecticut State University
New Britain, CT
www.ccsu.edu

Central Methodist University
Fayette, MO
www.centralmethodist.edu

Central Michigan University
Mount Pleasant, MI
www.cmich.edu

Central State University
Wilberforce, OH
www.centralstate.edu

Central Washington University
Ellensburg, WA
www.cwu.edu

Centre College
Danville, KY
www.centre.edu

Chadron State College
Chadron, NE
www.csc.edu

Chaminade University of Honolulu
Honolulu, HI
www.chaminade.edu

Champlain College
Burlington, VT
www.champlain.edu

Chapman University
Orange, CA
www.chapman.edu

Charleston Southern University
Charleston, SC
www.csuniv.edu

Chatham University
Pittsburgh, PA
www.chatham.edu

Chester College of New England
Chester, NH
www.chestercollege.edu

Chestnut Hill College
Philadelphia, PA
www.chc.edu

Cheyney University of Pennsylvania
Cheyney, PA
www.cheyney.edu

Chicago State University
Chicago, IL
www.csu.edu

Chowan University
Murfreesboro, NC
www.chowan.edu

Christian Brothers University
Memphis, TN
www.cbu.edu

Christopher Newport University
Newport News, VA
www.cnu.edu

Citadel, The
Charleston, SC
www.citadel.edu

City University
Bellevue, WA
www.cityu.edu

Claflin University
Orangeburg, SC
www.claflin.edu

Claremont McKenna College
Claremont, CA
www.claremont
mckenna.edu

Clarion University of Pennsylvania
Clarion, PA
www.clarion.edu

Clark Atlanta University
Atlanta, GA
www.cau.edu

Clark University
Worcester, MA
www.clarku.edu

Clarke College
Dubuque, IA
www.clarke.edu

Clarkson University
Potsdam, NY
www.clarkson.edu

Clayton State University
Morrow, GA
www.clayton.edu

Clearwater Christian College
Clearwater, FL
www.clearwater.edu

Cleary University
Ann Arbor, MI
www.cleary.edu

Clemson University
Clemson, SC
www.clemson.edu

Cleveland Institute of Art
Cleveland, OH
www.cia.edu

Cleveland Institute of Music
Cleveland, OH
www.cim.edu

Cleveland State University
Cleveland, OH
www.csuohio.edu

Coastal Carolina University
Conway, SC
www.coastal.edu

Coe College
Cedar Rapids, IA
www.coe.edu

Cogswell Polytechnical College
Sunnyvale, CA
www.cogswell.edu

Coker College
Hartsville, SC
www.coker.edu

Colby College
Waterville, ME
www.colby.edu

Colby-Sawyer College
New London, NH
www.colby-sawyer.edu

Colgate University
Hamilton, NY
www.colgate.edu

College for Creative Studies
Detroit, MI
www.ccscad.edu

College of Charleston
Charleston, SC
www.cofc.edu

College of Idaho
Caldwell, ID
www.collegeofidaho.
edu

College of Mount St. Joseph
Cincinnati, OH
www.msj.edu

College of Mount St. Vincent
Riverdale, NY
www.mountsaint
vincent.edu

College of New Jersey
Ewing, NJ
www.tcnj.edu

College of New Rochelle
New Rochelle, NY
www.cnr.edu

College of Notre Dame of Maryland
Baltimore, MD
www.ndm.edu

College of Santa Fe
Santa Fe, NM
www.csf.edu

College of St. Benedict
St. Joseph, MN
www.csbsju.edu

College of St. Catherine
St. Paul, MN
www.stkate.edu

College of St. Elizabeth
Morristown, NJ
www.cse.edu

College of St. Joseph
Rutland, VT
www.csj.edu

College of St. Mary
Omaha, NE
www.csm.edu

College of St. Rose
Albany, NY
www.strose.edu

College of St. Scholastica
Duluth, MN
www.css.edu

College of St. Thomas More
Fort Worth, TX
www.cstm.edu

College of the Atlantic
Bar Harbor, ME
www.coa.edu

College of the Holy Cross
Worcester, MA
www.holycross.edu

College of the Ozarks
Point Lookout, MO
www.cofo.edu

College of the Southwest
Hobbs, NM
www.csw.edu

College of Visual Arts
St. Paul, MN
www.cva.edu

College of William and Mary
Williamsburg, VA
www.wm.edu

College of Wooster
Wooster, OH
www.wooster.edu

Colorado Christian University
Lakewood, CO
www.ccu.edu

Colorado College
Colorado Springs, CO
www.coloradocollege.
edu

Colorado School of Mines
Golden, CO
www.mines.edu

Colorado State University
Fort Collins, CO
www.colostate.edu

Colorado State University—Pueblo
Pueblo, CO
www.colostate-pueblo.
edu

Columbia College
Chicago, IL
www.colum.edu

Columbia College
Columbia, MO
www.ccis.edu

Columbia College
Columbia, SC
www.columbiacollege
sc.edu

Columbia Union College
Takoma Park, MD
www.cuc.edu

Columbia University
New York, NY
www.columbia.edu

Columbus College of Art and Design
Columbus, OH
www.ccad.edu

Columbus State University
Columbus, GA
www.colstate.edu

Concord University
Athens, WV
www.concord.edu

Concordia College
Selma, AL
www.concordiaselma.edu

Concordia College
Bronxville, NY
www.concordia-ny.edu

Concordia College—Moorhead
Moorhead, MN
www.cord.edu

Concordia University
Irvine, CA
www.cui.edu

Concordia University
Ann Arbor, MI
www.cuaa.edu

Concordia University
Seward, NE
www.cune.edu

Concordia University
Portland, OR
www.cu-portland.edu

Concordia University Chicago
River Forest, IL
www.cuchicago.edu

Concordia University Wisconsin
Mequon, WI
www.cuw.edu

Concordia University—Austin
Austin, TX
www.concordia.edu

Concordia University—St. Paul
St. Paul, MN
www.csp.edu

Connecticut College
New London, CT
www.conncoll.edu

Converse College
Spartanburg, SC
www.converse.edu

Cooper Union
New York, NY
www.cooper.edu

Coppin State University
Baltimore, MD
www.coppin.edu

Corban College
Salem, OR
www.corban.edu

Corcoran College of Art and Design
Washington, DC
www.corcoran.edu

Cornell College
Mount Vernon, IA
www.cornellcollege.edu

Cornell University
Ithaca, NY
www.cornell.edu

Cornerstone University
Grand Rapids, MI
www.cornerstone.edu

Cornish College of the Arts
Seattle, WA
www.cornish.edu

Covenant College
Lookout Mountain, GA
www.covenant.edu

Creighton University
Omaha, NE
www.creighton.edu

Crichton College
Memphis, TN
www.crichton.edu

Crown College
St. Bonifacius, MN
www.crown.edu

Culver-Stockton College
Canton, MO
www.culver.edu

Cumberland University
Lebanon, TN
www.cumberland.edu

CUNY—Baruch College
New York, NY
www.baruch.cuny.edu

CUNY—Brooklyn College
Brooklyn, NY
www.brooklyn.cuny.edu

CUNY—City College
New York, NY
www.ccny.cuny.edu

CUNY—College of Staten Island
Staten Island, NY
www.csi.cuny.edu

CUNY—Hunter College
New York, NY
www.hunter.cuny.edu

CUNY—John Jay College of Criminal Justice
New York, NY
www.jjay.cuny.edu

CUNY—Lehman College
Bronx, NY
www.lehman.cuny.edu

CUNY—Medgar Evers College
Brooklyn, NY
www.mec.cuny.edu

CUNY—New York City College of Technology
Brooklyn, NY
www.citytech.cuny.edu

CUNY—Queens College
Flushing, NY
www.qc.edu

CUNY—York College
Jamaica, NY
www.york.cuny.edu

Curry College
Milton, MA
www.curry.edu

Curtis Institute of Music
Philadelphia, PA
www.curtis.edu

Daemen College
Amherst, NY
www.daemen.edu

Dakota State University
Madison, SD
www.dsu.edu

Dakota Wesleyan University
Mitchell, SD
www.dwu.edu

Dallas Baptist University
Dallas, TX
www.dbu.edu

Dalton State College
Dalton, GA
www.daltonstate.edu

Dana College
Blair, NE
www.dana.edu

Daniel Webster College
Nashua, NH
www.dwc.edu

Dartmouth College
Hanover, NH
www.dartmouth.edu

Davenport University
Grand Rapids, MI
www.davenport.edu

Davidson College
Davidson, NC
www.davidson.edu

Davis and Elkins College
Elkins, WV
www.davisandelkins.edu

Defiance College
Defiance, OH
www.defiance.edu

Delaware State University
Dover, DE
www.desu.edu

Delaware Valley College
Doylestown, PA
www.delval.edu

Delta State University
Cleveland, MS
www.deltastate.edu

Denison University
Granville, OH
www.denison.edu

DePaul University
Chicago, IL
www.depaul.edu

DePauw University
Greencastle, IN
www.depauw.edu

DeSales University
Center Valley, PA
www.desales.edu

Dickinson College
Carlisle, PA
www.dickinson.edu

Dickinson State University
Dickinson, ND
www.dickinsonstate.com

Dillard University
New Orleans, LA
www.dillard.edu

Dixie State College of Utah
Saint George, UT
www.dixie.edu

Doane College
Crete, NE
www.doane.edu

Dominican College
Orangeburg, NY
www.dc.edu

Dominican University
River Forest, IL
www.dom.edu

Dominican University of California
San Rafael, CA
www.dominican.edu

Dordt College
Sioux Center, IA
www.dordt.edu

Dowling College
Oakdale Long Island, NY
www.dowling.edu

Drake University
Des Moines, IA
www.drake.edu

Drew University
Madison, NJ
www.drew.edu

Drexel University
Philadelphia, PA
www.drexel.edu

Drury University
Springfield, MO
www.drury.edu

Duke University
Durham, NC
www.duke.edu

Duquesne University
Pittsburgh, PA
www.duq.edu

D'Youville College
Buffalo, NY
www.dyc.edu

Earlham College
Richmond, IN
www.earlham.edu

East Carolina University
Greenville, NC
www.ecu.edu

East Central University
Ada, OK
www.ecok.edu

East Stroudsburg University of Pennsylvania
East Stroudsburg, PA
www.esu.edu

East Tennessee State University
Johnson City, TN
www.etsu.edu

East Texas Baptist University
Marshall, TX
www.etbu.edu

Eastern Connecticut State University
Willimantic, CT
www.easternct.edu

Eastern Illinois University
Charleston, IL
www.eiu.edu

Eastern Kentucky University
Richmond, KY
www.eku.edu

Eastern Mennonite University
Harrisonburg, VA
www.emu.edu

Eastern Michigan University
Ypsilanti, MI
www.emich.edu

Eastern Nazarene College
Quincy, MA
www.enc.edu

Eastern New Mexico University
Portales, NM
www.enmu.edu

Eastern Oregon University
La Grande, OR
www.eou.edu

Eastern University
St. Davids, PA
www.eastern.edu

Eastern Washington University
Cheney, WA
www.ewu.edu

East-West University
Chicago, IL
www.eastwest.edu

Eckerd College
St. Petersburg, FL
www.eckerd.edu

Edgewood College
Madison, WI
www.edgewood.edu

**Edinboro University
of Pennsylvania**
Edinboro, PA
webs.edinboro.edu

**Edward Waters
College**
Jacksonville, FL
www.ewc.edu

**Elizabeth City State
University**
Elizabeth City, NC
www.ecsu.edu

**Elizabethtown
College**
Elizabethtown, PA
www.etown.edu

Elmhurst College
Elmhurst, IL
www.elmhurst.edu

Elmira College
Elmira, NY
www.elmira.edu

**Elms College (College
of Our Lady of the
Elms)**
Chicopee, MA
www.elms.edu

Elon University
Elon, NC
www.elon.edu

**Embry Riddle
Aeronautical
University**
Daytona Beach, FL
www.embryriddle.edu

Emerson College
Boston, MA
www.emerson.edu

Emmanuel College
Franklin Springs, GA
www.ec.edu

Emmanuel College
Boston, MA
www.emmanuel.edu

**Emory and Henry
College**
Emory, VA
www.ehc.edu

Emory University
Atlanta, GA
www.emory.edu

**Emporia State
University**
Emporia, KS
www.emporia.edu

Endicott College
Beverly, MA
www.endicott.edu

Erskine College
Due West, SC
www.erskine.edu

Eureka College
Eureka, IL
www.eureka.edu

Evangel University
Springfield, MO
www.evangel.edu

**Evergreen State
College**
Olympia, WA
www.evergreen.edu

Excelsior College
Albany, NY
www.excelsior.edu

Fairfield University
Fairfield, CT
www.fairfield.edu

**Fairleigh Dickinson
University**
Teaneck, NJ
www.fdu.edu

**Fairmont State
University**
Fairmont, WV
www.fairmontstate.edu

**Fashion Institute of
Technology**
New York, NY
www.fitnyc.edu

Faulkner University
Montgomery, AL
www.faulkner.edu

**Fayetteville State
University**
Fayetteville, NC
www.uncfsu.edu

Felician College
Lodi, NJ
www.felician.edu

Ferris State University
Big Rapids, MI
www.ferris.edu

Ferrum College
Ferrum, VA
www.ferrum.edu

Finlandia University
Hancock, MI
www.finlandia.edu

Fisher College
Boston, MA
www.fisher.edu

Fisk University
Nashville, TN
www.fisk.edu

Fitchburg State College
Fitchburg, MA
www.fsc.edu

Flagler College
St. Augustine, FL
www.flagler.edu

Florida A&M University
Tallahassee, FL
www.famu.edu

Florida Atlantic University
Boca Raton, FL
www.fau.edu

Florida Gulf Coast University
Fort Myers, FL
www.fgcu.edu

Florida Institute of Technology
Melbourne, FL
www.fit.edu

Florida International University
Miami, FL
www.fiu.edu

Florida Memorial College
Miami, FL
www.fmc.edu

Florida Southern College
Lakeland, FL
www.flsouthern.edu

Florida State University
Tallahassee, FL
www.fsu.edu

Fontbonne University
St. Louis, MO
www.fontbonne.edu

Fordham University
New York, NY
www.fordham.edu

Fort Hays State University
Hays, KS
www.fhsu.edu

Fort Lewis College
Durango, CO
www.fortlewis.edu

Fort Valley State University
Fort Valley, GA
www.fvsu.edu

Framingham State College
Framingham, MA
www.framingham.edu

Francis Marion University
Florence, SC
www.fmarion.edu

Franciscan University of Steubenville
Steubenville, OH
www.franciscan.edu

Franklin and Marshall College
Lancaster, PA
www.fandm.edu

Franklin College
Franklin, IN
www.franklincollege.edu

Franklin Pierce University
Rindge, NH
www.franklinpierce.edu

Franklin University
Columbus, OH
www.franklin.edu

Free Will Baptist Bible College
Nashville, TN
www.fwbbc.edu

Freed-Hardeman University
Henderson, TN
www.fhu.edu

Fresno Pacific University
Fresno, CA
www.fresno.edu

Friends University
Wichita, KS
www.friends.edu

Frostburg State University
Frostburg, MD
www.frostburg.edu

Furman University
Greenville, SC
www.furman.edu

Gallaudet University
Washington, DC
www.gallaudet.edu

Gannon University
Erie, PA
www.gannon.edu

Gardner-Webb University
Boiling Springs, NC
www.gardner-webb.edu

Geneva College
Beaver Falls, PA
www.geneva.edu

George Fox University
Newberg, OR
www.georgefox.edu

George Mason University
Fairfax, VA
www.gmu.edu

George Washington University
Washington, DC
www.gwu.edu

Georgetown College
Georgetown, KY
www.georgetown
college.edu

Georgetown University
Washington, DC
www.georgetown.edu

Georgia College and State University
Milledgeville, GA
www.gcsu.edu

Georgia Institute of Technology
Atlanta, GA
www.gatech.edu

Georgia Southern University
Statesboro, GA
www.georgiasouthern.edu

Georgia Southwestern State University
Americus, GA
www.gsw.edu

Georgia State University
Atlanta, GA
www.gsu.edu

Georgian Court University
Lakewood, NJ
www.georgian.edu

Gettysburg College
Gettysburg, PA
www.gettysburg.edu

Glenville State College
Glenville, WV
www.glenville.edu

Goddard College
Plainfield, VT
www.goddard.edu

Golden Gate University
San Francisco, CA
www.ggu.edu

Goldey Beacom College
Wilmington, DE
www.gbc.edu

Gonzaga University
Spokane, WA
www.gonzaga.edu

Gordon College
Wenham, MA
www.gordon.edu

Goshen College
Goshen, IN
www.goshen.edu

Goucher College
Baltimore, MD
www.goucher.edu

Grace Bible College
Grand Rapids, MI
www.gbcol.edu

Grace College and Seminary
Winona Lake, IN
www.grace.edu

Graceland University
Lamoni, IA
www.graceland.edu

Grambling State University
Grambling, LA
www.gram.edu

Grand Valley State University
Allendale, MI
www.gvsu.edu

Grand View College
Des Moines, IA
www.gvc.edu

Granite State College
Concord, NH
www.granite.edu

Gratz College
Melrose Park, PA
www.gratzcollege.edu

Great Basin College
Elko, NV
www.gbcnv.edu

Green Mountain College
Poultney, VT
www.greenmtn.edu

Greensboro College
Greensboro, NC
www.gborocollege.edu

Greenville College
Greenville, IL
www.greenville.edu

Grinnell College
Grinnell, IA
www.grinnell.edu

Grove City College
Grove City, PA
www.gcc.edu

Guilford College
Greensboro, NC
www.guilford.edu

Gustavus Adolphus College
St. Peter, MN
www.gac.edu

Gwynedd-Mercy College
Gwynedd Valley, PA
www.gmc.edu

Hamilton College
Clinton, NY
www.hamilton.edu

Hamline University
St. Paul, MN
www.hamline.edu

Hampden-Sydney College
Hampden-Sydney, VA
www.hsc.edu

Hampshire College
Amherst, MA
www.hampshire.edu

Hampton University
Hampton, VA
www.hamptonu.edu

Hannibal-LaGrange College
Hannibal, MO
www.hlg.edu

Hanover College
Hanover, IN
www.hanover.edu

Harding University
Searcy, AR
www.harding.edu

Hardin-Simmons University
Abilene, TX
www.hsutx.edu

Harris-Stowe State University
St. Louis, MO
www.hssu.edu

Hartwick College
Oneonta, NY
www.hartwick.edu

Harvard University
Cambridge, MA
www.college.harvard.edu

Harvey Mudd College
Claremont, CA
www.hmc.edu

Hastings College
Hastings, NE
www.hastings.edu

Haverford College
Haverford, PA
www.haverford.edu

Hawaii Pacific University
Honolulu, HI
www.hpu.edu

Heidelberg College
Tiffin, OH
www.heidelberg.edu

Henderson State University
Arkadelphia, AR
www.getreddie.com

Hendrix College
Conway, AR
www.hendrix.edu

Heritage University
Toppenish, WA
www.heritage.edu

High Point University
High Point, NC
www.highpoint.edu

Hilbert College
Hamburg, NY
www.hilbert.edu

Hillsdale College
Hillsdale, MI
www.hillsdale.edu

Hiram College
Hiram, OH
www.hiram.edu

Hobart and William Smith Colleges
Geneva, NY
www.hws.edu

Hodges University
Naples, FL
www.hodges.edu

Hofstra University
Hempstead, NY
www.hofstra.edu

Hollins University
Roanoke, VA
www.hollins.edu

Holy Family University
Philadelphia, PA
www.holyfamily.edu

Holy Names University
Oakland, CA
www.hnu.edu

Hood College
Frederick, MD
www.hood.edu

Hope College
Holland, MI
www.hope.edu

Hope International University
Fullerton, CA
www.hiu.edu

Houghton College
Houghton, NY
www.houghton.edu

Houston Baptist University
Houston, TX
www.hbu.edu

Howard Payne University
Brownwood, TX
www.hputx.edu

Howard University
Washington, DC
www.howard.edu

Humboldt State University
Arcata, CA
www.humboldt.edu

Humphreys College
Stockton, CA
www.humphreys.edu

Huntingdon College
Montgomery, AL
www.huntingdon.edu

Huntington University
Huntington, IN
www.huntington.edu

Husson College
Bangor, ME
www.husson.edu

Huston-Tillotson University
Austin, TX
www.htu.edu

Idaho State University
Pocatello, ID
www.isu.edu

Illinois College
Jacksonville, IL
www.ic.edu

Illinois Institute of Technology
Chicago, IL
www.iit.edu

Illinois State University
Normal, IL
www.ilstu.edu

Illinois Wesleyan University
Bloomington, IL
www.iwu.edu

Immaculata University
Immaculata, PA
www.immaculata.edu

Indiana Institute of Technology
Fort Wayne, IN
www.indianatech.edu

Indiana State University
Terre Haute, IN
web.indstate.edu

Indiana University East
Richmond, IN
www.iue.edu

Indiana University Northwest
Gary, IN
www.iun.edu

Indiana University of Pennsylvania
Indiana, PA
www.iup.edu

Indiana University Southeast
New Albany, IN
www.ius.edu

Indiana University— Bloomington
Bloomington, IN
www.iub.edu

Indiana University— Kokomo
Kokomo, IN
www.iuk.edu

Indiana University- Purdue University— Fort Wayne
Fort Wayne, IN
www.ipfw.edu

Indiana University- Purdue University— Indianapolis
Indianapolis, IN
www.iupui.edu

Indiana University— South Bend
South Bend, IN
www.iusb.edu

Indiana Wesleyan University
Marion, IN
www.indwes.edu

Iona College
New Rochelle, NY
www.iona.edu/info

Iowa State University
Ames, IA
www.iastate.edu

Iowa Wesleyan College
Mount Pleasant, IA
www.iwc.edu

Ithaca College
Ithaca, NY
www.ithaca.edu

Jackson State University
Jackson, MS
www.jsums.edu

Jacksonville State University
Jacksonville, AL
www.jsu.edu

Jacksonville University
Jacksonville, FL
www.jacksonville.edu

James Madison University
Harrisonburg, VA
www.jmu.edu

Jamestown College
Jamestown, ND
www.jc.edu

Jarvis Christian College
Hawkins, TX
www.jarvis.edu

John Brown University
Siloam Springs, AR
www.jbu.edu

John Carroll University
University Heights, OH
www.jcu.edu

John F. Kennedy University
Pleasant Hill, CA
www.jfku.edu

Johns Hopkins University
Baltimore, MD
www.jhu.edu

Johnson and Wales University
Providence, RI
www.jwu.edu

Johnson C. Smith University
Charlotte, NC
www.jcsu.edu

Johnson State College
Johnson, VT
www.johnsonstate
college.com

Judson College
Marion, AL
home.judson.edu

Judson University
Elgin, IL
www.judsonu.edu

Juilliard School
New York, NY
www.juilliard.edu

Juniata College
Huntingdon, PA
www.juniata.edu

Kalamazoo College
Kalamazoo, MI
www.kzoo.edu

Kansas City Art Institute
Kansas City, MO
www.kcai.edu

Kansas State University
Manhattan, KS
www.ksu.edu

Kansas Wesleyan University
Salina, KS
www.kwu.edu

Kean University
Union, NJ
www.kean.edu

Keene State College
Keene, NH
www.keene.edu

Kendall College
Chicago, IL
www.kendall.edu

Kennesaw State University
Kennesaw, GA
www.kennesaw.edu

Kent State University
Kent, OH
www.kent.edu

Kentucky State University
Frankfort, KY
www.kysu.edu

Kentucky Wesleyan College
Owensboro, KY
www.kwc.edu

Kenyon College
Gambier, OH
www.kenyon.edu

Kettering University
Flint, MI
www.kettering.edu

Keuka College
Keuka Park, NY
www.keuka.edu

Keystone College
La Plume, PA
www.keystone.edu

King College
Bristol, TN
www.king.edu

King's College
Wilkes-Barre, PA
www.kings.edu

Knox College
Galesburg, IL
www.knox.edu

Kutztown University of Pennsylvania
Kutztown, PA
www.kutztown.edu

La Roche College
Pittsburgh, PA
www.laroche.edu

La Salle University
Philadelphia, PA
www.lasalle.edu

La Sierra University
Riverside, CA
www.lasierra.edu

Lafayette College
Easton, PA
www.lafayette.edu

LaGrange College
LaGrange, GA
www.lagrange.edu

Laguna College of Art and Design
Laguna Beach, CA
www.lagunacollege.edu

Lake Erie College
Painesville, OH
www.lec.edu

Lake Forest College
Lake Forest, IL
www.lakeforest.edu

Lake Superior State University
Sault Ste. Marie, MI
www.lssu.edu

Lakeland College
Plymouth, WI
www.lakeland.edu

Lamar University
Beaumont, TX
www.lamar.edu

Lambuth University
Jackson, TN
www.lambuth.edu

Lander University
Greenwood, SC
www.lander.edu

Lane College
Jackson, TN
www.lanecollege.edu

Langston University
Langston, OK
www.lunet.edu

Lasell College
Newton, MA
www.lasell.edu

Lawrence Technological University
Southfield, MI
www.ltu.edu

Lawrence University
Appleton, WI
www.lawrence.edu

Le Moyne College
Syracuse, NY
www.lemoyne.edu

Lebanon Valley College
Annville, PA
www.lvc.edu

Lee University
Cleveland, TN
www.leeuniversity.edu

Lees-McRae College
Banner Elk, NC
www.lmc.edu

Lehigh University
Bethlehem, PA
www.lehigh.edu

LeMoyne-Owen College
Memphis, TN
www.loc.edu

Lenoir-Rhyne College
Hickory, NC
www.lrc.edu

Lesley University
Cambridge, MA
www.lesley.edu

LeTourneau University
Longview, TX
www.letu.edu

Lewis and Clark College
Portland, OR
www.lclark.edu

Lewis University
Romeoville, IL
www.lewisu.edu

Lewis-Clark State College
Lewiston, ID
www.lcsc.edu

Liberty University
Lynchburg, VA
www.liberty.edu

Life University
Marietta, GA
www.life.edu

Limestone College
Gaffney, SC
www.limestone.edu

Lincoln College
Normal, IL
www.lincolncollege.
edu

Lincoln Memorial University
Harrogate, TN
www.lmunet.edu

Lincoln University
Jefferson City, MO
www.lincolnu.edu

Lincoln University
Lincoln University, PA
www.lincoln.edu

Lindenwood University
St. Charles, MO
www.lindenwood.edu

Lindsey Wilson College
Columbia, KY
www.lindsey.edu

Linfield College
McMinnville, OR
www.linfield.edu

Lipscomb University
Nashville, TN
www.lipscomb.edu

Livingstone College
Salisbury, NC
www.livingstone.edu

Lock Haven University of Pennsylvania
Lock Haven, PA
www.lhup.edu

Long Island University—C.W. Post Campus
Brookville, NY
www.liu.edu

Longwood University
Farmville, VA
www.whylongwood.
com

Longy School of Music
Cambridge, MA
www.longy.edu

Loras College
Dubuque, IA
www.loras.edu

Louisiana College
Pineville, LA
www.lacollege.edu

Louisiana State University— Alexandria
Alexandria, LA
www.lsua.edu

Louisiana State University—Baton Rouge
Baton Rouge, LA
www.lsu.edu

Louisiana State University— Shreveport
Shreveport, LA
www.lsus.edu

Louisiana Tech University
Ruston, LA
www.latech.edu

Lourdes College
Sylvania, OH
www.lourdes.edu

Loyola College in Maryland
Baltimore, MD
www.loyola.edu

Loyola Marymount University
Los Angeles, CA
www.lmu.edu

Loyola University Chicago
Chicago, IL
www.luc.edu

Loyola University New Orleans
New Orleans, LA
www.loyno.edu

Lubbock Christian University
Lubbock, TX
www.lcu.edu

Luther College
Decorah, IA
www.luther.edu

Lycoming College
Williamsport, PA
www.lycoming.edu

Lynchburg College
Lynchburg, VA
www.lynchburg.edu

Lyndon State College
Lyndonville, VT
www.lyndonstate.edu

Lynn University
Boca Raton, FL
www.lynn.edu

Lyon College
Batesville, AR
www.lyon.edu

Macalester College
St. Paul, MN
www.macalester.edu

MacMurray College
Jacksonville, IL
www.mac.edu

Macon State College
Macon, GA
www.maconstate.edu

Madonna University
Livonia, MI
www.madonna.edu

Maharishi University of Management
Fairfield, IA
www.mum.edu

Maine College of Art
Portland, ME
www.meca.edu

Maine Maritime Academy
Castine, ME
www.mainemaritime.edu

Malone College
Canton, OH
www.malone.edu

Manchester College
North Manchester, IN
www.manchester.edu

Manhattan College
Riverdale, NY
www.manhattan.edu

Manhattan School of Music
New York, NY
www.msmnyc.edu

Manhattanville College
Purchase, NY
www.mville.edu

Mansfield University of Pennsylvania
Mansfield, PA
www.mansfield.edu

Maranatha Baptist Bible College
Watertown, WI
www.mbbc.edu

Marian College
Indianapolis, IN
www.marian.edu

Marian University
Fond du Lac, WI
www.mariancollege.
edu

Marietta College
Marietta, OH
www.marietta.edu

Marist College
Poughkeepsie, NY
www.marist.edu

Marlboro College
Marlboro, VT
www.marlboro.edu

Marquette University
Milwaukee, WI
www.marquette.edu

Mars Hill College
Mars Hill, NC
www.mhc.edu

Marshall University
Huntington, WV
www.marshall.edu

Martin Methodist College
Pulaski, TN
www.martinmethodist.
edu

Martin University
Indianapolis, IN
www.martin.edu

Mary Baldwin College
Staunton, VA
www.mbc.edu

Marygrove College
Detroit, MI
www.marygrove.edu

Maryland Institute College of Art
Baltimore, MD
www.mica.edu

Marylhurst University
Marylhurst, OR
www.marylhurst.edu

Marymount Manhattan College
New York, NY
www.mmm.edu

Marymount University
Arlington, VA
www.marymount.edu

Maryville College
Maryville, TN
www.maryvillecollege.
edu

Maryville University of St. Louis
St Louis, MO
www.maryville.edu

Marywood University
Scranton, PA
www.marywood.edu

Massachusetts College of Art and Design
Boston, MA
www.massart.edu

Massachusetts College of Liberal Arts
North Adams, MA
www.mcla.edu

Massachusetts Institute of Technology
Cambridge, MA
web.mit.edu

Massachusetts Maritime Academy
Buzzards Bay, MA
www.maritime.edu

Master's College and Seminary
Santa Clarita, CA
www.masters.edu

Mayville State University
Mayville, ND
www.mayvillestate.edu

McDaniel College
Westminster, MD
www.mcdaniel.edu

McKendree University
Lebanon, IL
www.mckendree.edu

McMurry University
Abilene, TX
www.mcm.edu

McNeese State University
Lake Charles, LA
www.mcneese.edu

McPherson College
McPherson, KS
www.mcpherson.edu

Medaille College
Buffalo, NY
www.medaille.edu

Memphis College of Art
Memphis, TN
www.mca.edu

Menlo College
Atherton, CA
www.menlo.edu

Mercer University
Macon, GA
www.mercer.edu

Mercy College
Dobbs Ferry, NY
www.mercy.edu

Mercyhurst College
Erie, PA
www.mercyhurst.edu

Meredith College
Raleigh, NC
www.meredith.edu

Merrimack College
North Andover, MA
www.merrimack.edu

Mesa State College
Grand Junction, CO
www.mesastate.edu

Messiah College
Grantham, PA
www.messiah.edu

Methodist University
Fayetteville, NC
www.methodist.edu

Metropolitan College of New York
New York, NY
www.metropolitan.edu

Metropolitan State College of Denver
Denver, CO
www.mscd.edu

Metropolitan State University
St. Paul, MN
www.metrostate.edu

Miami University—Oxford
Oxford, OH
www.muohio.edu

Michigan State University
East Lansing, MI
www.msu.edu

Michigan Technological University
Houghton, MI
www.mtu.edu

Mid-America Christian University
Oklahoma City, OK
www.macu.edu

MidAmerica Nazarene University
Olathe, KS
www.mnu.edu

Mid-Continent University
Mayfield, KY
www.midcontinent.edu

Middle Tennessee State University
Murfreesboro, TN
www.mtsu.edu

Middlebury College
Middlebury, VT
www.middlebury.edu

Midland Lutheran College
Fremont, NE
www.mlc.edu

Midway College
Midway, KY
www.midway.edu

Midwestern State University
Wichita Falls, TX
www.mwsu.edu

Miles College
Birmingham, AL
www.miles.edu

Millersville University of Pennsylvania
Millersville, PA
www.millersville.edu

Milligan College
Milligan College, TN
www.milligan.edu

Millikin University
Decatur, IL
www.millikin.edu

Mills College
Oakland, CA
www.mills.edu

Millsaps College
Jackson, MS
www.millsaps.edu

Milwaukee Institute of Art and Design
Milwaukee, WI
www.miad.edu

Milwaukee School of Engineering
Milwaukee, WI
www.msoe.edu

Minneapolis College of Art and Design
Minneapolis, MN
www.mcad.edu

Minnesota State University—Mankato
Mankato, MN
www.mnsu.edu

Minnesota State University— Moorhead
Moorhead, MN
www.mnstate.edu

Minot State University
Minot, ND
www.minotstateu.edu

Misericordia University
Dallas, PA
www.misericordia.edu

Mississippi College
Clinton, MS
www.mc.edu

Mississippi State University
Mississippi State, MS
www.msstate.edu

Mississippi University for Women
Columbus, MS
www.muw.edu

Mississippi Valley State University
Itta Bena, MS
www.mvsu.edu

Missouri Baptist University
St. Louis, MO
www.mobap.edu

Missouri Southern State University
Joplin, MO
www.mssu.edu

Missouri State University
Springfield, MO
www.missouristate.edu

Missouri University of Science & Technology
Rolla, MO
www.umr.edu

Missouri Valley College
Marshall, MO
www.moval.edu

Missouri Western State University
St. Joseph, MO
www.mwsc.edu

Mitchell College
New London, CT
www.mitchell.edu

Molloy College
Rockville Centre, NY
www.molloy.edu

Monmouth College
Monmouth, IL
www.monm.edu

Monmouth University
West Long Branch, NJ
www.monmouth.edu

Montana State University
Bozeman, MT
www.montana.edu

Montana State University—Billings
Billings, MT
www.msubillings.edu

Montana State University—Northern
Havre, MT
www.msun.edu

Montana Tech of the University of Montana
Butte, MT
www.mtech.edu

Montclair State University
Montclair, NJ
www.montclair.edu

Montreat College
Montreat, NC
www.montreat.edu

Montserrat College of Art
Beverly, MA
www.montserrat.edu

Moore College of Art and Design
Philadelphia, PA
www.moore.edu

Moravian College
Bethlehem, PA
www.moravian.edu

Morehead State University
Morehead, KY
www.moreheadstate.
edu

Morehouse College
Atlanta, GA
www.morehouse.edu

Morgan State University
Baltimore, MD
www.morgan.edu

Morningside College
Sioux City, IA
www.morningside.edu

Morris College
Sumter, SC
www.morris.edu

Mount Aloysius College
Cresson, PA
www.mtaloy.edu

Mount Holyoke College
South Hadley, MA
www.mtholyoke.edu

Mount Ida College
Newton, MA
www.mountida.edu

Mount Marty College
Yankton, SD
www.mtmc.edu

Mount Mary College
Milwaukee, WI
www.mtmary.edu

Mount Mercy College
Cedar Rapids, IA
www.mtmercy.edu

Mount Olive College
Mount Olive, NC
www.moc.edu

Mount St. Mary College
Newburgh, NY
www.msmc.edu

Mount St. Mary's College
Los Angeles, CA
www.msmc.la.edu

Mount St. Mary's University
Emmitsburg, MD
www.msmary.edu

Mount Union College
Alliance, OH
www2.muc.edu

Mount Vernon Nazarene University
Mount Vernon, OH
www.mvnu.edu

Mountain State University
Beckley, WV
www.mountainstate.edu

Muhlenberg College
Allentown, PA
www.muhlenberg.edu

Murray State University
Murray, KY
www.murraystate.edu

Muskingum College
New Concord, OH
www.muskingum.edu

Myers University
Cleveland, OH
www.myers.edu

Naropa University
Boulder, CO
www.naropa.edu

National Hispanic University
San Jose, CA
www.nhu.edu

National University
La Jolla, CA
www.nu.edu

National-Louis University
Chicago, IL
www.nl.edu

Nazareth College
Rochester, NY
www.naz.edu

Nebraska Wesleyan University
Lincoln, NE
www.nebrwesleyan.edu

Neumann College
Aston, PA
www.neumann.edu

New College of Florida
Sarasota, FL
www.ncf.edu

New England College
Henniker, NH
www.nec.edu

New England Conservatory of Music
Boston, MA
www.newenglandconservatory.edu

New Jersey City University
Jersey City, NJ
www.njcu.edu

**New Jersey Institute
of Technology**
Newark, NJ
www.njit.edu

**New Mexico
Highlands University**
Las Vegas, NM
www.nmhu.edu

**New Mexico Institute
of Mining and
Technology**
Socorro, NM
www.nmt.edu

**New Mexico State
University**
Las Cruces, NM
www.nmsu.edu

New School
New York, NY
www.newschool.edu

**New York Institute of
Technology**
Old Westbury, NY
www.nyit.edu

New York University
New York, NY
www.nyu.edu

Newberry College
Newberry, SC
www.newberry.edu

Newbury College
Brookline, MA
www.newbury.edu

Newman University
Wichita, KS
www.newmanu.edu

Niagara University
Niagara University, NY
www.niagara.edu

**Nicholls State
University**
Thibodaux, LA
www.nicholls.edu

Nichols College
Dudley, MA
www.nichols.edu

**Norfolk State
University**
Norfolk, VA
www.nsu.edu

**North Carolina A&T
State University**
Greensboro, NC
www.ncat.edu

**North Carolina
Central University**
Durham, NC
www.nccu.edu

**North Carolina School
of the Arts**
Winston-Salem, NC
www.ncarts.edu

**North Carolina State
University—Raleigh**
Raleigh, NC
www.ncsu.edu

**North Carolina
Wesleyan College**
Rocky Mount, NC
www.ncwc.edu

North Central College
Naperville, IL
www.noctrl.edu

**North Central
University**
Minneapolis, MN
www.northcentral.edu

**North Dakota State
University**
Fargo, ND
www.ndsu.edu

**North Georgia
College and State
University**
Dahlonega, GA
www.ngcsu.edu

**North Greenville
University**
Tigerville, SC
www.ngu.edu

North Park University
Chicago, IL
www.northpark.edu

**Northeastern Illinois
University**
Chicago, IL
www.neiu.edu

**Northeastern State
University**
Tahlequah, OK
www.nsuok.edu

**Northeastern
University**
Boston, MA
www.northeastern.edu

**Northern Arizona
University**
Flagstaff, AZ
www.nau.edu

**Northern Illinois
University**
DeKalb, IL
www.niu.edu

**Northern Kentucky
University**
Highland Heights, KY
www.nku.edu

Northern Michigan University
Marquette, MI
www.nmu.edu

Northern State University
Aberdeen, SD
www.northern.edu

Northland College
Ashland, WI
www.northland.edu

Northwest Christian College
Eugene, OR
www.nwcc.edu

Northwest Missouri State University
Maryville, MO
www.nwmissouri.edu

Northwest Nazarene University
Nampa, ID
www.nnu.edu

Northwest University
Kirkland, WA
www.northwestu.edu

Northwestern College
Orange City, IA
www.nwciowa.edu

Northwestern College
St. Paul, MN
www.nwc.edu

Northwestern Oklahoma State University
Alva, OK
www.nwosu.edu

Northwestern State University of Louisiana
Natchitoches, LA
www.nsula.edu

Northwestern University
Evanston, IL
www.northwestern.edu

Northwood University
Midland, MI
www.northwood.edu

Norwich University
Northfield, VT
www.norwich.edu

Notre Dame College of Ohio
Cleveland, OH
www.notredame
college.edu

Notre Dame de Namur University
Belmont, CA
www.ndnu.edu

Nova Southeastern University
Ft. Lauderdale, FL
www.nova.edu

Nyack College
Nyack, NY
www.nyack.edu

Oakland City University
Oakland City, IN
www.oak.edu

Oakland University
Rochester, MI
www.oakland.edu

Oakwood University
Huntsville, AL
www.oakwood.edu

Oberlin College
Oberlin, OH
www.oberlin.edu

Occidental College
Los Angeles, CA
www.oxy.edu

Oglethorpe University
Atlanta, GA
www.oglethorpe.edu

Ohio Dominican University
Columbus, OH
www.ohiodominican.
edu

Ohio Northern University
Ada, OH
www.onu.edu

Ohio State University—Columbus
Columbus, OH
www.osu.edu

Ohio University
Athens, OH
www.ohio.edu

Ohio Valley University
Vienna, WV
www.ovu.edu

Ohio Wesleyan University
Delaware, OH
web.owu.edu

Oklahoma Baptist University
Shawnee, OK
www.okbu.edu

Oklahoma Christian University
Oklahoma City, OK
www.oc.edu

Oklahoma City University
Oklahoma City, OK
www.okcu.edu

Oklahoma Panhandle State University
Goodwell, OK
www.opsu.edu

Oklahoma State University
Stillwater, OK
www.okstate.edu

Oklahoma Wesleyan University
Bartlesville, OK
www.okwu.edu

Old Dominion University
Norfolk, VA
www.odu.edu

Olivet College
Olivet, MI
www.olivetcollege.edu

Olivet Nazarene University
Bourbonnais, IL
www.olivet.edu

Oral Roberts University
Tulsa, OK
www.oru.edu

Oregon Institute of Technology
Klamath Falls, OR
www.oit.edu

Oregon State University
Corvallis, OR
oregonstate.edu

Otis College of Art and Design
Los Angeles, CA
www.otis.edu

Ottawa University
Ottawa, KS
www.ottawa.edu

Otterbein College
Westerville, OH
www.otterbein.edu

Ouachita Baptist University
Arkadelphia, AR
www.obu.edu

Our Lady of Holy Cross College
New Orleans, LA
www.olhcc.edu

Our Lady of the Lake University
San Antonio, TX
www.ollusa.edu

Pace University
New York, NY
www.pace.edu

Pacific Lutheran University
Tacoma, WA
www.plu.edu

Pacific Northwest College of Art
Portland, OR
www.pnca.edu

Pacific Union College
Angwin, CA
www.puc.edu

Pacific University
Forest Grove, OR
www.pacificu.edu

Paine College
Augusta, GA
www.paine.edu

Palm Beach Atlantic University
West Palm Beach, FL
www.pba.edu

Park University
Parkville, MO
www.park.edu

Patten University
Oakland, CA
www.patten.edu

Paul Quinn College
Dallas, TX
www.pqc.edu

Paul Smith's College
Paul Smiths, NY
www.paulsmiths.edu

Peace College
Raleigh, NC
www.peace.edu

Peirce College
Philadelphia, PA
www.peirce.edu

Pennsylvania College of Technology
Williamsport, PA
www.pct.edu

Pennsylvania State University—University Park
University Park, PA
www.psu.edu

Pepperdine University
Malibu, CA
www.pepperdine.edu

Peru State College
Peru, NE
www.peru.edu

Pfeiffer University
Misenheimer, NC
www.pfeiffer.edu

Philadelphia Biblical University
Langhorne, PA
www.pbu.edu

Philadelphia University
Philadelphia, PA
www.philau.edu

Philander Smith College
Little Rock, AR
www.philander.edu

Piedmont College
Demorest, GA
www.piedmont.edu

Pikeville College
Pikeville, KY
www.pc.edu

Pine Manor College
Chestnut Hill, MA
www.pmc.edu

Pittsburg State University
Pittsburg, KS
www.pittstate.edu

Pitzer College
Claremont, CA
www.pitzer.edu

Plymouth State University
Plymouth, NH
www.plymouth.edu

Point Loma Nazarene University
San Diego, CA
www.pointloma.edu

Point Park University
Pittsburgh, PA
www.pointpark.edu

Polytechnic University
Brooklyn, NY
www.poly.edu

Pomona College
Claremont, CA
www.pomona.edu

Portland State University
Portland, OR
www.pdx.edu

Prairie View A&M University
Prairie View, TX
www.pvamu.edu

Pratt Institute
Brooklyn, NY
www.pratt.edu

Presbyterian College
Clinton, SC
www.presby.edu

Prescott College
Prescott, AZ
www.prescott.edu

Princeton University
Princeton, NJ
www.princeton.edu

Principia College
Elsah, IL
www.prin.edu/college

Providence College
Providence, RI
www.providence.edu

Purdue University—Calumet
Hammond, IN
www.calumet.purdue.edu

Purdue University—North Central
Westville, IN
www.pnc.edu

Purdue University—West Lafayette
West Lafayette, IN
www.purdue.edu

Queens University of Charlotte
Charlotte, NC
www.queens.edu

Quincy University
Quincy, IL
www.quincy.edu

Quinnipiac University
Hamden, CT
www.quinnipiac.edu

Radford University
Radford, VA
www.radford.edu

Ramapo College of New Jersey
Mahwah, NJ
www.ramapo.edu

Randolph College
Lynchburg, VA
www.randolphcollege.
edu

Randolph-Macon College
Ashland, VA
www.rmc.edu

Reed College
Portland, OR
www.reed.edu

Regent University
Virginia Beach, VA
www.regent.edu

Regis College
Weston, MA
www.regiscollege.edu

Regis University
Denver, CO
www.regis.edu

Reinhardt College
Waleska, GA
www.reinhardt.edu

Rensselaer Polytechnic Institute
Troy, NY
www.rpi.edu

Rhode Island College
Providence, RI
www.ric.edu

Rhode Island School of Design
Providence, RI
www.risd.edu

Rhodes College
Memphis, TN
www.rhodes.edu

Rice University
Houston, TX
www.rice.edu

Richard Stockton College of New Jersey
Pomona, NJ
www.stockton.edu

Rider University
Lawrenceville, NJ
www.rider.edu

Ringling College of Art and Design
Sarasota, FL
www.ringling.edu

Ripon College
Ripon, WI
www.ripon.edu

Rivier College
Nashua, NH
www.rivier.edu

Roanoke College
Salem, VA
www.roanoke.edu

Robert Morris College
Chicago, IL
www.robertmorris.edu

Robert Morris University
Moon Township, PA
www.rmu.edu

Roberts Wesleyan College
Rochester, NY
www.roberts.edu

Rochester College
Rochester Hills, MI
www.rc.edu

Rochester Institute of Technology
Rochester, NY
www.rit.edu

Rockford College
Rockford, IL
www.rockford.edu

Rockhurst University
Kansas City, MO
www.rockhurst.edu

Rocky Mountain College
Billings, MT
www.rocky.edu

Roger Williams University
Bristol, RI
www.rwu.edu

Rogers State University
Claremore, OK
www.rsu.edu

Rollins College
Winter Park, FL
www.rollins.edu

Roosevelt University
Chicago, IL
www.roosevelt.edu

Rose-Hulman Institute of Technology
Terre Haute, IN
www.rose-hulman.edu

Rosemont College
Rosemont, PA
www.rosemont.edu

Rowan University
Glassboro, NJ
www.rowan.edu

Russell Sage College
Troy, NY
www.sage.edu

Rust College
Holly Springs, MS
www.rustcollege.edu

Rutgers, the State University of New Jersey—Camden
Camden, NJ
www.rutgers.edu

Rutgers, the State University of New Jersey—New Brunswick
Piscataway, NJ
www.rutgers.edu

Rutgers, the State University of New Jersey—Newark
Newark, NJ
rutgers-newark.rutgers.edu

Sacred Heart University
Fairfield, CT
www.sacredheart.edu

Sage Colleges—Albany
Albany, NY
www.sage.edu

Saginaw Valley State University
University Center, MI
www.svsu.edu

Salem College
Winston-Salem, NC
www.salem.edu

Salem State College
Salem, MA
www.salemstate.edu

Salisbury University
Salisbury, MD
www.salisbury.edu

Salve Regina University
Newport, RI
www.salve.edu

Sam Houston State University
Huntsville, TX
www.shsu.edu

Samford University
Birmingham, AL
www.samford.edu

San Diego State University
San Diego, CA
www.sdsu.edu

San Francisco Art Institute
San Francisco, CA
www.sfai.edu

San Francisco Conservatory of Music
San Francisco, CA
www.sfcm.edu

San Francisco State University
San Francisco, CA
www.sfsu.edu

San Jose State University
San Jose, CA
www.sjsu.edu

Santa Clara University
Santa Clara, CA
www.scu.edu

Sarah Lawrence College
Bronxville, NY
www.sarahlawrence.edu

Savannah College of Art and Design
Savannah, GA
www.scad.edu

Savannah State University
Savannah, GA
www.savstate.edu

School of the Art Institute of Chicago
Chicago, IL
www.saic.edu

Schreiner University
Kerrville, TX
www.schreiner.edu

Scripps College
Claremont, CA
www.scrippscol.edu

Seattle Pacific University
Seattle, WA
www.spu.edu

Seattle University
Seattle, WA
www.seattleu.edu

Seton Hall University
South Orange, NJ
www.shu.edu

Seton Hill University
Greensburg, PA
www.setonhill.edu

Sewanee—University of the South
Sewanee, TN
www.sewanee.edu

Shaw University
Raleigh, NC
www.shawu.edu

Shawnee State University
Portsmouth, OH
www.shawnee.edu

Shenandoah University
Winchester, VA
www.su.edu

Shepherd University
Shepherdstown, WV
www.shepherd.edu

Shimer College
Chicago, IL
www.shimer.edu

Shippensburg University of Pennsylvania
Shippensburg, PA
www.ship.edu

Shorter College
Rome, GA
www.shorter.edu

Siena College
Loudonville, NY
www.siena.edu

Siena Heights University
Adrian, MI
www.sienaheights.edu

Sierra Nevada College
Incline Village, NV
www.sierranevada.edu

Silver Lake College
Manitowoc, WI
www.sl.edu

Simmons College
Boston, MA
www.simmons.edu

Simpson College
Indianola, IA
www.simpson.edu

Simpson University
Redding, CA
www.simpsonuniversity.edu

Skidmore College
Saratoga Springs, NY
www.skidmore.edu

Slippery Rock University of Pennsylvania
Slippery Rock, PA
www.sru.edu

Smith College
Northampton, MA
www.smith.edu

Sojourner-Douglass College
Baltimore, MD
www.sdc.edu

Sonoma State University
Rohnert Park, CA
www.sonoma.edu

South Carolina State University
Orangeburg, SC
www.scsu.edu

South Dakota School of Mines and Technology
Rapid City, SD
www.sdsmt.edu

South Dakota State University
Brookings, SD
www3.sdstate.edu

Southeast Missouri State University
Cape Girardeau, MO
www.semo.edu

Southeastern Louisiana University
Hammond, LA
www.selu.edu

Southeastern Oklahoma State University
Durant, OK
www.sosu.edu

Southeastern University
Washington, DC
www.seu.edu

Southeastern University
Lakeland, FL
www.seuniversity.edu

Southern Adventist University
Collegedale, TN
www.southern.edu

Southern Arkansas University
Magnolia, AR
www.saumag.edu

Southern California Institute of Architecture
Los Angeles, CA
www.sciarc.edu

Southern Connecticut State University
New Haven, CT
www.southernct.edu

Southern Illinois University—Carbondale
Carbondale, IL
www.siuc.edu

Southern Illinois University—Edwardsville
Edwardsville, IL
www.siue.edu

Southern Methodist University
Dallas, TX
www.smu.edu

Southern Nazarene University
Bethany, OK
www.snu.edu

Southern New Hampshire University
Manchester, NH
www.snhu.edu

Southern Oregon University
Ashland, OR
www.sou.edu

Southern Polytechnic State University
Marietta, GA
www.spsu.edu

Southern University and A&M College
Baton Rouge, LA
www.subr.edu

Southern University—New Orleans
New Orleans, LA
www.suno.edu

Southern Utah University
Cedar City, UT
www.suu.edu

Southern Vermont College
Bennington, VT
www.svc.edu

Southern Wesleyan University
Central, SC
www.swu.edu

Southwest Baptist University
Bolivar, MO
www.sbuniv.edu

Southwest Minnesota State University
Marshall, MN
www.southwestmsu.edu

Southwestern Adventist University
Keene, TX
www.swau.edu

Southwestern Assemblies of God University
Waxahachie, TX
www.sagu.edu

Southwestern Christian College
Terrell, TX
www.swcc.edu

Southwestern College
Winfield, KS
www.sckans.edu

Southwestern Oklahoma State University
Weatherford, OK
www.swosu.edu

Southwestern University
Georgetown, TX
www.southwestern.edu

Spalding University
Louisville, KY
www.spalding.edu

Spelman College
Atlanta, GA
www.spelman.edu

Spring Arbor University
Spring Arbor, MI
www.arbor.edu

Spring Hill College
Mobile, AL
www.shc.edu

Springfield College
Springfield, MA
www.springfieldcollege.edu

St. Ambrose University
Davenport, IA
www.sau.edu

St. Andrews Presbyterian College
Laurinburg, NC
www.sapc.edu

St. Anselm College
Manchester, NH
www.anselm.edu

St. Augustine's College
Raleigh, NC
www.st-aug.edu

St. Bonaventure University
St. Bonaventure, NY
www.sbu.edu

St. Cloud State University
St. Cloud, MN
www.stcloudstate.edu

St. Edward's University
Austin, TX
www.gotostedwards.com

St. Francis College
Brooklyn Heights, NY
www.stfranciscollege.edu

St. Francis University
Loretto, PA
www.francis.edu

St. Gregory's University
Shawnee, OK
www.stgregorys.edu

St. John Fisher College
Rochester, NY
www.sjfc.edu

St. John's College
Annapolis, MD
www.sjca.edu

St. John's College
Santa Fe, NM
www.sjcsf.edu

St. John's University
Collegeville, MN
www.csbsju.edu

St. John's University
Queens, NY
www.stjohns.edu

St. Joseph College
West Hartford, CT
www.sjc.edu

St. Joseph's College
Rensselaer, IN
www.saintjoe.edu

St. Joseph's College
Standish, ME
www.sjcme.edu

St. Joseph's College New York
Brooklyn, NY
www.sjcny.edu

St. Joseph's University
Philadelphia, PA
www.sju.edu

St. Lawrence University
Canton, NY
www.stlawu.edu

St. Leo University
Saint Leo, FL
www.saintleo.edu

St. Louis University
St. Louis, MO
www.slu.edu

St. Martin's University
Lacey, WA
www.stmartin.edu

St. Mary-of-the-Woods College
St.Mary-of-the-Woods, IN
www.smwc.edu

St. Mary's College
Notre Dame, IN
www.saintmarys.edu

St. Mary's College of California
Moraga, CA
www.stmarys-ca.edu

St. Mary's College of Maryland
St. Mary's City, MD
www.smcm.edu

St. Mary's University of Minnesota
Winona, MN
www.smumn.edu

St. Mary's University of San Antonio
San Antonio, TX
www.stmarytx.edu

St. Michael's College
Colchester, VT
www.smcvt.edu

St. Norbert College
De Pere, WI
www.snc.edu

St. Olaf College
Northfield, MN
www.stolaf.edu

St. Paul's College
Lawrenceville, VA
www.saintpauls.edu

St. Peter's College
Jersey City, NJ
www.spc.edu

St. Thomas Aquinas College
Sparkill, NY
www.stac.edu

St. Thomas University
Miami Gardens, FL
www.stu.edu

St. Vincent College
Latrobe, PA
www.stvincent.edu

St. Xavier University
Chicago, IL
www.sxu.edu

Stanford University
Stanford, CA
www.stanford.edu

Stephen F. Austin State University
Nacogdoches, TX
www.sfasu.edu

Stephens College
Columbia, MO
www.stephens.edu

Sterling College
Sterling, KS
www.sterling.edu

Stetson University
Deland, FL
www.stetson.edu

Stevens Institute of Technology
Hoboken, NJ
www.stevens.edu

Stevenson University
Stevenson, MD
www.vjc.edu

Stillman College
Tuscaloosa, AL
www.stillman.edu

Stonehill College
Easton, MA
www.stonehill.edu

Suffolk University
Boston, MA
www.suffolk.edu

Sul Ross State University
Alpine, TX
www.sulross.edu

SUNY College of A&T—Cobleskill
Cobleskill, NY
www.cobleskill.edu

SUNY College of Arts and Sciences—Geneseo
Geneseo, NY
www.geneseo.edu

SUNY College of Arts and Sciences—New Paltz
New Paltz, NY
www.newpaltz.edu

SUNY College of Environmental Science and Forestry
Syracuse, NY
www.esf.edu

SUNY College of Technology—Alfred
Alfred, NY
www.alfredstate.edu

SUNY College of Technology—Delhi
Delhi, NY
www.delhi.edu

SUNY College—Brockport
Brockport, NY
www.brockport.edu

SUNY College—Cortland
Cortland, NY
www.cortland.edu

SUNY College—Old Westbury
Old Westbury, NY
www.oldwestbury.edu

SUNY College—Oneonta
Oneonta, NY
www.oneonta.edu

SUNY College—Potsdam
Potsdam, NY
www.potsdam.edu

SUNY Institute of Technology—Utica/Rome
Utica, NY
www.sunyit.edu

SUNY—Albany
Albany, NY
www.albany.edu

SUNY—Binghamton
Binghamton, NY
www.binghamton.edu

SUNY—Buffalo State College
Buffalo, NY
www.buffalostate.edu

SUNY—Empire State College
Saratoga Springs, NY
www.esc.edu

SUNY—Farmingdale
Farmingdale, NY
www.farmingdale.edu

SUNY—Fredonia
Fredonia, NY
www.fredonia.edu

SUNY—Maritime College
Throggs Neck, NY
www.sunymaritime.edu

SUNY—Oswego
Oswego, NY
www.oswego.edu

SUNY—Plattsburgh
Plattsburgh, NY
www.plattsburgh.edu

SUNY—Purchase College
Purchase, NY
www.purchase.edu

SUNY—Stony Brook
Stony Brook, NY
www.stonybrook.edu

Susquehanna University
Selinsgrove, PA
www.susqu.edu

Swarthmore College
Swarthmore, PA
www.swarthmore.edu

Sweet Briar College
Sweet Briar, VA
www.sbc.edu

Syracuse University
Syracuse, NY
www.syracuse.edu

Tabor College
Hillsboro, KS
www.tabor.edu

Talladega College
Talladega, AL
www.talladega.edu

Tarleton State University
Stephenville, TX
www.tarleton.edu

Taylor University
Upland, IN
www.taylor.edu

Temple University
Philadelphia, PA
www.temple.edu

Tennessee State University
Nashville, TN
www.tnstate.edu

Tennessee Technological University
Cookeville, TN
www.tntech.edu

Tennessee Wesleyan College
Athens, TN
www.twcnet.edu

Texas A&M International University
Laredo, TX
www.tamiu.edu

Texas A&M University—College Station
College Station, TX
www.tamu.edu

Texas A&M University—Commerce
Commerce, TX
www.tamu-commerce.edu

Texas A&M University—Corpus Christi
Corpus Christi, TX
www.tamucc.edu

Texas A&M University—Kingsville
Kingsville, TX
www.tamuk.edu

Texas Christian University
Fort Worth, TX
www.tcu.edu

Texas College
Tyler, TX
www.texascollege.edu

Texas Lutheran University
Seguin, TX
www.tlu.edu

Texas Southern University
Houston, TX
www.tsu.edu

Texas State University—San Marcos
San Marcos, TX
www.txstate.edu

Texas Tech University
Lubbock, TX
www.ttu.edu

Texas Wesleyan University
Fort Worth, TX
www.txwesleyan.edu

Texas Woman's University
Denton, TX
www.twu.edu

Thiel College
Greenville, PA
www.thiel.edu

Thomas Aquinas College
Santa Paula, CA
www.thomasaquinas.edu

Thomas College
Waterville, ME
www.thomas.edu

Thomas Edison State College
Trenton, NJ
www.tesc.edu

Thomas More College
Crestview Hills, KY
www.thomasmore.edu

Thomas More College of Liberal Arts
Merrimack, NH
www.thomasmorecollege.edu

Thomas University
Thomasville, GA
www.thomasu.edu

Tiffin University
Tiffin, OH
www.tiffin.edu

Toccoa Falls College
Toccoa Falls, GA
www.tfc.edu

Tougaloo College
Tougaloo, MS
www.tougaloo.edu

Touro College
New York, NY
www.touro.edu

Towson University
Towson, MD
www.towson.edu

Transylvania University
Lexington, KY
www.transy.edu

Trevecca Nazarene University
Nashville, TN
www.trevecca.edu

Trinity Christian College
Palos Heights, IL
www.trnty.edu

Trinity College
Hartford, CT
www.trincoll.edu

Trinity International University
Deerfield, IL
www.tiu.edu

Trinity University
Washington, DC
www.trinitydc.edu

Trinity University
San Antonio, TX
www.trinity.edu

Tri-State University
Angola, IN
www.trine.edu

Troy University
Troy, AL
www.troy.edu

Truman State University
Kirksville, MO
www.truman.edu

Tufts University
Medford, MA
www.tufts.edu

Tulane University
New Orleans, LA
www.tulane.edu

Tusculum College
Greeneville, TN
www.tusculum.edu

Tuskegee University
Tuskegee, AL
www.tuskegee.edu

Union College
Barbourville, KY
www.unionky.edu

Union College
Lincoln, NE
www.ucollege.edu

Union College
Schenectady, NY
www.union.edu

Union Institute and University
Cincinnati, OH
www.tui.edu

Union University
Jackson, TN
www.uu.edu

United States Air Force Academy
USAF Academy, CO
www.usafa.edu

United States Coast Guard Academy
New London, CT
www.uscga.edu

United States Merchant Marine Academy
Kings Point, NY
www.usmma.edu

United States Military Academy
West Point, NY
www.usma.edu

United States Naval Academy
Annapolis, MD
www.usna.edu

Unity College
Unity, ME
www.unity.edu

University at Buffalo—SUNY
Buffalo, NY
www.buffalo.edu

University of Akron
Akron, OH
www.uakron.edu

University of Alabama
Tuscaloosa, AL
www.ua.edu

University of Alabama—Birmingham
Birmingham, AL
www.uab.edu

University of Alabama—Huntsville
Huntsville, AL
www.uah.edu

University of Alaska—Anchorage
Anchorage, AK
www.uaa.alaska.edu

University of Alaska—Fairbanks
Fairbanks, AK
www.uaf.edu

University of Alaska—Southeast
Juneau, AK
www.uas.alaska.edu

University of Arizona
Tucson, AZ
www.arizona.edu

University of Arkansas
Fayetteville, AR
www.uark.edu

University of Arkansas—Fort Smith
Fort Smith, AR
www.uafortsmith.edu

University of Arkansas—Little Rock
Little Rock, AR
www.ualr.edu

University of Arkansas—Monticello
Monticello, AR
www.uamont.edu

University of Arkansas—Pine Bluff
Pine Bluff, AR
www.uapb.edu

University of Baltimore
Baltimore, MD
www.ubalt.edu

University of Bridgeport
Bridgeport, CT
www.bridgeport.edu

University of California—Berkeley
Berkeley, CA
www.berkeley.edu

University of California—Davis
Davis, CA
www.ucdavis.edu

University of California—Irvine
Irvine, CA
www.uci.edu

University of California—Los Angeles
Los Angeles, CA
www.ucla.edu

University of California—Riverside
Riverside, CA
www.ucr.edu

University of California—San Diego
La Jolla, CA
www.ucsd.edu

University of California—Santa Barbara
Santa Barbara, CA
www.ucsb.edu

University of California—Santa Cruz
Santa Cruz, CA
www.ucsc.edu

University of Central Arkansas
Conway, AR
www.uca.edu

University of Central Florida
Orlando, FL
www.ucf.edu

University of Central Missouri
Warrensburg, MO
www.ucmo.edu

University of Central Oklahoma
Edmond, OK
www.ucok.edu

University of Charleston
Charleston, WV
www.ucwv.edu

University of Chicago
Chicago, IL
www.uchicago.edu

University of Cincinnati
Cincinnati, OH
www.uc.edu

University of Colorado—Boulder
Boulder, CO
www.colorado.edu

University of Colorado—Colorado Springs
Colorado Springs, CO
www.uccs.edu

University of Colorado—Denver
Denver, CO
www.cudenver.edu

University of Connecticut
Storrs, CT
www.uconn.edu

University of Dallas
Irving, TX
www.udallas.edu

University of Dayton
Dayton, OH
www.udayton.edu

University of Delaware
Newark, DE
www.udel.edu

University of Denver
Denver, CO
www.du.edu

University of Detroit Mercy
Detroit, MI
www.udmercy.edu

University of Dubuque
Dubuque, IA
www.dbq.edu

University of Evansville
Evansville, IN
www.evansville.edu

University of Findlay
Findlay, OH
www.findlay.edu

University of Florida
Gainesville, FL
www.ufl.edu

University of Georgia
Athens, GA
www.uga.edu

University of Great Falls
Great Falls, MT
www.ugf.edu

University of Hartford
West Hartford, CT
www.hartford.edu

University of Hawaii—Hilo
Hilo, HI
www.uhh.hawaii.edu

University of Hawaii—Manoa
Honolulu, HI
www.manoa.hawaii.edu

University of Houston
Houston, TX
www.uh.edu

University of Houston—Downtown
Houston, TX
www.uhd.edu

University of Idaho
Moscow, ID
www.its.uidaho.edu

University of Illinois—Chicago
Chicago, IL
www.uic.edu

University of Illinois—Springfield
Springfield, IL
www.uis.edu

University of Illinois—Urbana-Champaign
Champaign, IL
www.uiuc.edu

University of Indianapolis
Indianapolis, IN
www.uindy.edu

University of Iowa
Iowa City, IA
www.uiowa.edu

University of Kansas
Lawrence, KS
www.ku.edu

University of Kentucky
Lexington, KY
www.uky.edu

University of La Verne
La Verne, CA
www.ulv.edu

University of Louisiana—Lafayette
Lafayette, LA
www.louisiana.edu

University of Louisiana—Monroe
Monroe, LA
www.ulm.edu

University of Louisville
Louisville, KY
www.louisville.edu

University of Maine
Orono, ME
www.umaine.edu

University of Maine—Augusta
Augusta, ME
www.uma.edu

University of Maine—Farmington
Farmington, ME
www.farmington.edu

University of Maine—Fort Kent
Fort Kent, ME
www.umfk.maine.edu

University of Maine—Machias
Machias, ME
www.umm.maine.edu

University of Maine—Presque Isle
Presque Isle, ME
www.umpi.maine.edu

University of Mary
Bismarck, ND
www.umary.edu

University of Mary Hardin-Baylor
Belton, TX
www.umhb.edu

University of Mary Washington
Fredericksburg, VA
www.umw.edu

University of Maryland—Baltimore County
Baltimore, MD
www.umbc.edu

University of Maryland—College Park
College Park, MD
www.maryland.edu

University of Maryland—Eastern Shore
Princess Anne, MD
www.umes.edu

University of Maryland—University College
Adelphi, MD
www.umuc.edu

University of Massachusetts—Amherst
Amherst, MA
www.umass.edu

University of Massachusetts—Boston
Boston, MA
www.umb.edu

**University of
Massachusetts—
Dartmouth**
North Dartmouth, MA
www.umassd.edu

**University of
Massachusetts—
Lowell**
Lowell, MA
www.uml.edu

**University of
Memphis**
Memphis, TN
www.memphis.edu

University of Miami
Coral Gables, FL
www.miami.edu

**University of
Michigan—Ann Arbor**
Ann Arbor, MI
www.umich.edu

**University of
Michigan—Dearborn**
Dearborn, MI
www.umd.umich.edu

**University of
Michigan—Flint**
Flint, MI
www.umflint.edu

**University of
Minnesota—
Crookston**
Crookston, MN
www.umcrookston.edu

**University of
Minnesota—Duluth**
Duluth, MN
www.d.umn.edu

**University of
Minnesota—Morris**
Morris, MN
www.morris.umn.edu

**University of
Minnesota—Twin
Cities**
Minneapolis, MN
www.umn.edu

**University of
Mississippi**
University, MS
www.olemiss.edu

**University of
Missouri—Columbia**
Columbia, MO
www.missouri.edu

**University of
Missouri—Kansas City**
Kansas City, MO
www.umkc.edu

**University of
Missouri—St. Louis**
St. Louis, MO
www.umsl.edu

University of Mobile
Mobile, AL
www.umobile.edu

**University of
Montana**
Missoula, MT
www.umt.edu

**University of
Montana—Western**
Dillon, MT
www.umwestern.edu

**University of
Montevallo**
Montevallo, AL
www.montevallo.edu

**University of
Nebraska—Kearney**
Kearney, NE
www.unk.edu

**University of
Nebraska—Lincoln**
Lincoln, NE
www.unl.edu

**University of
Nebraska—Omaha**
Omaha, NE
www.unomaha.edu

**University of
Nevada—Las Vegas**
Las Vegas, NV
www.unlv.edu

**University of
Nevada—Reno**
Reno, NV
www.unr.edu

**University of New
England**
Biddeford, ME
www.une.edu

**University of New
Hampshire**
Durham, NH
www.unh.edu

**University of New
Haven**
West Haven, CT
www.newhaven.edu

**University of New
Mexico**
Albuquerque, NM
www.unm.edu

**University of New
Orleans**
New Orleans, LA
www.uno.edu

University of North Alabama
Florence, AL
www.una.edu

University of North Carolina—Asheville
Asheville, NC
www.unca.edu

University of North Carolina—Chapel Hill
Chapel Hill, NC
www.unc.edu

University of North Carolina—Charlotte
Charlotte, NC
www.uncc.edu

University of North Carolina—Greensboro
Greensboro, NC
www.uncg.edu

University of North Carolina—Pembroke
Pembroke, NC
www.uncp.edu

University of North Carolina—Wilmington
Wilmington, NC
www.uncw.edu

University of North Dakota
Grand Forks, ND
www.go.und.edu

University of North Florida
Jacksonville, FL
www.unf.edu

University of North Texas
Denton, TX
www.unt.edu

University of Northern Colorado
Greeley, CO
www.unco.edu

University of Northern Iowa
Cedar Falls, IA
www.uni.edu

University of Northwestern Ohio
Lima, OH
www.unoh.edu

University of Notre Dame
Notre Dame, IN
www.nd.edu

University of Oklahoma
Norman, OK
www.ou.edu

University of Oregon
Eugene, OR
www.uoregon.edu

University of Pennsylvania
Philadelphia, PA
www.upenn.edu

University of Pittsburgh
Pittsburgh, PA
www.oafa.pitt.edu

University of Pittsburgh—Bradford
Bradford, PA
www.upb.pitt.edu

University of Pittsburgh—Johnstown
Johnstown, PA
www.upj.pitt.edu

University of Portland
Portland, OR
www.up.edu

University of Puget Sound
Tacoma, WA
www.ups.edu

University of Redlands
Redlands, CA
www.redlands.edu

University of Rhode Island
Kingston, RI
www.uri.edu

University of Richmond
Univ. of Richmond, VA
www.richmond.edu

University of Rio Grande
Rio Grande, OH
www.rio.edu

University of Rochester
Rochester, NY
www.rochester.edu

University of San Diego
San Diego, CA
www.SanDiego.edu

University of San Francisco
San Francisco, CA
www.usfca.edu

University of Science and Arts of Oklahoma
Chickasha, OK
www.usao.edu

University of Scranton
Scranton, PA
www.scranton.edu

University of Sioux Falls
Sioux Falls, SD
www.usiouxfalls.edu

University of South Alabama
Mobile, AL
www.southalabama.edu

University of South Carolina—Aiken
Aiken, SC
www.usca.edu

University of South Carolina—Columbia
Columbia, SC
www.sc.edu

University of South Carolina—Upstate
Spartanburg, SC
www.uscupstate.edu

University of South Dakota
Vermillion, SD
www.usd.edu

University of South Florida
Tampa, FL
www.usf.edu

University of Southern California
Los Angeles, CA
www.usc.edu

University of Southern Indiana
Evansville, IN
www.usi.edu

University of Southern Maine
Gorham, ME
www.usm.maine.edu

University of Southern Mississippi
Hattiesburg, MS
www.usm.edu

University of St. Francis
Joliet, IL
www.stfrancis.edu

University of St. Francis
Fort Wayne, IN
www.sf.edu

University of St. Mary
Leavenworth, KS
www.stmary.edu

University of St. Thomas
St. Paul, MN
www.stthomas.edu

University of St. Thomas
Houston, TX
www.stthom.edu

University of Tampa
Tampa, FL
www.ut.edu

University of Tennessee
Knoxville, TN
admissions.utk.edu

University of Tennessee—Chattanooga
Chattanooga, TN
www.utc.edu

University of Tennessee—Martin
Martin, TN
www.utm.edu

University of Texas of the Permian Basin
Odessa, TX
www.utpb.edu

University of Texas—Arlington
Arlington, TX
www.uta.edu

University of Texas—Austin
Austin, TX
www.utexas.edu

University of Texas—Brownsville
Brownsville, TX
www.utb.edu

University of Texas—Dallas
Richardson, TX
www.utdallas.edu

University of Texas—El Paso
El Paso, TX
www.utep.edu

University of Texas—Pan American
Edinburg, TX
www.utpa.edu

University of Texas—San Antonio
San Antonio, TX
www.utsa.edu

University of Texas—Tyler
Tyler, TX
www.uttyler.edu

University of the Arts
Philadelphia, PA
www.uarts.edu

University of the Cumberlands
Williamsburg, KY
www.ucumberlands.edu

University of the District of Columbia
Washington, DC
www.udc.edu

University of the Incarnate Word
San Antonio, TX
www.uiw.edu

University of the Ozarks
Clarksville, AR
www.ozarks.edu

University of the Pacific
Stockton, CA
www.pacific.edu

University of Toledo
Toledo, OH
www.utoledo.edu

University of Tulsa
Tulsa, OK
www.utulsa.edu

University of Utah
Salt Lake City, UT
www.utah.edu

University of Vermont
Burlington, VT
www.uvm.edu

University of Virginia
Charlottesville, VA
www.virginia.edu

University of Virginia—Wise
Wise, VA
www.uvawise.edu

University of Washington
Seattle, WA
www.washington.edu

University of West Alabama
Livingston, AL
www.uwa.edu

University of West Florida
Pensacola, FL
www.uwf.edu

University of West Georgia
Carrollton, GA
www.westga.edu

University of Wisconsin—Eau Claire
Eau Claire, WI
www.uwec.edu

University of Wisconsin—Green Bay
Green Bay, WI
www.uwgb.edu

University of Wisconsin—La Crosse
La Crosse, WI
www.uwlax.edu

University of Wisconsin—Madison
Madison, WI
www.wisc.edu

University of Wisconsin—Milwaukee
Milwaukee, WI
www.uwm.edu

University of Wisconsin—Oshkosh
Oshkosh, WI
www.uwosh.edu

University of Wisconsin—Parkside
Kenosha, WI
www.uwp.edu

University of Wisconsin—Platteville
Platteville, WI
www.uwplatt.edu

University of Wisconsin—River Falls
River Falls, WI
www.uwrf.edu

University of Wisconsin—Stevens Point
Stevens Point, WI
www.uwsp.edu

University of Wisconsin—Stout
Menomonie, WI
www.uwstout.edu

University of Wisconsin—Superior
Superior, WI
www.uwsuper.edu

University of Wisconsin—Whitewater
Whitewater, WI
www.uww.edu

University of Wyoming
Laramie, WY
www.uwyo.edu

Upper Iowa University
Fayette, IA
www.uiu.edu

Urbana University
Urbana, OH
www.urbana.edu

Ursinus College
Collegeville, PA
www.ursinus.edu

Ursuline College
Pepper Pike, OH
www.ursuline.edu

Utah State University
Logan, UT
www.usu.edu

Utah Valley State College
Orem, UT
www.uvsc.edu

Utica College
Utica, NY
www.utica.edu

Valdosta State University
Valdosta, GA
www.valdosta.edu

Valley City State University
Valley City, ND
www.vcsu.edu

Valley Forge Christian College
Phoenixville, PA
www.vfcc.edu

Valparaiso University
Valparaiso, IN
www.valpo.edu

Vanderbilt University
Nashville, TN
www.vanderbilt.edu

VanderCook College of Music
Chicago, IL
www.vandercook.edu

Vanguard University of Southern California
Costa Mesa, CA
www.vanguard.edu

Vassar College
Poughkeepsie, NY
www.vassar.edu

Vaughn College of Aeronautics and Technology
Flushing, NY
www.vaughn.edu

Vermont Technical College
Randolph Center, VT
www.vtc.edu

Villanova University
Villanova, PA
www.villanova.edu

Virginia Commonwealth University
Richmond, VA
www.vcu.edu

Virginia Intermont College
Bristol, VA
www.vic.edu

Virginia Military Institute
Lexington, VA
www.vmi.edu

Virginia State University
Petersburg, VA
www.vsu.edu

Virginia Tech
Blacksburg, VA
www.vt.edu

Virginia Union University
Richmond, VA
www.vuu.edu

Virginia Wesleyan College
Norfolk, VA
www.vwc.edu

Viterbo University
La Crosse, WI
www.viterbo.edu

Voorhees College
Denmark, SC
www.voorhees.edu

Wabash College
Crawfordsville, IN
www.wabash.edu

Wagner College
Staten Island, NY
www.wagner.edu

Wake Forest University
Winston-Salem, NC
www.wfu.edu

Waldorf College
Forest City, IA
www.waldorf.edu

Walla Walla University
College Place, WA
www.wallawalla.edu

Walsh College of Accountancy and Business Adm.
Troy, MI
www.walshcollege.edu

Walsh University
North Canton, OH
www.walsh.edu

Warner Pacific College
Portland, OR
www.warnerpacific.edu

Warner Southern College
Lake Wales, FL
www.warner.edu

Warren Wilson College
Asheville, NC
www.warren-wilson.edu

Wartburg College
Waverly, IA
www.wartburg.edu

Washburn University
Topeka, KS
www.washburn.edu

Washington and Jefferson College
Washington, PA
www.washjeff.edu

Washington and Lee University
Lexington, VA
www.wlu.edu

Washington College
Chestertown, MD
www.washcoll.edu

Washington State University
Pullman, WA
www.wsu.edu

Washington University in St. Louis
St. Louis, MO
www.wustl.edu

Wayland Baptist University
Plainview, TX
www.wbu.edu

Wayne State College
Wayne, NE
www.wsc.edu

Wayne State University
Detroit, MI
www.wayne.edu

Waynesburg University
Waynesburg, PA
www.waynesburg.edu

Webb Institute
Glen Cove, NY
www.webb-institute.edu

Webber International University
Babson Park, FL
www.webber.edu

Weber State University
Ogden, UT
www.weber.edu

Webster University
St. Louis, MO
www.webster.edu

Wellesley College
Wellesley, MA
www.wellesley.edu

Wells College
Aurora, NY
www.wells.edu

Wesley College
Dover, DE
www.wesley.edu

Wesleyan College
Macon, GA
www.wesleyancollege.edu

Wesleyan University
Middletown, CT
www.wesleyan.edu

West Chester University of Pennsylvania
West Chester, PA
www.wcupa.edu

West Liberty State College
West Liberty, WV
www.westliberty.edu

West Texas A&M University
Canyon, TX
www.wtamu.edu

West Virginia State University
Institute, WV
www.wvstateu.edu

West Virginia University
Morgantown, WV
www.wvu.edu

West Virginia University Institute of Technology
Montgomery, WV
www.wvutech.edu

West Virginia University—Parkersburg
Parkersburg, WV
www.wvup.edu

West Virginia Wesleyan College
Buckhannon, WV
www.wvwc.edu

Western Carolina University
Cullowhee, NC
www.wcu.edu

Western Connecticut State University
Danbury, CT
www.wcsu.edu

Western Governors University
Salt Lake City, UT
www.wgu.edu

Western Illinois University
Macomb, IL
www.wiu.edu

Western Kentucky University
Bowling Green, KY
www.wku.edu

Western Michigan University
Kalamazoo, MI
www.wmich.edu

Western New England College
Springfield, MA
www.wnec.edu

Western New Mexico University
Silver City, NM
www.wnmu.edu

Western Oregon University
Monmouth, OR
www.wou.edu

Western State College of Colorado
Gunnison, CO
www.western.edu

Western Washington University
Bellingham, WA
www.wwu.edu

Westfield State College
Westfield, MA
www.wsc.mass.edu

Westminster College
Fulton, MO
www.westminster-mo.edu

Westminster College
New Wilmington, PA
www.westminster.edu

Westminster College
Salt Lake City, UT
www.westminstercollege.edu

Westmont College
Santa Barbara, CA
www.westmont.edu

Wheaton College
Wheaton, IL
www.wheaton.edu

Wheaton College
Norton, MA
www.wheatoncollege.edu

Wheeling Jesuit University
Wheeling, WV
www.wju.edu

Wheelock College
Boston, MA
www.wheelock.edu

Whitman College
Walla Walla, WA
www.whitman.edu

Whittier College
Whittier, CA
www.whittier.edu

Whitworth University
Spokane, WA
www.whitworth.edu

Wichita State University
Wichita, KS
www.wichita.edu

Widener University
Chester, PA
www.widener.edu

Wilberforce University
Wilberforce, OH
www.wilberforce.edu

Wiley College
Marshall, TX
www.wileyc.edu

Wilkes University
Wilkes-Barre, PA
www.wilkes.edu

Willamette University
Salem, OR
www.willamette.edu

William Carey University
Hattiesburg, MS
www.wmcarey.edu

William Jewell College
Liberty, MO
www.jewell.edu

William Paterson University of New Jersey
Wayne, NJ
www.wpunj.edu

William Penn University
Oskaloosa, IA
www.wmpenn.edu

William Woods University
Fulton, MO
www.williamwoods.edu

Williams Baptist College
Walnut Ridge, AR
www.wbcoll.edu

Williams College
Williamstown, MA
www.williams.edu

Wilmington College
Wilmington, OH
www.wilmington.edu

Wilmington University
New Castle, DE
www.wilmu.edu

Wilson College
Chambersburg, PA
www.wilson.edu

Wingate University
Wingate, NC
www.wingate.edu

Winona State University
Winona, MN
www.winona.edu

Winston-Salem State University
Winston-Salem, NC
www.wssu.edu

Winthrop University
Rock Hill, SC
www.winthrop.edu

Wisconsin Lutheran College
Milwaukee, WI
www.wlc.edu

Wittenberg University
Springfield, OH
www.wittenberg.edu

Wofford College
Spartanburg, SC
www.wofford.edu

Woodbury College
Montpelier, VT
www.woodbury-college.edu

Woodbury University
Burbank, CA
www.woodbury.edu

Worcester Polytechnic Institute
Worcester, MA
www.wpi.edu

Worcester State College
Worcester, MA
www.worcester.edu

Wright State University
Dayton, OH
www.wright.edu

Xavier University
Cincinnati, OH
www.xavier.edu

Xavier University of Louisiana
New Orleans, LA
www.xula.edu

Yale University
New Haven, CT
www.yale.edu

Yeshiva University
New York, NY
www.yu.edu

York College
York, NE
www.york.edu

York College of Pennsylvania
York, PA
www.ycp.edu

Youngstown State University
Youngstown, OH
www.ysu.edu

Appendix 3

Women's Sports

These lists identify institutions that offer specific sports, as well as in which division the sport competes. Go to their websites for complete information.

ARCHERY
DIVISION I

Columbia U-Barnard College

BADMINTON
DIVISION III

Bryn Mawr College
Swarthmore College

BASKETBALL
DIVISION I

Alabama A&M U
Alabama State U
Alcorn State U
American U
Appalachian State U
Arizona State U
Arkansas State U
Auburn U
Austin Peay State U
Ball State U
Baylor U
Belmont U
Bethune-Cookman U
Birmingham-Southern
    College
Boise State U
Boston College
Boston U
Bowling Green State U
Bradley U

Brigham Young U
Brown U
Bryant U
Bucknell U
Butler U
California Polytechnic
    State U
California State U,
    Bakersfield
California State U, Fresno
California State U,
    Fullerton
California State U,
    Northridge
California State U,
    Sacramento
Campbell U
Canisius College
Centenary College (LA)
Central Connecticut State U
Central Michigan U
Charleston Southern U
Chicago State U
Clemson U
Cleveland State U
Coastal Carolina U
Colgate U
College of Charleston (SC)
College of the Holy Cross
College of William and
    Mary
Colorado State U
Columbia U-Barnard College
Coppin State U
Cornell U

Creighton U
Dartmouth College
Davidson College
Delaware State U
DePaul U
Drake U
Drexel U
Duke U
Duquesne U
East Carolina U
East Tennessee State U
Eastern Illinois U
Eastern Kentucky U
Eastern Michigan U
Eastern Washington U
Elon U
Fairfield U
Fairleigh Dickinson U,
    Metropolitan
Florida A&M U
Florida Atlantic U
Florida Gulf Coast U
Florida International U
Florida State U
Fordham U
Furman U
Gardner-Webb U
George Mason U
George Washington U
Georgetown U
Georgia Institute of
    Technology
Georgia Southern U
Georgia State U
Gonzaga U

Grambling State U
Hampton U
Harvard U
High Point U
Hofstra U
Houston Baptist U
Howard U
Idaho State U
Illinois State U
Indiana State U
Indiana U, Bloomington
Indiana U-Purdue U at
    Indianapolis
Indiana U-Purdue U, Fort
    Wayne
Iona College
Iowa State U
Jackson State U
Jacksonville State U
Jacksonville U
James Madison U
Kansas State U
Kennesaw State U
Kent State U
La Salle U
Lafayette College
Lamar U
Lehigh U
Liberty U
Lipscomb U
Long Beach State U
Long Island U-Brooklyn
    Campus
Longwood U
Louisiana State U
Louisiana Tech U
Loyola Marymount U
Loyola U (IL)
Loyola U (MD)
Manhattan College
Marist College
Marquette U
Marshall U
McNeese State U
Mercer U
Miami U (OH)
Michigan State U
Middle Tennessee State U

Mississippi State U
Mississippi Valley State U
Missouri State U
Monmouth U
Montana State U-Bozeman
Morehead State U
Morgan State U
Mount St. Mary's U
Murray State U
New Jersey Institute of
    Technology
New Mexico State U
Niagara U
Nicholls State U
Norfolk State U
North Carolina A&T State U
North Carolina Central U
North Carolina State U
North Dakota State U
Northeastern U
Northern Arizona U
Northern Illinois U
Northwestern State U
Northwestern U
Oakland U
Ohio U
The Ohio State U
Oklahoma State U
Old Dominion U
Oral Roberts U
Oregon State U
Pennsylvania State U
Pepperdine U
Portland State U
Prairie View A&M U
Presbyterian College
Princeton U
Providence College
Purdue U
Quinnipiac U
Radford U
Rice U
Rider U
Robert Morris U
Rutgers, State Univ of New
    Jersey, New Brunswick
Sacred Heart U
Saint Francis U (PA)

Saint Joseph's U
Saint Louis U
Sam Houston State U
Samford U
San Diego State U
San Jose State U
Santa Clara U
Savannah State U
Seattle U
Seton Hall U
Siena College
South Carolina State U
South Dakota State U
Southeast Missouri State U
Southeastern Louisiana U
Southern Illinois U at
    Carbondale
Southern Illinois U
    Edwardsville
Southern Methodist U
Southern U, Baton Rouge
Southern Utah U
St. Bonaventure U
St. Francis College (NY)
St. John's U (NY)
St. Mary's College of
    California
St. Peter's College
Stanford U
State U of New York at
    Binghamton
Stephen F. Austin State U
Stetson U
Stony Brook U
Syracuse U
Temple U
Tennessee State U
Tennessee Technological U
Texas A&M U, College
    Station
Texas A&M U-Corpus
    Christi
Texas Christian U
Texas Southern U
Texas State U-San Marcos
Texas Tech U
Towson U
Troy U

Tulane U
U.S. Air Force Academy
U.S. Military Academy
U.S. Naval Academy
U at Albany
U at Buffalo, the State U
  of New
U of Akron
U of Alabama at
  Birmingham
U of Alabama, Tuscaloosa
U of Arizona
U of Arkansas, Fayetteville
U of Arkansas, Little Rock
U of Arkansas, Pine Bluff
U of California, Berkeley
U of California, Davis
U of California, Irvine
U of California, Los
  Angeles
U of California, Riverside
U of California, Santa
  Barbara
U of Central Arkansas
U of Central Florida
U of Cincinnati
U of Colorado, Boulder
U of Connecticut
U of Dayton
U of Delaware
U of Denver
U of Detroit Mercy
U of Evansville
U of Florida
U of Georgia
U of Hartford
U of Hawaii, Manoa
U of Houston
U of Idaho
U of Illinois at Chicago
U of Illinois, Champaign
U of Iowa
U of Kansas
U of Kentucky
U of Louisiana at Lafayette
U of Louisiana at Monroe
U of Louisville

U of Maine, Orono
U of Maryland, Baltimore
  County
U of Maryland, College Park
U of Maryland, Eastern
  Shore
U of Massachusetts,
  Amherst
U of Memphis
U of Miami (FL)
U of Michigan
U of Minnesota, Twin Cities
U of Mississippi
U of Missouri, Columbia
U of Missouri, Kansas City
U of Montana
U of Nebraska, Lincoln
U of Nevada
U of Nevada, Las Vegas
U of New Hampshire
U of New Mexico
U of New Orleans
U of North Carolina at
  Greensboro
U of North Carolina,
  Asheville
U of North Carolina,
  Chapel Hill
U of North Carolina,
  Charlotte
U of North Carolina,
  Wilmington
U of North Dakota
U of North Florida
U of North Texas
U of Northern Colorado
U of Northern Iowa
U of Notre Dame
U of Oklahoma
U of Oregon
U of Pennsylvania
U of Pittsburgh
U of Portland
U of Rhode Island
U of Richmond
U of San Diego
U of San Francisco

U of South Alabama
U of South Carolina
  Upstate
U of South Carolina,
  Columbia
U of South Dakota
U of South Florida
U of Southern California
U of Southern Mississippi
U of Tennessee at
  Chattanooga
U of Tennessee at Martin
U of Tennessee, Knoxville
U of Texas at Arlington
U of Texas at Austin
U of Texas at El Paso
U of Texas at San Antonio
U of Texas, Pan American
U of the Pacific
U of Toledo
U of Tulsa
U of Utah
U of Vermont
U of Virginia
U of Washington
U of Wisconsin, Green Bay
U of Wisconsin, Madison
U of Wisconsin, Milwaukee
U of Wyoming
Utah State U
Utah Valley U
Valparaiso U
Vanderbilt U
Villanova U
Virginia Commonwealth U
Virginia Polytechnic
  Institute & State U
Wagner College
Wake Forest U
Washington State U
Weber State U
West Virginia U
Western Carolina U
Western Illinois U
Western Kentucky U
Western Michigan U
Wichita State U

Winston-Salem State U
Winthrop U
Wofford College
Wright State U
Xavier U
Yale U
Youngstown State U

BASKETBALL
DIVISION II

Abilene Christian U
Adams State College
Adelphi U
Albany State U (GA)
Alderson-Broaddus College
American International
  College
Anderson U (SC)
Angelo State U
Arkansas Tech U
Armstrong Atlantic State U
Ashland U
Assumption College
Augusta State U
Augustana College (SD)
Barry U
Barton College
Bellarmine U
Belmont Abbey College
Bemidji State U
Benedict College
Bentley College
Bloomfield College
Bloomsburg U of
  Pennsylvania
Bluefield State College
Bowie State U
Brevard College
Brigham Young U, Hawaii
Bryant U
C.W. Post Campus/Long
  Island U
Caldwell College
California State
  Polytechnic U, Pomona
California State U,
  Bakersfield

California State U, Chico
California State U,
  Dominguez Hills
California State U, Los
  Angeles
California State U,
  Monterey Bay
California State U, San
  Bernardino
California State U,
  Stanislaus
California U of Pennsylvania
Cameron U
Carson-Newman College
Catawba College
Central State U
Central Washington U
Chadron State College
Chaminade U
Chestnut Hill College
Cheyney U of Pennsylvania
Chowan U
Christian Brothers U
Claflin U
Clarion U of Pennsylvania
Clark Atlanta U
Clayton State U
Coker College
College of Saint Rose
Colorado Christian U
Colorado School of Mines
Colorado State U-Pueblo
Columbia Union College
Columbus State U
Concord U
Concordia College (NY)
Concordia U, St. Paul
Converse College
Davis and Elkins College
Delta State U
Dixie State College of Utah
Dominican College (NY)
Dowling College
Drury U
East Central U
East Stroudsburg U of
  Pennsylvania
Eastern New Mexico U

Eckerd College
Edinboro U of Pennsylvania
Elizabeth City State U
Emporia State U
Erskine College
Fairmont State U
Fayetteville State U
Felician College
Ferris State U
Flagler College
Florida Gulf Coast U
Florida Institute of
  Technology
Florida Southern College
Fort Hays State U
Fort Lewis College
Fort Valley State U
Francis Marion U
Franklin Pierce U
Gannon U
Georgia Southwestern
  State U
The Georgia College &
  State U
Georgian Court U
Glenville State College
Goldey-Beacom College
Grand Canyon U
Grand Valley State U
Harding U
Hawaii Pacific U
Henderson State U
Hillsdale College
Holy Family U
Humboldt State U
Indiana U of Pennsylvania
Johnson C. Smith U
Kennesaw State U
Kentucky State U
Kentucky Wesleyan College
Kutztown U of
  Pennsylvania
Lake Superior State U
Lander U
Lane College
Le Moyne College
Lees-McRae College
LeMoyne-Owen College

Lenoir-Rhyne College
Lewis U
Limestone College
Lincoln Memorial U
Lincoln U (MO)
Livingstone College
Lock Haven U of
   Pennsylvania
Lynn U
Mansfield U of Pennsylvania
Mars Hill College
Mercy College
Mercyhurst College
Merrimack College
Mesa State College
Metropolitan State College
   of Denver
Michigan Technological U
Midwestern State U
Miles College
Millersville U of
   Pennsylvania
Minnesota State U
   Moorhead
Minnesota State U, Mankato
Missouri Southern State U
Missouri U of Science and
   Technology
Missouri Western State U
Molloy College
Montana State U-Billings
Mount Olive College
New Jersey Institute of
   Technology
New Mexico Highlands U
New York Institute of
   Technology
Newberry College
Newman U
North Carolina Central U
North Georgia College &
   State U
North Greenville U
Northeastern State U
Northern Kentucky U
Northern Michigan U
Northern State U
Northwest Missouri State U

Northwest Nazarene U
Northwood U (MI)
Notre Dame de Namur U
Nova Southeastern U
Nyack College
Oakland City U
Ohio Valley U
Oklahoma Panhandle
   State U
Ouachita Baptist U
Pace U
Paine College
Palm Beach Atlantic U
Pfeiffer U
Philadelphia U
Pittsburg State U
Post U
Presbyterian College
Queens College (NY)
Queens U of Charlotte
Quincy U
Regis U (CO)
Rockhurst U
Rollins College
Saginaw Valley State U
Saint Anselm College
Saint Joseph's College (IN)
Saint Leo U
Saint Michael's College
Salem International U
San Francisco State U
Seattle Pacific U
Seattle U
Seton Hill U
Shaw U
Shepherd U
Shippensburg U of
   Pennsylvania
Slippery Rock U of
   Pennsylvania
Sonoma State U
Southeastern Oklahoma
   State U
Southern Arkansas U
Southern Connecticut
   State U
Southern Illinois U
   Edwardsville

Southern New Hampshire U
Southwest Baptist U
Southwest Minnesota
   State U
Southwestern Oklahoma
   State U
St. Andrews Presbyterian
   College
St. Augustine's College
St. Cloud State U
St. Edward's U
St. Martin's U
St. Mary's U (TX)
St. Paul's College
St. Thomas Aquinas
   College
Stillman College
Stonehill College
Tarleton State U
Texas A&M International U
Texas A&M U-Commerce
Texas A&M U-Kingsville
Texas Woman's U
Tiffin U
Truman State U
Tusculum College
Tuskegee U
U of Alabama in Huntsville
U of Alaska Anchorage
U of Alaska Fairbanks
U of Arkansas, Monticello
U of Bridgeport
U of California, San Diego
U of Central Arkansas
U of Central Missouri
U of Central Oklahoma
U of Charleston (WV)
U of Colorado, Colorado
   Springs
U of Findlay
U of Hawaii at Hilo
U of Indianapolis
U of Mary
U of Massachusetts at
   Lowell
U of Minnesota Duluth
U of Minnesota, Crookston
U of Missouri, St. Louis

U of Montevallo
U of Nebraska at Kearney
U of Nebraska at Omaha
U of New Haven
U of North Alabama
U of North Carolina at
  Pembroke
U of North Dakota
U of North Florida
U of Pittsburgh, Johnstown
U of Puerto Rico, Bayamon
U of Puerto Rico, Cayey
U of Puerto Rico,
  Mayaguez Campus
U of Puerto Rico, Rio
  Piedras
U of South Carolina Aiken
U of South Carolina
  Upstate
U of South Dakota
U of Southern Indiana
U of Tampa
U of Texas of the Permian
  Basin
U of the District of
  Columbia
U of the Incarnate Word
U of the Sciences in
  Philadelphia
U of West Alabama
U of West Florida
U of West Georgia
U of Wisconsin, Parkside
Upper Iowa U
Valdosta State U
Virginia State U
Virginia Union U
Washburn U of Topeka
Wayne State College (NE)
Wayne State U (MI)
West Chester U of
  Pennsylvania
West Liberty State College
West Texas A&M U
West Virginia State U
West Virginia Wesleyan
  College

Western New Mexico U
Western Oregon U
Western State College of
  Colorado
Western Washington U
Wheeling Jesuit U
Wilmington U (DE)
Wingate U
Winona State U
Winston-Salem State U

BASKETBALL
DIVISION III

Adrian College
Agnes Scott College
Albertus Magnus College
Albion College
Albright College
Alfred U
Allegheny College
Alma College
Alvernia U
Alverno College
Amherst College
Anderson U (IN)
Anna Maria College
Arcadia U
Augsburg College
Augustana College (IL)
Aurora U
Austin College
Averett U
Babson College
Baldwin-Wallace College
Baptist Bible College
Bard College
Baruch College
Bates College
Bay Path College
Becker College
Beloit College
Benedictine U (IL)
Bethany College (WV)
Bethany Lutheran College
Bethel U (MN)
Blackburn College

Bluffton U
Bowdoin College
Brandeis U
Bridgewater College (VA)
Bridgewater State College
Brooklyn College
Bryn Mawr College
Buena Vista U
Buffalo State College
Cabrini College
California Institute of
  Technology
California Lutheran U
California State U, East Bay
Calvin College
Capital U
Carleton College
Carnegie Mellon U
Carroll U (WI)
Carthage College
Case Western Reserve U
Castleton State College
Catholic U
Cazenovia College
Cedar Crest College
Centenary College (NJ)
Central College (IA)
Centre College
Chapman U
Chatham U
Christopher Newport U
The City College of New
  York
Claremont McKenna-
  Harvey Mudd-Scripps
  Colleges
Clark U (MA)
Clarkson U
Coe College
Colby College
Colby-Sawyer College
College of Brockport, State
  U of New York
College of Mount St.
  Joseph
College of Mount St.
  Vincent

The College of New Jersey
College of New Rochelle
College of Notre Dame (MD)
College of Saint Elizabeth
College of St. Benedict
College of St. Catherine
The College of St.
  Scholastica
College of Staten Island
College of Wooster
Colorado College
Concordia College,
  Moorhead
Concordia U (WI)
Concordia U Chicago
Concordia U Texas
Connecticut College
Cornell College
Crown College (MN)
Curry College
Daniel Webster College
Defiance College
Delaware Valley College
Denison U
DePauw U
DeSales U
Dickinson College
Dominican U (IL)
Drew U
D'Youville College
Earlham College
East Texas Baptist U
Eastern Connecticut State U
Eastern Mennonite U
Eastern Nazarene College
Eastern U
Edgewood College
Elizabethtown College
Elmhurst College
Elmira College
Elms College
Emerson College
Emmanuel College (MA)
Emory and Henry College
Emory U
Endicott College
Eureka College

Fairleigh Dickinson U,
  Florham
Ferrum College
Finlandia U
Fitchburg State College
Fontbonne U
Framingham State College
Franciscan U of
  Steubenville
Franklin & Marshall College
Franklin College
Frostburg State U
Gallaudet U
Geneva College
George Fox U
Gettysburg College
Gordon College
Goucher College
Green Mountain College
Greensboro College
Greenville College
Grinnell College
Grove City College
Guilford College
Gustavus Adolphus College
Gwynedd-Mercy College
Hamilton College
Hamline U
Hanover College
Hardin-Simmons U
Hartwick College
Haverford College
Heidelberg College
Hendrix College
Hilbert College
Hiram College
Hollins U
Hood College
Hope College
Howard Payne U
Hunter College
Huntingdon College
Husson College
Illinois College
Illinois Wesleyan U
Immaculata U
Ithaca College

John Carroll U
John Jay College of
  Criminal Justice
Johns Hopkins U
Johnson and Wales U
Johnson State College
Juniata College
Kalamazoo College
Kean U
Keene State College
Kenyon College
Keuka College
Keystone College
King's College (PA)
Knox College
La Grange College
La Roche College
La Sierra U
Lake Erie College
Lake Forest College
Lakeland College
Lancaster Bible College
Lasell College
Lawrence U
Lebanon Valley College
Lehman College, City U of
  New York
Lesley U
LeTourneau U
Lewis & Clark College
Lincoln U (PA)
Linfield College
Loras College
Louisiana College
Luther College
Lycoming College
Lynchburg College
Lyndon State College
Macalester College
MacMurray College
Maine Maritime Academy
Manchester College
Manhattanville College
Maranatha Baptist Bible
  College
Marian U (WI)
Marietta College

Martin Luther College
Mary Baldwin College
Marymount U (VA)
Maryville College (TN)
Maryville U of Saint Louis
Marywood U
Massachusetts College of
Liberal Arts
Massachusetts Institute of
Technology
McDaniel College
McMurry U
Medaille College
Medgar Evers College
Menlo College
Meredith College
Messiah College
Methodist U
Middlebury College
Millikin U
Millsaps College
Milwaukee School of
Engineering
Misericordia U
Mississippi College
Mitchell College
Monmouth College (IL)
Montclair State U
Moravian College
Mount Aloysius College
Mount Holyoke College
Mount Ida College
Mount Mary College
Mount Saint Mary College
(NY)
Mount Union College
Muhlenberg College
Muskingum College
Nazareth College
Nebraska Wesleyan U
Neumann College
New England College
New Jersey City U
New York City College of
Technology
New York U
Newbury College

Nichols College
North Carolina Wesleyan
College
North Central College
North Central U
North Park U
Northland College
Northwestern College
Norwich U
Oberlin College
Occidental College
Oglethorpe U
Ohio Northern U
Ohio Wesleyan U
Olivet College
Otterbein College
Pacific Lutheran U
Pacific U (OR)
Peace College
Penn State Berks College
Penn State Harrisburg
Penn State U, Altoona
Pennsylvania State Univ.
Erie, the Behrend College
Philadelphia Biblical U
Piedmont College
Pine Manor College
Plattsburgh State U of
New York
Plymouth State U
Polytechnic Institute of
New York U
Pomona-Pitzer Colleges
Presentation College
Principia College
Purchase College, State U
of New York
Ramapo College
Randolph College
Randolph-Macon College
Regis College (MA)
Rensselaer Polytechnic
Institute
Rhode Island College
Rhodes College
Richard Stockton College
of New Jersey

Ripon College
Rivier College
Roanoke College
Rochester Institute of
Technology
Rockford College
Roger Williams U
Rose-Hulman Institute of
Technology
Rosemont College
Rowan U
Rust College
Rutgers, The State Univ. of
New Jersey, Camden
Rutgers, The State Univ. of
New Jersey, Newark
The Sage Colleges
Saint Joseph's College (ME)
Saint Mary's College (IN)
Saint Mary's U of
Minnesota
Saint Vincent College
Salem College
Salem State College
Salisbury U
Salve Regina U
Schreiner U
Shenandoah U
Simmons College
Simpson College
Skidmore College
Smith College
Southern Vermont College
Southwestern U (TX)
Spalding U
Spelman College
Springfield College
St. John Fisher College
St. Joseph College (CT)
St. Joseph's College (Long
Island)
St. Joseph's College, New
York
St. Lawrence U
St. Mary's College of
Maryland
St. Norbert College

St. Olaf College
State U College at Cortland
State U College at Fredonia
State U College at Geneseo
State U College at New Paltz
State U College at Old Westbury
State U College at Oneonta
State U of New York at Cobleskill
State U of New York at Farmingdale
State U of New York at Morrisville
State U of New York at Oswego
State U of New York at Potsdam
State U of New York Institute of Technolo
Stevens Institute of Technology
Stevenson U
Suffolk U
Sul Ross State U
Susquehanna U
Swarthmore College
Texas Lutheran U
Thiel College
Thomas College
Thomas More College
Transylvania U
Trine U
Trinity College (CT)
Trinity College (District of Columbia)
Trinity U (TX)
Tufts U
U.S. Coast Guard Academy
U.S. Merchant Marine Academy
Union College (NY)
U of California, Santa Cruz
U of Chicago
U of Dallas

U of Dubuque
U of La Verne
U of Maine at Presque Isle
U of Maine, Farmington
U of Mary Hardin-Baylor
U of Mary Washington
U of Massachusetts, Boston
U of Massachusetts, Dartmouth
U of Minnesota, Morris
U of New England
U of Pittsburgh, Bradford
U of Pittsburgh, Greensburg
U of Puget Sound
U of Redlands
U of Rochester
U of Scranton
U of Southern Maine
U of St. Thomas (MN)
U of Texas at Dallas
U of Texas at Tyler
U of the Ozarks (AR)
U of the South
U of Wisconsin, Eau Claire
U of Wisconsin, La Crosse
U of Wisconsin, Oshkosh
U of Wisconsin, Platteville
U of Wisconsin, River Falls
U of Wisconsin, Stevens Point
U of Wisconsin, Stout
U of Wisconsin, Superior
U of Wisconsin, Whitewater
Ursinus College
Utica College
Vassar College
Virginia Wesleyan College
Wartburg College
Washington and Jefferson College
Washington and Lee U
Washington College (MD)
Washington U (MO)
Waynesburg U
Webster U

Wellesley College
Wentworth Institute of Technology
Wesley College
Wesleyan College (GA)
Wesleyan U (CT)
Western Connecticut State U
Western New England College
Westfield State College
Westminster College (MO)
Westminster College (PA)
Wheaton College (IL)
Wheaton College (MA)
Wheelock College
Whitman College
Whittier College
Whitworth U
Widener U
Wilkes U
Willamette U
William Paterson U of New Jersey
William Smith College
Williams College
Wilmington College (OH)
Wilson College
Wisconsin Lutheran College
Wittenberg U
Worcester Polytechnic Institute
Worcester State College
Yeshiva U
York College (NY)
York College (PA)

BOWLING
DIVISION I

Alabama A&M U
Alabama State U
Arkansas State U
Bethune-Cookman U
Coppin State U
Delaware State U

Fairleigh Dickinson U,
Metropolitan
Florida A&M U
Grambling State U
Hampton U
Howard U
Jackson State U
Long Island U-Brooklyn
Campus
Louisiana Tech U
Mississippi Valley State U
Morgan State U
Norfolk State U
North Carolina A&T State
U
North Carolina Central U
Prairie View A&M U
Sacred Heart U
Sam Houston State U
South Carolina State U
Southern U, Baton Rouge
St. Francis College (NY)
St. Peter's College
Texas Southern U
U of Arkansas, Pine Bluff
U of Maryland, Eastern
Shore
U of Nebraska, Lincoln
Vanderbilt U
Winston-Salem State U

BOWLING
DIVISION II

Adelphi U
Bowie State U
Cheyney U of Pennsylvania
Elizabeth City State U
Fayetteville State U
Grand Canyon U
Johnson C. Smith U
Kutztown U of
Pennsylvania
Livingstone College
Minnesota State U, Mankato
North Carolina Central U
Shaw U

St. Augustine's College
St. Paul's College
U of Central Missouri
Virginia State U
Virginia Union U
Winston-Salem State U

BOWLING
DIVISION III

Adrian College
Elmhurst College
Fontbonne U
Lincoln U (PA)
Medaille College
New Jersey City U
Spalding U
State U of New York
Institute of Technolo
U of Wisconsin,
Whitewater

CROSS-COUNTRY
DIVISION I

Alabama A&M U
Alabama State U
Alcorn State U
American U
Appalachian State U
Arizona State U
Arkansas State U
Auburn U
Austin Peay State U
Ball State U
Baylor U
Belmont U
Bethune-Cookman U
Birmingham-Southern
College
Boise State U
Boston College
Boston U
Bowling Green State U
Bradley U

Brigham Young U
Brown U
Bryant U
Bucknell U
Butler U
California Polytechnic
State U
California State U,
Bakersfield
California State U, Fresno
California State U,
Fullerton
California State U,
Northridge
California State U,
Sacramento
Campbell U
Canisius College
Centenary College (LA)
Central Connecticut State
U
Central Michigan U
Charleston Southern U
Chicago State U
The Citadel
Clemson U
Cleveland State U
Coastal Carolina U
Colgate U
College of Charleston (SC)
College of the Holy Cross
College of William and
Mary
Colorado State U
Columbia U-Barnard
College
Coppin State U
Cornell U
Creighton U
Dartmouth College
Davidson College
Delaware State U
DePaul U
Drake U
Duke U
Duquesne U
East Carolina U

East Tennessee State U
Eastern Illinois U
Eastern Kentucky U
Eastern Michigan U
Eastern Washington U
Elon U
Fairfield U
Fairleigh Dickinson U,
    Metropolitan
Florida A&M U
Florida Atlantic U
Florida Gulf Coast U
Florida International U
Florida State U
Fordham U
Furman U
Gardner-Webb U
George Mason U
George Washington U
Georgetown U
Georgia Institute of
    Technology
Georgia Southern U
Georgia State U
Gonzaga U
Grambling State U
Hampton U
Harvard U
High Point U
Hofstra U
Howard U
Idaho State U
Illinois State U
Indiana State U
Indiana U, Bloomington
Indiana U-Purdue U at
    Indianapolis
Indiana U-Purdue U, Fort
    Wayne
Iona College
Iowa State U
Jackson State U
Jacksonville State U
Jacksonville U
James Madison U
Kansas State U

Kennesaw State U
Kent State U
La Salle U
Lafayette College
Lamar U
Lehigh U
Liberty U
Lipscomb U
Long Beach State U
Long Island U-Brooklyn
    Campus
Longwood U
Louisiana State U
Louisiana Tech U
Loyola Marymount U
Loyola U (IL)
Loyola U (MD)
Manhattan College
Marist College
Marquette U
Marshall U
McNeese State U
Mercer U
Miami U (OH)
Michigan State U
Middle Tennessee State U
Mississippi State U
Mississippi Valley State U
Missouri State U
Monmouth U
Montana State U-Bozeman
Morehead State U
Morgan State U
Mount St. Mary's U
Murray State U
New Jersey Institute of
    Technology
New Mexico State U
Niagara U
Nicholls State U
Norfolk State U
North Carolina A&T State U
North Carolina Central U
North Carolina State U
North Dakota State U
Northeastern U

Northern Arizona U
Northern Illinois U
Northwestern State U
Northwestern U
Oakland U
Ohio U
The Ohio State U
Oklahoma State U
Oral Roberts U
Oregon State U
Pennsylvania State U
Pepperdine U
Portland State U
Prairie View A&M U
Presbyterian College
Princeton U
Providence College
Purdue U
Quinnipiac U
Radford U
Rice U
Rider U
Robert Morris U
Rutgers, State Univ of New
    Jersey, New Brunswick
Sacred Heart U
Saint Francis U (PA)
Saint Joseph's U
Saint Louis U
Sam Houston State U
Samford U
San Diego State U
San Jose State U
Santa Clara U
Savannah State U
Seattle U
Seton Hall U
Siena College
South Carolina State U
South Dakota State U
Southeast Missouri State U
Southeastern Louisiana U
Southern Illinois U at
    Carbondale
Southern Illinois U
    Edwardsville

Southern Methodist U
Southern U, Baton Rouge
Southern Utah U
St. Bonaventure U
St. Francis College (NY)
St. John's U (NY)
St. Mary's College of
 California
St. Peter's College
Stanford U
State U of New York at
 Binghamton
Stephen F. Austin State U
Stetson U
Stony Brook U
Syracuse U
Temple U
Tennessee State U
Tennessee Technological U
Texas A&M U, College
 Station
Texas A&M U-Corpus
 Christi
Texas Christian U
Texas State U-San Marcos
Texas Tech U
Towson U
Troy U
Tulane U
U.S. Air Force Academy
U.S. Military Academy
U.S. Naval Academy
U at Albany
U at Buffalo, the State U
 of New
U of Akron
U of Alabama at
 Birmingham
U of Alabama, Tuscaloosa
U of Arizona
U of Arkansas, Fayetteville
U of Arkansas, Little Rock
U of Arkansas, Pine Bluff
U of California, Berkeley
U of California, Davis
U of California, Irvine
U of California, Los

Angeles
U of California, Riverside
U of California, Santa
 Barbara
U of Central Arkansas
U of Central Florida
U of Cincinnati
U of Colorado, Boulder
U of Connecticut
U of Dayton
U of Delaware
U of Detroit Mercy
U of Evansville
U of Florida
U of Georgia
U of Hartford
U of Hawaii, Manoa
U of Houston
U of Idaho
U of Illinois at Chicago
U of Illinois, Champaign
U of Iowa
U of Kansas
U of Kentucky
U of Louisiana at Lafayette
U of Louisiana at Monroe
U of Louisville
U of Maine, Orono
U of Maryland, Baltimore
 County
U of Maryland, College Park
U of Maryland, Eastern
 Shore
U of Massachusetts,
 Amherst
U of Memphis
U of Miami (FL)
U of Michigan
U of Minnesota, Twin
 Cities
U of Mississippi
U of Missouri, Columbia
U of Missouri, Kansas City
U of Montana
U of Nebraska, Lincoln
U of Nevada
U of Nevada, Las Vegas

U of New Hampshire
U of New Mexico
U of North Carolina at
 Greensboro
U of North Carolina,
 Asheville
U of North Carolina,
 Chapel Hill
U of North Carolina,
 Charlotte
U of North Carolina,
 Wilmington
U of North Dakota
U of North Florida
U of North Texas
U of Northern Colorado
U of Northern Iowa
U of Notre Dame
U of Oklahoma
U of Oregon
U of Pennsylvania
U of Pittsburgh
U of Portland
U of Rhode Island
U of Richmond
U of San Diego
U of San Francisco
U of South Alabama
U of South Carolina
 Upstate
U of South Carolina,
 Columbia
U of South Dakota
U of South Florida
U of Southern California
U of Southern Mississippi
U of Tennessee at
 Chattanooga
U of Tennessee at Martin
U of Tennessee, Knoxville
U of Texas at Arlington
U of Texas at Austin
U of Texas at El Paso
U of Texas at San Antonio
U of Texas, Pan American
U of the Pacific
U of Toledo

U of Tulsa
U of Utah
U of Vermont
U of Virginia
U of Washington
U of Wisconsin, Green Bay
U of Wisconsin, Madison
U of Wisconsin, Milwaukee
U of Wyoming
Utah State U
Utah Valley U
Valparaiso U
Vanderbilt U
Villanova U
Virginia Commonwealth U
Virginia Military Institute
Virginia Polytechnic
    Institute & State U
Wagner College
Wake Forest U
Washington State U
Weber State U
West Virginia U
Western Carolina U
Western Illinois U
Western Kentucky U
Western Michigan U
Wichita State U
Winston-Salem State U
Winthrop U
Wofford College
Wright State U
Xavier U
Yale U
Youngstown State U

CROSS-COUNTRY
DIVISION II

Abilene Christian U
Adams State College
Adelphi U
Albany State U (GA)
Alderson-Broaddus College
American International
    College

Anderson U (SC)
Angelo State U
Arkansas Tech U
Ashland U
Assumption College
Augusta State U
Augustana College (SD)
Barton College
Bellarmine U
Belmont Abbey College
Bemidji State U
Benedict College
Bentley College
Bloomfield College
Bloomsburg U of
    Pennsylvania
Bluefield State College
Bowie State U
Brevard College
Brigham Young U, Hawaii
Bryant U
C.W. Post Campus/Long
    Island U
Caldwell College
California State
    Polytechnic U, Pomona
California State U,
    Bakersfield
California State U, Chico
California State U,
    Dominguez Hills
California State U, Los
    Angeles
California State U,
    Monterey Bay
California State U, San
    Bernardino
California State U,
    Stanislaus
California U of
    Pennsylvania
Carson-Newman College
Catawba College
Central State U
Central Washington U
Chaminade U
Chestnut Hill College

Cheyney U of Pennsylvania
Christian Brothers U
Claflin U
Clarion U of Pennsylvania
Clark Atlanta U
Clayton State U
Coker College
College of Saint Rose
Colorado Christian U
Colorado School of Mines
Colorado State U-Pueblo
Columbia Union College
Columbus State U
Concord U
Concordia College (NY)
Concordia U, St. Paul
Converse College
Dallas Baptist U
Davis and Elkins College
Delta State U
Dixie State College of Utah
Dominican College (NY)
Dowling College
Drury U
East Central U
East Stroudsburg U of
    Pennsylvania
Eastern New Mexico U
Edinboro U of
    Pennsylvania
Elizabeth City State U
Emporia State U
Erskine College
Fairmont State U
Fayetteville State U
Felician College
Ferris State U
Flagler College
Florida Gulf Coast U
Florida Institute of
    Technology
Florida Southern College
Fort Hays State U
Fort Lewis College
Fort Valley State U
Francis Marion U
Franklin Pierce U

Gannon U
The Georgia College & State U
Georgia Southwestern State U
Georgian Court U
Glenville State College
Goldey-Beacom College
Grand Canyon U
Grand Valley State U
Harding U
Hawaii Pacific U
Henderson State U
Hillsdale College
Holy Family U
Humboldt State U
Indiana U of Pennsylvania
Johnson C. Smith U
Kennesaw State U
Kentucky State U
Kentucky Wesleyan College
Kutztown U of Pennsylvania
Lake Superior State U
Lander U
Lane College
Le Moyne College
Lees-McRae College
LeMoyne-Owen College
Lenoir-Rhyne College
Lewis U
Limestone College
Lincoln Memorial U
Lincoln U (MO)
Livingstone College
Lock Haven U of Pennsylvania
Mansfield U of Pennsylvania
Mars Hill College
Mercy College
Mercyhurst College
Merrimack College
Mesa State College
Metropolitan State College of Denver
Michigan Technological U

Midwestern State U
Miles College
Millersville U of Pennsylvania
Minnesota State U Moorhead
Minnesota State U, Mankato
Missouri Southern State U
Missouri U of Science and Technology
Molloy College
Montana State U-Billings
Mount Olive College
New Jersey Institute of Technology
New Mexico Highlands U
New York Institute of Technology
Newberry College
Newman U
North Carolina Central U
North Georgia College & State U
North Greenville U
Northern Kentucky U
Northern Michigan U
Northern State U
Northwest Missouri State U
Northwest Nazarene U
Northwood U (MI)
Notre Dame de Namur U
Nova Southeastern U
Nyack College
Oakland City U
Ohio Valley U
Oklahoma Panhandle State U
Ouachita Baptist U
Pace U
Paine College
Palm Beach Atlantic U
Pfeiffer U
Philadelphia U
Pittsburg State U
Post U
Presbyterian College

Queens College (NY)
Queens U of Charlotte
Regis U (CO)
Rollins College
Saginaw Valley State U
Saint Anselm College
Saint Joseph's College (IN)
Saint Leo U
Saint Michael's College
San Francisco State U
Seattle Pacific U
Seattle U
Seton Hill U
Shaw U
Shippensburg U of Pennsylvania
Slippery Rock U of Pennsylvania
Sonoma State U
Southeastern Oklahoma State U
Southern Arkansas U
Southern Connecticut State U
Southern Illinois U Edwardsville
Southern New Hampshire U
Southwest Baptist U
Southwestern Oklahoma State U
St. Andrews Presbyterian College
St. Augustine's College
St. Cloud State U
St. Edward's U
St. Martin's U
St. Mary's U (TX)
St. Paul's College
St. Thomas Aquinas College
Stillman College
Stonehill College
Tarleton State U
Texas A&M International U
Texas A&M U-Commerce
Texas A&M U-Kingsville
Tiffin U
Truman State U

Tusculum College
Tuskegee U
U of Alabama in Huntsville
U of Alaska Anchorage
U of Alaska Fairbanks
U of Arkansas, Monticello
U of Bridgeport
U of California, San Diego
U of Central Arkansas
U of Central Missouri
U of Central Oklahoma
U of Charleston (WV)
U of Colorado, Colorado
  Springs
U of Findlay
U of Hawaii at Hilo
U of Indianapolis
U of Mary
U of Massachusetts at Lowell
U of Minnesota Duluth
U of Montevallo
U of Nebraska at Kearney
U of Nebraska at Omaha
U of New Haven
U of North Alabama
U of North Carolina at
  Pembroke
U of North Dakota
U of North Florida
U of Pittsburgh, Johnstown
U of Puerto Rico, Bayamon
U of Puerto Rico, Cayey
U of Puerto Rico,
  Mayaguez Campus
U of Puerto Rico, Rio
  Piedras
U of South Carolina Aiken
U of South Carolina
  Upstate
U of South Dakota
U of Southern Indiana
U of Tampa
U of Texas of the Permian
  Basin
U of the District of Columbia
U of the Incarnate Word
U of the Sciences in
  Philadelphia

U of West Alabama
U of West Florida
U of West Georgia
U of Wisconsin, Parkside
Valdosta State U
Virginia State U
Virginia Union U
Wayne State College (NE)
Wayne State U (MI)
West Chester U of
  Pennsylvania
West Liberty State College
West Texas A&M U
West Virginia Wesleyan
  College
Western New Mexico U
Western Oregon U
Western State College of
  Colorado
Western Washington U
Wheeling Jesuit U
Wilmington U (DE)
Wingate U
Winona State U
Winston-Salem State U

CROSS-COUNTRY
DIVISION III

Adrian College
Agnes Scott College
Albion College
Albright College
Alfred U
Allegheny College
Alma College
Alvernia U
Alverno College
Amherst College
Anderson U (IN)
Augsburg College
Augustana College (IL)
Aurora U
Averett U
Babson College
Baldwin-Wallace College

Baptist Bible College
Bard College
Baruch College
Bates College
Bay Path College
Beloit College
Benedictine U (IL)
Bethany College (WV)
Bethel U (MN)
Blackburn College
Bluffton U
Bowdoin College
Brandeis U
Bridgewater College (VA)
Bridgewater State College
Brooklyn College
Bryn Mawr College
Buena Vista U
Buffalo State College
Cabrini College
California Institute of
  Technology
California Lutheran U
California State U, East Bay
Calvin College
Capital U
Carleton College
Carnegie Mellon U
Carroll U (WI)
Carthage College
Case Western Reserve U
Castleton State College
Catholic U
Cazenovia College
Cedar Crest College
Centenary College (NJ)
Central College (IA)
Centre College
Chapman U
Chatham U
Christopher Newport U
Claremont McKenna-
  Harvey Mudd-Scripps
  Colleges
Clark U (MA)
Clarkson U
Coe College
Colby College

College of Brockport, State U of New York

College of Mount St. Joseph

College of Mount St. Vincent

The College of New Jersey

College of New Rochelle

College of St. Benedict

College of St. Catherine

The College of St. Scholastica

College of Wooster

Colorado College

Concordia College, Moorhead

Concordia U (WI)

Concordia U Chicago

Concordia U Texas

Connecticut College

Cornell College

Crown College (MN)

Curry College

Daniel Webster College

Defiance College

Delaware Valley College

Denison U

DePauw U

DeSales U

Dickinson College

Dominican U (IL)

Drew U

D'Youville College

Earlham College

East Texas Baptist U

Eastern Connecticut State U

Eastern Mennonite U

Eastern Nazarene College

Eastern U

Edgewood College

Elizabethtown College

Elmhurst College

Elms College

Emerson College

Emmanuel College (MA)

Emory and Henry College

Emory U

Endicott College

Eureka College

Fairleigh Dickinson U, Florham

Ferrum College

Finlandia U

Fitchburg State College

Fontbonne U

Framingham State College

Franciscan U of Steubenville

Franklin & Marshall College

Franklin College

Frostburg State U

Geneva College

George Fox U

Gettysburg College

Gordon College

Goucher College

Green Mountain College

Greensboro College

Greenville College

Grinnell College

Grove City College

Guilford College

Gustavus Adolphus College

Gwynedd-Mercy College

Hamilton College

Hamline U

Hanover College

Hardin-Simmons U

Hartwick College

Haverford College

Heidelberg College

Hendrix College

Hilbert College

Hiram College

Hood College

Hope College

Hunter College

Huntingdon College

Illinois College

Illinois Wesleyan U

Immaculata U

Ithaca College

John Carroll U

John Jay College of Criminal Justice

Johns Hopkins U

Johnson and Wales U

Johnson State College

Juniata College

Kalamazoo College

Keene State College

Kenyon College

Keuka College

Keystone College

King's College (PA)

Knox College

La Grange College

La Roche College

Lake Erie College

Lake Forest College

Lakeland College

Lancaster Bible College

Lasell College

Lawrence U

Lebanon Valley College

Lehman College, City U of New York

Lesley U

Lewis & Clark College

Lincoln U (PA)

Linfield College

Loras College

Louisiana College

Luther College

Lycoming College

Lynchburg College

Lyndon State College

Macalester College

Maine Maritime Academy

Manchester College

Manhattanville College

Maranatha Baptist Bible College

Marian U (WI)

Marietta College

Martin Luther College

Mary Baldwin College

Marymount U (VA)

Maryville College (TN)

Maryville U of Saint Louis

Marywood U
Massachusetts College of Liberal Arts
Massachusetts Institute of Technology
Massachusetts Maritime Academy
McDaniel College
McMurry U
Medaille College
Medgar Evers College
Menlo College
Meredith College
Messiah College
Methodist U
Middlebury College
Millikin U
Mills College
Millsaps College
Milwaukee School of Engineering
Misericordia U
Mississippi College
Mitchell College
Monmouth College (IL)
Moravian College
Mount Aloysius College
Mount Holyoke College
Mount Ida College
Mount Mary College
Mount Saint Mary College (NY)
Mount Union College
Muhlenberg College
Muskingum College
Nazareth College
Nebraska Wesleyan U
New England College
New Jersey City U
New York City College of Technology
New York U
Newbury College
North Carolina Wesleyan College
North Central College
North Central U

North Park U
Northland College
Northwestern College
Norwich U
Oberlin College
Occidental College
Oglethorpe U
Ohio Northern U
Ohio Wesleyan U
Olivet College
Otterbein College
Pacific Lutheran U
Pacific U (OR)
Peace College
Penn State Berks College
Penn State Harrisburg
Penn State U, Altoona
Pennsylvania State Univ. Erie, the Behrend College
Piedmont College
Pine Manor College
Plattsburgh State U of New York
Polytechnic Institute of New York U
Pomona-Pitzer Colleges
Principia College
Purchase College, State U of New York
Ramapo College
Randolph College
Rensselaer Polytechnic Institute
Rhode Island College
Rhodes College
Richard Stockton College of New Jersey
Ripon College
Rivier College
Roanoke College
Rochester Institute of Technology
Rockford College
Roger Williams U
Rose-Hulman Institute of Technology
Rowan U

Rust College
Rutgers, The State Univ. of New Jersey, Camden
Rutgers, The State Univ. of New Jersey, Newark
Saint Joseph's College (ME)
Saint Mary's College (IN)
Saint Mary's U of Minnesota
Saint Vincent College
Salem College
Salem State College
Salisbury U
Salve Regina U
Schreiner U
Shenandoah U
Simpson College
Smith College
Southern Vermont College
Southwestern U (TX)
Spalding U
Spelman College
Springfield College
St. Joseph College (CT)
St. Joseph's College (Long Island)
St. Joseph's College, New York
St. Lawrence U
St. Norbert College
St. Olaf College
State U College at Cortland
State U College at Fredonia
State U College at Geneseo
State U College at New Paltz
State U College at Old Westbury
State U College at Oneonta
State U of New York at Cobleskill
State U of New York at Farmingdale
State U of New York at Oswego
State U of New York at Potsdam

State U of New York Institute of Technolo
State U of New York Maritime College
Stevens Institute of Technology
Stevenson U
Suffolk U
Sul Ross State U
Susquehanna U
Swarthmore College
Texas Lutheran U
Thiel College
Thomas More College
Transylvania U
Trine U
Trinity College (CT)
Trinity U (TX)
Tufts U
U.S. Coast Guard Academy
U.S. Merchant Marine Academy
Union College (NY)
U of California, Santa Cruz
U of Chicago
U of Dallas
U of Dubuque
U of La Verne
U of Maine at Presque Isle
U of Maine, Farmington
U of Mary Washington
U of Massachusetts, Boston
U of Massachusetts, Dartmouth
U of Minnesota, Morris
U of New England
U of Pittsburgh, Bradford
U of Pittsburgh, Greensburg
U of Puget Sound
U of Redlands
U of Rochester
U of Scranton
U of Southern Maine
U of St. Thomas (MN)
U of Texas at Dallas
U of Texas at Tyler

U of the Ozarks (AR)
U of the South
U of Wisconsin, Eau Claire
U of Wisconsin, La Crosse
U of Wisconsin, Oshkosh
U of Wisconsin, Platteville
U of Wisconsin, River Falls
U of Wisconsin, Stevens Point
U of Wisconsin, Stout
U of Wisconsin, Superior
U of Wisconsin, Whitewater
Ursinus College
Utica College
Vassar College
Virginia Wesleyan College
Wartburg College
Washington and Jefferson College
Washington and Lee U
Washington U (MO)
Waynesburg U
Webster U
Wellesley College
Wells College
Wesley College
Wesleyan College (GA)
Wesleyan U (CT)
Western New England College
Westfield State College
Westminster College (MO)
Westminster College (PA)
Wheaton College (IL)
Wheaton College (MA)
Whitman College
Whittier College
Whitworth U
Widener U
Willamette U
William Smith College
Williams College
Wilmington College (OH)
Wisconsin Lutheran College
Wittenberg U
Worcester Polytechnic Institute

Worcester State College
Yeshiva U
York College (NY)
York College (PA)

EQUESTRIAN
DIVISION I

Auburn U
Baylor U
Brown U
California State U, Fresno
College of Charleston (SC)
Cornell U
Delaware State U
Kansas State U
New Mexico State U
Oklahoma State U
Sacred Heart U
South Dakota State U
Southern Methodist U
Texas A&M U, College Station
Texas Christian U
U of Georgia
U of South Carolina, Columbia
U of Tennessee at Martin

EQUESTRIAN
DIVISION II

Pace U
Seton Hill U
Stonehill College
U of Minnesota, Crookston
West Texas A&M U

EQUESTRIAN
DIVISION III

Arcadia U
Becker College
Drew U
Goucher College
Hartwick College
Mississippi College

Mount Holyoke College
Nazareth College
Skidmore College
St. Joseph's College (Long Island)
State U College at Geneseo
State U of New York at Morrisville
State U of New York at Potsdam
Stevens Institute of Technology
U of Massachusetts, Dartmouth

FENCING
DIVISION I

Boston College
Brown U
Cleveland State U
Columbia U-Barnard College
Cornell U
Duke U
Fairleigh Dickinson U, Metropolitan
Harvard U
New Jersey Institute of Technology
Northwestern U
The Ohio State U
Pennsylvania State U
Princeton U
Sacred Heart U
St. Francis College (NY)
St. John's U (NY)
Stanford U
Temple U
U.S. Air Force Academy
U of Detroit Mercy
U of North Carolina, Chapel Hill
U of Notre Dame
U of Pennsylvania
Yale U

FENCING
DIVISION II

New Jersey Institute of Technology
Queens College (NY)
U of California, San Diego
Wayne State U (MI)

FENCING
DIVISION III

Brandeis U
California Institute of Technology
The City College of New York
Drew U
Haverford College
Hunter College
Johns Hopkins U
Lawrence U
Massachusetts Institute of Technology
New York U
Stevens Institute of Technology
Tufts U
Vassar College
Wellesley College
Yeshiva U

FIELD HOCKEY
DIVISION I

American U
Appalachian State U
Ball State U
Boston College
Boston U
Brown U
Bryant U
Bucknell U
Central Michigan U
Colgate U

College of the Holy Cross
College of William and Mary
Columbia U-Barnard College
Cornell U
Dartmouth College
Davidson College
Drexel U
Duke U
Fairfield U
Georgetown U
Harvard U
Hofstra U
Indiana U, Bloomington
James Madison U
Kent State U
La Salle U
Lafayette College
Lehigh U
Lock Haven U of Pennsylvania
Longwood U
Miami U (OH)
Michigan State U
Missouri State U
Monmouth U
Northeastern U
Northwestern U
Ohio U
The Ohio State U Old Dominion U
Pennsylvania State U
Princeton U
Providence College
Quinnipiac U
Radford U
Rider U
Robert Morris U
Rutgers, State Univ of New Jersey, New Brunswick
Sacred Heart U
Saint Francis U (PA)
Saint Joseph's U
Saint Louis U
Siena College
Stanford U

Syracuse U
Temple U
Towson U
U at Albany
U of California, Berkeley
U of Connecticut
U of Delaware
U of Iowa
U of Louisville
U of Maine, Orono
U of Maryland, College Park
U of Massachusetts, Amherst
U of Michigan
U of New Hampshire
U of North Carolina,
   Chapel Hill
U of Pennsylvania
U of Richmond
U of the Pacific
U of Vermont
U of Virginia
Villanova U
Virginia Commonwealth U
Wake Forest U
West Chester U of
   Pennsylvania
Yale U

FIELD HOCKEY
DIVISION II

Adelphi U
American International
   College
Assumption College
Bellarmine U
Bentley College
Bloomsburg U of
   Pennsylvania
Bryant U
C.W. Post Campus/Long
   Island U
Catawba College
East Stroudsburg U of
   Pennsylvania
Franklin Pierce U

Indiana U of Pennsylvania
Kutztown U of
   Pennsylvania
Mansfield U of
   Pennsylvania
Mercyhurst College
Merrimack College
Millersville U of Pennsylvania
Philadelphia U
Saint Anselm College
Saint Michael's College
Seton Hill U
Shippensburg U of
   Pennsylvania
Slippery Rock U of
   Pennsylvania
Southern Connecticut
   State U
Stonehill College
U of Massachusetts at Lowell

FIELD HOCKEY
DIVISION III

Albright College
Alvernia U
Amherst College
Anna Maria College
Arcadia U
Babson College
Bates College
Becker College
Bowdoin College
Bridgewater College (VA)
Bridgewater State College
Bryn Mawr College
Cabrini College
Castleton State College
Catholic U
Cedar Crest College
Centre College
Christopher Newport U
Clark U (MA)
Colby College
College of Brockport, State
   U of New York

The College of New Jersey
College of Notre Dame (MD)
College of Wooster
Connecticut College
Daniel Webster College
Delaware Valley College
Denison U
DePauw U
DeSales U
Dickinson College
Drew U
Earlham College
Eastern Connecticut State U
Eastern Mennonite U
Eastern U
Elizabethtown College
Elmira College
Elms College
Endicott College
Fairleigh Dickinson U,
   Florham
Fitchburg State College
Fontbonne U
Framingham State College
Franklin & Marshall
   College
Frostburg State U
Gettysburg College
Gordon College
Goucher College
Gwynedd-Mercy College
Hamilton College
Hartwick College
Haverford College
Hendrix College
Hood College
Husson College
Immaculata U
Ithaca College
Johns Hopkins U
Juniata College
Kean U
Keene State College
Kenyon College
Keystone College
King's College (PA)
Lasell College

Lebanon Valley College
Lynchburg College
Manhattanville College
Marywood U
Massachusetts Institute of
    Technology
McDaniel College
Messiah College
Middlebury College
Misericordia U
Montclair State U
Moravian College
Mount Holyoke College
Muhlenberg College
Nazareth College
Neumann College
New England College
Nichols College
Oberlin College
Ohio Wesleyan U
Philadelphia Biblical U
Plymouth State U
Ramapo College
Randolph-Macon College
Regis College (MA)
Rensselaer Polytechnic
    Institute
Rhodes College
Richard Stockton College
    of New Jersey
Roanoke College
Rosemont College
Rowan U
Saint Joseph's College (ME)
Saint Vincent College
Salem State College
Salisbury U
Salve Regina U
Shenandoah U
Simmons College
Skidmore College
Smith College
Springfield College
St. Lawrence U
St. Mary's College of
    Maryland
State U College at Cortland
State U College at Geneseo

State U College at New
    Paltz
State U College at Oneonta
State U of New York at
    Morrisville
State U of New York at
    Oswego
Stevens Institute of
    Technology
Stevenson U
Susquehanna U
Swarthmore College
Sweet Briar College
Thomas College
Transylvania U
Trinity College (CT)
Tufts U
Union College (NY)
U of Maine, Farmington
U of Mary Washington
U of Massachusetts,
    Dartmouth
U of New England
U of Rochester
U of Scranton
U of Southern Maine
U of the South
Ursinus College
Utica College
Vassar College
Virginia Wesleyan College
Washington and Jefferson
    College
Washington and Lee U
Washington College (MD)
Wellesley College
Wells College
Wesley College
Wesleyan U (CT)
Western Connecticut
    State U
Western New England
    College
Westfield State College
Wheaton College (MA)
Wheelock College
Widener U
Wilkes U

William Paterson U of New
    Jersey
William Smith College
Williams College
Wilson College
Wittenberg U
Worcester Polytechnic
    Institute
Worcester State College
York College (PA)

GOLF
DIVISION I

Alabama State U
Alcorn State U
Appalachian State U
Arizona State U
Arkansas State U
Auburn U
Augusta State U
Austin Peay State U
Ball State U
Baylor U
Belmont U
Bethune-Cookman U
Birmingham-Southern
    College
Boise State U
Boston College
Boston U
Bowling Green State U
Bradley U
Brigham Young U
Brown U
Bucknell U
Butler U
California Polytechnic
    State U
California State U,
    Bakersfield
California State U, Fresno
California State U,
    Northridge
California State U,
    Sacramento
Campbell U

Centenary College (LA)
Central Connecticut State U
Charleston Southern U
Chicago State U
The Citadel
Cleveland State U
Coastal Carolina U
College of Charleston (SC)
College of the Holy Cross
College of William and Mary
Colorado State U
Columbia U-Barnard
  College
Creighton U
Dartmouth College
Drake U
Duke U
East Carolina U
East Tennessee State U
Eastern Illinois U
Eastern Kentucky U
Eastern Michigan U
Eastern Washington U
Elon U
Fairfield U
Fairleigh Dickinson U,
  Metropolitan
Florida Atlantic U
Florida Gulf Coast U
Florida International U
Florida State U
Furman U
Gardner-Webb U
Georgetown U
Georgia State U
Gonzaga U
Grambling State U
Hampton U
Harvard U
High Point U
Hofstra U
Houston Baptist U
Idaho State U
Illinois State U
Indiana State U
Indiana U, Bloomington
Indiana U-Purdue U at
  Indianapolis

Indiana U-Purdue U, Fort
  Wayne
Iowa State U
Jackson State U
Jacksonville State U
Jacksonville U
James Madison U
Kansas State U
Kennesaw State U
Kent State U
Lamar U
Lehigh U
Lipscomb U
Long Beach State U
Long Island U-Brooklyn
  Campus
Longwood U
Louisiana State U
Loyola U (IL)
Marshall U
McNeese State U
Mercer U
Michigan State U
Middle Tennessee State U
Mississippi State U
Mississippi Valley State U
Missouri State U
Monmouth U
Montana State U-Bozeman
Morehead State U
Mount St. Mary's U
Murray State U
New Mexico State U
Nicholls State U
North Carolina State U
North Dakota State U
Northern Arizona U
Northern Illinois U
Northwestern U
Oakland U
Ohio U
The Ohio State U
Oklahoma State U
Old Dominion U
Oral Roberts U
Oregon State U
Pennsylvania State U
Pepperdine U

Portland State U
Prairie View A&M U
Presbyterian College
Princeton U
Purdue U
Radford U
Robert Morris U
Rutgers, State Univ of New
  Jersey, New Brunswick
Sacred Heart U
Saint Francis U (PA)
Sam Houston State U
Samford U
San Diego State U
San Jose State U
Santa Clara U
Savannah State U
Siena College
South Carolina State U
South Dakota State U
Southern Illinois U at
  Carbondale
Southern Illinois U
  Edwardsville
Southern Methodist U
Southern U, Baton Rouge
Southern Utah U
St. Francis College (NY)
St. John's U (NY)
Stanford U
Stetson U
Tennessee State U
Tennessee Technological U
Texas A&M U, College
  Station
Texas A&M U-Corpus
  Christi
Texas Christian U
Texas Southern U
Texas State U-San Marcos
Texas Tech U
Towson U
Troy U
Tulane U
U at Albany
U of Alabama at
  Birmingham
U of Alabama, Tuscaloosa

U of Arizona
U of Arkansas, Fayetteville
U of Arkansas, Little Rock
U of Arkansas, Pine Bluff
U of California, Berkeley
U of California, Davis
U of California, Irvine
U of California, Los
  Angeles
U of California, Riverside
U of Central Arkansas
U of Central Florida
U of Cincinnati
U of Colorado, Boulder
U of Dayton
U of Denver
U of Detroit Mercy
U of Evansville
U of Florida
U of Georgia
U of Hartford
U of Hawaii, Manoa
U of Idaho
U of Illinois, Champaign
U of Iowa
U of Kansas
U of Kentucky
U of Louisiana at Monroe
U of Louisville
U of Maryland, College
  Park
U of Memphis
U of Miami (FL)
U of Michigan
U of Minnesota, Twin
  Cities
U of Mississippi
U of Missouri, Columbia
U of Missouri, Kansas City
U of Montana
U of Nebraska, Lincoln
U of Nevada
U of Nevada, Las Vegas
U of New Mexico
U of North Carolina at
  Greensboro
U of North Carolina,
  Chapel Hill

U of North Carolina,
  Wilmington
U of North Dakota
U of North Texas
U of Northern Colorado
U of Northern Iowa
U of Notre Dame
U of Oklahoma
U of Oregon
U of Pennsylvania
U of Portland
U of Richmond
U of San Francisco
U of South Alabama
U of South Carolina Upstate
U of South Carolina,
  Columbia
U of South Dakota
U of South Florida
U of Southern California
U of Southern Mississippi
U of Tennessee at
  Chattanooga
U of Tennessee, Knoxville
U of Texas at Austin
U of Texas at El Paso
U of Texas at San Antonio
U of Texas, Pan American
U of Toledo
U of Tulsa
U of Virginia
U of Washington
U of Wisconsin, Green Bay
U of Wisconsin, Madison
U of Wyoming
Utah Valley U
Vanderbilt U
Wagner College
Wake Forest U
Washington State U
Weber State U
Western Carolina U
Western Illinois U
Western Kentucky U
Western Michigan U
Wichita State U
Winthrop U
Wofford College

Xavier U
Yale U
Youngstown State U

GOLF
DIVISION II

Adams State College
Albany State U (GA)
Anderson U (SC)
Angelo State U
Arkansas Tech U
Armstrong Atlantic State U
Ashland U
Augustana College (SD)
Barry U
Bellarmine U
Belmont Abbey College
Bemidji State U
Benedict College
Brevard College
California State U,
  Bakersfield
California State U, Chico
California State U,
  Monterey Bay
California U of
  Pennsylvania
Cameron U
Catawba College
Central State U
Chadron State College
Chestnut Hill College
Christian Brothers U
Clarion U of Pennsylvania
Colorado Christian U
Colorado State U-Pueblo
Concord U
Concordia U, St. Paul
Dallas Baptist U
Drury U
East Central U
East Stroudsburg U of
  Pennsylvania
Eckerd College
Erskine College
Fairmont State U
Ferris State U

Flagler College
Florida Gulf Coast U
Florida Institute of
Technology
Florida Southern College
Fort Hays State U
Gannon U
Glenville State College
Grand Canyon U
Grand Valley State U
Harding U
Henderson State U
Kennesaw State U
Kentucky Wesleyan
College
Kutztown U of
Pennsylvania
Lenoir-Rhyne College
Lewis U
Limestone College
Lincoln Memorial U
Lynn U
Mars Hill College
Mercyhurst College
Mesa State College
Minnesota State U
Moorhead
Minnesota State U,
Mankato
Missouri Western State U
Montana State U-Billings
Mount Olive College
Newberry College
Newman U
Northeastern State U
Northern Kentucky U
Northern State U
Northwest Missouri State U
Northwood U (MI)
Notre Dame de Namur U
Nova Southeastern U
Oakland City U
Ohio Valley U
Oklahoma Panhandle
State U
Pfeiffer U
Presbyterian College
Queens U of Charlotte

Quincy U
Regis U (CO)
Rockhurst U
Rollins College
Saint Joseph's College (IN)
Saint Leo U
Salem International U
Seton Hill U
Sonoma State U
Southern Arkansas U
Southern Illinois U
Edwardsville
Southwest Minnesota
State U
Southwestern Oklahoma
State U
St. Andrews Presbyterian
College
St. Cloud State U
St. Edward's U
St. Martin's U
St. Mary's U (TX)
Tarleton State U
Texas A&M International U
Texas A&M U-Commerce
Tiffin U
Truman State U
Tusculum College
U of Arkansas, Monticello
U of Central Arkansas
U of Central Oklahoma
U of Findlay
U of Hawaii at Hilo
U of Indianapolis
U of Mary
U of Minnesota, Crookston
U of Missouri, St. Louis
U of Montevallo
U of Nebraska at Kearney
U of Nebraska at Omaha
U of North Carolina at
Pembroke
U of North Dakota
U of Pittsburgh, Johnstown
U of South Carolina Upstate
U of South Dakota
U of Southern Indiana
U of the Incarnate Word

U of West Florida
U of West Georgia
Upper Iowa U
Wayne State College (NE)
West Chester U of
Pennsylvania
West Liberty State College
West Texas A&M U
West Virginia State U
Western New Mexico U
Western Washington U
Wheeling Jesuit U
Wingate U
Winona State U

GOLF
DIVISION III

Adrian College
Albion College
Allegheny College
Alma College
Amherst College
Anderson U (IN)
Augsburg College
Augustana College (IL)
Aurora U
Baldwin-Wallace College
Bates College
Beloit College
Benedictine U (IL)
Bethany Lutheran College
Bethel U (MN)
Bowdoin College
Buena Vista U
California State U, East Bay
Calvin College
Capital U
Carleton College
Carroll U (WI)
Carthage College
Central College (IA)
Centre College
Claremont McKenna-
Harvey Mudd-Scripps
Colleges
Coe College
College of Mount St. Joseph

College of St. Benedict
Concordia College,
    Moorhead
Concordia U (WI)
Concordia U Texas
Cornell College
Defiance College
Denison U
DePauw U
Dickinson College
Edgewood College
Elmhurst College
Elmira College
Fontbonne U
Franklin & Marshall College
Franklin College
George Fox U
Gettysburg College
Grinnell College
Grove City College
Gustavus Adolphus College
Hanover College
Hardin-Simmons U
Heidelberg College
Hendrix College
Hiram College
Hollins U
Hood College
Hope College
Huntingdon College
Illinois College
Illinois Wesleyan U
Ithaca College
John Carroll U
Kalamazoo College
Knox College
Lake Erie College
Lakeland College
LeTourneau U
Lewis & Clark College
Linfield College
Loras College
Luther College
Macalester College
Manchester College
Marian U (WI)
Maryville U of Saint Louis
McDaniel College

McMurry U
Methodist U
Middlebury College
Millikin U
Millsaps College
Milwaukee School of
    Engineering
Monmouth College (IL)
Mount Holyoke College
Mount Union College
Muhlenberg College
Muskingum College
Nazareth College
Nebraska Wesleyan U
New York U
North Central College
North Park U
Northwestern College
Occidental College
Oglethorpe U
Ohio Northern U
Olivet College
Otterbein College
Pacific Lutheran U
Pacific U (OR)
Pennsylvania State Univ.
    Erie, the Behrend College
Piedmont College
Presentation College
Rhodes College
Ripon College
Rose-Hulman Institute of
    Technology
Saint Mary's College (IN)
Saint Mary's U of
    Minnesota
Saint Vincent College
Schreiner U
Simpson College
Southwestern U (TX)
Spelman College
St. John Fisher College
St. Lawrence U
St. Norbert College
St. Olaf College
State U College at Cortland
State U of New York at
    Cobleskill

Stevenson U
Susquehanna U
Texas Lutheran U
Thiel College
Thomas More College
Transylvania U
Trine U
Trinity U (TX)
U of California, Santa Cruz
U of Dubuque
U of Mary Hardin-Baylor
U of Minnesota, Morris
U of Pittsburgh, Bradford
U of Puget Sound
U of Redlands
U of St. Thomas (MN)
U of Texas at Dallas
U of Texas at Tyler
U of the South
U of Wisconsin, Eau Claire
U of Wisconsin, Oshkosh
U of Wisconsin, Platteville
U of Wisconsin, River Falls
U of Wisconsin, Stevens
    Point
U of Wisconsin, Stout
U of Wisconsin, Superior
U of Wisconsin, Whitewater
Vassar College
Wartburg College
Washington and Jefferson
    College
Washington U (MO)
Waynesburg U
Wellesley College
Westfield State College
Westminster College (MO)
Westminster College (PA)
Wheaton College (IL)
Whitman College
Whitworth U
Willamette U
William Smith College
Williams College
Wilmington College (OH)
Wisconsin Lutheran College
Wittenberg U

GYMNASTICS
DIVISION I

Arizona State U
Auburn U
Ball State U
Boise State U
Bowling Green State U
Brigham Young U
Brown U
California State U, Fullerton
California State U, Sacramento
Centenary College (LA)
Central Michigan U
College of William and Mary
Cornell U
Eastern Michigan U
George Washington U
Illinois State U
Iowa State U
Kent State U
Louisiana State U
Michigan State U
North Carolina State U
Northern Illinois U
The Ohio State U
Oregon State U
Pennsylvania State U
Rutgers, State Univ of New Jersey, New Brunswick
San Jose State U
Southeast Missouri State U
Southern Utah U
Stanford U
Temple U
Towson U
U.S. Air Force Academy
U of Alabama, Tuscaloosa
U of Alaska Anchorage
U of Arizona
U of Arkansas, Fayetteville
U of California, Berkeley
U of California, Davis
U of California, Los Angeles
U of Denver
U of Florida

U of Georgia
U of Illinois at Chicago
U of Illinois, Champaign
U of Iowa
U of Kentucky
U of Maryland, College Park
U of Michigan
U of Minnesota, Twin Cities
U of Missouri, Columbia
U of Nebraska, Lincoln
U of New Hampshire
U of North Carolina, Chapel Hill
U of Oklahoma
U of Pennsylvania
U of Pittsburgh
U of Utah
U of Washington
Utah State U
West Virginia U
Western Michigan U
Yale U

GYMNASTICS
DIVISION II

Seattle Pacific U
Southern Connecticut State U
Texas Woman's U
U of Bridgeport

GYMNASTICS
DIVISION III

College of Brockport, State U of New York
Gustavus Adolphus College
Hamline U
Ithaca College
Massachusetts Institute of Technology
Rhode Island College
Springfield College
State U College at Cortland
U of Wisconsin, Eau Claire

U of Wisconsin, La Crosse
U of Wisconsin, Oshkosh
U of Wisconsin, Stout
U of Wisconsin, Whitewater
Ursinus College
Wilson College
Winona State U

ICE HOCKEY
DIVISION I

Bemidji State U
Boston College
Boston U
Brown U
Clarkson U
Colgate U
College of the Holy Cross
Cornell U
Dartmouth College
Harvard U
Mercyhurst College
Minnesota State U, Mankato
Niagara U
Northeastern U
The Ohio State U
Princeton U
Providence College
Quinnipiac U
Rensselaer Polytechnic Institute
Robert Morris U
Sacred Heart U
St. Cloud State U
St. Lawrence U
Syracuse U
Union College (NY)
U of Connecticut
U of Maine, Orono
U of Minnesota Duluth
U of Minnesota, Twin Cities
U of New Hampshire
U of North Dakota
U of Vermont
U of Wisconsin, Madison
Wayne State U (MI)
Yale U

ICE HOCKEY
DIVISION II

Saint Anselm College
Saint Michael's College

ICE HOCKEY
DIVISION III

Adrian College
Amherst College
Augsburg College
Bethel U (MN)
Bowdoin College
Buffalo State College
Castleton State College
Chatham U
Colby College
College of St. Benedict
College of St. Catherine
Concordia College,
    Moorhead
Concordia U (WI)
Connecticut College
Elmira College
Finlandia U
Gustavus Adolphus College
Hamilton College
Hamline U
Lake Forest College
Manhattanville College
Massachusetts Institute of
    Technology
Middlebury College
Neumann College
New England College
Nichols College
Norwich U
Plattsburgh State U of
    New York
Plymouth State U
Rochester Institute of
    Technology
Saint Mary's U of
    Minnesota
Salve Regina U
St. Olaf College

State U College at Cortland
State U of New York at
    Oswego
State U of New York at
    Potsdam
Trinity College (CT)
U of Massachusetts, Boston
U of Southern Maine
U of St. Thomas (MN)
U of Wisconsin, Eau Claire
U of Wisconsin, River Falls
U of Wisconsin, Stevens
    Point
U of Wisconsin, Superior
Utica College
Wesleyan U (CT)
Williams College

LACROSSE
DIVISION I

American U
Boston College
Boston U
Brown U
Bryant U
Bucknell U
California State U, Fresno
Canisius College
Central Connecticut State U
Colgate U
College of the Holy Cross
College of William and Mary
Columbia U-Barnard College
Cornell U
Dartmouth College
Davidson College
Drexel U
Duke U
Duquesne U
Fairfield U
George Mason U
George Washington U
Georgetown U
Harvard U
Hofstra U
Howard U

Iona College
James Madison U
Johns Hopkins U
La Salle U
Lafayette College
Le Moyne College
Lehigh U
Long Island U-Brooklyn
    Campus
Longwood U
Loyola U (MD)
Manhattan College
Marist College
Monmouth U
Mount St. Mary's U
Niagara U
Northwestern U
The Ohio State U
Old Dominion U
Pennsylvania State U
Presbyterian College
Princeton U
Quinnipiac U
Robert Morris U
Rutgers, State Univ of New
    Jersey, New Brunswick
Sacred Heart U
Saint Francis U (PA)
Saint Joseph's U
Siena College
St. Bonaventure U
St. Mary's College of
    California
Stanford U
State U of New York at
    Binghamton
Stony Brook U
Syracuse U
Temple U
Towson U
U.S. Naval Academy
U at Albany
U of California, Berkeley
U of California, Davis
U of Cincinnati
U of Connecticut
U of Delaware

U of Denver
U of Detroit Mercy
U of Louisville
U of Maryland, Baltimore
County
U of Maryland, College Park
U of Massachusetts, Amherst
U of New Hampshire
U of North Carolina,
Chapel Hill
U of Notre Dame
U of Oregon
U of Pennsylvania
U of Richmond
U of Vermont
U of Virginia
Vanderbilt U
Villanova U
Virginia Polytechnic
Institute & State U
Wagner College
Yale U

LACROSSE
DIVISION II

Adelphi U
American International
College
Assumption College
Belmont Abbey College
Bentley College
Bloomsburg U of
Pennsylvania
Bryant U
C.W. Post Campus/Long
Island U
Chestnut Hill College
Converse College
Dominican College (NY)
Dowling College
East Stroudsburg U of
Pennsylvania
Edinboro U of Pennsylvania
Erskine College
Fort Lewis College
Franklin Pierce U

Gannon U
Georgian Court U
Holy Family U
Indiana U of Pennsylvania
Kutztown U of
Pennsylvania
Lees-McRae College
Limestone College
Lock Haven U of
Pennsylvania
Mercyhurst College
Merrimack College
Millersville U of
Pennsylvania
Molloy College
Pfeiffer U
Philadelphia U
Presbyterian College
Queens U of Charlotte
Regis U (CO)
Rollins College
Saint Anselm College
Saint Michael's College
Seton Hill U
Shippensburg U of
Pennsylvania
Slippery Rock U of
Pennsylvania
Southern Connecticut
State U
Southern New Hampshire U
St. Andrews Presbyterian
College
St. Thomas Aquinas College
Stonehill College
U of New Haven
West Chester U of
Pennsylvania
Wilmington U (DE)

LACROSSE
DIVISION III

Adrian College
Alfred U
Allegheny College
Alvernia U

Amherst College
Anna Maria College
Arcadia U
Babson College
Bates College
Becker College
Bowdoin College
Bridgewater College (VA)
Bridgewater State College
Bryn Mawr College
Buffalo State College
Cabrini College
Castleton State College
Catholic U
Cazenovia College
Cedar Crest College
Centenary College (NJ)
Christopher Newport U
Claremont McKenna-
Harvey Mudd-Scripps
Colleges
Clarkson U
Colby College
Colby-Sawyer College
College of Brockport, State
U of New York
College of Mount St.
Joseph
College of Mount St.
Vincent
The College of New Jersey
College of Notre Dame (MD)
College of Wooster
Colorado College
Connecticut College
Curry College
Daniel Webster College
Denison U
Dickinson College
Drew U
Eastern Connecticut State U
Eastern U
Elizabethtown College
Elmira College
Elms College
Emerson College
Endicott College

Fairleigh Dickinson U, Florham
Ferrum College
Fitchburg State College
Fontbonne U
Framingham State College
Franklin & Marshall College
Frostburg State U
Gettysburg College
Gordon College
Goucher College
Green Mountain College
Greensboro College
Guilford College
Gwynedd-Mercy College
Hamilton College
Hartwick College
Haverford College
Hollins U
Hood College
Immaculata U
Ithaca College
Kean U
Keene State College
Kenyon College
Keuka College
King's College (PA)
Lancaster Bible College
Lasell College
Linfield College
Lycoming College
Lynchburg College
Manhattanville College
Marymount U (VA)
Marywood U
Massachusetts Institute of Technology
McDaniel College
Medaille College
Messiah College
Methodist U
Middlebury College
Misericordia U
Montclair State U
Moravian College
Mount Holyoke College

Muhlenberg College
Nazareth College
Neumann College
New England College
Nichols College
Norwich U
Oberlin College
Ohio Wesleyan U
Pacific U (OR)
Pine Manor College
Plymouth State U
Polytechnic Institute of New York U
Pomona-Pitzer Colleges
Ramapo College
Randolph-Macon College
Rensselaer Polytechnic Institute
Rhode Island College
Roanoke College
Rochester Institute of Technology
Roger Williams U
Rowan U
The Sage Colleges
Saint Joseph's College (ME)
Saint Vincent College
Salisbury U
Salve Regina U
Shenandoah U
Simmons College
Skidmore College
Smith College
Springfield College
St. John Fisher College
St. Joseph College (CT)
St. Lawrence U
St. Mary's College of Maryland
State U College at Cortland
State U College at Fredonia
State U College at Geneseo
State U College at Oneonta
State U of New York at Farmingdale
State U of New York at Morrisville

State U of New York at Oswego
State U of New York at Potsdam
State U of New York Maritime College
Stevens Institute of Technology
Stevenson U
Susquehanna U
Swarthmore College
Sweet Briar College
Thomas College
Trine U
Trinity College (CT)
Trinity College (District of Columbia)
Tufts U
Union College (NY)
U of Dallas
U of Maine, Farmington
U of Mary Washington
U of Massachusetts, Dartmouth
U of New England
U of Puget Sound
U of Redlands
U of Rochester
U of Scranton
U of Southern Maine
U of the South
Ursinus College
Utica College
Vassar College
Virginia Wesleyan College
Washington and Jefferson College
Washington and Lee U
Washington College (MD)
Waynesburg U
Wellesley College
Wells College
Wesley College
Wesleyan U (CT)
Western Connecticut State U

Western New England
  College
Westfield State College
Wheaton College (MA)
Whittier College
Widener U
Wilkes U
William Smith College
Williams College
Wilson College
Wittenberg U
Worcester State College
York College (PA)

RIFLE
DIVISION I

Birmingham-Southern
  College
The Citadel
Texas Christian U
U of Alabama at
  Birmingham
U of Mississippi
U of Nebraska, Lincoln
U of Tennessee at Martin
U of Texas at El Paso

RIFLE
DIVISION II

U of the Sciences in
  Philadelphia

RIFLE
DIVISION III

State U of New York
  Maritime College
Wentworth Institute of
  Technology

ROWING
DIVISION I

Boston College
Boston U

Brown U
Bucknell U
California State U,
  Sacramento
Clemson U
Colgate U
College of the Holy Cross
Columbia U-Barnard College
Cornell U
Creighton U
Dartmouth College
Drake U
Drexel U
Duke U
Duquesne U
Eastern Michigan U
Fairfield U
Fordham U
George Mason U
George Washington U
Georgetown U
Gonzaga U
Harvard U
Indiana U, Bloomington
Iona College
Jacksonville U
Kansas State U
La Salle U
Lehigh U
Loyola Marymount U
Loyola U (MD)
Marist College
Massachusetts Institute of
  Technology
Michigan State U
Northeastern U
The Ohio State U
Old Dominion U
Oregon State U
Princeton U
Robert Morris U
Rutgers, State Univ of New
  Jersey, New Brunswick
Sacred Heart U
Saint Joseph's U
San Diego State U
Santa Clara U

Southern Methodist U
St. Mary's College of
  California
Stanford U
Stetson U
Syracuse U
Temple U
U.S. Naval Academy
U at Buffalo, the State U
  of New
U of Alabama, Tuscaloosa
U of California, Berkeley
U of California, Davis
U of California, Irvine
U of California, Los
  Angeles
U of Central Florida
U of Connecticut
U of Dayton
U of Delaware
U of Iowa
U of Kansas
U of Louisville
U of Massachusetts,
  Amherst
U of Miami (FL)
U of Michigan
U of Minnesota, Twin
  Cities
U of North Carolina,
  Chapel Hill
U of Notre Dame
U of Oklahoma
U of Pennsylvania
U of Rhode Island
U of San Diego
U of Southern California
U of Tennessee, Knoxville
U of Texas at Austin
U of Tulsa
U of Virginia
U of Washington
U of Wisconsin, Madison
Villanova U
Washington State U
West Virginia U
Yale U

ROWING
DIVISION II

Assumption College
Barry U
Dowling College
Florida Institute of
   Technology
Franklin Pierce U
Humboldt State U
Mercyhurst College
Nova Southeastern U
Philadelphia U
Rollins College
Seattle Pacific U
U of California, San Diego
U of Central Oklahoma
U of Charleston (WV)
U of Tampa
Western Washington U

ROWING
DIVISION III

Bates College
Bryn Mawr College
Cazenovia College
Chapman U
Clark U (MA)
Colby College
Connecticut College
D'Youville College
Franklin & Marshall College
Hamilton College
Ithaca College
Johns Hopkins U
Lesley U
Lewis & Clark College
Marietta College
Massachusetts Maritime
   Academy
Mills College
Mount Holyoke College
North Park U
Pacific Lutheran U
Richard Stockton College
   of New Jersey

Rochester Institute of
   Technology
Rutgers, The State Univ. of
   New Jersey, Camden
Simmons College
Skidmore College
Smith College
St. Lawrence U
State U of New York
   Maritime College
Trinity College (CT)
Tufts U
U.S. Coast Guard Academy
U.S. Merchant Marine
   Academy
Union College (NY)
U of Mary Washington
U of Puget Sound
Vassar College
Washington College (MD)
Wellesley College
Wesleyan U (CT)
Willamette U
William Smith College
Williams College
Worcester Polytechnic
   Institute

RUGBY
DIVISION I

Eastern Illinois U

RUGBY
DIVISION II

West Chester U of
   Pennsylvania

RUGBY
DIVISION III

Bowdoin College
Norwich U
Southern Vermont College

SKIING
DIVISION I

Boston College
Brown U
Dartmouth College
Harvard U
Montana State U-Bozeman
U of Colorado, Boulder
U of Denver
U of Massachusetts, Amherst
U of Nevada
U of New Hampshire
U of New Mexico
U of Utah
U of Vermont
U of Wisconsin, Green Bay

SKIING
DIVISION II

Michigan Technological U
Northern Michigan U
Saint Anselm College
Saint Michael's College
St. Cloud State U
U of Alaska Anchorage
U of Alaska Fairbanks

SKIING
DIVISION III

Babson College
Bates College
Bowdoin College
Clarkson U
Colby College
Colby-Sawyer College
College of St. Benedict
The College of St. Scholastica
Green Mountain College
Gustavus Adolphus College
Middlebury College
Northland College
Plymouth State U
Smith College

St. Lawrence U
St. Olaf College
U of Maine at Presque Isle
Whitman College
Williams College

SOCCER
DIVISION I

Alabama A&M U
Alabama State U
Alcorn State U
American U
Appalachian State U
Arizona State U
Arkansas State U
Auburn U
Austin Peay State U
Ball State U
Baylor U
Belmont U
Birmingham-Southern
   College
Boise State U
Boston College
Boston U
Bowling Green State U
Brigham Young U
Brown U
Bryant U
Bucknell U
Butler U
California Polytechnic
   State U
California State U,
   Bakersfield
California State U, Fresno
California State U, Fullerton
California State U,
   Northridge
California State U,
   Sacramento
Campbell U
Canisius College
Centenary College (LA)
Central Connecticut State U
Central Michigan U

Charleston Southern U
The Citadel
Clemson U
Cleveland State U
Coastal Carolina U
Colgate U
College of Charleston (SC)
College of the Holy Cross
College of William and Mary
Colorado College
Columbia U-Barnard
   College
Cornell U
Creighton U
Dartmouth College
Davidson College
Delaware State U
DePaul U
Drake U
Drexel U
Duke U
Duquesne U
East Carolina U
East Tennessee State U
Eastern Illinois U
Eastern Kentucky U
Eastern Michigan U
Eastern Washington U
Elon U
Fairfield U
Fairleigh Dickinson U,
   Metropolitan
Florida Atlantic U
Florida Gulf Coast U
Florida International U
Florida State U
Fordham U
Francis Marion U
Furman U
Gardner-Webb U
George Mason U
George Washington U
Georgetown U
Georgia Southern U
Georgia State U
Gonzaga U
Grambling State U

Harvard U
High Point U
Hofstra U
Houston Baptist U
Howard U
Idaho State U
Illinois State U
Indiana State U
Indiana U, Bloomington
Indiana U-Purdue U at
   Indianapolis
Indiana U-Purdue U, Fort
   Wayne
Iona College
Iowa State U
Jackson State U
Jacksonville State U
Jacksonville U
James Madison U
Kennesaw State U
Kent State U
La Salle U
Lafayette College
Lamar U
Lehigh U
Liberty U
Lipscomb U
Long Beach State U
Long Island U-Brooklyn
   Campus
Longwood U
Louisiana State U
Louisiana Tech U
Loyola Marymount U
Loyola U (IL)
Loyola U (MD)
Manhattan College
Marist College
Marquette U
Marshall U
McNeese State U
Mercer U
Miami U (OH)
Michigan State U
Middle Tennessee State U
Mississippi State U
Mississippi Valley State U

Missouri State U
Monmouth U
Morehead State U
Mount St. Mary's U
Murray State U
New Jersey Institute of
Technology
Niagara U
Nicholls State U
North Carolina State U
North Dakota State U
Northeastern U
Northern Arizona U
Northern Illinois U
Northwestern State U
Northwestern U
Oakland U
Ohio U
The Ohio State U
Oklahoma State U
Old Dominion U
Oral Roberts U
Oregon State U
Pennsylvania State U
Pepperdine U
Portland State U
Prairie View A&M U
Presbyterian College
Princeton U
Providence College
Purdue U
Quinnipiac U
Radford U
Rice U
Rider U
Robert Morris U
Rutgers, State Univ of New
Jersey, New Brunswick
Sacred Heart U
Saint Francis U (PA)
Saint Joseph's U
Saint Louis U
Sam Houston State U
Samford U
San Diego State U
San Jose State U
Santa Clara U

Seattle U
Seton Hall U
Siena College
South Carolina State U
South Dakota State U
Southeast Missouri State U
Southeastern Louisiana U
Southern Illinois U
Edwardsville
Southern Methodist U
Southern U, Baton Rouge
Southern Utah U
St. Bonaventure U
St. John's U (NY)
St. Mary's College of
California
St. Peter's College
Stanford U
State U of New York at
Binghamton
Stephen F. Austin State U
Stetson U
Stony Brook U
Syracuse U
Temple U
Tennessee Technological U
Texas A&M U, College
Station
Texas Christian U
Texas Southern U
Texas State U-San Marcos
Texas Tech U
Towson U
Troy U
U.S. Air Force Academy
U.S. Military Academy
U.S. Naval Academy
U at Albany
U at Buffalo, the State U
of New
U of Akron
U of Alabama at
Birmingham
U of Alabama, Tuscaloosa
U of Arizona
U of Arkansas, Fayetteville
U of Arkansas, Little Rock

U of Arkansas, Pine Bluff
U of California, Berkeley
U of California, Davis
U of California, Irvine
U of California, Los Angeles
U of California, Riverside
U of California, Santa
Barbara
U of Central Arkansas
U of Central Florida
U of Cincinnati
U of Colorado, Boulder
U of Connecticut
U of Dayton
U of Delaware
U of Denver
U of Detroit Mercy
U of Evansville
U of Florida
U of Georgia
U of Hartford
U of Hawaii, Manoa
U of Houston
U of Idaho
U of Illinois, Champaign
U of Iowa
U of Kansas
U of Kentucky
U of Louisiana at Lafayette
U of Louisiana at Monroe
U of Louisville
U of Maine, Orono
U of Maryland, Baltimore
County
U of Maryland, College
Park
U of Massachusetts,
Amherst
U of Memphis
U of Miami (FL)
U of Michigan
U of Minnesota, Twin Cities
U of Mississippi
U of Missouri, Columbia
U of Montana
U of Nebraska, Lincoln
U of Nevada

U of Nevada, Las Vegas
U of New Hampshire
U of New Mexico
U of North Carolina at
Greensboro
U of North Carolina,
Asheville
U of North Carolina,
Chapel Hill
U of North Carolina,
Charlotte
U of North Carolina,
Wilmington
U of North Dakota
U of North Florida
U of North Texas
U of Northern Colorado
U of Northern Iowa
U of Notre Dame
U of Oklahoma
U of Oregon
U of Pennsylvania
U of Pittsburgh
U of Portland
U of Rhode Island
U of Richmond
U of San Diego
U of San Francisco
U of South Alabama
U of South Carolina
Upstate
U of South Carolina,
Columbia
U of South Dakota
U of South Florida
U of Southern California
U of Southern Mississippi
U of Tennessee at
Chattanooga
U of Tennessee at Martin
U of Tennessee, Knoxville
U of Texas at Austin
U of Texas at El Paso
U of Texas at San Antonio
U of the Pacific
U of Toledo
U of Tulsa

U of Utah
U of Vermont
U of Virginia
U of Washington
U of Wisconsin, Green Bay
U of Wisconsin, Madison
U of Wisconsin, Milwaukee
U of Wyoming
Utah State U
Utah Valley U
Valparaiso U
Vanderbilt U
Villanova U
Virginia Commonwealth U
Virginia Military Institute
Virginia Polytechnic
Institute & State U
Wagner College
Wake Forest U
Washington State U
Weber State U
West Virginia U
Western Carolina U
Western Illinois U
Western Kentucky U
Western Michigan U
Winthrop U
Wofford College
Wright State U
Xavier U
Yale U
Youngstown State U

SOCCER
DIVISION II

Abilene Christian U
Adams State College
Adelphi U
Alderson-Broaddus College
American International
College
Anderson U (SC)
Angelo State U
Armstrong Atlantic State U
Ashland U
Assumption College

Augustana College (SD)
Barry U
Barton College
Bellarmine U
Belmont Abbey College
Bemidji State U
Bentley College
Bloomfield College
Bloomsburg U of
Pennsylvania
Brevard College
Brigham Young U, Hawaii
Bryant U
C.W. Post Campus/Long
Island U
Caldwell College
California State
Polytechnic U, Pomona
California State U,
Bakersfield
California State U, Chico
California State U,
Dominguez Hills
California State U, Los
Angeles
California State U,
Monterey Bay
California State U, San
Bernardino
California State U,
Stanislaus
California U of
Pennsylvania
Carson-Newman College
Catawba College
Central Washington U
Chaminade U
Chestnut Hill College
Chowan U
Christian Brothers U
Clarion U of Pennsylvania
Clayton State U
Coker College
College of Saint Rose
Colorado Christian U
Colorado School of Mines
Colorado State U-Pueblo

Columbia Union College
Columbus State U
Concord U
Concordia College (NY)
Concordia U, St. Paul
Converse College
Dallas Baptist U
Davis and Elkins College
Delta State U
Dixie State College of Utah
Dominican College (NY)
Dowling College
Drury U
East Central U
East Stroudsburg U of
   Pennsylvania
Eastern New Mexico U
Eckerd College
Edinboro U of
   Pennsylvania
Emporia State U
Erskine College
Felician College
Ferris State U
Flagler College
Florida Gulf Coast U
Florida Institute of
   Technology
Florida Southern College
Fort Lewis College
Franklin Pierce U
Gannon U
The Georgia College &
   State U
Georgia Southwestern
   State U
Georgian Court U
Goldey-Beacom College
Grand Canyon U
Grand Valley State U
Harding U
Hawaii Pacific U
Holy Family U
Humboldt State U
Indiana U of Pennsylvania
Kentucky Wesleyan
   College

Kutztown U of
   Pennsylvania
Lander U
Le Moyne College
Lees-McRae College
Lenoir-Rhyne College
Lewis U
Limestone College
Lincoln Memorial U
Lock Haven U of
   Pennsylvania
Lynn U
Mansfield U of
   Pennsylvania
Mars Hill College
Mercy College
Mercyhurst College
Merrimack College
Mesa State College
Metropolitan State College
   of Denver
Midwestern State U
Millersville U of
   Pennsylvania
Minnesota State U
   Moorhead
Minnesota State U,
   Mankato
Missouri Southern State U
Missouri U of Science and
   Technology
Missouri Western State U
Molloy College
Montana State U-Billings
Mount Olive College
New Mexico Highlands U
New York Institute of
   Technology
Newberry College
Newman U
North Georgia College &
   State U
North Greenville U
Northeastern State U
Northern Kentucky U
Northern Michigan U
Northern State U

Northwest Missouri State U
Northwest Nazarene U
Northwood U (MI)
Notre Dame de Namur U
Nova Southeastern U
Nyack College
Oakland City U
Ohio Valley U
Ouachita Baptist U
Pace U
Palm Beach Atlantic U
Pfeiffer U
Philadelphia U
Post U
Presbyterian College
Queens College (NY)
Queens U of Charlotte
Quincy U
Regis U (CO)
Rockhurst U
Rollins College
Saginaw Valley State U
Saint Anselm College
Saint Joseph's College (IN)
Saint Leo U
Saint Michael's College
Salem International U
San Francisco State U
Seattle Pacific U
Seattle U
Seton Hill U
Shepherd U
Shippensburg U of
   Pennsylvania
Slippery Rock U of
   Pennsylvania
Sonoma State U
Southern Connecticut
   State U
Southern Illinois U
   Edwardsville
Southern New Hampshire U
Southwest Baptist U
Southwest Minnesota
   State U
Southwestern Oklahoma
   State U

St. Andrews Presbyterian
College
St. Cloud State U
St. Edward's U
St. Martin's U
St. Mary's U (TX)
St. Thomas Aquinas College
Stonehill College
Texas A&M International U
Texas A&M U-Commerce
Texas Woman's U
Tiffin U
Truman State U
Tusculum College
U of Alabama in Huntsville
U of Bridgeport
U of California, San Diego
U of Central Arkansas
U of Central Missouri
U of Central Oklahoma
U of Charleston (WV)
U of Colorado, Colorado
Springs
U of Findlay
U of Hawaii at Hilo
U of Indianapolis
U of Mary
U of Massachusetts at
Lowell
U of Minnesota Duluth
U of Minnesota, Crookston
U of Missouri, St. Louis
U of Montevallo
U of Nebraska at Omaha
U of New Haven
U of North Alabama
U of North Carolina at
Pembroke
U of North Dakota
U of North Florida
U of Pittsburgh, Johnstown
U of South Carolina Aiken
U of South Carolina Upstate
U of South Dakota
U of Southern Indiana
U of Tampa
U of Texas of the Permian
Basin

U of the Incarnate Word
U of West Florida
U of West Georgia
U of Wisconsin, Parkside
Upper Iowa U
Washburn U of Topeka
Wayne State College (NE)
West Chester U of
Pennsylvania
West Texas A&M U
West Virginia Wesleyan
College
Western Oregon U
Western Washington U
Wheeling Jesuit U
Wilmington U (DE)
Wingate U
Winona State U

SOCCER
DIVISION III

Adrian College
Agnes Scott College
Albertus Magnus College
Albion College
Albright College
Alfred U
Allegheny College
Alma College
Alvernia U
Alverno College
Amherst College
Anderson U (IN)
Anna Maria College
Arcadia U
Augsburg College
Augustana College (IL)
Aurora U
Austin College
Averett U
Babson College
Baldwin-Wallace College
Baptist Bible College
Bard College
Bates College
Bay Path College
Becker College

Beloit College
Benedictine U (IL)
Bethany College (WV)
Bethany Lutheran College
Bethel U (MN)
Blackburn College
Bluffton U
Bowdoin College
Brandeis U
Bridgewater College (VA)
Bridgewater State College
Bryn Mawr College
Buena Vista U
Buffalo State College
Cabrini College
California Lutheran U
California State U, East Bay
Calvin College
Capital U
Carleton College
Carnegie Mellon U
Carroll U (WI)
Carthage College
Case Western Reserve U
Castleton State College
Catholic U
Cazenovia College
Cedar Crest College
Centenary College (NJ)
Central College (IA)
Centre College
Chapman U
Chatham U
Christopher Newport U
The City College of New
York
Claremont McKenna-
Harvey Mudd-Scripps
Colleges
Clark U (MA)
Clarkson U
Coe College
Colby College
Colby-Sawyer College
College of Brockport, State
U of New York
College of Mount St.
Joseph

College of Mount St. Vincent
The College of New Jersey
College of Notre Dame (MD)
College of Saint Elizabeth
College of St. Benedict
College of St. Catherine
The College of St. Scholastica
College of Staten Island
College of Wooster
Concordia College, Moorhead
Concordia U (WI)
Concordia U Chicago
Concordia U Texas
Connecticut College
Cornell College
Crown College (MN)
Curry College
Daniel Webster College
Defiance College
Delaware Valley College
Denison U
DePauw U
DeSales U
Dickinson College
Dominican U (IL)
Drew U
D'Youville College
Earlham College
East Texas Baptist U
Eastern Connecticut State U
Eastern Mennonite U
Eastern Nazarene College
Eastern U
Edgewood College
Elizabethtown College
Elmhurst College
Elmira College
Elms College
Emerson College
Emmanuel College (MA)
Emory and Henry College
Emory U
Endicott College
Eureka College
Fairleigh Dickinson U, Florham

Ferrum College
Finlandia U
Fitchburg State College
Fontbonne U
Framingham State College
Franciscan U of Steubenville
Franklin & Marshall College
Franklin College
Frostburg State U
Gallaudet U
Geneva College
George Fox U
Gettysburg College
Gordon College
Goucher College
Green Mountain College
Greensboro College
Greenville College
Grinnell College
Grove City College
Guilford College
Gustavus Adolphus College
Gwynedd-Mercy College
Hamilton College
Hamline U
Hanover College
Hardin-Simmons U
Hartwick College
Haverford College
Heidelberg College
Hendrix College
Hilbert College
Hiram College
Hollins U
Hood College
Hope College
Howard Payne U
Huntingdon College
Husson College
Illinois College
Illinois Wesleyan U
Immaculata U
Ithaca College
John Carroll U
Johns Hopkins U
Johnson and Wales U
Johnson State College
Juniata College

Kalamazoo College
Kean U
Keene State College
Kenyon College
Keuka College
Keystone College
King's College (PA)
Knox College
La Grange College
La Roche College
La Sierra U
Lake Erie College
Lake Forest College
Lakeland College
Lancaster Bible College
Lasell College
Lawrence U
Lebanon Valley College
Lesley U
LeTourneau U
Lewis & Clark College
Lincoln U (PA)
Linfield College
Loras College
Louisiana College
Luther College
Lycoming College
Lynchburg College
Lyndon State College
Macalester College
MacMurray College
Maine Maritime Academy
Manchester College
Manhattanville College
Maranatha Baptist Bible College
Marian U (WI)
Marietta College
Martin Luther College
Mary Baldwin College
Marymount U (VA)
Maryville College (TN)
Maryville U of Saint Louis
Marywood U
Massachusetts College of Liberal Arts
Massachusetts Institute of Technology

Massachusetts Maritime
  Academy
McDaniel College
McMurry U
Medaille College
Medgar Evers College
Menlo College
Meredith College
Messiah College
Methodist U
Middlebury College
Millikin U
Mills College
Millsaps College
Milwaukee School of
  Engineering
Misericordia U
Mississippi College
Mitchell College
Monmouth College (IL)
Montclair State U
Moravian College
Mount Aloysius College
Mount Holyoke College
Mount Ida College
Mount Mary College
Mount Saint Mary College
  (NY)
Mount Union College
Muhlenberg College
Muskingum College
Nazareth College
Nebraska Wesleyan U
Neumann College
New England College
New Jersey City U
New York U
Newbury College
Nichols College
North Carolina Wesleyan
  College
North Central College
North Central U
North Park U
Northland College
Northwestern College
Norwich U
Oberlin College

Occidental College
Oglethorpe U
Ohio Northern U
Ohio Wesleyan U
Olivet College
Otterbein College
Pacific Lutheran U
Pacific U (OR)
Peace College
Penn State Berks College
Penn State Harrisburg
Penn State U, Altoona
Pennsylvania State Univ.
  Erie, the Behrend
  College
Philadelphia Biblical U
Piedmont College
Pine Manor College
Plattsburgh State U of
  New York
Plymouth State U
Pomona-Pitzer Colleges
Presentation College
Principia College
Purchase College, State U
  of New York
Ramapo College
Randolph College
Randolph-Macon College
Regis College (MA)
Rensselaer Polytechnic
  Institute
Rhode Island College
Rhodes College
Richard Stockton College
  of New Jersey
Ripon College
Rivier College
Roanoke College
Rochester Institute of
  Technology
Rockford College
Roger Williams U
Rose-Hulman Institute of
  Technology
Rowan U
Rutgers, The State Univ. of
  New Jersey, Camden

Rutgers, The State Univ. of
  New Jersey, Newark
The Sage Colleges
Saint Joseph's College (ME)
Saint Mary's College (IN)
Saint Mary's U of
  Minnesota
Saint Vincent College
Salem College
Salem State College
Salisbury U
Salve Regina U
Schreiner U
Shenandoah U
Simmons College
Simpson College
Skidmore College
Smith College
Southern Vermont College
Southwestern U (TX)
Spalding U
Spelman College
Springfield College
St. John Fisher College
St. Joseph College (CT)
St. Joseph's College (Long
  Island)
St. Lawrence U
St. Mary's College of
  Maryland
St. Norbert College
St. Olaf College
State U College at Cortland
State U College at Fredonia
State U College at Geneseo
State U College at New
  Paltz
State U College at Old
  Westbury
State U College at Oneonta
State U of New York at
  Cobleskill
State U of New York at
  Farmingdale
State U of New York at
  Morrisville
State U of New York at
  Oswego

State U of New York at
Potsdam
State U of New York
Institute of Technolo
State U of New York
Maritime College
Stevens Institute of
Technology
Stevenson U
Suffolk U
Susquehanna U
Swarthmore College
Sweet Briar College
Texas Lutheran U
Thiel College
Thomas College
Thomas More College
Transylvania U
Trine U
Trinity College (CT)
Trinity College (District of
Columbia)
Trinity U (TX)
Tufts U
U.S. Coast Guard Academy
Union College (NY)
U of California, Santa Cruz
U of Chicago
U of Dallas
U of Dubuque
U of La Verne
U of Maine at Presque Isle
U of Maine, Farmington
U of Mary Hardin-Baylor
U of Mary Washington
U of Massachusetts, Boston
U of Massachusetts,
Dartmouth
U of Minnesota, Morris
U of New England
U of Pittsburgh, Bradford
U of Pittsburgh, Greensburg
U of Puget Sound
U of Redlands
U of Rochester
U of Scranton
U of Southern Maine
U of St. Thomas (MN)

U of Texas at Dallas
U of Texas at Tyler
U of the Ozarks (AR)
U of the South
U of Wisconsin, Eau Claire
U of Wisconsin, La Crosse
U of Wisconsin, Oshkosh
U of Wisconsin, Platteville
U of Wisconsin, River Falls
U of Wisconsin, Stevens
Point
U of Wisconsin, Stout
U of Wisconsin, Superior
U of Wisconsin,
Whitewater
Ursinus College
Utica College
Vassar College
Virginia Wesleyan College
Wartburg College
Washington and Jefferson
College
Washington and Lee U
Washington College (MD)
Washington U (MO)
Waynesburg U
Webster U
Wellesley College
Wells College
Wentworth Institute of
Technology
Wesley College
Wesleyan College (GA)
Wesleyan U (CT)
Western Connecticut
State U
Western New England
College
Westfield State College
Westminster College (MO)
Westminster College (PA)
Wheaton College (IL)
Wheaton College (MA)
Wheelock College
Whitman College
Whittier College
Whitworth U
Widener U

Wilkes U
Willamette U
William Paterson U of New
Jersey
William Smith College
Williams College
Wilmington College (OH)
Wilson College
Wisconsin Lutheran College
Wittenberg U
Worcester Polytechnic
Institute
Worcester State College
Yeshiva U
York College (PA)

SOFTBALL
DIVISION I

Alabama A&M U
Alabama State U
Alcorn State U
Appalachian State U
Arizona State U
Auburn U
Austin Peay State U
Ball State U
Baylor U
Belmont U
Bethune-Cookman U
Birmingham-Southern
College
Boise State U
Boston College
Boston U
Bowling Green State U
Bradley U
Brigham Young U
Brown U
Bryant U
Bucknell U
Butler U
California Polytechnic
State U
California State U,
Bakersfield
California State U, Fresno

California State U, Fullerton
California State U, Northridge
California State U, Sacramento
Campbell U
Canisius College
Centenary College (LA)
Central Connecticut State U
Central Michigan U
Charleston Southern U
Cleveland State U
Coastal Carolina U
Colgate U
College of Charleston (SC)
College of the Holy Cross
Colorado State U
Columbia U-Barnard College
Coppin State U
Cornell U
Creighton U
Dartmouth College
Delaware State U
DePaul U
Drake U
Drexel U
East Carolina U
East Tennessee State U
Eastern Illinois U
Eastern Kentucky U
Eastern Michigan U
Elon U
Fairfield U
Fairleigh Dickinson U, Metropolitan
Florida A&M U
Florida Atlantic U
Florida Gulf Coast U
Florida International U
Florida State U
Fordham U
Furman U
Gardner-Webb U
George Mason U
George Washington U
Georgetown U
Georgia Institute of Technology

Georgia Southern U
Georgia State U
Grambling State U
Hampton U
Harvard U
Hofstra U
Houston Baptist U
Howard U
Idaho State U
Illinois State U
Indiana State U
Indiana U, Bloomington
Indiana U-Purdue U at Indianapolis
Indiana U-Purdue U, Fort Wayne
Iona College
Iowa State U
Jackson State U
Jacksonville State U
Jacksonville U
James Madison U
Kennesaw State U
Kent State U
La Salle U
Lafayette College
Lehigh U
Liberty U
Lipscomb U
Long Beach State U
Long Island U-Brooklyn Campus
Longwood U
Louisiana State U
Louisiana Tech U
Loyola Marymount U
Loyola U (IL)
Manhattan College
Marist College
Marshall U
McNeese State U
Mercer U
Miami U (OH)
Michigan State U
Middle Tennessee State U
Mississippi State U
Mississippi Valley State U
Missouri State U

Monmouth U
Morehead State U
Morgan State U
Mount St. Mary's U
New Mexico State U
Niagara U
Nicholls State U
Norfolk State U
North Carolina A&T State U
North Carolina Central U
North Carolina State U
North Dakota State U
Northern Illinois U
Northwestern State U
Northwestern U
Oakland U
Ohio U
The Ohio State U
Oklahoma State U
Oregon State U
Pennsylvania State U
Portland State U
Prairie View A&M U
Presbyterian College
Princeton U
Providence College
Purdue U
Quinnipiac U
Radford U
Rider U
Robert Morris U
Rutgers, State Univ of New Jersey, New Brunswick
Sacred Heart U
Saint Francis U (PA)
Saint Joseph's U
Saint Louis U
Sam Houston State U
Samford U
San Diego State U
San Jose State U
Santa Clara U
Savannah State U
Seattle U
Seton Hall U
Siena College
South Carolina State U
South Dakota State U

Southeast Missouri State U
Southeastern Louisiana U
Southern Illinois U at
Carbondale
Southern Illinois U
Edwardsville
Southern U, Baton Rouge
Southern Utah U
St. Bonaventure U
St. John's U (NY)
St. Mary's College of
California
St. Peter's College
Stanford U
State U of New York at
Binghamton
Stephen F. Austin State U
Stetson U
Stony Brook U
Syracuse U
Temple U
Tennessee State U
Tennessee Technological U
Texas A&M U, College
Station
Texas A&M U-Corpus Christi
Texas Southern U
Texas State U-San Marcos
Texas Tech U
Towson U
Troy U
U.S. Military Academy
U at Albany
U at Buffalo, the State U
of New
U of Akron
U of Alabama at
Birmingham
U of Alabama, Tuscaloosa
U of Arizona
U of Arkansas, Fayetteville
U of Arkansas, Pine Bluff
U of California, Berkeley
U of California, Davis
U of California, Los Angeles
U of California, Riverside
U of California, Santa
Barbara

U of Central Arkansas
U of Central Florida
U of Connecticut
U of Dayton
U of Delaware
U of Detroit Mercy
U of Evansville
U of Florida
U of Georgia
U of Hartford
U of Hawaii, Manoa
U of Houston
U of Illinois at Chicago
U of Illinois, Champaign
U of Iowa
U of Kansas
U of Kentucky
U of Louisiana at Lafayette
U of Louisiana at Monroe
U of Louisville
U of Maine, Orono
U of Maryland, Baltimore
County
U of Maryland, College Park
U of Maryland, Eastern
Shore
U of Massachusetts,
Amherst
U of Memphis
U of Michigan
U of Minnesota, Twin Cities
U of Mississippi
U of Missouri, Columbia
U of Missouri, Kansas City
U of Nebraska, Lincoln
U of Nevada
U of Nevada, Las Vegas
U of New Mexico
U of North Carolina at
Greensboro
U of North Carolina,
Chapel Hill
U of North Carolina,
Charlotte
U of North Carolina,
Wilmington
U of North Dakota
U of North Florida

U of North Texas
U of Northern Colorado
U of Northern Iowa
U of Notre Dame
U of Oklahoma
U of Oregon
U of Pennsylvania
U of Pittsburgh
U of Rhode Island
U of San Diego
U of South Alabama
U of South Carolina Upstate
U of South Carolina,
Columbia
U of South Dakota
U of South Florida
U of Southern Mississippi
U of Tennessee at
Chattanooga
U of Tennessee at Martin
U of Tennessee, Knoxville
U of Texas at Arlington
U of Texas at Austin
U of Texas at El Paso
U of Texas at San Antonio
U of the Pacific
U of Toledo
U of Tulsa
U of Utah
U of Vermont
U of Virginia
U of Washington
U of Wisconsin, Green Bay
U of Wisconsin, Madison
Utah State U
Utah Valley U
Valparaiso U
Villanova U
Virginia Polytechnic
Institute & State U
Wagner College
Western Carolina U
Western Illinois U
Western Kentucky U
Western Michigan U
Wichita State U
Winston-Salem State U
Winthrop U

Wright State U
Yale U
Youngstown State U

SOFTBALL
DIVISION II

Abilene Christian U
Adams State College
Adelphi U
Albany State U (GA)
Alderson-Broaddus College
American International
  College
Anderson U (SC)
Angelo State U
Arkansas Tech U
Armstrong Atlantic State U
Ashland U
Assumption College
Augusta State U
Augustana College (SD)
Barry U
Barton College
Bellarmine U
Belmont Abbey College
Bemidji State U
Benedict College
Bentley College
Bloomfield College
Bloomsburg U of
  Pennsylvania
Bluefield State College
Bowie State U
Brevard College
Brigham Young U, Hawaii
Bryant U
C.W. Post Campus/Long
  Island U
Caldwell College
California State U,
  Bakersfield
California State U, Chico
California State U,
  Dominguez Hills
California State U,
  Monterey Bay

California State U, San
  Bernardino
California State U,
  Stanislaus
California U of
  Pennsylvania
Cameron U
Carson-Newman College
Catawba College
Central Washington U
Chadron State College
Chaminade U
Chestnut Hill College
Chowan U
Christian Brothers U
Claflin U
Clarion U of Pennsylvania
Clark Atlanta U
Coker College
College of Saint Rose
Colorado School of Mines
Colorado State U-Pueblo
Columbia Union College
Columbus State U
Concord U
Concordia College (NY)
Concordia U, St. Paul
Davis and Elkins College
Delta State U
Dixie State College of Utah
Dominican College (NY)
Dowling College
Drury U
East Central U
East Stroudsburg U of
  Pennsylvania
Eastern New Mexico U
Eckerd College
Edinboro U of
  Pennsylvania
Elizabeth City State U
Emporia State U
Erskine College
Fairmont State U
Fayetteville State U
Felician College
Ferris State U

Flagler College
Florida Gulf Coast U
Florida Institute of
  Technology
Florida Southern College
Fort Hays State U
Fort Lewis College
Fort Valley State U
Francis Marion U
Franklin Pierce U
Gannon U
The Georgia College &
  State U
Georgia Southwestern
  State U
Georgian Court U
Glenville State College
Goldey-Beacom College
Grand Canyon U
Grand Valley State U
Hawaii Pacific U
Henderson State U
Hillsdale College
Holy Family U
Humboldt State U
Indiana U of Pennsylvania
Johnson C. Smith U
Kennesaw State U
Kentucky State U
Kentucky Wesleyan College
Kutztown U of
  Pennsylvania
Lake Superior State U
Lander U
Lane College
Le Moyne College
Lees-McRae College
LeMoyne-Owen College
Lenoir-Rhyne College
Lewis U
Limestone College
Lincoln Memorial U
Lincoln U (MO)
Livingstone College
Lock Haven U of
  Pennsylvania
Lynn U

Mansfield U of Pennsylvania
Mars Hill College
Mercy College
Mercyhurst College
Merrimack College
Mesa State College
Metropolitan State College
of Denver
Midwestern State U
Miles College
Millersville U of
Pennsylvania
Minnesota State U
Moorhead
Minnesota State U, Mankato
Missouri Southern State U
Missouri U of Science and
Technology
Missouri Western State U
Molloy College
Montana State U-Billings
Mount Olive College
New Mexico Highlands U
New York Institute of
Technology
Newberry College
Newman U
North Carolina Central U
North Georgia College &
State U
North Greenville U
Northeastern State U
Northern Kentucky U
Northern State U
Northwest Missouri State U
Northwest Nazarene U
Northwood U (MI)
Notre Dame de Namur U
Nova Southeastern U
Nyack College
Oakland City U
Ohio Valley U
Oklahoma Panhandle
State U
Ouachita Baptist U
Pace U
Paine College

Palm Beach Atlantic U
Pfeiffer U
Philadelphia U
Pittsburg State U
Post U
Presbyterian College
Queens College (NY)
Queens U of Charlotte
Quincy U
Regis U (CO)
Rockhurst U
Rollins College
Saginaw Valley State U
Saint Anselm College
Saint Joseph's College (IN)
Saint Leo U
Saint Michael's College
Salem International U
San Francisco State U
Seattle U
Seton Hill U
Shaw U
Shepherd U
Shippensburg U of
Pennsylvania
Slippery Rock U of
Pennsylvania
Sonoma State U
Southeastern Oklahoma
State U
Southern Arkansas U
Southern Connecticut
State U
Southern Illinois U
Edwardsville
Southern New Hampshire
U
Southwest Baptist U
Southwest Minnesota
State U
Southwestern Oklahoma
State U
St. Andrews Presbyterian
College
St. Augustine's College
St. Cloud State U
St. Edward's U

St. Martin's U
St. Mary's U (TX)
St. Paul's College
St. Thomas Aquinas
College
Stillman College
Stonehill College
Tarleton State U
Texas A&M International U
Texas A&M U-Kingsville
Texas Woman's U
Tiffin U
Truman State U
Tusculum College
Tuskegee U
U of Alabama in Huntsville
U of Arkansas, Monticello
U of Bridgeport
U of California, San Diego
U of Central Arkansas
U of Central Missouri
U of Central Oklahoma
U of Charleston (WV)
U of Colorado, Colorado
Springs
U of Findlay
U of Hawaii at Hilo
U of Indianapolis
U of Mary
U of Massachusetts at
Lowell
U of Minnesota Duluth
U of Minnesota, Crookston
U of Missouri, St. Louis
U of Nebraska at Kearney
U of Nebraska at Omaha
U of New Haven
U of North Alabama
U of North Carolina at
Pembroke
U of North Dakota
U of North Florida
U of Puerto Rico, Cayey
U of Puerto Rico,
Mayaguez Campus
U of Puerto Rico, Rio
Piedras

U of South Carolina Aiken
U of South Carolina Upstate
U of South Dakota
U of Southern Indiana
U of Tampa
U of Texas of the Permian
  Basin
U of the Incarnate Word
U of the Sciences in
  Philadelphia
U of West Alabama
U of West Florida
U of West Georgia
U of Wisconsin, Parkside
Upper Iowa U
Valdosta State U
Virginia State U
Virginia Union U
Washburn U of Topeka
Wayne State College (NE)
Wayne State U (MI)
West Chester U of
  Pennsylvania
West Liberty State College
West Texas A&M U
West Virginia State U
West Virginia Wesleyan
  College
Western New Mexico U
Western Oregon U
Western Washington U
Wheeling Jesuit U
Wilmington U (DE)
Wingate U
Winona State U
Winston-Salem State U

SOFTBALL
DIVISION III

Adrian College
Agnes Scott College
Albertus Magnus College
Albion College
Albright College
Alfred U
Allegheny College

Alma College
Alvernia U
Alverno College
Amherst College
Anderson U (IN)
Anna Maria College
Arcadia U
Augsburg College
Augustana College (IL)
Aurora U
Austin College
Averett U
Babson College
Baldwin-Wallace College
Baptist Bible College
Baruch College
Bates College
Bay Path College
Becker College
Beloit College
Benedictine U (IL)
Bethany College (WV)
Bethany Lutheran College
Bethel U (MN)
Blackburn College
Bluffton U
Bowdoin College
Brandeis U
Bridgewater College (VA)
Bridgewater State College
Brooklyn College
Buena Vista U
Buffalo State College
Cabrini College
California Lutheran U
California State U, East Bay
Calvin College
Capital U
Carleton College
Carroll U (WI)
Carthage College
Case Western Reserve U
Castleton State College
Catholic U
Cazenovia College
Cedar Crest College
Centenary College (NJ)

Central College (IA)
Centre College
Chapman U
Chatham U
Christopher Newport U
Claremont McKenna-
  Harvey Mudd-Scripps
  Colleges
Clark U (MA)
Coe College
Colby College
College of Brockport, State
  U of New York
College of Mount St.
  Joseph
College of Mount St.
  Vincent
The College of New Jersey
College of New Rochelle
College of Notre Dame (MD)
College of Saint Elizabeth
College of St. Benedict
College of St. Catherine
The College of St.
  Scholastica
College of Staten Island
College of Wooster
Colorado College
Concordia College,
  Moorhead
Concordia U (WI)
Concordia U Chicago
Concordia U Texas
Cornell College
Crown College (MN)
Curry College
Daniel Webster College
Defiance College
Delaware Valley College
Denison U
DePauw U
DeSales U
Dickinson College
Dominican U (IL)
Drew U
D'Youville College
East Texas Baptist U

Eastern Connecticut State U
Eastern Mennonite U
Eastern Nazarene College
Eastern U
Edgewood College
Elizabethtown College
Elmhurst College
Elmira College
Elms College
Emerson College
Emmanuel College (MA)
Emory and Henry College
Emory U
Endicott College
Eureka College
Fairleigh Dickinson U, Florham
Ferrum College
Finlandia U
Fitchburg State College
Fontbonne U
Framingham State College
Franciscan U of Steubenville
Franklin & Marshall College
Franklin College
Frostburg State U
Gallaudet U
Geneva College
George Fox U
Gettysburg College
Gordon College
Green Mountain College
Greensboro College
Greenville College
Grinnell College
Grove City College
Guilford College
Gustavus Adolphus College
Gwynedd-Mercy College
Hamilton College
Hamline U
Hanover College
Hardin-Simmons U
Haverford College
Heidelberg College
Hendrix College
Hilbert College

Hiram College
Hood College
Hope College
Howard Payne U
Hunter College
Huntingdon College
Husson College
Illinois College
Illinois Wesleyan U
Immaculata U
Ithaca College
John Carroll U
John Jay College of Criminal Justice
Johnson and Wales U
Johnson State College
Juniata College
Kalamazoo College
Kean U
Keene State College
Kenyon College
Keuka College
Keystone College
King's College (PA)
Knox College
La Grange College
La Roche College
La Sierra U
Lake Erie College
Lake Forest College
Lakeland College
Lasell College
Lawrence U
Lebanon Valley College
Lehman College, City U of New York
Lesley U
LeTourneau U
Lewis & Clark College
Lincoln U (PA)
Linfield College
Loras College
Louisiana College
Luther College
Lycoming College
Lynchburg College
Lyndon State College

Macalester College
MacMurray College
Maine Maritime Academy
Manchester College
Manhattanville College
Maranatha Baptist Bible College
Marian U (WI)
Marietta College
Martin Luther College
Mary Baldwin College
Maryville College (TN)
Maryville U of Saint Louis
Marywood U
Massachusetts College of Liberal Arts
Massachusetts Institute of Technology
Massachusetts Maritime Academy
McDaniel College
Medaille College
Menlo College
Meredith College
Messiah College
Methodist U
Middlebury College
Millikin U
Millsaps College
Milwaukee School of Engineering
Misericordia U
Mississippi College
Mitchell College
Monmouth College (IL)
Montclair State U
Moravian College
Mount Aloysius College
Mount Ida College
Mount Mary College
Mount Saint Mary College (NY)
Mount Union College
Muhlenberg College
Muskingum College
Nazareth College
Nebraska Wesleyan U

Neumann College
New England College
New Jersey City U
New York City College of
Technology
Newbury College
Nichols College
North Carolina Wesleyan
College
North Central College
North Central U
North Park U
Northland College
Northwestern College
Norwich U
Oberlin College
Occidental College
Ohio Northern U
Ohio Wesleyan U
Olivet College
Otterbein College
Pacific Lutheran U
Pacific U (OR)
Peace College
Penn State Berks College
Penn State Harrisburg
Penn State U, Altoona
Pennsylvania State Univ.
Erie, the Behrend College
Philadelphia Biblical U
Piedmont College
Pine Manor College
Plattsburgh State U of
New York
Plymouth State U
Polytechnic Institute of
New York U
Pomona-Pitzer Colleges
Presentation College
Purchase College, State U
of New York
Ramapo College
Randolph College
Randolph-Macon College
Regis College (MA)
Rensselaer Polytechnic
Institute
Rhode Island College

Rhodes College
Richard Stockton College
of New Jersey
Ripon College
Rivier College
Roanoke College
Rochester Institute of
Technology
Rockford College
Roger Williams U
Rose-Hulman Institute of
Technology
Rosemont College
Rowan U
Rust College
Rutgers, The State Univ. of
New Jersey, Camden
Rutgers, The State Univ. of
New Jersey, Newark
The Sage Colleges
Saint Joseph's College (ME)
Saint Mary's College (IN)
Saint Mary's U of
Minnesota
Saint Vincent College
Salem State College
Salisbury U
Salve Regina U
Schreiner U
Shenandoah U
Simmons College
Simpson College
Skidmore College
Smith College
Southern Vermont College
Southwestern U (TX)
Spalding U
Spelman College
Springfield College
St. John Fisher College
St. Joseph College (CT)
St. Joseph's College (Long
Island)
St. Joseph's College, New
York
St. Lawrence U
St. Norbert College
St. Olaf College

State U College at Cortland
State U College at Fredonia
State U College at Geneseo
State U College at New
Paltz
State U College at Old
Westbury
State U College at Oneonta
State U of New York at
Cobleskill
State U of New York at
Farmingdale
State U of New York at
Morrisville
State U of New York at
Oswego
State U of New York at
Potsdam
State U of New York
Institute of Technolo
Stevenson U
Suffolk U
Sul Ross State U
Susquehanna U
Swarthmore College
Sweet Briar College
Texas Lutheran U
Thiel College
Thomas College
Thomas More College
Transylvania U
Trine U
Trinity College (CT)
Trinity U (TX)
Tufts U
U.S. Coast Guard Academy
U.S. Merchant Marine
Academy
Union College (NY)
U of Chicago
U of Dallas
U of Dubuque
U of La Verne
U of Maine at Presque Isle
U of Maine, Farmington
U of Mary Hardin-Baylor
U of Mary Washington
U of Massachusetts, Boston

U of Massachusetts,
Dartmouth
U of Minnesota, Morris
U of New England
U of Pittsburgh, Bradford
U of Pittsburgh, Greensburg
U of Puget Sound
U of Redlands
U of Rochester
U of Scranton
U of Southern Maine
U of St. Thomas (MN)
U of Texas at Dallas
U of Texas at Tyler
U of the Ozarks (AR)
U of the South
U of Wisconsin, Eau Claire
U of Wisconsin, La Crosse
U of Wisconsin, Oshkosh
U of Wisconsin, Platteville
U of Wisconsin, River Falls
U of Wisconsin, Stevens
Point
U of Wisconsin, Stout
U of Wisconsin, Superior
U of Wisconsin,
Whitewater
Ursinus College
Utica College
Virginia Wesleyan College
Wartburg College
Washington and Jefferson
College
Washington College (MD)
Washington U (MO)
Waynesburg U
Webster U
Wellesley College
Wells College
Wentworth Institute of
Technology
Wesley College
Wesleyan College (GA)
Wesleyan U (CT)
Western Connecticut
State U
Western New England
College

Westfield State College
Westminster College (MO)
Westminster College (PA)
Wheaton College (IL)
Wheaton College (MA)
Wheelock College
Whittier College
Whitworth U
Widener U
Wilkes U
Willamette U
William Paterson U of New
Jersey
Williams College
Wilmington College (OH)
Wilson College
Wisconsin Lutheran
College
Wittenberg U
Worcester Polytechnic
Institute
Worcester State College
York College (NY)
York College (PA)

SQUASH
DIVISION I

Brown U
Cornell U
Dartmouth College
George Washington U
Harvard U
Princeton U
Stanford U
U of Pennsylvania
Yale U

SQUASH
DIVISION III

Amherst College
Bates College
Bowdoin College
Colby College
Connecticut College
Franklin & Marshall
College

Hamilton College
Haverford College
Middlebury College
Mount Holyoke College
Smith College
St. Lawrence U
Trinity College (CT)
Tufts U
Vassar College
Wellesley College
Wesleyan U (CT)
William Smith College
Williams College

SWIMMING
DIVISION I

American U
Arizona State U
Auburn U
Ball State U
Boise State U
Boston College
Boston U
Bowling Green State U
Brigham Young U
Brown U
Bryant U
Bucknell U
Butler U
California Polytechnic
State U
California State U,
Bakersfield
California State U, Fresno
California State U,
Northridge
Campbell U
Canisius College
Centenary College (LA)
Central Connecticut State U
Clemson U
Cleveland State U
Colgate U
College of Charleston (SC)
College of the Holy Cross
College of William and
Mary

Colorado State U
Columbia U-Barnard College
Cornell U
Dartmouth College
Davidson College
Drexel U
Duke U
Duquesne U
East Carolina U
Eastern Illinois U
Eastern Michigan U
Fairfield U
Florida A&M U
Florida Atlantic U
Florida Gulf Coast U
Florida International U
Florida State U
Fordham U
Gardner-Webb U
George Mason U
George Washington U
Georgetown U
Georgia Institute of
   Technology
Georgia Southern U
Harvard U
Howard U
Illinois State U
Indiana U, Bloomington
Indiana U-Purdue U at
   Indianapolis
Iona College
Iowa State U
James Madison U
La Salle U
Lafayette College
Lehigh U
Louisiana State U
Loyola Marymount U
Loyola U (MD)
Manhattan College
Marist College
Marshall U
Miami U (OH)
Michigan State U
Missouri State U
Mount St. Mary's U

New Jersey Institute of
   Technology
New Mexico State U
Niagara U
North Carolina A&T State U
North Carolina State U
Northeastern U
Northern Arizona U
Northwestern U
Oakland U
Ohio U
The Ohio State U
Old Dominion U
Oregon State U
Pennsylvania State U
Pepperdine U
Princeton U
Providence College
Purdue U
Radford U
Rice U
Rider U
Rutgers, State Univ of New
   Jersey, New Brunswick
Sacred Heart U
Saint Francis U (PA)
Saint Louis U
San Diego State U
San Jose State U
Seattle U
Seton Hall U
Siena College
South Dakota State U
Southern Illinois U at
   Carbondale
Southern Methodist U
St. Bonaventure U
St. Francis College (NY)
St. Peter's College
Stanford U
State U of New York at
   Binghamton
Stony Brook U
Syracuse U
Texas A&M U, College
   Station
Texas Christian U

Towson U
U.S. Air Force Academy
U.S. Military Academy
U.S. Naval Academy
U at Buffalo, the State U
   of New
U of Akron
U of Alabama, Tuscaloosa
U of Arizona
U of Arkansas, Fayetteville
U of Arkansas, Little Rock
U of California, Berkeley
U of California, Davis
U of California, Irvine
U of California, Los
   Angeles
U of California, Santa
   Barbara
U of Cincinnati
U of Connecticut
U of Delaware
U of Denver
U of Evansville
U of Florida
U of Georgia
U of Hawaii, Manoa
U of Houston
U of Idaho
U of Illinois at Chicago
U of Illinois, Champaign
U of Iowa
U of Kansas
U of Kentucky
U of Louisville
U of Maine, Orono
U of Maryland, Baltimore
   County
U of Maryland, College
   Park
U of Massachusetts,
   Amherst
U of Miami (FL)
U of Michigan
U of Minnesota, Twin Cities
U of Missouri, Columbia
U of Nebraska, Lincoln
U of Nevada

U of Nevada, Las Vegas
U of New Hampshire
U of New Mexico
U of New Orleans
U of North Carolina,
  Chapel Hill
U of North Carolina,
  Wilmington
U of North Dakota
U of North Florida
U of North Texas
U of Northern Colorado
U of Northern Iowa
U of Notre Dame
U of Pennsylvania
U of Pittsburgh
U of Rhode Island
U of Richmond
U of San Diego
U of South Carolina,
  Columbia
U of South Dakota
U of Southern California
U of Tennessee, Knoxville
U of Texas at Austin
U of the Pacific
U of Toledo
U of Utah
U of Vermont
U of Virginia
U of Washington
U of Wisconsin, Green Bay
U of Wisconsin, Madison
U of Wisconsin, Milwaukee
U of Wyoming
Valparaiso U
Vanderbilt U
Villanova U
Virginia Military Institute
Virginia Polytechnic
  Institute & State U
Wagner College
Washington State U
West Virginia U
Western Illinois U
Western Kentucky U
Wright State U

Xavier U
Yale U
Youngstown State U

SWIMMING
DIVISION II

Adelphi U
Ashland U
Bentley College
Bloomsburg U of
  Pennsylvania
Bryant U
C.W. Post Campus/Long
  Island U
California State U,
  Bakersfield
California U of
  Pennsylvania
Catawba College
Clarion U of Pennsylvania
College of Saint Rose
Colorado School of Mines
Converse College
Delta State U
Drury U
East Stroudsburg U of
  Pennsylvania
Edinboro U of
  Pennsylvania
Fairmont State U
Florida Gulf Coast U
Florida Southern College
Gannon U
Grand Canyon U
Grand Valley State U
Henderson State U
Hillsdale College
Indiana U of Pennsylvania
Kutztown U of
  Pennsylvania
Le Moyne College
Lenoir-Rhyne College
Lewis U
Limestone College
Lock Haven U of
  Pennsylvania

Mansfield U of Pennsylvania
Mars Hill College
Mesa State College
Millersville U of Pennsylvania
Minnesota State U
  Moorhead
Minnesota State U, Mankato
New Jersey Institute of
  Technology
Northern Michigan U
Ouachita Baptist U
Pace U
Pfeiffer U
Queens College (NY)
Rollins College
Saint Leo U
Saint Michael's College
Seattle U
Shippensburg U of
  Pennsylvania
Slippery Rock U of
  Pennsylvania
Southern Connecticut
  State U
St. Cloud State U
Truman State U
U of Alaska Fairbanks
U of Bridgeport
U of California, San Diego
U of Findlay
U of Indianapolis
U of Nebraska at Kearney
U of Nebraska at Omaha
U of North Dakota
U of Puerto Rico,
  Mayaguez Campus
U of Puerto Rico, Rio Piedras
U of South Dakota
U of Tampa
U of Texas of the Permian
  Basin
U of the Incarnate Word
Wayne State U (MI)
West Chester U of
  Pennsylvania
West Virginia Wesleyan
  College

Wheeling Jesuit U
Wingate U

SWIMMING
DIVISION III

Agnes Scott College
Albion College
Albright College
Alfred U
Allegheny College
Alma College
Amherst College
Arcadia U
Augsburg College
Augustana College (IL)
Austin College
Babson College
Baldwin-Wallace College
Baruch College
Bates College
Beloit College
Bethany College (WV)
Bowdoin College
Brandeis U
Bridgewater College (VA)
Bridgewater State College
Bryn Mawr College
Buffalo State College
Cabrini College
California Institute of
    Technology
California Lutheran U
California State U, East Bay
Calvin College
Carleton College
Carnegie Mellon U
Carroll U (WI)
Carthage College
Case Western Reserve U
Catholic U
Cazenovia College
Centre College
Chapman U
Chatham U
Claremont McKenna-Harvey
    Mudd-Scripps Colleges

Clark U (MA)
Clarkson U
Coe College
Colby College
Colby-Sawyer College
College of Brockport, State
    U of New York
College of Mount St.
    Vincent
The College of New Jersey
College of New Rochelle
College of Notre Dame (MD)
College of Saint Elizabeth
College of St. Benedict
College of St. Catherine
College of Staten Island
College of Wooster
Colorado College
Concordia College,
    Moorhead
Connecticut College
Denison U
DePauw U
Dickinson College
Drew U
Eastern Connecticut State U
Elizabethtown College
Elms College
Emory and Henry College
Emory U
Eureka College
Fairleigh Dickinson U,
    Florham
Franklin & Marshall
    College
Frostburg State U
Gallaudet U
Gettysburg College
Gordon College
Goucher College
Greensboro College
Grinnell College
Grove City College
Guilford College
Gustavus Adolphus College
Hamilton College
Hamline U

Hartwick College
Hendrix College
Hiram College
Hollins U
Hood College
Hope College
Hunter College
Husson College
Illinois College
Illinois Wesleyan U
Ithaca College
John Carroll U
John Jay College of
    Criminal Justice
Johns Hopkins U
Juniata College
Kalamazoo College
Keene State College
Kenyon College
King's College (PA)
Knox College
La Grange College
Lake Forest College
Lawrence U
Lebanon Valley College
Lehman College, City U of
    New York
Lewis & Clark College
Linfield College
Loras College
Luther College
Lycoming College
Macalester College
Marymount U (VA)
Massachusetts Institute of
    Technology
McDaniel College
McMurry U
Middlebury College
Millikin U
Mills College
Misericordia U
Monmouth College (IL)
Montclair State U
Mount Holyoke College
Mount Saint Mary College
    (NY)

Mount Union College
Nazareth College
New York U
North Central College
Norwich U
Oberlin College
Occidental College
Ohio Northern U
Ohio Wesleyan U
Olivet College
Pacific Lutheran U
Pacific U (OR)
Penn State U, Altoona
Pennsylvania State Univ.
Erie, the Behrend College
Plymouth State U
Pomona-Pitzer Colleges
Principia College
Purchase College, State U
of New York
Ramapo College
Randolph College
Randolph-Macon College
Regis College (MA)
Rensselaer Polytechnic
Institute
Rhodes College
Ripon College
Rochester Institute of
Technology
Roger Williams U
Rose-Hulman Institute of
Technology
Rowan U
Saint Joseph's College (ME)
Saint Mary's College (IN)
Saint Mary's U of
Minnesota
Saint Vincent College
Salem College
Salisbury U
Simmons College
Simpson College
Skidmore College
Smith College
Southwestern U (TX)
Springfield College

St. Joseph College (CT)
St. Joseph's College (Long
Island)
St. Lawrence U
St. Mary's College of
Maryland
St. Norbert College
St. Olaf College
State U College at Cortland
State U College at Fredonia
State U College at Geneseo
State U College at New Paltz
State U College at Old
Westbury
State U College at Oneonta
State U of New York at
Cobleskill
State U of New York at
Oswego
State U of New York at
Potsdam
State U of New York
Maritime College
Stevens Institute of
Technology
Susquehanna U
Swarthmore College
Sweet Briar College
Transylvania U
Trinity College (CT)
Trinity U (TX)
Tufts U
U.S. Coast Guard Academy
U.S. Merchant Marine
Academy
Union College (NY)
U of California, Santa Cruz
U of Chicago
U of La Verne
U of Mary Washington
U of Massachusetts,
Dartmouth
U of Minnesota, Morris
U of New England
U of Pittsburgh, Bradford
U of Puget Sound
U of Redlands

U of Rochester
U of Scranton
U of St. Thomas (MN)
U of the South
U of Wisconsin, Eau Claire
U of Wisconsin, La Crosse
U of Wisconsin, Oshkosh
U of Wisconsin, River Falls
U of Wisconsin, Stevens
Point
U of Wisconsin, Whitewater
Ursinus College
Utica College
Vassar College
Washington and Jefferson
College
Washington and Lee U
Washington College (MD)
Washington U (MO)
Wellesley College
Wells College
Wesleyan U (CT)
Western Connecticut
State U
Western New England
College
Westfield State College
Westminster College (PA)
Wheaton College (IL)
Wheaton College (MA)
Wheelock College
Whitman College
Whittier College
Whitworth U
Widener U
Willamette U
William Paterson U of New
Jersey
William Smith College
Williams College
Wilmington College (OH)
Wittenberg U
Worcester Polytechnic
Institute
York College (NY)
York College (PA)

SYNCHRONIZED SWIMMING
DIVISION I

Canisius College
The Ohio State U
Stanford U
U of Alabama at
  Birmingham

SYNCHRONIZED SWIMMING
DIVISION II

U of the Incarnate Word

SYNCHRONIZED SWIMMING
DIVISION III

Carleton College
Keuka College
Wheaton College (MA)

TENNIS
DIVISION I

Alabama A&M U
Alabama State U
Alcorn State U
Appalachian State U
Arizona State U
Arkansas State U
Auburn U
Austin Peay State U
Ball State U
Baylor U
Belmont U
Bethune-Cookman U
Birmingham-Southern
  College

Boise State U
Boston College
Boston U
Bowling Green State U
Bradley U
Brigham Young U
Brown U
Bryant U
Bucknell U
Butler U
California Polytechnic
  State U
California State U,
  Bakersfield
California State U, Fresno
California State U, Fullerton
California State U,
  Northridge
California State U,
  Sacramento
Campbell U
Centenary College (LA)
Charleston Southern U
Chicago State U
Clemson U
Cleveland State U
Coastal Carolina U
Colgate U
College of Charleston (SC)
College of the Holy Cross
College of William and Mary
Colorado State U
Columbia U-Barnard
  College
Coppin State U
Cornell U
Creighton U
Dartmouth College
Davidson College
Delaware State U
DePaul U
Drake U
Drexel U
Duke U
Duquesne U
East Carolina U
East Tennessee State U

Eastern Illinois U
Eastern Kentucky U
Eastern Michigan U
Eastern Washington U
Elon U
Fairfield U
Fairleigh Dickinson U,
  Metropolitan
Florida A&M U
Florida Atlantic U
Florida Gulf Coast U
Florida International U
Florida State U
Fordham U
Furman U
Gardner-Webb U
George Mason U
George Washington U
Georgetown U
Georgia Institute of
  Technology
Georgia Southern U
Georgia State U
Gonzaga U
Grambling State U
Hampton U
Harvard U
Hofstra U
Howard U
Idaho State U
Illinois State U
Indiana State U
Indiana U, Bloomington
Indiana U-Purdue U at
  Indianapolis
Indiana U-Purdue U, Fort
  Wayne
Iowa State U
Jackson State U
Jacksonville State U
Jacksonville U
James Madison U
Kansas State U
Kennesaw State U
La Salle U
Lafayette College
Lamar U

Lehigh U
Liberty U
Lipscomb U
Long Beach State U
Long Island U-Brooklyn
   Campus
Longwood U
Louisiana State U
Louisiana Tech U
Loyola Marymount U
Loyola U (MD)
Manhattan College
Marist College
Marquette U
Marshall U
McNeese State U
Mercer U
Miami U (OH)
Michigan State U
Middle Tennessee State U
Mississippi State U
Mississippi Valley State U
Monmouth U
Montana State U-Bozeman
Morehead State U
Morgan State U
Mount St. Mary's U
Murray State U
New Jersey Institute of
   Technology
New Mexico State U
Niagara U
Nicholls State U
Norfolk State U
North Carolina A&T State U
North Carolina Central U
North Carolina State U
Northern Arizona U
Northern Illinois U
Northwestern State U
Northwestern U
Oakland U
Oklahoma State U
The Ohio State U
Old Dominion U
Oral Roberts U
Pennsylvania State U

Pepperdine U
Portland State U
Prairie View A&M U
Presbyterian College
Princeton U
Providence College
Purdue U
Quinnipiac U
Radford U
Rice U
Rider U
Robert Morris U
Rutgers, State Univ of New
   Jersey, New Brunswick
Sacred Heart U
Saint Francis U (PA)
Saint Joseph's U
Saint Louis U
Sam Houston State U
Samford U
San Diego State U
San Jose State U
Santa Clara U
Savannah State U
Seton Hall U
Siena College
South Carolina State U
South Dakota State U
Southeast Missouri State U
Southeastern Louisiana U
Southern Illinois U at
   Carbondale
Southern Illinois U
   Edwardsville
Southern Methodist U
Southern U, Baton Rouge
Southern Utah U
St. Bonaventure U
St. Francis College (NY)
St. John's U (NY)
St. Mary's College of
   California
St. Peter's College
Stanford U
State U of New York at
   Binghamton
Stephen F. Austin State U

Stetson U
Stony Brook U
Syracuse U
Temple U
Tennessee State U
Tennessee Technological U
Texas A&M U, College
   Station
Texas A&M U-Corpus Christi
Texas Christian U
Texas State U-San Marcos
Texas Tech U
Towson U
Troy U
Tulane U
U.S. Air Force Academy
U.S. Military Academy
U at Albany
U at Buffalo, the State U
   of New
U of Akron
U of Alabama at
   Birmingham
U of Alabama, Tuscaloosa
U of Arizona
U of Arkansas, Fayetteville
U of Arkansas, Little Rock
U of Arkansas, Pine Bluff
U of California, Berkeley
U of California, Davis
U of California, Irvine
U of California, Los Angeles
U of California, Riverside
U of California, Santa
   Barbara
U of Central Arkansas
U of Central Florida
U of Cincinnati
U of Colorado, Boulder
U of Connecticut
U of Dayton
U of Delaware
U of Denver
U of Detroit Mercy
U of Evansville
U of Florida
U of Georgia

U of Hartford
U of Hawaii, Manoa
U of Houston
U of Idaho
U of Illinois at Chicago
U of Illinois, Champaign
U of Iowa
U of Kansas
U of Kentucky
U of Louisiana at Lafayette
U of Louisiana at Monroe
U of Louisville
U of Maryland, Baltimore County
U of Maryland, College Park
U of Maryland, Eastern Shore
U of Massachusetts, Amherst
U of Memphis
U of Miami (FL)
U of Michigan
U of Minnesota, Twin Cities
U of Mississippi
U of Missouri, Columbia
U of Missouri, Kansas City
U of Montana
U of Nebraska, Lincoln
U of Nevada
U of Nevada, Las Vegas
U of New Mexico
U of New Orleans
U of North Carolina at Greensboro
U of North Carolina, Asheville
U of North Carolina, Chapel Hill
U of North Carolina, Charlotte
U of North Carolina, Wilmington
U of North Dakota
U of North Florida
U of North Texas
U of Northern Colorado
U of Northern Iowa
U of Notre Dame

U of Oklahoma
U of Oregon
U of Pennsylvania
U of Pittsburgh
U of Portland
U of Rhode Island
U of Richmond
U of San Diego
U of San Francisco
U of South Alabama
U of South Carolina Upstate
U of South Carolina, Columbia
U of South Dakota
U of South Florida
U of Southern California
U of Southern Mississippi
U of Tennessee at Chattanooga
U of Tennessee at Martin
U of Tennessee, Knoxville
U of Texas at Arlington
U of Texas at Austin
U of Texas at El Paso
U of Texas at San Antonio
U of Texas, Pan American
U of the Pacific
U of Toledo
U of Tulsa
U of Utah
U of Virginia
U of Washington
U of Wisconsin, Green Bay
U of Wisconsin, Madison
U of Wisconsin, Milwaukee
U of Wyoming
Utah State U
Valparaiso U
Vanderbilt U
Villanova U
Virginia Commonwealth U
Virginia Polytechnic Institute & State U
Wagner College
Wake Forest U
Washington State U
Weber State U
West Virginia U

Western Carolina U
Western Illinois U
Western Kentucky U
Western Michigan U
Wichita State U
Winston-Salem State U
Winthrop U
Wofford College
Wright State U
Xavier U
Yale U
Youngstown State U

TENNIS
DIVISION II

Abilene Christian U
Adelphi U
Albany State U (GA)
American International College
Anderson U (SC)
Arkansas Tech U
Armstrong Atlantic State U
Ashland U
Assumption College
Augusta State U
Augustana College (SD)
Barry U
Barton College
Bellarmine U
Bemidji State U
Benedict College
Bentley College
Bloomsburg U of Pennsylvania
Bluefield State College
Bowie State U
Brevard College
Brigham Young U, Hawaii
Bryant U
C.W. Post Campus/Long Island U
Caldwell College
California State Polytechnic U, Pomona
California State U, Bakersfield

California State U, Los
  Angeles
California State U, San
  Bernardino
California State U, Stanislaus
California U of
  Pennsylvania
Cameron U
Carson-Newman College
Catawba College
Central State U
Chaminade U
Chestnut Hill College
Cheyney U of Pennsylvania
Chowan U
Christian Brothers U
Clarion U of Pennsylvania
Clark Atlanta U
Clayton State U
Coker College
College of Saint Rose
Colorado Christian U
Colorado State U-Pueblo
Columbus State U
Concord U
Concordia College (NY)
Converse College
Dallas Baptist U
Delta State U
Dixie State College of Utah
Dowling College
Drury U
East Central U
East Stroudsburg U of
  Pennsylvania
Eckerd College
Elizabeth City State U
Emporia State U
Erskine College
Fairmont State U
Fayetteville State U
Ferris State U
Flagler College
Florida Gulf Coast U
Florida Institute of
  Technology
Florida Southern College
Fort Hays State U

Fort Valley State U
Francis Marion U
Franklin Pierce U
The Georgia College &
  State U
Georgia Southwestern
  State U
Georgian Court U
Goldey-Beacom College
Grand Canyon U
Grand Valley State U
Harding U
Hawaii Pacific U
Henderson State U
Holy Family U
Indiana U of Pennsylvania
Johnson C. Smith U
Kennesaw State U
Kentucky Wesleyan College
Kutztown U of
  Pennsylvania
Lake Superior State U
Lander U
Lane College
Le Moyne College
Lees-McRae College
LeMoyne-Owen College
Lenoir-Rhyne College
Lewis U
Limestone College
Lincoln Memorial U
Lincoln U (MO)
Livingstone College
Lynn U
Mars Hill College
Mercyhurst College
Merrimack College
Mesa State College
Metropolitan State College
  of Denver
Michigan Technological U
Midwestern State U
Millersville U of
  Pennsylvania
Minnesota State U
  Moorhead
Minnesota State U, Mankato
Missouri Southern State U

Missouri Western State U
Molloy College
Montana State U-Billings
Mount Olive College
New Jersey Institute of
  Technology
Newberry College
Newman U
North Carolina Central U
North Georgia College &
  State U
North Greenville U
Northeastern State U
Northern Kentucky U
Northern State U
Northwest Missouri State U
Northwood U (MI)
Notre Dame de Namur U
Nova Southeastern U
Oakland City U
Ouachita Baptist U
Pace U
Palm Beach Atlantic U
Pfeiffer U
Philadelphia U
Post U
Presbyterian College
Queens College (NY)
Queens U of Charlotte
Quincy U
Rockhurst U
Rollins College
Saginaw Valley State U
Saint Anselm College
Saint Joseph's College (IN)
Saint Leo U
Saint Michael's College
Seton Hill U
Shaw U
Shepherd U
Shippensburg U of
  Pennsylvania
Slippery Rock U of
  Pennsylvania
Sonoma State U
Southeastern Oklahoma
  State U
Southern Arkansas U

Southern Illinois U
  Edwardsville
Southern New Hampshire U
Southwest Baptist U
Southwest Minnesota
  State U
St. Augustine's College
St. Cloud State U
St. Edward's U
St. Mary's U (TX)
St. Paul's College
St. Thomas Aquinas College
Stillman College
Stonehill College
Tarleton State U
Tiffin U
Truman State U
Tusculum College
Tuskegee U
U of Alabama in Huntsville
U of California, San Diego
U of Central Arkansas
U of Central Oklahoma
U of Charleston (WV)
U of Findlay
U of Hawaii at Hilo
U of Indianapolis
U of Mary
U of Minnesota Duluth
U of Minnesota, Crookston
U of Missouri, St. Louis
U of Montevallo
U of Nebraska at Kearney
U of Nebraska at Omaha
U of New Haven
U of North Alabama
U of North Carolina at
  Pembroke
U of North Dakota
U of North Florida
U of Puerto Rico, Bayamon
U of Puerto Rico, Cayey
U of Puerto Rico,
  Mayaguez Campus
U of Puerto Rico, Rio Piedras
U of South Carolina Aiken
U of South Carolina Upstate

U of South Dakota
U of Southern Indiana
U of Tampa
U of the District of
  Columbia
U of the Incarnate Word
U of the Sciences in
  Philadelphia
U of West Alabama
U of West Florida
Upper Iowa U
Valdosta State U
Virginia State U
Virginia Union U
Washburn U of Topeka
Wayne State U (MI)
West Chester U of
  Pennsylvania
West Liberty State College
West Virginia State U
West Virginia Wesleyan
  College
Western New Mexico U
Wingate U
Winona State U
Winston-Salem State U

TENNIS
DIVISION III

Adrian College
Agnes Scott College
Albertus Magnus College
Albion College
Albright College
Alfred U
Allegheny College
Alma College
Alvernia U
Amherst College
Anderson U (IN)
Anna Maria College
Arcadia U
Augustana College (IL)
Aurora U
Austin College
Averett U

Babson College
Baldwin-Wallace College
Baptist Bible College
Bard College
Baruch College
Bates College
Bay Path College
Becker College
Beloit College
Benedictine U (IL)
Bethany College (WV)
Bethany Lutheran College
Bethel U (MN)
Blackburn College
Bluffton U
Bowdoin College
Brandeis U
Bridgewater College (VA)
Bridgewater State College
Brooklyn College
Bryn Mawr College
Buena Vista U
Cabrini College
California Institute of
  Technology
California Lutheran U
Calvin College
Capital U
Carleton College
Carnegie Mellon U
Carroll U (WI)
Carthage College
Case Western Reserve U
Castleton State College
Catholic U
Cedar Crest College
Central College (IA)
Centre College
Chapman U
Chatham U
Christopher Newport U
The City College of New
  York
Claremont McKenna-Harvey
  Mudd-Scripps Colleges
Clark U (MA)
Coe College

Colby College

Colby-Sawyer College

College of Brockport, State U of New York

College of Mount St. Joseph

College of Mount St. Vincent

The College of New Jersey

College of New Rochelle

College of Notre Dame (MD)

College of Saint Elizabeth

College of St. Benedict

College of St. Catherine

The College of St. Scholastica

College of Staten Island

College of Wooster

Colorado College

Concordia College, Moorhead

Concordia U (WI)

Concordia U Chicago

Concordia U Texas

Connecticut College

Cornell College

Curry College

Defiance College

Denison U

DePauw U

DeSales U

Dickinson College

Dominican U (IL)

Drew U

Earlham College

Eastern Nazarene College

Eastern U

Edgewood College

Elizabethtown College

Elmhurst College

Elmira College

Emerson College

Emmanuel College (MA)

Emory and Henry College

Emory U

Endicott College

Eureka College

Fairleigh Dickinson U, Florham

Ferrum College

Fontbonne U

Franklin & Marshall College

Franklin College

Frostburg State U

Geneva College

George Fox U

Gettysburg College

Gordon College

Goucher College

Greensboro College

Greenville College

Grinnell College

Grove City College

Guilford College

Gustavus Adolphus College

Gwynedd-Mercy College

Hamilton College

Hamline U

Hanover College

Hardin-Simmons U

Hartwick College

Haverford College

Heidelberg College

Hendrix College

Hiram College

Hollins U

Hood College

Hope College

Howard Payne U

Hunter College

Huntingdon College

Illinois College

Illinois Wesleyan U

Immaculata U

Ithaca College

John Carroll U

John Jay College of Criminal Justice

Johns Hopkins U

Johnson and Wales U

Johnson State College

Juniata College

Kalamazoo College

Kean U

Kenyon College

Keuka College

Keystone College

King's College (PA)

Knox College

La Grange College

La Roche College

La Sierra U

Lake Forest College

Lakeland College

Lancaster Bible College

Lawrence U

Lebanon Valley College

Lehman College, City U of New York

LeTourneau U

Lewis & Clark College

Lincoln U (PA)

Linfield College

Loras College

Louisiana College

Luther College

Lycoming College

Lynchburg College

Lyndon State College

Macalester College

Manchester College

Manhattanville College

Marian U (WI)

Marietta College

Martin Luther College

Mary Baldwin College

Maryville College (TN)

Maryville U of Saint Louis

Marywood U

Massachusetts College of Liberal Arts

Massachusetts Institute of Technology

McDaniel College

McMurry U

Medgar Evers College

Meredith College

Messiah College

Methodist U

Middlebury College

Millikin U
Mills College
Millsaps College
Milwaukee School of
  Engineering
Misericordia U
Mississippi College
Mitchell College
Monmouth College (IL)
Moravian College
Mount Holyoke College
Mount Mary College
Mount Saint Mary College
  (NY)
Mount Union College
Muhlenberg College
Muskingum College
Nazareth College
Nebraska Wesleyan U
Neumann College
New York City College of
  Technology
New York U
Newbury College
Nichols College
North Carolina Wesleyan
  College
North Central College
North Central U
Northwestern College
Oberlin College
Occidental College
Oglethorpe U
Ohio Northern U
Ohio Wesleyan U
Olivet College
Otterbein College
Pacific Lutheran U
Pacific U (OR)
Peace College
Penn State Berks College
Penn State Harrisburg
Penn State U, Altoona
Pennsylvania State Univ.
  Erie, the Behrend College
Philadelphia Biblical U
Piedmont College
Pine Manor College

Plattsburgh State U of
  New York
Plymouth State U
Polytechnic Institute of
  New York U
Pomona-Pitzer Colleges
Principia College
Purchase College, State U
  of New York
Ramapo College
Randolph College
Randolph-Macon College
Regis College (MA)
Rensselaer Polytechnic
  Institute
Rhode Island College
Rhodes College
Richard Stockton College
  of New Jersey
Ripon College
Roanoke College
Rochester Institute of
  Technology
Rockford College
Roger Williams U
Rose-Hulman Institute of
  Technology
Rosemont College
Rust College
Rutgers, The State Univ. of
  New Jersey, Newark
The Sage Colleges
Saint Mary's College (IN)
Saint Mary's U of
  Minnesota
Saint Vincent College
Salem College
Salem State College
Salisbury U
Salve Regina U
Schreiner U
Shenandoah U
Simmons College
Simpson College
Skidmore College
Smith College
Southwestern U (TX)
Spelman College

Springfield College
St. John Fisher College
St. Joseph College (CT)
St. Joseph's College (Long
  Island)
St. Joseph's College, New
  York
St. Lawrence U
St. Mary's College of
  Maryland
St. Norbert College
St. Olaf College
State U College at Cortland
State U College at Fredonia
State U College at Geneseo
State U College at New Paltz
State U College at Oneonta
State U of New York at
  Cobleskill
State U of New York at
  Farmingdale
State U of New York at
  Oswego
Stevens Institute of
  Technology
Stevenson U
Suffolk U
Sul Ross State U
Susquehanna U
Swarthmore College
Sweet Briar College
Texas Lutheran U
Thomas More College
Transylvania U
Trine U
Trinity College (CT)
Trinity College (District of
  Columbia)
Trinity U (TX)
Tufts U
Union College (NY)
U of California, Santa Cruz
U of Chicago
U of Dubuque
U of La Verne
U of Mary Hardin-Baylor
U of Mary Washington
U of Massachusetts, Boston

U of Massachusetts, Dartmouth
U of Minnesota, Morris
U of Pittsburgh, Bradford
U of Puget Sound
U of Redlands
U of Rochester
U of Scranton
U of Southern Maine
U of St. Thomas (MN)
U of Texas at Dallas
U of Texas at Tyler
U of the Ozarks (AR)
U of the South
U of Wisconsin, Eau Claire
U of Wisconsin, La Crosse
U of Wisconsin, Oshkosh
U of Wisconsin, River Falls
U of Wisconsin, Stevens Point
U of Wisconsin, Stout
U of Wisconsin, Whitewater
Ursinus College
Utica College
Vassar College
Virginia Wesleyan College
Wartburg College
Washington and Jefferson College
Washington and Lee U
Washington College (MD)
Washington U (MO)
Waynesburg U
Webster U
Wellesley College
Wells College
Wentworth Institute of Technology
Wesley College
Wesleyan College (GA)
Wesleyan U (CT)
Western Connecticut State U
Western New England College
Westminster College (MO)
Westminster College (PA)
Wheaton College (IL)

Wheaton College (MA)
Whitman College
Whittier College
Whitworth U
Wilkes U
Willamette U
William Paterson U of New Jersey
William Smith College
Williams College
Wilmington College (OH)
Wilson College
Wisconsin Lutheran College
Wittenberg U
Worcester State College
Yeshiva U
York College (PA)

TRACK, INDOOR
DIVISION I

Alabama State U
American U
Appalachian State U
Arizona State U
Arkansas State U
Auburn U
Austin Peay State U
Ball State U
Baylor U
Belmont U
Bethune-Cookman U
Boise State U
Boston College
Boston U
Bowling Green State U
Bradley U
Brigham Young U
Brown U
Bryant U
Bucknell U
Butler U
California Polytechnic State U
California State U, Bakersfield

California State U, Fresno
California State U, Fullerton
California State U, Northridge
California State U, Sacramento
Campbell U
Central Connecticut State U
Central Michigan U
Charleston Southern U
Chicago State U
The Citadel
Clemson U
Coastal Carolina U
Colgate U
College of Charleston (SC)
College of the Holy Cross
College of William and Mary
Colorado State U
Columbia U-Barnard College
Coppin State U
Cornell U
Dartmouth College
Davidson College
Delaware State U
DePaul U
Drake U
Duke U
Duquesne U
East Carolina U
East Tennessee State U
Eastern Illinois U
Eastern Kentucky U
Eastern Michigan U
Eastern Washington U
Elon U
Fairleigh Dickinson U, Metropolitan
Florida A&M U
Florida Atlantic U
Florida International U
Florida State U
Fordham U
Furman U
Gardner-Webb U
George Mason U
Georgetown U

Georgia Institute of
Technology
Georgia Southern U
Georgia State U
Grambling State U
Hampton U
Harvard U
High Point U
Howard U
Idaho State U
Illinois State U
Indiana State U
Indiana U, Bloomington
Indiana U-Purdue U, Fort
Wayne
Iona College
Iowa State U
Jackson State U
Jacksonville State U
Jacksonville U
James Madison U
Kansas State U
Kennesaw State U
Kent State U
La Salle U
Lafayette College
Lamar U
Lehigh U
Liberty U
Lipscomb U
Long Beach State U
Long Island U-Brooklyn
Campus
Louisiana State U
Louisiana Tech U
Loyola U (IL)
Loyola U (MD)
Manhattan College
Marist College
Marquette U
Marshall U
McNeese State U
Miami U (OH)
Michigan State U
Middle Tennessee State U
Mississippi State U
Mississippi Valley State U

Missouri State U
Monmouth U
Montana State U-Bozeman
Morgan State U
Mount St. Mary's U
Murray State U
New Jersey Institute of
Technology
New Mexico State U
Nicholls State U
Norfolk State U
North Carolina A&T State U
North Carolina Central U
North Carolina State U
North Dakota State U
Northeastern U
Northern Arizona U
Northern Illinois U
Northwestern State U
Oakland U
Ohio U
The Ohio State U
Oklahoma State U
Oral Roberts U
Pennsylvania State U
Portland State U
Prairie View A&M U
Princeton U
Providence College
Purdue U
Quinnipiac U
Radford U
Rice U
Rider U
Robert Morris U
Rutgers, State Univ of New
Jersey, New Brunswick
Sacred Heart U
Saint Francis U (PA)
Saint Joseph's U
Saint Louis U
Sam Houston State U
Samford U
San Diego State U
Savannah State U
Seattle U
Seton Hall U

South Carolina State U
South Dakota State U
Southeast Missouri State U
Southeastern Louisiana U
Southern Illinois U at
Carbondale
Southern Illinois U
Edwardsville
Southern Methodist U
Southern U, Baton Rouge
Southern Utah U
St. Francis College (NY)
St. John's U (NY)
St. Peter's College
Stanford U
State U of New York at
Binghamton
Stephen F. Austin State U
Stony Brook U
Syracuse U
Temple U
Tennessee State U
Tennessee Technological U
Texas A&M U, College
Station
Texas A&M U-Corpus Christi
Texas Christian U
Texas Southern U
Texas State U-San Marcos
Texas Tech U
Towson U
Troy U
Tulane U
U.S. Air Force Academy
U.S. Military Academy
U.S. Naval Academy
U at Albany
U at Buffalo, the State U
of New
U of Akron
U of Alabama at
Birmingham
U of Alabama, Tuscaloosa
U of Arizona
U of Arkansas, Fayetteville
U of Arkansas, Little Rock
U of Arkansas, Pine Bluff

U of California, Berkeley
U of California, Davis
U of California, Irvine
U of California, Los Angeles
U of California, Riverside
U of California, Santa
    Barbara
U of Central Arkansas
U of Central Florida
U of Cincinnati
U of Colorado, Boulder
U of Connecticut
U of Dayton
U of Delaware
U of Detroit Mercy
U of Florida
U of Georgia
U of Hartford
U of Hawaii, Manoa
U of Houston
U of Idaho
U of Illinois at Chicago
U of Illinois, Champaign
U of Iowa
U of Kansas
U of Kentucky
U of Louisiana at Lafayette
U of Louisiana at Monroe
U of Louisville
U of Maine, Orono
U of Maryland, Baltimore
    County
U of Maryland, College Park
U of Maryland, Eastern
    Shore
U of Massachusetts,
    Amherst
U of Memphis
U of Miami (FL)
U of Michigan
U of Minnesota, Twin Cities
U of Mississippi
U of Missouri, Columbia
U of Missouri, Kansas City
U of Montana
U of Nebraska, Lincoln
U of Nevada

U of Nevada, Las Vegas
U of New Hampshire
U of New Mexico
U of North Carolina,
    Asheville
U of North Carolina,
    Chapel Hill
U of North Carolina,
    Charlotte
U of North Carolina,
    Wilmington
U of North Dakota
U of North Florida
U of North Texas
U of Northern Colorado
U of Northern Iowa
U of Notre Dame
U of Oklahoma
U of Oregon
U of Pennsylvania
U of Pittsburgh
U of Portland
U of Rhode Island
U of Richmond
U of South Alabama
U of South Carolina Upstate
U of South Carolina,
    Columbia
U of South Dakota
U of South Florida
U of Southern California
U of Southern Mississippi
U of Tennessee at
    Chattanooga
U of Tennessee, Knoxville
U of Texas at Arlington
U of Texas at Austin
U of Texas at El Paso
U of Texas at San Antonio
U of Texas, Pan American
U of Toledo
U of Tulsa
U of Utah
U of Vermont
U of Virginia
U of Washington
U of Wisconsin, Madison

U of Wisconsin, Milwaukee
U of Wyoming
Utah State U
Utah Valley U
Valparaiso U
Vanderbilt U
Villanova U
Virginia Commonwealth U
Virginia Military Institute
Virginia Polytechnic
    Institute & State U
Wagner College
Wake Forest U
Washington State U
Weber State U
West Virginia U
Western Carolina U
Western Illinois U
Western Kentucky U
Western Michigan U
Wichita State U
Winston-Salem State U
Winthrop U
Wofford College
Wright State U
Xavier U
Yale U
Youngstown State U

TRACK, INDOOR
DIVISION II

Abilene Christian U
Adams State College
Adelphi U
Alderson-Broaddus College
American International
    College
Anderson U (SC)
Ashland U
Assumption College
Augustana College (SD)
Bellarmine U
Bemidji State U
Bentley College

Bloomsburg U of
Pennsylvania
Bowie State U
Bryant U
C.W. Post Campus/Long
Island U
California State U,
Bakersfield
California State U,
Dominguez Hills
California State U, Los
Angeles
California State U,
Stanislaus
California U of
Pennsylvania
Carson-Newman College
Central State U
Central Washington U
Chadron State College
Cheyney U of Pennsylvania
Claflin U
Clarion U of Pennsylvania
Clayton State U
College of Saint Rose
Colorado School of Mines
Colorado State U-Pueblo
Concord U
Concordia U, St. Paul
Dallas Baptist U
East Stroudsburg U of
Pennsylvania
Edinboro U of Pennsylvania
Emporia State U
Ferris State U
Fort Hays State U
Grand Valley State U
Harding U
Hillsdale College
Indiana U of Pennsylvania
Johnson C. Smith U
Kennesaw State U
Kentucky State U
Kutztown U of
Pennsylvania
Lake Superior State U
Lees-McRae College
Lewis U

Lincoln U (MO)
Livingstone College
Lock Haven U of
Pennsylvania
Mansfield U of
Pennsylvania
Mercy College
Mesa State College
Metropolitan State College
of Denver
Millersville U of
Pennsylvania
Minnesota State U
Moorhead
Minnesota State U, Mankato
Missouri Southern State U
Missouri U of Science and
Technology
Montana State U-Billings
New Jersey Institute of
Technology
New Mexico Highlands U
North Carolina Central U
Northern Kentucky U
Northern Michigan U
Northern State U
Northwest Missouri State U
Northwest Nazarene U
Northwood U (MI)
Pittsburg State U
Queens College (NY)
Queens U of Charlotte
Saginaw Valley State U
Saint Joseph's College (IN)
San Francisco State U
Seattle Pacific U
Seattle U
Seton Hill U
Shippensburg U of
Pennsylvania
Slippery Rock U of
Pennsylvania
Southern Connecticut
State U
Southern Illinois U
Edwardsville
Southwest Baptist U
St. Augustine's College

St. Cloud State U
St. Martin's U
St. Paul's College
St. Thomas Aquinas
College
Stonehill College
Tiffin U
Truman State U
U of Alabama in Huntsville
U of Central Arkansas
U of Central Missouri
U of Colorado, Colorado
Springs
U of Findlay
U of Indianapolis
U of Mary
U of Massachusetts at
Lowell
U of Minnesota Duluth
U of Nebraska at Kearney
U of Nebraska at Omaha
U of New Haven
U of North Dakota
U of North Florida
U of Pittsburgh, Johnstown
U of South Carolina Upstate
U of South Dakota
U of Southern Indiana
U of the District of
Columbia
U of the Incarnate Word
U of Wisconsin, Parkside
Virginia State U
Virginia Union U
Wayne State College (NE)
West Chester U of
Pennsylvania
West Texas A&M U
West Virginia State U
Western Oregon U
Western State College of
Colorado
Western Washington U
Wheeling Jesuit U
Winona State U
Winston-Salem State U

TRACK, INDOOR
DIVISION III

Adrian College
Albion College
Albright College
Alfred U
Allegheny College
Alma College
Amherst College
Anderson U (IN)
Augsburg College
Augustana College (IL)
Aurora U
Baldwin-Wallace College
Bates College
Beloit College
Benedictine U (IL)
Bethany College (WV)
Bethel U (MN)
Birmingham-Southern College
Bluffton U
Bowdoin College
Brandeis U
Bridgewater College (VA)
Bridgewater State College
Bryn Mawr College
Buena Vista U
Buffalo State College
Cabrini College
Calvin College
Capital U
Carleton College
Carnegie Mellon U
Carroll U (WI)
Carthage College
Case Western Reserve U
Catholic U
Central College (IA)
Centre College
Christopher Newport U
The City College of New York
Coe College
Colby College

College of Brockport, State U of New York
College of Mount St. Joseph
The College of New Jersey
College of St. Benedict
College of St. Catherine
The College of St. Scholastica
College of Wooster
Colorado College
Concordia College, Moorhead
Concordia U (WI)
Concordia U Chicago
Connecticut College
Cornell College
Defiance College
Delaware Valley College
Denison U
DePauw U
DeSales U
Dickinson College
Earlham College
Eastern Connecticut State U
Eastern Mennonite U
Edgewood College
Elizabethtown College
Elmhurst College
Emmanuel College (MA)
Emory U
Fitchburg State College
Franklin & Marshall College
Franklin College
Frostburg State U
Geneva College
Gettysburg College
Gordon College
Goucher College
Greenville College
Grinnell College
Gustavus Adolphus College
Gwynedd-Mercy College
Hamilton College
Hamline U
Hanover College
Hardin-Simmons U
Haverford College
Heidelberg College

Hiram College
Hunter College
Illinois College
Illinois Wesleyan U
Ithaca College
John Carroll U
Johns Hopkins U
Juniata College
Kean U
Keene State College
Kenyon College
Keystone College
Knox College
Lake Erie College
Lawrence U
Lebanon Valley College
Lehman College, City U of New York
Lewis & Clark College
Lincoln U (PA)
Linfield College
Loras College
Luther College
Lynchburg College
Macalester College
Manchester College
Manhattanville College
Marietta College
Massachusetts Institute of Technology
McDaniel College
McMurry U
Medgar Evers College
Messiah College
Methodist U
Middlebury College
Millikin U
Milwaukee School of Engineering
Misericordia U
Mississippi College
Monmouth College (IL)
Montclair State U
Moravian College
Mount Holyoke College
Mount Union College
Muhlenberg College
Muskingum College

Nazareth College
Nebraska Wesleyan U
New Jersey City U
New York City College of
  Technology
New York U
North Central College
North Park U
Northwestern College
Oberlin College
Occidental College
Ohio Northern U
Ohio Wesleyan U
Otterbein College
Pennsylvania State Univ.
  Erie, the Behrend College
Plattsburgh State U of
  New York
Principia College
Ramapo College
Regis College (MA)
Rensselaer Polytechnic
  Institute
Rhode Island College
Rhodes College
Richard Stockton College
  of New Jersey
Ripon College
Roanoke College
Rochester Institute of
  Technology
Rockford College
Rose-Hulman Institute of
  Technology
Rowan U
Rutgers, The State Univ. of
  New Jersey, Camden
Rutgers, The State Univ. of
  New Jersey, Newark
Saint Mary's U of
  Minnesota
Salem State College
Salisbury U
Simpson College
Smith College
Springfield College
St. Joseph's College (Long
  Island)

St. Lawrence U
St. Norbert College
St. Olaf College
State U College at Cortland
State U College at Fredonia
State U College at Geneseo
State U College at Oneonta
State U of New York at
  Farmingdale
State U of New York at
  Oswego
Stevens Institute of
  Technology
Susquehanna U
Swarthmore College
Texas Lutheran U
Thiel College
Trine U
Trinity College (CT)
Trinity U (TX)
Tufts U
U.S. Coast Guard Academy
U.S. Merchant Marine
  Academy
Union College (NY)
U of Chicago
U of Dubuque
U of La Verne
U of Mary Washington
U of Massachusetts, Boston
U of Massachusetts,
  Dartmouth
U of Minnesota, Morris
U of Puget Sound
U of Rochester
U of Southern Maine
U of St. Thomas (MN)
U of the South
U of Wisconsin, Eau Claire
U of Wisconsin, La Crosse
U of Wisconsin, Oshkosh
U of Wisconsin, Platteville
U of Wisconsin, River Falls
U of Wisconsin, Stevens
  Point
U of Wisconsin, Stout
U of Wisconsin, Superior
U of Wisconsin, Whitewater

Ursinus College
Virginia Wesleyan College
Wartburg College
Washington and Jefferson
  College
Washington and Lee U
Washington U (MO)
Waynesburg U
Wellesley College
Wesley College
Wesleyan U (CT)
Westfield State College
Westminster College (PA)
Wheaton College (IL)
Wheaton College (MA)
Whitworth U
Widener U
Willamette U
Williams College
Wilmington College (OH)
Wisconsin Lutheran College
Wittenberg U
Worcester Polytechnic
  Institute
Worcester State College
York College (NY)

TRACK, OUTDOOR
DIVISION I

Alabama A&M U
Alabama State U
Alcorn State U
American U
Appalachian State U
Arizona State U
Arkansas State U
Auburn U
Austin Peay State U
Ball State U
Baylor U
Belmont U
Bethune-Cookman U
Boise State U
Boston College
Boston U

Bowling Green State U
Bradley U
Brigham Young U
Brown U
Bryant U
Bucknell U
Butler U
California Polytechnic
State U
California State U,
Bakersfield
California State U, Fresno
California State U, Fullerton
California State U,
Northridge
California State U,
Sacramento
Campbell U
Central Connecticut State U
Central Michigan U
Charleston Southern U
Chicago State U
The Citadel
Clemson U
Coastal Carolina U
Colgate U
College of Charleston (SC)
College of the Holy Cross
College of William and Mary
Colorado State U
Columbia U-Barnard College
Coppin State U
Cornell U
Dartmouth College
Davidson College
Delaware State U
DePaul U
Drake U
Duke U
Duquesne U
East Carolina U
East Tennessee State U
Eastern Illinois U
Eastern Kentucky U
Eastern Michigan U
Eastern Washington U
Elon U

Fairleigh Dickinson U,
Metropolitan
Florida A&M U
Florida Atlantic U
Florida International U
Florida State U
Fordham U
Furman U
Gardner-Webb U
George Mason U
Georgetown U
Georgia Institute of
Technology
Georgia Southern U
Georgia State U
Gonzaga U
Grambling State U
Hampton U
Harvard U
High Point U
Houston Baptist U
Howard U
Idaho State U
Illinois State U
Indiana State U
Indiana U, Bloomington
Indiana U-Purdue U, Fort
Wayne
Iona College
Iowa State U
Jackson State U
Jacksonville State U
Jacksonville U
James Madison U
Kansas State U
Kennesaw State U
Kent State U
La Salle U
Lafayette College
Lamar U
Lehigh U
Liberty U
Lipscomb U
Long Beach State U
Long Island U-Brooklyn
Campus
Louisiana State U

Louisiana Tech U
Loyola Marymount U
Loyola U (IL)
Loyola U (MD)
Manhattan College
Marist College
Marquette U
Marshall U
McNeese State U
Miami U (OH)
Michigan State U
Middle Tennessee State U
Mississippi State U
Mississippi Valley State U
Missouri State U
Monmouth U
Montana State U-Bozeman
Morehead State U
Morgan State U
Mount St. Mary's U
Murray State U
New Jersey Institute of
Technology
New Mexico State U
Nicholls State U
Norfolk State U
North Carolina A&T State U
North Carolina Central U
North Carolina State U
North Dakota State U
Northeastern U
Northern Arizona U
Northern Illinois U
Northwestern State U
Oakland U
Ohio U
The Ohio State U
Oklahoma State U
Oral Roberts U
Oregon State U
Pennsylvania State U
Pepperdine U
Portland State U
Prairie View A&M U
Princeton U
Providence College
Purdue U

Quinnipiac U
Radford U
Rice U
Rider U
Robert Morris U
Rutgers, State Univ of New Jersey, New Brunswick
Sacred Heart U
Saint Francis U (PA)
Saint Joseph's U
Saint Louis U
Sam Houston State U
Samford U
San Diego State U
Santa Clara U
Savannah State U
Seattle U
Seton Hall U
South Carolina State U
South Dakota State U
Southeast Missouri State U
Southeastern Louisiana U
Southern Illinois U at Carbondale
Southern Illinois U Edwardsville
Southern Methodist U
Southern U, Baton Rouge
Southern Utah U
St. Francis College (NY)
St. John's U (NY)
St. Peter's College
Stanford U
State U of New York at Binghamton
Stephen F. Austin State U
Stony Brook U
Syracuse U
Temple U
Tennessee State U
Tennessee Technological U
Texas A&M U, College Station
Texas A&M U-Corpus Christi
Texas Christian U
Texas Southern U
Texas State U-San Marcos

Texas Tech U
Towson U
Troy U
Tulane U
U.S. Air Force Academy
U.S. Military Academy
U.S. Naval Academy
U at Albany
U at Buffalo, the State U of New
U of Akron
U of Alabama at Birmingham
U of Alabama, Tuscaloosa
U of Arizona
U of Arkansas, Fayetteville
U of Arkansas, Little Rock
U of Arkansas, Pine Bluff
U of California, Berkeley
U of California, Davis
U of California, Irvine
U of California, Los Angeles
U of California, Riverside
U of California, Santa Barbara
U of Central Arkansas
U of Central Florida
U of Cincinnati
U of Colorado, Boulder
U of Connecticut
U of Dayton
U of Delaware
U of Detroit Mercy
U of Florida
U of Georgia
U of Hartford
U of Hawaii, Manoa
U of Houston
U of Idaho
U of Illinois at Chicago
U of Illinois, Champaign
U of Iowa
U of Kansas
U of Kentucky
U of Louisiana at Lafayette
U of Louisiana at Monroe

U of Louisville
U of Maine, Orono
U of Maryland, Baltimore County
U of Maryland, College Park
U of Maryland, Eastern Shore
U of Massachusetts, Amherst
U of Memphis
U of Miami (FL)
U of Michigan
U of Minnesota, Twin Cities
U of Mississippi
U of Missouri, Columbia
U of Missouri, Kansas City
U of Montana
U of Nebraska, Lincoln
U of Nevada
U of Nevada, Las Vegas
U of New Hampshire
U of New Mexico
U of North Carolina at Greensboro
U of North Carolina, Asheville
U of North Carolina, Chapel Hill
U of North Carolina, Charlotte
U of North Carolina, Wilmington
U of North Dakota
U of North Florida
U of North Texas
U of Northern Colorado
U of Northern Iowa
U of Notre Dame
U of Oklahoma
U of Oregon
U of Pennsylvania
U of Pittsburgh
U of Portland
U of Rhode Island
U of Richmond
U of San Diego
U of San Francisco

U of South Alabama
U of South Carolina Upstate
U of South Carolina, Columbia
U of South Dakota
U of South Florida
U of Southern California
U of Southern Mississippi
U of Tennessee at Chattanooga
U of Tennessee, Knoxville
U of Texas at Arlington
U of Texas at Austin
U of Texas at El Paso
U of Texas at San Antonio
U of Texas, Pan American
U of Toledo
U of Tulsa
U of Utah
U of Vermont
U of Virginia
U of Washington
U of Wisconsin, Madison
U of Wisconsin, Milwaukee
U of Wyoming
Utah State U
Utah Valley U
Valparaiso U
Vanderbilt U
Villanova U
Virginia Commonwealth U
Virginia Military Institute
Virginia Polytechnic Institute & State U
Wagner College
Wake Forest U
Washington State U
Weber State U
West Virginia U
Western Carolina U
Western Illinois U
Western Kentucky U
Western Michigan U
Wichita State U
Winston-Salem State U
Winthrop U
Wofford College

Wright State U
Xavier U
Yale U
Youngstown State U

TRACK, OUTDOOR
DIVISION II

Abilene Christian U
Adams State College
Adelphi U
Albany State U (GA)
Alderson-Broaddus College
American International College
Anderson U (SC)
Angelo State U
Ashland U
Assumption College
Augustana College (SD)
Bellarmine U
Bemidji State U
Benedict College
Bentley College
Bloomsburg U of Pennsylvania
Bowie State U
Brevard College
Bryant U
C.W. Post Campus/Long Island U
California State Polytechnic U, Pomona
California State U, Bakersfield
California State U, Chico
California State U, Dominguez Hills
California State U, Los Angeles
California State U, Stanislaus
California U of Pennsylvania
Carson-Newman College
Central State U

Central Washington U
Chadron State College
Cheyney U of Pennsylvania
Claflin U
Clarion U of Pennsylvania
Clark Atlanta U
Clayton State U
College of Saint Rose
Colorado School of Mines
Colorado State U-Pueblo
Columbia Union College
Concord U
Concordia U, St. Paul
Dallas Baptist U
Dominican College (NY)
Drury U
East Stroudsburg U of Pennsylvania
Eastern New Mexico U
Edinboro U of Pennsylvania
Emporia State U
Ferris State U
Florida Southern College
Fort Hays State U
Fort Valley State U
Francis Marion U
Georgian Court U
Glenville State College
Grand Valley State U
Harding U
Hillsdale College
Humboldt State U
Indiana U of Pennsylvania
Johnson C. Smith U
Kennesaw State U
Kentucky State U
Kutztown U of Pennsylvania
Lake Superior State U
Lane College
Lees-McRae College
Lenoir-Rhyne College
Lewis U
Limestone College
Lincoln U (MO)
Livingstone College

Lock Haven U of
Pennsylvania
Mansfield U of
Pennsylvania
Mars Hill College
Mercy College
Mesa State College
Metropolitan State College
of Denver
Michigan Technological U
Miles College
Millersville U of
Pennsylvania
Minnesota State U
Moorhead
Minnesota State U, Mankato
Missouri Southern State U
Missouri U of Science and
Technology
Montana State U-Billings
Mount Olive College
New Jersey Institute of
Technology
New Mexico Highlands U
North Carolina Central U
Northern Kentucky U
Northern Michigan U
Northern State U
Northwest Missouri State U
Northwest Nazarene U
Northwood U (MI)
Nova Southeastern U
Pace U
Paine College
Pittsburg State U
Queens College (NY)
Queens U of Charlotte
Saginaw Valley State U
Saint Joseph's College (IN)
San Francisco State U
Seattle Pacific U
Seattle U
Seton Hill U
Shaw U
Shippensburg U of
Pennsylvania
Slippery Rock U of
Pennsylvania

Southern Arkansas U
Southern Connecticut
State U
Southern Illinois U
Edwardsville
Southwest Baptist U
St. Andrews Presbyterian
College
St. Augustine's College
St. Cloud State U
St. Martin's U
St. Paul's College
St. Thomas Aquinas College
Stillman College
Stonehill College
Tarleton State U
Texas A&M U-Commerce
Texas A&M U-Kingsville
Tiffin U
Truman State U
Tuskegee U
U of Alabama in Huntsville
U of Alaska Anchorage
U of California, San Diego
U of Central Arkansas
U of Central Missouri
U of Charleston (WV)
U of Colorado, Colorado
Springs
U of Findlay
U of Indianapolis
U of Mary
U of Massachusetts at
Lowell
U of Minnesota Duluth
U of Nebraska at Kearney
U of Nebraska at Omaha
U of New Haven
U of North Carolina at
Pembroke
U of North Dakota
U of North Florida
U of Pittsburgh, Johnstown
U of Puerto Rico, Bayamon
U of Puerto Rico, Cayey
U of Puerto Rico,
Mayaguez Campus
U of Puerto Rico, Rio Piedras

U of South Carolina Upstate
U of South Dakota
U of Southern Indiana
U of Tampa
U of the District of Columbia
U of the Incarnate Word
U of Wisconsin, Parkside
Virginia State U
Virginia Union U
Wayne State College (NE)
West Chester U of
Pennsylvania
West Liberty State College
West Texas A&M U
West Virginia State U
West Virginia Wesleyan
College
Western Oregon U
Western State College of
Colorado
Western Washington U
Wheeling Jesuit U
Winona State U
Winston-Salem State U

TRACK, OUTDOOR
DIVISION III

Adrian College
Albion College
Albright College
Alfred U
Allegheny College
Alma College
Amherst College
Anderson U (IN)
Augsburg College
Augustana College (IL)
Aurora U
Babson College
Baldwin-Wallace College
Bard College
Bates College
Beloit College
Benedictine U (IL)
Bethany College (WV)

Bethel U (MN)
Birmingham-Southern
  College
Bluffton U
Bowdoin College
Brandeis U
Bridgewater College (VA)
Bridgewater State College
Bryn Mawr College
Buena Vista U
Buffalo State College
Cabrini College
California Institute of
  Technology
California Lutheran U
California State U, East Bay
Calvin College
Capital U
Carleton College
Carnegie Mellon U
Carroll U (WI)
Carthage College
Case Western Reserve U
Catholic U
Central College (IA)
Centre College
Chapman U
Christopher Newport U
The City College of New
  York
Claremont McKenna-Harvey
  Mudd-Scripps Colleges
Coe College
Colby College
Colby-Sawyer College
College of Brockport, State
  U of New York
College of Mount St. Joseph
The College of New Jersey
College of St. Benedict
College of St. Catherine
The College of St.
  Scholastica
College of Wooster
Colorado College
Concordia College,
  Moorhead
Concordia U (WI)

Concordia U Chicago
Connecticut College
Cornell College
Defiance College
Delaware Valley College
Denison U
DePauw U
DeSales U
Dickinson College
Earlham College
Eastern Connecticut State U
Eastern Mennonite U
Edgewood College
Elizabethtown College
Elmhurst College
Emmanuel College (MA)
Emory U
Eureka College
Fitchburg State College
Fontbonne U
Franciscan U of Steubenville
Franklin & Marshall College
Franklin College
Frostburg State U
Gallaudet U
Geneva College
George Fox U
Gettysburg College
Gordon College
Goucher College
Greenville College
Grinnell College
Grove City College
Gustavus Adolphus College
Gwynedd-Mercy College
Hamilton College
Hamline U
Hanover College
Hardin-Simmons U
Haverford College
Heidelberg College
Hendrix College
Hiram College
Hood College
Hope College
Hunter College
Illinois College
Illinois Wesleyan U

Ithaca College
John Carroll U
Johns Hopkins U
Juniata College
Kean U
Keene State College
Kenyon College
Keystone College
Knox College
Lake Erie College
Lakeland College
Lawrence U
Lebanon Valley College
Lehman College, City U of
  New York
Lewis & Clark College
Lincoln U (PA)
Linfield College
Loras College
Luther College
Lynchburg College
Macalester College
Manchester College
Manhattanville College
Marietta College
Martin Luther College
Massachusetts Institute of
  Technology
Massachusetts Maritime
  Academy
McDaniel College
McMurry U
Medgar Evers College
Messiah College
Methodist U
Middlebury College
Millikin U
Mills College
Milwaukee School of
  Engineering
Misericordia U
Mississippi College
Monmouth College (IL)
Montclair State U
Moravian College
Mount Holyoke College
Mount Union College
Muhlenberg College

Muskingum College
Nazareth College
Nebraska Wesleyan U
New Jersey City U
New York City College of
  Technology
New York U
North Central College
North Central U
North Park U
Northwestern College
Oberlin College
Occidental College
Oglethorpe U
Ohio Northern U
Ohio Wesleyan U
Olivet College
Otterbein College
Pacific Lutheran U
Pacific U (OR)
Pennsylvania State Univ.
  Erie, the Behrend College
Plattsburgh State U of
  New York
Pomona-Pitzer Colleges
Principia College
Ramapo College
Regis College (MA)
Rensselaer Polytechnic
  Institute
Rhode Island College
Rhodes College
Richard Stockton College
  of New Jersey
Ripon College
Roanoke College
Rochester Institute of
  Technology
Rockford College
Rose-Hulman Institute of
  Technology
Rowan U
Rust College
Rutgers, The State Univ. of
  New Jersey, Camden
Rutgers, The State Univ. of

New Jersey, Newark
Saint Mary's U of
  Minnesota
Salem State College
Salisbury U
Salve Regina U
Simpson College
Smith College
Southwestern U (TX)
Springfield College
St. Joseph's College (Long
  Island)
St. Lawrence U
St. Norbert College
St. Olaf College
State U College at Cortland
State U College at Fredonia
State U College at Geneseo
State U College at Oneonta
State U of New York at
  Cobleskill
State U of New York at
  Farmingdale
State U of New York at
  Oswego
Stevens Institute of
  Technology
Sul Ross State U
Susquehanna U
Swarthmore College
Texas Lutheran U
Thiel College
Transylvania U
Trine U
Trinity College (CT)
Trinity U (TX)
Tufts U
U.S. Coast Guard Academy
U.S. Merchant Marine
  Academy
Union College (NY)
U of Chicago
U of Dallas
U of Dubuque
U of La Verne
U of Mary Washington

U of Massachusetts, Boston
U of Massachusetts,
  Dartmouth
U of Minnesota, Morris
U of Puget Sound
U of Redlands
U of Rochester
U of Southern Maine
U of St. Thomas (MN)
U of Texas at Tyler
U of the South
U of Wisconsin, Eau Claire
U of Wisconsin, La Crosse
U of Wisconsin, Oshkosh
U of Wisconsin, Platteville
U of Wisconsin, River Falls
U of Wisconsin, Stevens
  Point
U of Wisconsin, Stout
U of Wisconsin, Superior
U of Wisconsin, Whitewater
Ursinus College
Vassar College
Virginia Wesleyan College
Wartburg College
Washington and Jefferson
  College
Washington and Lee U
Washington U (MO)
Waynesburg U
Webster U
Wellesley College
Wesley College
Wesleyan U (CT)
Westfield State College
Westminster College (PA)
Wheaton College (IL)
Wheaton College (MA)
Whittier College
Whitworth U
Widener U
Willamette U
Williams College
Wilmington College (OH)
Wisconsin Lutheran College
Wittenberg U

Worcester Polytechnic
 Institute
Worcester State College
York College (NY)
York College (PA)

VOLLEYBALL
DIVISION I

Alabama A&M U
Alabama State U
Alcorn State U
American U
Appalachian State U
Arizona State U
Arkansas State U
Auburn U
Austin Peay State U
Ball State U
Baylor U
Belmont U
Bethune-Cookman U
Birmingham-Southern
 College
Boise State U
Boston College
Bowling Green State U
Bradley U
Brigham Young U
Brown U
Bryant U
Bucknell U
Butler U
California Polytechnic
 State U
California State U,
 Bakersfield
California State U, Fresno
California State U, Fullerton
California State U,
 Northridge
California State U,
 Sacramento
Campbell U
Canisius College
Centenary College (LA)

Central Connecticut State U
Central Michigan U
Charleston Southern U
Chicago State U
The Citadel
Clemson U
Cleveland State U
Coastal Carolina U
Colgate U
College of Charleston (SC)
College of the Holy Cross
College of William and Mary
Colorado State U
Columbia U-Barnard College
Coppin State U
Cornell U
Creighton U
Dartmouth College
Davidson College
Delaware State U
DePaul U
Drake U
Duke U
Duquesne U
East Carolina U
East Tennessee State U
Eastern Illinois U
Eastern Kentucky U
Eastern Michigan U
Eastern Washington U
Elon U
Fairfield U
Fairleigh Dickinson U,
 Metropolitan
Florida A&M U
Florida Atlantic U
Florida Gulf Coast U
Florida International U
Florida State U
Fordham U
Furman U
Gardner-Webb U
George Mason U
George Washington U
Georgetown U
Georgia Institute of
 Technology

Georgia Southern U
Georgia State U
Gonzaga U
Grambling State U
Hampton U
Harvard U
High Point U
Hofstra U
Houston Baptist U
Howard U
Idaho State U
Illinois State U
Indiana State U
Indiana U, Bloomington
Indiana U-Purdue U at
 Indianapolis
Indiana U-Purdue U, Fort
 Wayne
Iona College
Iowa State U
Jackson State U
Jacksonville State U
Jacksonville U
James Madison U
Kansas State U
Kennesaw State U
Kent State U
La Salle U
Lafayette College
Lamar U
Lehigh U
Liberty U
Lipscomb U
Long Beach State U
Long Island U-Brooklyn
 Campus
Louisiana State U
Louisiana Tech U
Loyola Marymount U
Loyola U (IL)
Loyola U (MD)
Manhattan College
Marist College
Marquette U
Marshall U
McNeese State U
Mercer U

Miami U (OH)
Michigan State U
Middle Tennessee State U
Mississippi State U
Mississippi Valley State U
Missouri State U
Montana State U-Bozeman
Morehead State U
Morgan State U
Murray State U
New Jersey Institute of
    Technology
New Mexico State U
Niagara U
Nicholls State U
Norfolk State U
North Carolina A&T State U
North Carolina Central U
North Carolina State U
North Dakota State U
Northeastern U
Northern Arizona U
Northern Illinois U
Northwestern State U
Northwestern U
Oakland U
Ohio U
The Ohio State U
Oral Roberts U
Oregon State U
Pennsylvania State U
Pepperdine U
Portland State U
Prairie View A&M U
Presbyterian College
Princeton U
Providence College
Purdue U
Quinnipiac U
Radford U
Rice U
Rider U
Robert Morris U
Rutgers, State Univ of New
    Jersey, New Brunswick
Sacred Heart U

Saint Francis U (PA)
Saint Louis U
Sam Houston State U
Samford U
San Diego State U
San Jose State U
Santa Clara U
Savannah State U
Seattle U
Seton Hall U
Siena College
South Carolina State U
South Dakota State U
Southeast Missouri State U
Southeastern Louisiana U
Southern Illinois U at
    Carbondale
Southern Illinois U
    Edwardsville
Southern Methodist U
Southern U, Baton Rouge
St. Francis College (NY)
St. John's U (NY)
St. Mary's College of
    California
St. Peter's College
Stanford U
State U of New York at
    Binghamton
Stephen F. Austin State U
Stetson U
Stony Brook U
Syracuse U
Temple U
Tennessee State U
Tennessee Technological U
Texas A&M U, College
    Station
Texas A&M U-Corpus Christi
Texas Christian U
Texas Southern U
Texas State U-San Marcos
Texas Tech U
Towson U
Troy U
Tulane U

U.S. Air Force Academy
U.S. Military Academy
U.S. Naval Academy
U at Albany
U at Buffalo, the State U
    of New
U of Akron
U of Alabama at
    Birmingham
U of Alabama, Tuscaloosa
U of Arizona
U of Arkansas, Fayetteville
U of Arkansas, Little Rock
U of Arkansas, Pine Bluff
U of California, Berkeley
U of California, Davis
U of California, Irvine
U of California, Los Angeles
U of California, Riverside
U of California, Santa
    Barbara
U of Central Arkansas
U of Central Florida
U of Cincinnati
U of Colorado, Boulder
U of Connecticut
U of Dayton
U of Delaware
U of Denver
U of Evansville
U of Florida
U of Georgia
U of Hartford
U of Hawaii, Manoa
U of Houston
U of Idaho
U of Illinois at Chicago
U of Illinois, Champaign
U of Iowa
U of Kansas
U of Kentucky
U of Louisiana at Lafayette
U of Louisiana at Monroe
U of Louisville
U of Maine, Orono
U of Maryland, Baltimore

County
U of Maryland, College Park
U of Maryland, Eastern
Shore
U of Memphis
U of Miami (FL)
U of Michigan
U of Minnesota, Twin Cities
U of Mississippi
U of Missouri, Columbia
U of Missouri, Kansas City
U of Montana
U of Nebraska, Lincoln
U of Nevada
U of Nevada, Las Vegas
U of New Hampshire
U of New Mexico
U of New Orleans
U of North Carolina at
Greensboro
U of North Carolina,
Asheville
U of North Carolina,
Chapel Hill
U of North Carolina,
Charlotte
U of North Carolina,
Wilmington
U of North Dakota
U of North Florida
U of North Texas
U of Northern Colorado
U of Northern Iowa
U of Notre Dame
U of Oklahoma
U of Oregon
U of Pennsylvania
U of Pittsburgh
U of Portland
U of Rhode Island
U of San Diego
U of San Francisco
U of South Alabama
U of South Carolina Upstate
U of South Carolina,
Columbia
U of South Dakota

U of South Florida
U of Southern California
U of Southern Mississippi
U of Tennessee at
Chattanooga
U of Tennessee at Martin
U of Tennessee, Knoxville
U of Texas at Arlington
U of Texas at Austin
U of Texas at El Paso
U of Texas at San Antonio
U of Texas, Pan American
U of the Pacific
U of Toledo
U of Tulsa
U of Utah
U of Virginia
U of Washington
U of Wisconsin, Green Bay
U of Wisconsin, Madison
U of Wisconsin, Milwaukee
U of Wyoming
Utah State U
Utah Valley U
Valparaiso U
Villanova U
Virginia Commonwealth U
Virginia Polytechnic
Institute & State U
Wagner College
Wake Forest U
Washington State U
Weber State U
West Virginia U
Western Carolina U
Western Illinois U
Western Kentucky U
Western Michigan U
Wichita State U
Winston-Salem State U
Winthrop U
Wofford College
Wright State U
Xavier U
Yale U
Youngstown State U

VOLLEYBALL
DIVISION II

Abilene Christian U
Adams State College
Adelphi U
Albany State U (GA)
Alderson-Broaddus College
American International
College
Anderson U (SC)
Angelo State U
Arkansas Tech U
Armstrong Atlantic State U
Ashland U
Assumption College
Augusta State U
Augustana College (SD)
Barry U
Barton College
Bellarmine U
Belmont Abbey College
Bemidji State U
Benedict College
Bentley College
Bloomfield College
Bluefield State College
Bowie State U
Brevard College
Brigham Young U, Hawaii
Bryant U
C.W. Post Campus/Long
Island U
Caldwell College
California State
Polytechnic U, Pomona
California State U,
Bakersfield
California State U, Chico
California State U,
Dominguez Hills
California State U, Los
Angeles
California State U,
Monterey Bay
California State U, San
Bernardino

California State U, Stanislaus
California U of
 Pennsylvania
Cameron U
Carson-Newman College
Catawba College
Central State U
Central Washington U
Chadron State College
Chaminade U
Chestnut Hill College
Cheyney U of Pennsylvania
Chowan U
Christian Brothers U
Claflin U
Clarion U of Pennsylvania
Clark Atlanta U
Coker College
College of Saint Rose
Colorado Christian U
Colorado School of Mines
Colorado State U-Pueblo
Concord U
Concordia College (NY)
Concordia U, St. Paul
Converse College
Dallas Baptist U
Davis and Elkins College
Dixie State College of Utah
Dominican College (NY)
Dowling College
Drury U
East Central U
East Stroudsburg U of
 Pennsylvania
Eastern New Mexico U
Eckerd College
Edinboro U of Pennsylvania
Elizabeth City State U
Emporia State U
Fairmont State U
Fayetteville State U
Felician College
Ferris State U
Flagler College
Florida Gulf Coast U
Florida Institute of
 Technology

Florida Southern College
Fort Hays State U
Fort Lewis College
Fort Valley State U
Francis Marion U
Franklin Pierce U
Gannon U
Georgian Court U
Glenville State College
Goldey-Beacom College
Grand Canyon U
Grand Valley State U
Harding U
Hawaii Pacific U
Henderson State U
Hillsdale College
Holy Family U
Humboldt State U
Indiana U of Pennsylvania
Johnson C. Smith U
Kennesaw State U
Kentucky State U
Kentucky Wesleyan College
Kutztown U of
 Pennsylvania
Lake Superior State U
Lander U
Lane College
Le Moyne College
Lees-McRae College
LeMoyne-Owen College
Lenoir-Rhyne College
Lewis U
Limestone College
Lincoln Memorial U
Livingstone College
Lock Haven U of
 Pennsylvania
Lynn U
Mars Hill College
Mercy College
Mercyhurst College
Merrimack College
Mesa State College
Metropolitan State College
 of Denver
Michigan Technological U
Midwestern State U

Miles College
Millersville U of
 Pennsylvania
Minnesota State U
 Moorhead
Minnesota State U, Mankato
Missouri Southern State U
Missouri U of Science and
 Technology
Missouri Western State U
Molloy College
Montana State U-Billings
Mount Olive College
New Jersey Institute of
 Technology
New Mexico Highlands U
New York Institute of
 Technology
Newberry College
Newman U
North Carolina Central U
North Greenville U
Northern Kentucky U
Northern Michigan U
Northern State U
Northwest Missouri State U
Northwest Nazarene U
Northwood U (MI)
Notre Dame de Namur U
Nova Southeastern U
Nyack College
Oakland City U
Ohio Valley U
Oklahoma Panhandle
 State U
Ouachita Baptist U
Pace U
Paine College
Palm Beach Atlantic U
Pfeiffer U
Philadelphia U
Pittsburg State U
Post U
Presbyterian College
Queens College (NY)
Queens U of Charlotte
Quincy U
Regis U (CO)

Rockhurst U
Rollins College
Saginaw Valley State U
Saint Anselm College
Saint Joseph's College (IN)
Saint Leo U
Saint Michael's College
Salem International U
San Francisco State U
Seattle Pacific U
Seattle U
Seton Hill U
Shaw U
Shepherd U
Shippensburg U of
   Pennsylvania
Slippery Rock U of
   Pennsylvania
Sonoma State U
Southeastern Oklahoma
   State U
Southern Arkansas U
Southern Connecticut
   State U
Southern Illinois U
   Edwardsville
Southern New Hampshire U
Southwest Baptist U
Southwest Minnesota
   State U
Southwestern Oklahoma
   State U
St. Andrews Presbyterian
   College
St. Augustine's College
St. Cloud State U
St. Edward's U
St. Martin's U
St. Mary's U (TX)
St. Paul's College
Stillman College
Stonehill College
Tarleton State U
Texas A&M International U
Texas A&M U-Commerce
Texas A&M U-Kingsville
Texas Woman's U
Tiffin U

Truman State U
Tusculum College
Tuskegee U
U of Alabama in Huntsville
U of Alaska Anchorage
U of Alaska Fairbanks
U of Arkansas, Monticello
U of Bridgeport
U of California, San Diego
U of Central Arkansas
U of Central Missouri
U of Central Oklahoma
U of Charleston (WV)
U of Colorado, Colorado
   Springs
U of Findlay
U of Hawaii at Hilo
U of Indianapolis
U of Mary
U of Massachusetts at
   Lowell
U of Minnesota Duluth
U of Minnesota, Crookston
U of Missouri, St. Louis
U of Montevallo
U of Nebraska at Kearney
U of Nebraska at Omaha
U of New Haven
U of North Alabama
U of North Carolina at
   Pembroke
U of North Dakota
U of North Florida
U of Pittsburgh, Johnstown
U of Puerto Rico, Bayamon
U of Puerto Rico, Cayey
U of Puerto Rico,
   Mayaguez Campus
U of Puerto Rico, Rio Piedras
U of South Carolina Aiken
U of South Carolina Upstate
U of South Dakota
U of Southern Indiana
U of Tampa
U of Texas of the Permian
   Basin
U of the District of
   Columbia

U of the Incarnate Word
U of the Sciences in
   Philadelphia
U of West Alabama
U of West Florida
U of West Georgia
U of Wisconsin, Parkside
Upper Iowa U
Valdosta State U
Virginia State U
Virginia Union U
Washburn U of Topeka
Wayne State College (NE)
Wayne State U (MI)
West Chester U of
   Pennsylvania
West Liberty State College
West Texas A&M U
West Virginia State U
West Virginia Wesleyan
   College
Western New Mexico U
Western Oregon U
Western State College of
   Colorado
Western Washington U
Wheeling Jesuit U
Wilmington U (DE)
Wingate U
Winona State U
Winston-Salem State U

VOLLEYBALL
DIVISION III

Adrian College
Albertus Magnus College
Albion College
Albright College
Alfred U
Allegheny College
Alma College
Alvernia U
Alverno College
Amherst College
Anderson U (IN)
Anna Maria College

Arcadia U
Augsburg College
Augustana College (IL)
Aurora U
Austin College
Averett U
Babson College
Baldwin-Wallace College
Baptist Bible College
Bard College
Baruch College
Bates College
Bay Path College
Becker College
Beloit College
Benedictine U (IL)
Bethany College (WV)
Bethany Lutheran College
Bethel U (MN)
Blackburn College
Bluffton U
Bowdoin College
Brandeis U
Bridgewater College (VA)
Bridgewater State College
Brooklyn College
Bryn Mawr College
Buena Vista U
Buffalo State College
Cabrini College
California Institute of
    Technology
California Lutheran U
California State U, East Bay
Calvin College
Capital U
Carleton College
Carnegie Mellon U
Carroll U (WI)
Carthage College
Case Western Reserve U
Castleton State College
Catholic U
Cazenovia College
Cedar Crest College
Centenary College (NJ)
Central College (IA)

Centre College
Chapman U
Chatham U
Christopher Newport U
The City College of New
    York
Claremont McKenna-Harvey
    Mudd-Scripps Colleges
Clark U (MA)
Clarkson U
Coe College
Colby College
Colby-Sawyer College
College of Brockport, State
    U of New York
College of Mount St. Joseph
College of Mount St.
    Vincent
College of New Rochelle
College of Notre Dame (MD)
College of Saint Elizabeth
College of St. Benedict
College of St. Catherine
The College of St. Scholastica
College of Staten Island
College of Wooster
Colorado College
Concordia College,
    Moorhead
Concordia U (WI)
Concordia U Chicago
Concordia U Texas
Connecticut College
Cornell College
Crown College (MN)
Daniel Webster College
Defiance College
Delaware Valley College
Denison U
DePauw U
DeSales U
Dickinson College
Dominican U (IL)
D'Youville College
Earlham College
East Texas Baptist U
Eastern Connecticut State U

Eastern Mennonite U
Eastern Nazarene College
Eastern U
Edgewood College
Elizabethtown College
Elmhurst College
Elmira College
Elms College
Emerson College
Emmanuel College (MA)
Emory and Henry College
Emory U
Endicott College
Eureka College
Fairleigh Dickinson U,
    Florham
Ferrum College
Finlandia U
Fontbonne U
Framingham State College
Franciscan U of Steubenville
Franklin & Marshall College
Franklin College
Frostburg State U
Gallaudet U
Geneva College
George Fox U
Gettysburg College
Gordon College
Goucher College
Green Mountain College
Greensboro College
Greenville College
Grinnell College
Grove City College
Guilford College
Gustavus Adolphus College
Gwynedd-Mercy College
Hamilton College
Hamline U
Hanover College
Hardin-Simmons U
Hartwick College
Haverford College
Heidelberg College
Hendrix College
Hilbert College

Hiram College
Hood College
Hope College
Howard Payne U
Hunter College
Huntingdon College
Husson College
Illinois College
Illinois Wesleyan U
Immaculata U
Ithaca College
John Carroll U
John Jay College of
    Criminal Justice
Johns Hopkins U
Johnson and Wales U
Juniata College
Kalamazoo College
Kean U
Keene State College
Kenyon College
Keuka College
King's College (PA)
Knox College
La Grange College
La Roche College
La Sierra U
Lake Erie College
Lake Forest College
Lakeland College
Lancaster Bible College
Lasell College
Lawrence U
Lebanon Valley College
Lehman College, City U of
    New York
Lesley U
LeTourneau U
Lewis & Clark College
Lincoln U (PA)
Linfield College
Loras College
Luther College
Lycoming College
Lynchburg College
Lyndon State College
Macalester College

MacMurray College
Maine Maritime Academy
Manchester College
Manhattanville College
Maranatha Baptist Bible
    College
Marian U (WI)
Marietta College
Martin Luther College
Mary Baldwin College
Marymount U (VA)
Maryville College (TN)
Maryville U of Saint Louis
Marywood U
Massachusetts College of
    Liberal Arts
Massachusetts Institute of
    Technology
Massachusetts Maritime
    Academy
McDaniel College
McMurry U
Medaille College
Medgar Evers College
Menlo College
Meredith College
Messiah College
Methodist U
Middlebury College
Millikin U
Mills College
Millsaps College
Milwaukee School of
    Engineering
Misericordia U
Mississippi College
Mitchell College
Monmouth College (IL)
Montclair State U
Moravian College
Mount Aloysius College
Mount Holyoke College
Mount Ida College
Mount Mary College
Mount Saint Mary College
    (NY)
Mount Union College

Muhlenberg College
Muskingum College
Nazareth College
Nebraska Wesleyan U
Neumann College
New Jersey City U
New York City College of
    Technology
New York U
Newbury College
North Carolina Wesleyan
    College
North Central College
North Central U
North Park U
Northland College
Northwestern College
Norwich U
Oberlin College
Occidental College
Oglethorpe U
Ohio Northern U
Ohio Wesleyan U
Olivet College
Otterbein College
Pacific Lutheran U
Pacific U (OR)
Peace College
Penn State Berks College
Penn State Harrisburg
Penn State U, Altoona
Pennsylvania State Univ.
    Erie, the Behrend College
Philadelphia Biblical U
Piedmont College
Pine Manor College
Plattsburgh State U of
    New York
Plymouth State U
Polytechnic Institute of
    New York U
Pomona-Pitzer Colleges
Presentation College
Principia College
Purchase College, State U
    of New York
Ramapo College

Randolph College

Randolph-Macon College

Regis College (MA)

Rhode Island College

Rhodes College

Richard Stockton College of New Jersey

Ripon College

Rivier College

Roanoke College

Rochester Institute of Technology

Rockford College

Roger Williams U

Rose-Hulman Institute of Technology

Rosemont College

Rowan U

Rust College

Rutgers, The State Univ. of New Jersey, Camden

Rutgers, The State Univ. of New Jersey, Newark

The Sage Colleges

Saint Joseph's College (ME)

Saint Mary's College (IN)

Saint Mary's U of Minnesota

Saint Vincent College

Salem College

Salem State College

Salisbury U

Salve Regina U

Schreiner U

Shenandoah U

Simmons College

Simpson College

Skidmore College

Smith College

Southern Vermont College

Southwestern U (TX)

Spalding U

Spelman College

Springfield College

St. John Fisher College

St. Joseph College (CT)

St. Joseph's College (Long Island)

St. Joseph's College, New York

St. Lawrence U

St. Mary's College of Maryland

St. Norbert College

St. Olaf College

State U College at Cortland

State U College at Fredonia

State U College at Geneseo

State U College at New Paltz

State U College at Old Westbury

State U College at Oneonta

State U of New York at Cobleskill

State U of New York at Farmingdale

State U of New York at Morrisville

State U of New York at Oswego

State U of New York at Potsdam

State U of New York Institute of Technolo

State U of New York Maritime College

Stevens Institute of Technology

Stevenson U

Suffolk U

Sul Ross State U

Susquehanna U

Swarthmore College

Sweet Briar College

Texas Lutheran U

Thiel College

Thomas College

Thomas More College

Transylvania U

Trine U

Trinity College (CT)

Trinity College (District of Columbia)

Trinity U (TX)

Tufts U

U.S. Coast Guard Academy

U.S. Merchant Marine Academy

Union College (NY)

U of California, Santa Cruz

U of Chicago

U of Dallas

U of Dubuque

U of La Verne

U of Maine at Presque Isle

U of Maine, Farmington

U of Mary Hardin-Baylor

U of Mary Washington

U of Massachusetts, Boston

U of Massachusetts, Dartmouth

U of Minnesota, Morris

U of New England

U of Pittsburgh, Bradford

U of Pittsburgh, Greensburg

U of Puget Sound

U of Redlands

U of Rochester

U of Scranton

U of St. Thomas (MN)

U of Texas at Dallas

U of Texas at Tyler

U of the South

U of Wisconsin, Eau Claire

U of Wisconsin, La Crosse

U of Wisconsin, Oshkosh

U of Wisconsin, Platteville

U of Wisconsin, River Falls

U of Wisconsin, Stevens Point

U of Wisconsin, Stout

U of Wisconsin, Superior

U of Wisconsin, Whitewater

Ursinus College

Utica College

Vassar College

Virginia Wesleyan College

Wartburg College

Washington and Jefferson College

Washington and Lee U

Washington College (MD)

Washington U (MO)

Waynesburg U

Webster U
Wellesley College
Wentworth Institute of
   Technology
Wesley College
Wesleyan U (CT)
Western Connecticut
   State U
Western New England
   College
Westfield State College
Westminster College (MO)
Westminster College (PA)
Wheaton College (IL)
Wheaton College (MA)
Whitman College
Whittier College
Whitworth U
Widener U
Wilkes U
Willamette U
William Paterson U of New
   Jersey
Williams College
Wilmington College (OH)
Wisconsin Lutheran College
Wittenberg U
Worcester Polytechnic
   Institute
Worcester State College
Yeshiva U
York College (NY)
York College (PA)

WATER POLO
DIVISION I

Arizona State U
Brown U
Bucknell U
California State U,
   Bakersfield
California State U,
   Northridge
Colorado State U
George Washington U
Hartwick College

Harvard U
Indiana U, Bloomington
Iona College
Long Beach State U
Loyola Marymount U
Marist College
Princeton U
San Diego State U
San Jose State U
Santa Clara U
Siena College
St. Francis College (NY)
Stanford U
U of California, Berkeley
U of California, Davis
U of California, Irvine
U of California, Los Angeles
U of California, Santa
   Barbara
U of Hawaii, Manoa
U of Maryland, College Park
U of Michigan
U of Southern California
U of the Pacific
Villanova U
Wagner College

WATER POLO
DIVISION II

California State U,
   Bakersfield
California State U,
   Monterey Bay
California State U, San
   Bernardino
Gannon U
Mercyhurst College
Sonoma State U
U of California, San Diego

WATER POLO
DIVISION III

California Institute of
   Technology
California Lutheran U

California State U, East Bay
Carthage College
Chapman U
Claremont McKenna-Harvey
   Mudd-Scripps Colleges
Colorado College
Connecticut College
Grove City College
Macalester College
Occidental College
Pennsylvania State Univ.
   Erie, the Behrend College
Pomona-Pitzer Colleges
U of California, Santa Cruz
U of La Verne
U of Redlands
Utica College
Washington and Jefferson
   College
Wheaton College (IL)
Whittier College

Men's Sports

These lists identify institutions that offer specific sports, as well as in which division the sport competes. Go to their websites for complete information.

BASEBALL
DIVISION I

Alabama A&M U
Alabama State U
Alcorn State U
Appalachian State U
Arizona State U
Arkansas State U
Auburn U
Austin Peay State U
Ball State U
Baylor U
Belmont U
Bethune-Cookman U
Boston College
Bowling Green State U
Bradley U
Brigham Young U
Brown U
Bryant U
Bucknell U
Butler U
California Polytechnic
   State U
California State U, Fresno
California State U, Fullerton
California State U,
   Northridge
California State U,
   Sacramento
Campbell U
Canisius College
Centenary College (LA)

Central Connecticut State U
Central Michigan U
Charleston Southern U
Chicago State U
The Citadel
Clemson U
Cleveland State U
Coastal Carolina U
College of Charleston (SC)
College of the Holy Cross
College of William and Mary
Columbia U-Barnard College
Coppin State U
Cornell U
Creighton U
Dallas Baptist U
Dartmouth College
Davidson College
Delaware State U
Duke U
Duquesne U
East Carolina U
East Tennessee State U
Eastern Illinois U
Eastern Kentucky U
Eastern Michigan U
Elon U
Fairfield U
Fairleigh Dickinson U,
   Metropolitan
Florida A&M U
Florida Atlantic U
Florida Gulf Coast U
Florida International U

Florida State U
Fordham U
Furman U
Gardner-Webb U
George Mason U
George Washington U
Georgetown U
Georgia Institute of
   Technology
Georgia Southern U
Georgia State U
Gonzaga U
Grambling State U
Harvard U
High Point U
Hofstra U
Houston Baptist U
Illinois State U
Indiana State U
Indiana U, Bloomington
Indiana U-Purdue U, Fort
   Wayne
Iona College
Jackson State U
Jacksonville State U
Jacksonville U
James Madison U
Kansas State U
Kennesaw State U
Kent State U
La Salle U
Lafayette College
Lamar U
Le Moyne College

Lehigh U
Liberty U
Lipscomb U
Long Beach State U
Long Island U-Brooklyn
  Campus
Longwood U
Louisiana State U
Louisiana Tech U
Loyola Marymount U
Manhattan College
Marist College
Marshall U
McNeese State U
Mercer U
Miami U (OH)
Michigan State U
Middle Tennessee State U
Mississippi State U
Mississippi Valley State U
Missouri State U
Monmouth U
Morehead State U
Mount St. Mary's U
Murray State U
New Jersey Institute of
  Technology
New Mexico State U
New York Institute of
  Technology
Niagara U
Nicholls State U
Norfolk State U
North Carolina A&T State U
North Carolina Central U
North Carolina State U
North Dakota State U
Northeastern U
Northern Illinois U
Northwestern State U
Northwestern U
Oakland U
Ohio U
Oklahoma State U
Old Dominion U
Oral Roberts U
Oregon State U
Pennsylvania State U

Pepperdine U
Prairie View A&M U
Presbyterian College
Princeton U
Purdue U
Quinnipiac U
Radford U
Rice U
Rider U
Rutgers, State Univ of New
  Jersey, New Brunswick
Sacred Heart U
Saint Joseph's U
Saint Louis U
Sam Houston State U
Samford U
San Diego State U
San Jose State U
Santa Clara U
Savannah State U
Seton Hall U
Siena College
South Dakota State U
Southeast Missouri State U
Southeastern Louisiana U
Southern Illinois U at
  Carbondale
Southern Illinois U
  Edwardsville
Southern U, Baton Rouge
Southern Utah U
St. Bonaventure U
St. John's U (NY)
St. Mary's College of
  California
St. Peter's College
Stanford U
State U of New York at
  Binghamton
Stephen F. Austin State U
Stetson U
Stony Brook U
Temple U
Tennessee Technological U
Texas A&M U, College
  Station
Texas A&M U-Corpus Christi
Texas Christian U

Texas Southern U
Texas State U-San Marcos
Texas Tech U
 The Ohio State U
Towson U
Troy U
Tulane U
U.S. Air Force Academy
U.S. Military Academy
U.S. Naval Academy
U at Albany
U at Buffalo, the State U
  of New
U of Akron
U of Alabama at
  Birmingham
U of Alabama, Tuscaloosa
U of Arizona
U of Arkansas, Fayetteville
U of Arkansas, Little Rock
U of Arkansas, Pine Bluff
U of California, Berkeley
U of California, Davis
U of California, Irvine
U of California, Los Angeles
U of California, Riverside
U of California, Santa
  Barbara
U of Central Arkansas
U of Central Florida
U of Cincinnati
U of Connecticut
U of Dayton
U of Delaware
U of Evansville
U of Florida
U of Georgia
U of Hartford
U of Hawaii at Hilo
U of Hawaii, Manoa
U of Houston
U of Illinois at Chicago
U of Illinois, Champaign
U of Iowa
U of Kansas
U of Kentucky
U of Louisiana at Lafayette
U of Louisiana at Monroe

U of Louisville
U of Maine, Orono
U of Maryland, Baltimore County
U of Maryland, College Park
U of Maryland, Eastern Shore
U of Massachusetts, Amherst
U of Memphis
U of Miami (FL)
U of Michigan
U of Minnesota, Twin Cities
U of Mississippi
U of Missouri, Columbia
U of Nebraska, Lincoln
U of Nevada
U of Nevada, Las Vegas
U of New Mexico
U of New Orleans
U of North Carolina at Greensboro
U of North Carolina, Asheville
U of North Carolina, Chapel Hill
U of North Carolina, Charlotte
U of North Carolina, Wilmington
U of North Dakota
U of North Florida
U of Northern Colorado
U of Northern Iowa
U of Notre Dame
U of Oklahoma
U of Oregon
U of Pennsylvania
U of Pittsburgh
U of Portland
U of Rhode Island
U of Richmond
U of San Diego
U of San Francisco
U of South Alabama
U of South Carolina Upstate
U of South Carolina, Columbia

U of South Florida
U of Southern California
U of Southern Mississippi
U of Tennessee at Martin
U of Tennessee, Knoxville
U of Texas at Arlington
U of Texas at Austin
U of Texas at San Antonio
U of Texas, Pan American
U of the Pacific
U of Toledo
U of Utah
U of Vermont
U of Virginia
U of Washington
U of Wisconsin, Milwaukee
Utah Valley U
Valparaiso U
Vanderbilt U
Villanova U
Virginia Commonwealth U
Virginia Military Institute
Virginia Polytechnic Institute & State U
Wagner College
Wake Forest U
Washington State U
West Virginia U
Western Carolina U
Western Illinois U
Western Kentucky U
Western Michigan U
Wichita State U
Winthrop U
Wofford College
Wright State U
Xavier U
Yale U
Youngstown State U

BASEBALL
DIVISION II

Abilene Christian U
Adelphi U
Albany State U (GA)
Alderson-Broaddus College

American International College
Anderson U (SC)
Angelo State U
Arkansas Tech U
Armstrong Atlantic State U
Ashland U
Assumption College
Augusta State U
Augustana College (SD)
Barry U
Barton College
Bellarmine U
Belmont Abbey College
Bemidji State U
Benedict College
Bentley College
Bloomfield College
Bloomsburg U of Pennsylvania
Bluefield State College
Brevard College
Bryant U
C.W. Post Campus/Long Island U
Caldwell College
California State Polytechnic U, Pomona
California State U, Chico
California State U, Dominguez Hills
California State U, Los Angeles
California State U, Monterey Bay
California State U, San Bernardino
California State U, Stanislaus
California U of Pennsylvania
Cameron U
Carson-Newman College
Catawba College
Central Washington U
Chestnut Hill College
Chowan U
Christian Brothers U

Claflin U
Clarion U of Pennsylvania
Clark Atlanta U
Coker College
College of Saint Rose
Colorado Christian U
Colorado School of Mines
Colorado State U-Pueblo
Columbia Union College
Columbus State U
Concord U
Concordia College (NY)
Concordia U, St. Paul
Davis and Elkins College
Delta State U
Dixie State College of Utah
Dominican College (NY)
Dowling College
Drury U
East Central U
East Stroudsburg U of
   Pennsylvania
Eastern New Mexico U
Eckerd College
Elizabeth City State U
Emporia State U
Erskine College
Fairmont State U
Felician College
Flagler College
Florida Gulf Coast U
Florida Institute of
   Technology
Florida Southern College
Fort Hays State U
Francis Marion U
Franklin Pierce U
Gannon U
The Georgia College &
   State U
Georgia Southwestern
   State U
Grand Canyon U
Grand Valley State U
Harding U
Hawaii Pacific U

Henderson State U
Hillsdale College
Indiana U of Pennsylvania
Kennesaw State U
Kentucky State U
Kentucky Wesleyan
   College
Kutztown U of
   Pennsylvania
Lander U
Lane College
LeMoyne-Owen College
Lenoir-Rhyne College
Lewis U
Limestone College
Lincoln Memorial U
Lincoln U (MO)
Lock Haven U of
   Pennsylvania
Lynn U
Mansfield U of
   Pennsylvania
Mars Hill College
Mercy College
Mercyhurst College
Merrimack College
Mesa State College
Metropolitan State College
   of Denver
Miles College
Millersville U of
   Pennsylvania
Minnesota State U,
   Mankato
Missouri Southern State U
Missouri U of Science and
   Technology
Missouri Western State U
Molloy College
Montana State U-Billings
Morehouse College
Mount Olive College
New Jersey Institute of
   Technology
New Mexico Highlands U
Newberry College

Newman U
North Carolina Central U
North Georgia College &
   State U
North Greenville U
Northeastern State U
Northern Kentucky U
Northern State U
Northwest Missouri State U
Northwest Nazarene U
Northwood U (MI)
Nova Southeastern U
Nyack College
Oakland City U
Ohio Valley U
Oklahoma Panhandle
   State U
Ouachita Baptist U
Pace U
Paine College
Palm Beach Atlantic U
Pfeiffer U
Philadelphia U
Pittsburg State U
Post U
Presbyterian College
Queens College (NY)
Quincy U
Regis U (CO)
Rockhurst U
Rollins College
Saginaw Valley State U
Saint Anselm College
Saint Joseph's College (IN)
Saint Leo U
Saint Michael's College
Salem International U
San Francisco State U
Seton Hill U
Shaw U
Shepherd U
Shippensburg U of
   Pennsylvania
Slippery Rock U of
   Pennsylvania
Sonoma State U

Southeastern Oklahoma
State U
Southern Arkansas U
Southern Connecticut
State U
Southern Illinois U
Edwardsville
Southern New Hampshire U
Southwest Baptist U
Southwest Minnesota
State U
Southwestern Oklahoma
State U
St. Andrews Presbyterian
College
St. Augustine's College
St. Cloud State U
St. Edward's U
St. Martin's U
St. Mary's U (TX)
St. Paul's College
St. Thomas Aquinas College
Stillman College
Stonehill College
Tarleton State U
Texas A&M International U
Texas A&M U-Kingsville
Tiffin U
Truman State U
Tusculum College
Tuskegee U
U of Alabama in Huntsville
U of Arkansas, Monticello
U of Bridgeport
U of California, San Diego
U of Central Arkansas
U of Central Missouri
U of Central Oklahoma
U of Charleston (WV)
U of Findlay
U of Hawaii at Hilo
U of Indianapolis
U of Mary
U of Massachusetts at
Lowell
U of Minnesota Duluth
U of Minnesota, Crookston

U of Missouri, St. Louis
U of Montevallo
U of Nebraska at Kearney
U of Nebraska at Omaha
U of New Haven
U of North Alabama
U of North Carolina at
Pembroke
U of North Dakota
U of North Florida
U of Pittsburgh, Johnstown
U of Puerto Rico, Cayey
U of Puerto Rico,
Mayaguez Campus
U of Puerto Rico, Rio Piedras
U of South Carolina Aiken
U of South Carolina Upstate
U of Southern Indiana
U of Tampa
U of Texas of the Permian
Basin
U of the Incarnate Word
U of the Sciences in
Philadelphia
U of West Alabama
U of West Florida
U of West Georgia
U of Wisconsin, Parkside
Upper Iowa U
Valdosta State U
Virginia State U
Washburn U of Topeka
Wayne State College (NE)
Wayne State U (MI)
West Chester U of
Pennsylvania
West Liberty State College
West Texas A&M U
West Virginia State U
West Virginia Wesleyan
College
Western Oregon U
Wheeling Jesuit U
Wilmington U (Delaware)
Wingate U
Winona State U

BASEBALL
DIVISION III

Adrian College
Albertus Magnus College
Albion College
Albright College
Allegheny College
Alma College
Alvernia U
Amherst College
Anderson U (IN)
Anna Maria College
Arcadia U
Augsburg College
Augustana College (IL)
Aurora U
Austin College
Averett U
Babson College
Baldwin-Wallace College
Baptist Bible College
Baruch College
Bates College
Becker College
Beloit College
Benedictine U (IL)
Bethany College (WV)
Bethany Lutheran College
Bethel U (MN)
Birmingham-Southern
College
Blackburn College
Bluffton U
Bowdoin College
Brandeis U
Bridgewater College (VA)
Bridgewater State College
Buena Vista U
California Institute of
Technology
California Lutheran U
California State U, East Bay
Calvin College
Capital U
Carleton College
Carroll U (WI)

Carthage College
Case Western Reserve U
Castleton State College
Catholic U
Cazenovia College
Centenary College (NJ)
Central College (IA)
Centre College
Chapman U
Christopher Newport U
The City College of New
    York
Claremont McKenna-
    Harvey Mudd-Scripps
    Colleges
Clark U (MA)
Clarkson U
Coe College
Colby College
Colby-Sawyer College
College of Brockport, State
    U of New York
College of Mount St. Joseph
College of Mount St.
    Vincent
The College of New Jersey
The College of St.
    Scholastica
College of Staten Island
College of Wooster
Concordia College,
    Moorhead
Concordia U (WI)
Concordia U Chicago
Concordia U Texas
Cornell College
Crown College (MN)
Curry College
Daniel Webster College
Defiance College
Delaware Valley College
Denison U
DePauw U
DeSales U
Dickinson College
Dominican U (IL)
Drew U

D'Youville College
Earlham College
East Texas Baptist U
Eastern Connecticut State U
Eastern Mennonite U
Eastern Nazarene College
Eastern U
Edgewood College
Elizabethtown College
Elmhurst College
Elms College
Emerson College
Emory and Henry College
Emory U
Endicott College
Eureka College
Fairleigh Dickinson U,
    Florham
Ferrum College
Finlandia U
Fitchburg State College
Fontbonne U
Framingham State College
Franciscan U of Steubenville
Franklin & Marshall College
Franklin College
Frostburg State U
Gallaudet U
Geneva College
George Fox U
Gettysburg College
Gordon College
Greensboro College
Greenville College
Grinnell College
Grove City College
Guilford College
Gustavus Adolphus College
Gwynedd-Mercy College
Hamilton College
Hamline U
Hampden-Sydney College
Hanover College
Hardin-Simmons U
Haverford College
Heidelberg College
Hendrix College

Hilbert College
Hiram College
Hope College
Howard Payne U
Huntingdon College
Husson College
Illinois College
Illinois Wesleyan U
Ithaca College
John Carroll U
John Jay College of
    Criminal Justice
Johns Hopkins U
Johnson and Wales U
Juniata College
Kalamazoo College
Kean U
Keene State College
Kenyon College
Keuka College
Keystone College
King's College (PA)
Knox College
La Grange College
La Roche College
La Sierra U
Lake Erie College
Lakeland College
Lancaster Bible College
Lasell College
Lawrence U
Lebanon Valley College
Lehman College, City U of
    New York
LeTourneau U
Lewis & Clark College
Lincoln U (PA)
Linfield College
Loras College
Louisiana College
Luther College
Lynchburg College
Lyndon State College
Macalester College
MacMurray College
Manchester College
Manhattanville College

Maranatha Baptist Bible
College
Marian U (WI)
Marietta College
Martin Luther College
Maryville College (TN)
Maryville U of Saint Louis
Marywood U
Massachusetts College of
Liberal Arts
Massachusetts Institute of
Technology
Massachusetts Maritime
Academy
McDaniel College
McMurry U
Medaille College
Menlo College
Messiah College
Methodist U
Middlebury College
Millikin U
Millsaps College
Milwaukee School of
Engineering
Misericordia U
Mississippi College
Mitchell College
Monmouth College (IL)
Montclair State U
Moravian College
Mount Aloysius College
Mount Saint Mary College
(NY)
Mount Union College
Muhlenberg College
Muskingum College
Nebraska Wesleyan U
Neumann College
New England College
New Jersey City U
Newbury College
Nichols College
North Carolina Wesleyan
College
North Central College
North Central U

North Park U
Northland College
Northwestern College
Norwich U
Oberlin College
Occidental College
Oglethorpe U
Ohio Northern U
Ohio Wesleyan U
Olivet College
Otterbein College
Pacific Lutheran U
Pacific U (OR)
Penn State Berks College
Penn State Harrisburg
Penn State U, Altoona
Pennsylvania State Univ.
Erie, the Behrend College
Philadelphia Biblical U
Piedmont College
Plattsburgh State U of
New York
Plymouth State U
Polytechnic Institute of
New York U
Pomona-Pitzer Colleges
Presentation College
Principia College
Purchase College, State U
of New York
Ramapo College
Randolph-Macon College
Rensselaer Polytechnic
Institute
Rhode Island College
Rhodes College
Richard Stockton College
of New Jersey
Ripon College
Rivier College
Roanoke College
Rochester Institute of
Technology
Rockford College
Roger Williams U
Rose-Hulman Institute of
Technology

Rowan U
Rust College
Rutgers, The State Univ. of
New Jersey, Camden
Rutgers, The State Univ. of
New Jersey, Newark
Saint Joseph's College (ME)
Saint Mary's U of Minnesota
Saint Vincent College
Salem State College
Salisbury U
Salve Regina U
Schreiner U
Shenandoah U
Simpson College
Skidmore College
Southern Vermont College
Southwestern U (TX)
Spalding U
Springfield College
St. John Fisher College
St. John's U (MN)
St. Joseph's College (Long
Island)
St. Joseph's College, New
York
St. Lawrence U
St. Mary's College of
Maryland
St. Norbert College
St. Olaf College
State U College at Cortland
State U College at Fredonia
State U College at New Paltz
State U College at Old
Westbury
State U College at Oneonta
State U of New York at
Cobleskill
State U of New York at
Farmingdale
State U of New York at
Oswego
State U of New York
Institute of Technolo
State U of New York
Maritime College

Stevens Institute of
Technology
Stevenson U
Suffolk U
Sul Ross State U
Susquehanna U
Swarthmore College
Texas Lutheran U
Thiel College
Thomas College
Thomas More College
Transylvania U
Trine U
Trinity College (CT)
Trinity U (TX)
Tufts U
U.S. Coast Guard Academy
U.S. Merchant Marine
Academy
Union College (NY)
U of Chicago
U of Dallas
U of Dubuque
U of La Verne
U of Maine at Presque Isle
U of Maine, Farmington
U of Mary Hardin-Baylor
U of Mary Washington
U of Massachusetts, Boston
U of Massachusetts,
Dartmouth
U of Minnesota, Morris
U of Pittsburgh, Bradford
U of Pittsburgh, Greensburg
U of Puget Sound
U of Redlands
U of Rochester
U of Scranton
U of Southern Maine
U of St. Thomas (MN)
U of Texas at Dallas
U of Texas at Tyler
U of the Ozarks (AR)
U of the South
U of Wisconsin, La Crosse
U of Wisconsin, Oshkosh
U of Wisconsin, Platteville

U of Wisconsin, Stevens
Point
U of Wisconsin, Stout
U of Wisconsin, Superior
U of Wisconsin, Whitewater
Ursinus College
Utica College
Vassar College
Virginia Wesleyan College
Wabash College
Wartburg College
Washington and Jefferson
College
Washington and Lee U
Washington College (MD)
Washington U (MO)
Waynesburg U
Webster U
Wentworth Institute of
Technology
Wesley College
Wesleyan U (CT)
Western Connecticut
State U
Western New England
College
Westfield State College
Westminster College (MO)
Westminster College (PA)
Wheaton College (IL)
Wheaton College (MA)
Whitman College
Whittier College
Whitworth U
Widener U
Wilkes U
Willamette U
William Paterson U of New
Jersey
Williams College
Wilmington College (OH)
Wisconsin Lutheran
College
Wittenberg U
Worcester Polytechnic
Institute
Worcester State College

Yeshiva U
York College (PA)

BASKETBALL
DIVISION I

Alabama A&M U
Alabama State U
Alcorn State U
American U
Appalachian State U
Arizona State U
Arkansas State U
Auburn U
Austin Peay State U
Ball State U
Baylor U
Belmont U
Bethune-Cookman U
Boise State U
Boston College
Boston U
Bowling Green State U
Bradley U
Brigham Young U
Brown U
Bryant U
Bucknell U
Butler U
California Polytechnic
State U
California State U,
Bakersfield
California State U, Fresno
California State U, Fullerton
California State U,
Northridge
California State U,
Sacramento
Campbell U
Canisius College
Centenary College (LA)
Central Connecticut State U
Central Michigan U
Charleston Southern U
Chicago State U
The Citadel

Clemson U
Cleveland State U
Coastal Carolina U
Colgate U
College of Charleston (SC)
College of the Holy Cross
College of William and Mary
Colorado State U
Columbia U-Barnard College
Coppin State U
Cornell U
Creighton U
Dartmouth College
Davidson College
Delaware State U
DePaul U
Drake U
Drexel U
Duke U
Duquesne U
East Carolina U
East Tennessee State U
Eastern Illinois U
Eastern Kentucky U
Eastern Michigan U
Eastern Washington U
Elon U
Fairfield U
Fairleigh Dickinson U,
    Metropolitan
Florida A&M U
Florida Atlantic U
Florida Gulf Coast U
Florida International U
Florida State U
Fordham U
Furman U
Gardner-Webb U
George Mason U
George Washington U
Georgetown U
Georgia Institute of
    Technology
Georgia Southern U
Georgia State U
Gonzaga U
Grambling State U

Hampton U
Harvard U
High Point U
Hofstra U
Houston Baptist U
Howard U
Idaho State U
Illinois State U
Indiana State U
Indiana U, Bloomington
Indiana U-Purdue U at
    Indianapolis
Indiana U-Purdue U, Fort
    Wayne
Iona College
Iowa State U
Jackson State U
Jacksonville State U
Jacksonville U
James Madison U
Kansas State U
Kennesaw State U
Kent State U
La Salle U
Lafayette College
Lamar U
Lehigh U
Liberty U
Lipscomb U
Long Beach State U
Long Island U-Brooklyn
    Campus
Longwood U
Louisiana State U
Louisiana Tech U
Loyola Marymount U
Loyola U (IL)
Loyola U (MD)
Manhattan College
Marist College
Marquette U
Marshall U
McNeese State U
Mercer U
Miami U (OH)
Michigan State U
Middle Tennessee State U

Mississippi State U
Mississippi Valley State U
Missouri State U
Monmouth U
Montana State U-Bozeman
Morehead State U
Morgan State U
Mount St. Mary's U
Murray State U
New Jersey Institute of
    Technology
New Mexico State U
Niagara U
Nicholls State U
Norfolk State U
North Carolina A&T State U
North Carolina Central U
North Carolina State U
North Dakota State U
Northeastern U
Northern Arizona U
Northern Illinois U
Northwestern State U
Northwestern U
Oakland U
The Ohio State U
Ohio U
Oklahoma State U
Old Dominion U
Oral Roberts U
Oregon State U
Pennsylvania State U
Pepperdine U
Portland State U
Prairie View A&M U
Presbyterian College
Princeton U
Providence College
Purdue U
Quinnipiac U
Radford U
Rice U
Rider U
Robert Morris U
Rutgers, State Univ of New
    Jersey, New Brunswick
Sacred Heart U

Saint Francis U (PA)
Saint Joseph's U
Saint Louis U
Sam Houston State U
Samford U
San Diego State U
San Jose State U
Santa Clara U
Savannah State U
Seattle U
Seton Hall U
Siena College
South Carolina State U
South Dakota State U
Southeast Missouri State U
Southeastern Louisiana U
Southern Illinois U at
  Carbondale
Southern Illinois U
  Edwardsville
Southern Methodist U
Southern U, Baton Rouge
Southern Utah U
St. Bonaventure U
St. Francis College (NY)
St. John's U (NY)
St. Mary's College of
  California
St. Peter's College
Stanford U
State U of New York at
  Binghamton
Stephen F. Austin State U
Stetson U
Stony Brook U
Syracuse U
Temple U
Tennessee State U
Tennessee Technological U
Texas A&M U, College
  Station
Texas A&M U-Corpus Christi
Texas Christian U
Texas Southern U
Texas State U-San Marcos
Texas Tech U
Towson U
Troy U

Tulane U
U.S. Air Force Academy
U.S. Military Academy
U.S. Naval Academy
U at Albany
U at Buffalo, the State U
  of New
U of Akron
U of Alabama at
  Birmingham
U of Alabama, Tuscaloosa
U of Arizona
U of Arkansas, Fayetteville
U of Arkansas, Little Rock
U of Arkansas, Pine Bluff
U of California, Berkeley
U of California, Davis
U of California, Irvine
U of California, Los
  Angeles
U of California, Riverside
U of California, Santa
  Barbara
U of Central Arkansas
U of Central Florida
U of Cincinnati
U of Colorado, Boulder
U of Connecticut
U of Dayton
U of Delaware
U of Denver
U of Detroit Mercy
U of Evansville
U of Florida
U of Georgia
U of Hartford
U of Hawaii, Manoa
U of Houston
U of Idaho
U of Illinois at Chicago
U of Illinois, Champaign
U of Iowa
U of Kansas
U of Kentucky
U of Louisiana at Lafayette
U of Louisiana at Monroe
U of Louisville
U of Maine, Orono

U of Maryland, Baltimore
  County
U of Maryland, College Park
U of Maryland, Eastern
  Shore
U of Massachusetts,
  Amherst
U of Memphis
U of Miami (FL)
U of Michigan
U of Minnesota, Twin Cities
U of Mississippi
U of Missouri, Columbia
U of Missouri, Kansas City
U of Montana
U of Nebraska, Lincoln
U of Nevada
U of Nevada, Las Vegas
U of New Hampshire
U of New Mexico
U of New Orleans
U of North Carolina at
  Greensboro
U of North Carolina,
  Asheville
U of North Carolina,
  Chapel Hill
U of North Carolina,
  Charlotte
U of North Carolina,
  Wilmington
U of North Dakota
U of North Florida
U of North Texas
U of Northern Colorado
U of Northern Iowa
U of Notre Dame
U of Oklahoma
U of Oregon
U of Pennsylvania
U of Pittsburgh
U of Portland
U of Rhode Island
U of Richmond
U of San Diego
U of San Francisco
U of South Alabama
U of South Carolina Upstate

U of South Carolina, Columbia
U of South Dakota
U of South Florida
U of Southern California
U of Southern Mississippi
U of Tennessee at Chattanooga
U of Tennessee at Martin
U of Tennessee, Knoxville
U of Texas at Arlington
U of Texas at Austin
U of Texas at El Paso
U of Texas at San Antonio
U of Texas, Pan American
U of the Pacific
U of Toledo
U of Tulsa
U of Utah
U of Vermont
U of Virginia
U of Washington
U of Wisconsin, Green Bay
U of Wisconsin, Madison
U of Wisconsin, Milwaukee
U of Wyoming
Utah State U
Utah Valley U
Valparaiso U
Vanderbilt U
Villanova U
Virginia Commonwealth U
Virginia Military Institute
Virginia Polytechnic Institute & State U
Wagner College
Wake Forest U
Washington State U
Weber State U
West Virginia U
Western Carolina U
Western Illinois U
Western Kentucky U
Western Michigan U
Wichita State U
Winston-Salem State U
Winthrop U
Wofford College

Wright State U
Xavier U
Yale U
Youngstown State U

BASKETBALL
DIVISION II

Abilene Christian U
Adams State College
Adelphi U
Albany State U (GA)
Alderson-Broaddus College
American International College
Anderson U (SC)
Angelo State U
Arkansas Tech U
Armstrong Atlantic State U
Ashland U
Assumption College
Augusta State U
Augustana College (SD)
Barry U
Barton College
Bellarmine U
Belmont Abbey College
Bemidji State U
Benedict College
Bentley College
Bloomfield College
Bloomsburg U of Pennsylvania
Bluefield State College
Bowie State U
Brevard College
Brigham Young U, Hawaii
Bryant U
C.W. Post Campus/Long Island U
Caldwell College
California State Polytechnic U, Pomona
California State U, Bakersfield
California State U, Chico
California State U, Dominguez Hills

California State U, Los Angeles
California State U, Monterey Bay
California State U, San Bernardino
California State U, Stanislaus
California U of Pennsylvania
Cameron U
Carson-Newman College
Catawba College
Central State U
Central Washington U
Chadron State College
Chaminade U
Chestnut Hill College
Cheyney U of Pennsylvania
Chowan U
Christian Brothers U
Claflin U
Clarion U of Pennsylvania
Clark Atlanta U
Clayton State U
Coker College
College of Saint Rose
Colorado Christian U
Colorado School of Mines
Colorado State U-Pueblo
Columbia Union College
Columbus State U
Concord U
Concordia College (NY)
Concordia U, St. Paul
Dallas Baptist U
Davis and Elkins College
Delta State U
Dixie State College of Utah
Dominican College (NY)
Dowling College
Drury U
East Central U
East Stroudsburg U of Pennsylvania
Eastern New Mexico U
Eckerd College
Edinboro U of Pennsylvania
Elizabeth City State U

Emporia State U
Erskine College
Fairmont State U
Fayetteville State U
Felician College
Ferris State U
Flagler College
Florida Gulf Coast U
Florida Institute of
Technology
Florida Southern College
Fort Hays State U
Fort Lewis College
Fort Valley State U
Francis Marion U
Franklin Pierce U
Gannon U
The Georgia College &
State U
Georgia Southwestern
State U
Glenville State College
Goldey-Beacom College
Grand Canyon U
Grand Valley State U
Harding U
Hawaii Pacific U
Henderson State U
Hillsdale College
Holy Family U
Humboldt State U
Indiana U of Pennsylvania
Johnson C. Smith U
Kennesaw State U
Kentucky State U
Kentucky Wesleyan College
Kutztown U of
Pennsylvania
Lake Superior State U
Lander U
Lane College
Le Moyne College
Lees-McRae College
LeMoyne-Owen College
Lenoir-Rhyne College
Lewis U
Limestone College
Lincoln Memorial U

Lincoln U (MO)
Livingstone College
Lock Haven U of
Pennsylvania
Lynn U
Mansfield U of
Pennsylvania
Mars Hill College
Mercy College
Mercyhurst College
Merrimack College
Mesa State College
Metropolitan State College
of Denver
Michigan Technological U
Midwestern State U
Miles College
Millersville U of
Pennsylvania
Minnesota State U
Moorhead
Minnesota State U, Mankato
Missouri Southern State U
Missouri U of Science and
Technology
Missouri Western State U
Molloy College
Montana State U-Billings
Morehouse College
Mount Olive College
New Jersey Institute of
Technology
New Mexico Highlands U
New York Institute of
Technology
Newberry College
Newman U
North Carolina Central U
North Georgia College &
State U
North Greenville U
Northeastern State U
Northern Kentucky U
Northern Michigan U
Northern State U
Northwest Missouri State U
Northwest Nazarene U
Northwood U (MI)

Notre Dame de Namur U
Nova Southeastern U
Nyack College
Oakland City U
Ohio Valley U
Oklahoma Panhandle
State U
Ouachita Baptist U
Pace U
Paine College
Palm Beach Atlantic U
Pfeiffer U
Philadelphia U
Pittsburg State U
Post U
Presbyterian College
Queens College (NY)
Queens U of Charlotte
Quincy U
Regis U (CO)
Rockhurst U
Rollins College
Saginaw Valley State U
Saint Anselm College
Saint Joseph's College (IN)
Saint Leo U
Saint Michael's College
Salem International U
San Francisco State U
Seattle Pacific U
Seattle U
Seton Hill U
Shaw U
Shepherd U
Shippensburg U of
Pennsylvania
Slippery Rock U of
Pennsylvania
Sonoma State U
Southeastern Oklahoma
State U
Southern Arkansas U
Southern Connecticut
State U
Southern Illinois U
Edwardsville
Southern New Hampshire U
Southwest Baptist U

Southwest Minnesota
State U
Southwestern Oklahoma
State U
St. Andrews Presbyterian
College
St. Augustine's College
St. Cloud State U
St. Edward's U
St. Martin's U
St. Mary's U (TX)
St. Paul's College
St. Thomas Aquinas College
Stillman College
Stonehill College
Tarleton State U
Texas A&M International U
Texas A&M U-Commerce
Texas A&M U-Kingsville
Tiffin U
Truman State U
Tusculum College
Tuskegee U
U of Alabama in Huntsville
U of Alaska Anchorage
U of Alaska Fairbanks
U of Arkansas, Monticello
U of Bridgeport
U of California, San Diego
U of Central Arkansas
U of Central Missouri
U of Central Oklahoma
U of Charleston (WV)
U of Colorado, Colorado
Springs
U of Findlay
U of Hawaii at Hilo
U of Indianapolis
U of Mary
U of Massachusetts at
Lowell
U of Minnesota Duluth
U of Minnesota, Crookston
U of Missouri, St. Louis
U of Montevallo
U of Nebraska at Kearney
U of Nebraska at Omaha
U of New Haven

U of North Alabama
U of North Carolina at
Pembroke
U of North Dakota
U of North Florida
U of Pittsburgh, Johnstown
U of Puerto Rico, Bayamon
U of Puerto Rico, Cayey
U of Puerto Rico,
Mayaguez Campus
U of Puerto Rico, Rio Piedras
U of South Carolina Aiken
U of South Carolina Upstate
U of South Dakota
U of Southern Indiana
U of Tampa
U of Texas of the Permian
Basin
U of the District of Columbia
U of the Incarnate Word
U of the Sciences in
Philadelphia
U of West Alabama
U of West Florida
U of West Georgia
U of Wisconsin, Parkside
Upper Iowa U
Valdosta State U
Virginia State U
Virginia Union U
Washburn U of Topeka
Wayne State College (NE)
Wayne State U (MI)
West Chester U of
Pennsylvania
West Liberty State College
West Texas A&M U
West Virginia State U
West Virginia Wesleyan
College
Western New Mexico U
Western Oregon U
Western State College of
Colorado
Western Washington U
Wheeling Jesuit U
Wilmington U (Delaware)
Wingate U

Winona State U
Winston-Salem State U

BASKETBALL
DIVISION III

Adrian College
Albertus Magnus College
Albion College
Albright College
Alfred U
Allegheny College
Alma College
Alvernia U
Amherst College
Anderson U (IN)
Anna Maria College
Arcadia U
Augsburg College
Augustana College (IL)
Aurora U
Austin College
Averett U
Babson College
Baldwin-Wallace College
Baptist Bible College
Bard College
Baruch College
Bates College
Becker College
Beloit College
Benedictine U (IL)
Bethany College (WV)
Bethany Lutheran College
Bethel U (MN)
Birmingham-Southern
College
Blackburn College
Bluffton U
Bowdoin College
Brandeis U
Bridgewater College (VA)
Bridgewater State College
Brooklyn College
Buena Vista U
Buffalo State College
Cabrini College

California Institute of
   Technology
California Lutheran U
California State U, East Bay
Calvin College
Capital U
Carleton College
Carnegie Mellon U
Carroll U (WI)
Carthage College
Case Western Reserve U
Castleton State College
Catholic U
Cazenovia College
Centenary College (NJ)
Central College (IA)
Centre College
Chapman U
Christopher Newport U
The City College of New
   York
Claremont McKenna-
   Harvey Mudd-Scripps
   Colleges
Clark U (MA)
Clarkson U
Coe College
Colby College
Colby-Sawyer College
College of Brockport, State
   U of New York
College of Mount St. Joseph
College of Mount St.
   Vincent
The College of New Jersey
The College of St. Scholastica
College of Staten Island
College of Wooster
Colorado College
Concordia College,
   Moorhead
Concordia U (WI)
Concordia U Chicago
Concordia U Texas
Connecticut College
Cornell College
Crown College (MN)
Curry College

Daniel Webster College
Defiance College
Delaware Valley College
Denison U
DePauw U
DeSales U
Dickinson College
Dominican U (IL)
Drew U
D'Youville College
Earlham College
East Texas Baptist U
Eastern Connecticut State U
Eastern Mennonite U
Eastern Nazarene College
Eastern U
Edgewood College
Elizabethtown College
Elmhurst College
Elmira College
Elms College
Emerson College
Emmanuel College (MA)
Emory and Henry College
Emory U
Endicott College
Eureka College
Fairleigh Dickinson U,
   Florham
Ferrum College
Finlandia U
Fitchburg State College
Fontbonne U
Framingham State College
Franciscan U of
   Steubenville
Franklin & Marshall College
Franklin College
Frostburg State U
Gallaudet U
Geneva College
George Fox U
Gettysburg College
Gordon College
Goucher College
Green Mountain College
Greensboro College
Greenville College

Grinnell College
Grove City College
Guilford College
Gustavus Adolphus College
Gwynedd-Mercy College
Hamilton College
Hamline U
Hampden-Sydney College
Hanover College
Hardin-Simmons U
Hartwick College
Haverford College
Heidelberg College
Hendrix College
Hilbert College
Hiram College
Hobart College
Hood College
Hope College
Howard Payne U
Hunter College
Huntingdon College
Husson College
Illinois College
Illinois Wesleyan U
Immaculata U
Ithaca College
John Carroll U
John Jay College of
   Criminal Justice
Johns Hopkins U
Johnson and Wales U
Johnson State College
Juniata College
Kalamazoo College
Kean U
Keene State College
Kenyon College
Keuka College
Keystone College
King's College (PA)
Knox College
La Grange College
La Roche College
La Sierra U
Lake Erie College
Lake Forest College
Lakeland College

Lancaster Bible College
Lasell College
Lawrence U
Lebanon Valley College
Lehman College, City U of
New York
Lesley U
LeTourneau U
Lewis & Clark College
Lincoln U (PA)
Linfield College
Loras College
Louisiana College
Luther College
Lycoming College
Lynchburg College
Lyndon State College
Macalester College
MacMurray College
Maine Maritime Academy
Manchester College
Manhattanville College
Maranatha Baptist Bible
College
Marian U (WI)
Marietta College
Martin Luther College
Marymount U (VA)
Maryville College (TN)
Maryville U of Saint Louis
Marywood U
Massachusetts College of
Liberal Arts
Massachusetts Institute of
Technology
McDaniel College
McMurry U
Medaille College
Medgar Evers College
Menlo College
Messiah College
Methodist U
Middlebury College
Millikin U
Millsaps College
Milwaukee School of
Engineering
Misericordia U

Mississippi College
Mitchell College
Monmouth College (IL)
Montclair State U
Moravian College
Mount Aloysius College
Mount Ida College
Mount Saint Mary College
(NY)
Mount Union College
Muhlenberg College
Muskingum College
Nazareth College
Nebraska Wesleyan U
Neumann College
New England College
New Jersey City U
New York City College of
Technology
New York U
Newbury College
Nichols College
North Carolina Wesleyan
College
North Central College
North Central U
North Park U
Northland College
Northwestern College
Norwich U
Oberlin College
Occidental College
Oglethorpe U
Ohio Northern U
Ohio Wesleyan U
Olivet College
Otterbein College
Pacific Lutheran U
Pacific U (OR)
Penn State Berks College
Penn State Harrisburg
Penn State U, Altoona
Pennsylvania State Univ.
Erie, the Behrend College
Philadelphia Biblical U
Piedmont College
Plattsburgh State U of
New York

Plymouth State U
Polytechnic Institute of
New York U
Pomona-Pitzer Colleges
Presentation College
Principia College
Purchase College, State U
of New York
Ramapo College
Randolph College
Randolph-Macon College
Regis College (MA)
Rensselaer Polytechnic
Institute
Rhode Island College
Rhodes College
Richard Stockton College
of New Jersey
Ripon College
Rivier College
Roanoke College
Rochester Institute of
Technology
Rockford College
Roger Williams U
Rose-Hulman Institute of
Technology
Rowan U
Rust College
Rutgers, The State Univ. of
New Jersey, Camden
Rutgers, The State Univ. of
New Jersey, Newark
Saint Joseph's College (ME)
Saint Mary's U of
Minnesota
Saint Vincent College
Salem State College
Salisbury U
Salve Regina U
Schreiner U
Shenandoah U
Simpson College
Skidmore College
Southern Vermont College
Southwestern U (TX)
Spalding U
Springfield College

St. John Fisher College
St. John's U (MN)
St. Joseph's College (Long Island)
St. Joseph's College, New York
St. Lawrence U
St. Mary's College of Maryland
St. Norbert College
St. Olaf College
State U College at Cortland
State U College at Fredonia
State U College at Geneseo
State U College at New Paltz
State U College at Old Westbury
State U College at Oneonta
State U of New York at Cobleskill
State U of New York at Farmingdale
State U of New York at Morrisville
State U of New York at Oswego
State U of New York at Potsdam
State U of New York Institute of Technolo
State U of New York Maritime College
Stevens Institute of Technology
Stevenson U
Suffolk U
Sul Ross State U
Susquehanna U
Swarthmore College
Texas Lutheran U
Thiel College
Thomas College
Thomas More College
Transylvania U
Trine U
Trinity College (CT)
Trinity U (TX)
Tufts U

U.S. Coast Guard Academy
U.S. Merchant Marine Academy
Union College (NY)
U of California, Santa Cruz
U of Chicago
U of Dallas
U of Dubuque
U of La Verne
U of Maine at Presque Isle
U of Maine, Farmington
U of Mary Hardin-Baylor
U of Mary Washington
U of Massachusetts, Boston
U of Massachusetts, Dartmouth
U of Minnesota, Morris
U of New England
U of Pittsburgh, Bradford
U of Pittsburgh, Greensburg
U of Puget Sound
U of Redlands
U of Rochester
U of Scranton
U of Southern Maine
U of St. Thomas (MN)
U of Texas at Dallas
U of Texas at Tyler
U of the Ozarks (AR)
U of the South
U of Wisconsin, Eau Claire
U of Wisconsin, La Crosse
U of Wisconsin, Oshkosh
U of Wisconsin, Platteville
U of Wisconsin, River Falls
U of Wisconsin, Stevens Point
U of Wisconsin, Stout
U of Wisconsin, Superior
U of Wisconsin, Whitewater
Ursinus College
Utica College
Vassar College
Virginia Wesleyan College
Wabash College
Wartburg College
Washington and Jefferson College

Washington and Lee U
Washington College (MD)
Washington U (MO)
Waynesburg U
Webster U
Wells College
Wentworth Institute of Technology
Wesley College
Wesleyan U (CT)
Western Connecticut State U
Western New England College
Westfield State College
Westminster College (MO)
Westminster College (PA)
Wheaton College (IL)
Wheaton College (MA)
Wheelock College
Whitman College
Whittier College
Whitworth U
Widener U
Wilkes U
Willamette U
William Paterson U of New Jersey
Williams College
Wilmington College (OH)
Wisconsin Lutheran College
Wittenberg U
Worcester Polytechnic Institute
Worcester State College
Yeshiva U
York College (NY)
York College (PA)

CROSS-COUNTRY
DIVISION I

Alabama State U
Alcorn State U
American U
Appalachian State U

Arizona State U
Arkansas State U
Auburn U
Austin Peay State U
Baylor U
Belmont U
Bethune-Cookman U
Birmingham-Southern
    College
Boise State U
Boston College
Boston U
Bowling Green State U
Bradley U
Brigham Young U
Brown U
Bryant U
Bucknell U
Butler U
California Polytechnic
    State U
California State U, Fresno
California State U,
    Fullerton
California State U,
    Northridge
California State U,
    Sacramento
Campbell U
Canisius College
Centenary College (LA)
Central Connecticut State U
Central Michigan U
Charleston Southern U
Chicago State U
The Citadel
Clemson U
Coastal Carolina U
Colgate U
College of Charleston (SC)
College of the Holy Cross
College of William and Mary
Colorado State U
Columbia U-Barnard
    College
Coppin State U
Cornell U
Creighton U

Dartmouth College
Davidson College
Delaware State U
DePaul U
Drake U
Duke U
Duquesne U
East Carolina U
East Tennessee State U
Eastern Illinois U
Eastern Kentucky U
Eastern Michigan U
Eastern Washington U
Elon U
Fairfield U
Fairleigh Dickinson U,
    Metropolitan
Florida A&M U
Florida Atlantic U
Florida Gulf Coast U
Florida International U
Florida State U
Fordham U
Furman U
Gardner-Webb U
George Mason U
George Washington U
Georgetown U
Georgia Institute of
    Technology
Georgia State U
Gonzaga U
Grambling State U
Hampton U
Harvard U
High Point U
Hofstra U
Howard U
Idaho State U
Illinois State U
Indiana State U
Indiana U, Bloomington
Indiana U-Purdue U at
    Indianapolis
Indiana U-Purdue U, Fort
    Wayne
Iona College
Iowa State U

Jackson State U
Jacksonville State U
Jacksonville U
Kansas State U
Kennesaw State U
Kent State U
La Salle U
Lafayette College
Lamar U
Lehigh U
Liberty U
Lipscomb U
Long Beach State U
Long Island U-Brooklyn
    Campus
Longwood U
Louisiana State U
Louisiana Tech U
Loyola Marymount U
Loyola U (IL)
Loyola U (MD)
Manhattan College
Marist College
Marquette U
Marshall U
McNeese State U
Mercer U
Miami U (OH)
Michigan State U
Middle Tennessee State U
Mississippi State U
Mississippi Valley State U
Monmouth U
Montana State U-Bozeman
Morehead State U
Morgan State U
Mount St. Mary's U
Murray State U
New Jersey Institute of
    Technology
New Mexico State U
Niagara U
Nicholls State U
Norfolk State U
North Carolina A&T State U
North Carolina Central U
North Carolina State U
North Dakota State U

Northeastern U
Northern Arizona U
Northwestern State U
Oakland U
Ohio U
Oklahoma State U
The Ohio State U
Oral Roberts U
Pennsylvania State U
Pepperdine U
Portland State U
Prairie View A&M U
Presbyterian College
Princeton U
Providence College
Purdue U
Quinnipiac U
Radford U
Rice U
Rider U
Robert Morris U
Rutgers, State Univ of New
  Jersey, New Brunswick
Sacred Heart U
Saint Francis U (PA)
Saint Joseph's U
Saint Louis U
Sam Houston State U
Samford U
San Jose State U
Santa Clara U
Savannah State U
Seattle U
Seton Hall U
Siena College
South Carolina State U
South Dakota State U
Southeast Missouri State U
Southeastern Louisiana U
Southern Illinois U at
  Carbondale
Southern Illinois U
  Edwardsville
Southern U, Baton Rouge
Southern Utah U
St. Bonaventure U
St. Francis College (NY)

St. Mary's College of
  California
St. Peter's College
Stanford U
State U of New York at
  Binghamton
Stephen F. Austin State U
Stetson U
Stony Brook U
Syracuse U
Temple U
Tennessee State U
Tennessee Technological U
Texas A&M U, College
  Station
Texas A&M U-Corpus Christi
Texas Christian U
Texas State U-San Marcos
Texas Tech U
Troy U
Tulane U
U.S. Air Force Academy
U.S. Military Academy
U.S. Naval Academy
U at Albany
U at Buffalo, the State U
  of New
U of Akron
U of Alabama, Tuscaloosa
U of Arizona
U of Arkansas, Fayetteville
U of Arkansas, Little Rock
U of California, Berkeley
U of California, Davis
U of California, Irvine
U of California, Los Angeles
U of California, Riverside
U of California, Santa
  Barbara
U of Central Arkansas
U of Cincinnati
U of Colorado, Boulder
U of Connecticut
U of Dayton
U of Delaware
U of Detroit Mercy
U of Evansville

U of Florida
U of Georgia
U of Hartford
U of Houston
U of Idaho
U of Illinois at Chicago
U of Illinois, Champaign
U of Iowa
U of Kansas
U of Kentucky
U of Louisiana at Lafayette
U of Louisiana at Monroe
U of Louisville
U of Maine, Orono
U of Maryland, Baltimore
  County
U of Maryland, College Park
U of Maryland, Eastern
  Shore
U of Massachusetts,
  Amherst
U of Memphis
U of Miami (FL)
U of Michigan
U of Minnesota, Twin Cities
U of Mississippi
U of Missouri, Columbia
U of Missouri, Kansas City
U of Montana
U of Nebraska, Lincoln
U of New Hampshire
U of New Mexico
U of North Carolina at
  Greensboro
U of North Carolina,
  Asheville
U of North Carolina,
  Chapel Hill
U of North Carolina,
  Charlotte
U of North Carolina,
  Wilmington
U of North Dakota
U of North Florida
U of North Texas
U of Northern Colorado
U of Northern Iowa

U of Notre Dame
U of Oklahoma
U of Oregon
U of Pennsylvania
U of Pittsburgh
U of Portland
U of Rhode Island
U of Richmond
U of San Diego
U of San Francisco
U of South Alabama
U of South Carolina Upstate
U of South Dakota
U of South Florida
U of Tennessee at
Chattanooga
U of Tennessee at Martin
U of Tennessee, Knoxville
U of Texas at Arlington
U of Texas at Austin
U of Texas at El Paso
U of Texas at San Antonio
U of Texas, Pan American
U of Toledo
U of Tulsa
U of Vermont
U of Virginia
U of Washington
U of Wisconsin, Green Bay
U of Wisconsin, Madison
U of Wisconsin, Milwaukee
U of Wyoming
Utah State U
Utah Valley U
Valparaiso U
Vanderbilt U
Villanova U
Virginia Commonwealth U
Virginia Military Institute
Virginia Polytechnic
Institute & State U
Wagner College
Wake Forest U
Washington State U
Weber State U
Western Carolina U
Western Illinois U

Western Kentucky U
Wichita State U
Winston-Salem State U
Winthrop U
Wofford College
Wright State U
Xavier U
Yale U
Youngstown State U

CROSS-COUNTRY
DIVISION II

Abilene Christian U
Adams State College
Adelphi U
Albany State U (GA)
Alderson-Broaddus College
American International
College
Anderson U (SC)
Angelo State U
Ashland U
Assumption College
Augustana College (SD)
Barton College
Bellarmine U
Belmont Abbey College
Benedict College
Bentley College
Bloomfield College
Bloomsburg U of
Pennsylvania
Bluefield State College
Bowie State U
Brevard College
Brigham Young U, Hawaii
Bryant U
C.W. Post Campus/Long
Island U
California State Polytechnic
U, Pomona
California State U, Chico
California State U,
Monterey Bay

California State U, Stanislaus
California U of
Pennsylvania
Cameron U
Carson-Newman College
Catawba College
Central State U
Central Washington U
Chaminade U
Chestnut Hill College
Cheyney U of Pennsylvania
Christian Brothers U
Claflin U
Clark Atlanta U
Clayton State U
Coker College
College of Saint Rose
Colorado Christian U
Colorado School of Mines
Columbia Union College
Columbus State U
Concord U
Concordia College (NY)
Concordia U, St. Paul
Dallas Baptist U
Davis and Elkins College
Dixie State College of Utah
Dowling College
Drury U
East Central U
East Stroudsburg U of
Pennsylvania
Eastern New Mexico U
Edinboro U of Pennsylvania
Elizabeth City State U
Emporia State U
Erskine College
Fairmont State U
Fayetteville State U
Felician College
Ferris State U
Flagler College
Florida Gulf Coast U
Florida Institute of
Technology
Florida Southern College
Fort Hays State U

Fort Lewis College
Fort Valley State U
Francis Marion U
Gannon U
The Georgia College &
   State U
Glenville State College
Goldey-Beacom College
Grand Canyon U
Grand Valley State U
Harding U
Hawaii Pacific U
Henderson State U
Hillsdale College
Holy Family U
Humboldt State U
Indiana U of Pennsylvania
Johnson C. Smith U
Kennesaw State U
Kentucky State U
Kentucky Wesleyan College
Kutztown U of
   Pennsylvania
Lake Superior State U
Lane College
Le Moyne College
Lees-McRae College
LeMoyne-Owen College
Lenoir-Rhyne College
Lewis U
Limestone College
Lincoln Memorial U
Livingstone College
Lock Haven U of
   Pennsylvania
Mansfield U of
   Pennsylvania
Mars Hill College
Mercy College
Mercyhurst College
Merrimack College
Metropolitan State College
   of Denver
Michigan Technological U
Miles College
Millersville U of Pennsylvania
Minnesota State U
   Moorhead

Minnesota State U, Mankato
Missouri Southern State U
Missouri U of Science and
   Technology
Molloy College
Montana State U-Billings
Morehouse College
Mount Olive College
New Jersey Institute of
   Technology
New Mexico Highlands U
New York Institute of
   Technology
Newberry College
Newman U
North Carolina Central U
North Georgia College &
   State U
North Greenville U
Northern Kentucky U
Northern State U
Northwest Missouri State U
Northwest Nazarene U
Northwood U (MI)
Notre Dame de Namur U
Nova Southeastern U
Nyack College
Oakland City U
Ohio Valley U
Oklahoma Panhandle
   State U
Pace U
Paine College
Palm Beach Atlantic U
Pfeiffer U
Philadelphia U
Pittsburg State U
Post U
Presbyterian College
Queens College (NY)
Queens U of Charlotte
Regis U (CO)
Rollins College
Saginaw Valley State U
Saint Anselm College
Saint Joseph's College (IN)
Saint Leo U
Saint Michael's College

San Francisco State U
Seattle Pacific U
Seattle U
Seton Hill U
Shaw U
Shippensburg U of
   Pennsylvania
Slippery Rock U of
   Pennsylvania
Southern Arkansas U
Southern Connecticut
   State U
Southern Illinois U
   Edwardsville
Southern New Hampshire U
Southwest Baptist U
St. Andrews Presbyterian
   College
St. Augustine's College
St. Cloud State U
St. Edward's U
St. Martin's U
St. Paul's College
St. Thomas Aquinas College
Stillman College
Stonehill College
Tarleton State U
Texas A&M International U
Texas A&M U-Commerce
Texas A&M U-Kingsville
Tiffin U
Truman State U
Tusculum College
Tuskegee U
U of Alabama in Huntsville
U of Alaska Anchorage
U of Alaska Fairbanks
U of Arkansas, Monticello
U of Bridgeport
U of California, San Diego
U of Central Arkansas
U of Central Missouri
U of Charleston (WV)
U of Colorado, Colorado
   Springs
U of Findlay
U of Hawaii at Hilo
U of Indianapolis

U of Mary
U of Massachusetts at Lowell
U of Minnesota Duluth
U of Nebraska at Kearney
U of New Haven
U of North Alabama
U of North Carolina at
  Pembroke
U of North Dakota
U of North Florida
U of Puerto Rico, Bayamon
U of Puerto Rico, Cayey
U of Puerto Rico,
  Mayaguez Campus
U of Puerto Rico, Rio Piedras
U of South Carolina Upstate
U of South Dakota
U of Southern Indiana
U of Tampa
U of Texas of the Permian
  Basin
U of the District of
  Columbia
U of the Incarnate Word
U of the Sciences in
  Philadelphia
U of West Alabama
U of West Florida
U of West Georgia
U of Wisconsin, Parkside
Valdosta State U
Virginia State U
Virginia Union U
Wayne State College (NE)
Wayne State U (MI)
West Chester U of
  Pennsylvania
West Liberty State College
West Texas A&M U
West Virginia Wesleyan
  College
Western New Mexico U
Western Oregon U
Western State College of
  Colorado
Western Washington U
Wheeling Jesuit U
Wilmington U (Delaware)

Wingate U
Winona State U
Winston-Salem State U

CROSS-COUNTRY
DIVISION III

Adrian College
Albertus Magnus College
Albion College
Albright College
Alfred U
Allegheny College
Alma College
Alvernia U
Amherst College
Anderson U (IN)
Anna Maria College
Augsburg College
Augustana College (IL)
Aurora U
Averett U
Babson College
Baldwin-Wallace College
Baptist Bible College
Bard College
Baruch College
Bates College
Beloit College
Benedictine U (IL)
Bethany College (WV)
Bethel U (MN)
Blackburn College
Bluffton U
Bowdoin College
Brandeis U
Bridgewater College (VA)
Bridgewater State College
Brooklyn College
Buena Vista U
Buffalo State College
Cabrini College
California Institute of
  Technology
California Lutheran U
California State U, East Bay

Calvin College
Capital U
Carleton College
Carnegie Mellon U
Carroll U (WI)
Carthage College
Case Western Reserve U
Castleton State College
Catholic U
Cazenovia College
Centenary College (NJ)
Central College (IA)
Centre College
Chapman U
Christopher Newport U
The City College of New
  York
Claremont McKenna-
  Harvey Mudd-Scripps
  Colleges
Clark U (MA)
Clarkson U
Coe College
Colby College
College of Brockport, State
  U of New York
College of Mount St. Joseph
The College of New Jersey
The College of St.
  Scholastica
College of Mount St.
  Vincent
College of Wooster
Colorado College
Concordia College,
  Moorhead
Concordia U (WI)
Concordia U Chicago
Concordia U Texas
Connecticut College
Cornell College
Crown College (MN)
Daniel Webster College
Defiance College
Delaware Valley College
Denison U
DePauw U
DeSales U

Dickinson College
Dominican U (IL)
Drew U
Earlham College
East Texas Baptist U
Eastern Connecticut State U
Eastern Mennonite U
Eastern Nazarene College
Eastern U
Edgewood College
Elizabethtown College
Elmhurst College
Elms College
Emerson College
Emmanuel College (MA)
Emory and Henry College
Emory U
Endicott College
Eureka College
Fairleigh Dickinson U,
   Florham
Ferrum College
Finlandia U
Fitchburg State College
Fontbonne U
Framingham State College
Franciscan U of Steubenville
Franklin & Marshall College
Franklin College
Frostburg State U
Geneva College
George Fox U
Gettysburg College
Gordon College
Goucher College
Green Mountain College
Greensboro College
Greenville College
Grinnell College
Grove City College
Guilford College
Gustavus Adolphus College
Gwynedd-Mercy College
Hamilton College
Hamline U
Hampden-Sydney College
Hanover College

Hardin-Simmons U
Hartwick College
Haverford College
Heidelberg College
Hendrix College
Hilbert College
Hiram College
Hobart College
Hood College
Hope College
Hunter College
Huntingdon College
Illinois College
Illinois Wesleyan U
Immaculata U
Ithaca College
John Carroll U
John Jay College of
   Criminal Justice
Johns Hopkins U
Johnson and Wales U
Johnson State College
Juniata College
Kalamazoo College
Keene State College
Kenyon College
Keuka College
Keystone College
King's College (PA)
Knox College
La Grange College
La Roche College
Lake Erie College
Lake Forest College
Lakeland College
Lancaster Bible College
Lasell College
Lawrence U
Lebanon Valley College
Lehman College, City U of
   New York
Lesley U
Lewis & Clark College
Lincoln U (PA)
Linfield College
Loras College
Louisiana College

Luther College
Lycoming College
Lynchburg College
Lyndon State College
Macalester College
Maine Maritime Academy
Manchester College
Manhattanville College
Maranatha Baptist Bible
   College
Marian U (WI)
Marietta College
Martin Luther College
Marymount U (VA)
Maryville College (TN)
Maryville U of Saint Louis
Marywood U
Massachusetts College of
   Liberal Arts
Massachusetts Institute of
   Technology
Massachusetts Maritime
   Academy
McDaniel College
McMurry U
Medaille College
Medgar Evers College
Menlo College
Messiah College
Methodist U
Middlebury College
Millikin U
Millsaps College
Milwaukee School of
   Engineering
Misericordia U
Mississippi College
Mitchell College
Monmouth College (IL)
Moravian College
Mount Aloysius College
Mount Saint Mary College
   (NY)
Mount Union College
Muhlenberg College
Muskingum College
Nazareth College

Nebraska Wesleyan U
New England College
New Jersey City U
New York City College of
Technology
New York U
Newbury College
North Central College
North Central U
North Park U
Northland College
Northwestern College
Norwich U
Oberlin College
Occidental College
Oglethorpe U
Ohio Northern U
Ohio Wesleyan U
Olivet College
Otterbein College
Pacific Lutheran U
Pacific U (OR)
Penn State Berks College
Penn State Harrisburg
Penn State U, Altoona
Pennsylvania State Univ.
Erie, the Behrend College
Philadelphia Biblical U
Piedmont College
Plattsburgh State U of
New York
Polytechnic Institute of
New York U
Pomona-Pitzer Colleges
Presentation College
Principia College
Purchase College, State U
of New York
Ramapo College
Randolph College
Rensselaer Polytechnic
Institute
Rhode Island College
Rhodes College
Richard Stockton College
of New Jersey
Ripon College
Rivier College

Roanoke College
Rochester Institute of
Technology
Rockford College
Roger Williams U
Rose-Hulman Institute of
Technology
Rowan U
Rust College
Rutgers, The State Univ. of
New Jersey, Camden
Rutgers, The State Univ. of
New Jersey, Newark
Saint Joseph's College (ME)
Saint Mary's U of
Minnesota
Saint Vincent College
Salem State College
Salisbury U
Salve Regina U
Schreiner U
Shenandoah U
Simpson College
Southern Vermont College
Southwestern U (TX)
Spalding U
Springfield College
St. John's U (MN)
St. Joseph's College (Long
Island)
St. Joseph's College, New
York
St. Lawrence U
St. Norbert College
St. Olaf College
State U College at Cortland
State U College at Fredonia
State U College at Geneseo
State U College at New Paltz
State U College at Old
Westbury
State U College at Oneonta
State U of New York at
Cobleskill
State U of New York at
Farmingdale
State U of New York at
Oswego

State U of New York at
Potsdam
State U of New York
Institute of Technolo
State U of New York
Maritime College
Stevens Institute of
Technology
Stevenson U
Suffolk U
Sul Ross State U
Susquehanna U
Swarthmore College
Thiel College
Thomas More College
Transylvania U
Trine U
Trinity College (CT)
Trinity U (TX)
Tufts U
U.S. Coast Guard Academy
U.S. Merchant Marine
Academy
Union College (NY)
U of Chicago
U of Dallas
U of Dubuque
U of La Verne
U of Maine at Presque Isle
U of Maine, Farmington
U of Mary Washington
U of Massachusetts, Boston
U of Massachusetts,
Dartmouth
U of Minnesota, Morris
U of New England
U of Pittsburgh, Bradford
U of Pittsburgh, Greensburg
U of Puget Sound
U of Redlands
U of Rochester
U of Scranton
U of Southern Maine
U of St. Thomas (MN)
U of Texas at Dallas
U of Texas at Tyler
U of the Ozarks (AR)
U of the South

U of Wisconsin, Eau Claire
U of Wisconsin, La Crosse
U of Wisconsin, Oshkosh
U of Wisconsin, Platteville
U of Wisconsin, River Falls
U of Wisconsin, Stevens
 Point
U of Wisconsin, Stout
U of Wisconsin, Superior
U of Wisconsin,
 Whitewater
Ursinus College
Utica College
Vassar College
Virginia Wesleyan College
Wabash College
Wartburg College
Washington and Jefferson
 College
Washington and Lee U
Washington U (MO)
Waynesburg U
Wells College
Wesley College
Wesleyan U (CT)
Western New England
 College
Westfield State College
Westminster College (MO)
Westminster College (PA)
Wheaton College (IL)
Wheaton College (MA)
Whitman College
Whittier College
Whitworth U
Widener U
Willamette U
Williams College
Wilmington College (OH)
Wisconsin Lutheran College
Wittenberg U
Worcester Polytechnic
 Institute
Worcester State College
Yeshiva U
York College (NY)
York College (PA)

FENCING
DIVISION I

Boston College
Brown U
Cleveland State U
Columbia U-Barnard College
Duke U
Harvard U
New Jersey Institute of
 Technology
The Ohio State U
Pennsylvania State U
Princeton U
Sacred Heart U
St. John's U (NY)
Stanford U
U.S. Air Force Academy
U of Detroit Mercy
U of North Carolina,
 Chapel Hill
U of Notre Dame
U of Pennsylvania
Yale U

FENCING
DIVISION II

New Jersey Institute of
 Technology
U of California, San Diego
Wayne State U (MI)

FENCING
DIVISION III

Brandeis U
California Institute of
 Technology
Drew U
Haverford College
Hunter College
Johns Hopkins U
Lawrence U
Massachusetts Institute of
 Technology
New York U

Stevens Institute of
 Technology
Vassar College
Yeshiva U

FOOTBALL
DIVISION I: FBS

Arizona State U
Arkansas State U
Auburn U
Ball State U
Baylor U
Boise State U
Boston College
Bowling Green State U
Brigham Young U
California State U, Fresno
Central Michigan U
Clemson U
Colorado State U
Duke U
East Carolina U
Eastern Michigan U
Florida Atlantic U
Florida International U
Florida State U
Georgia Institute of
 Technology
Indiana U, Bloomington
Iowa State U
Kansas State U
Kent State U
Louisiana State U
Louisiana Tech U
Marshall U
Miami U (OH)
Michigan State U
Middle Tennessee State U
Mississippi State U
New Mexico State U
North Carolina State U
Northern Illinois U
Northwestern U
Ohio U
The Ohio State U
Oklahoma State U

Oregon State U
Pennsylvania State U
Purdue U
Rice U
Rutgers, State Univ of New
Jersey, New Brunswick
San Diego State U
San Jose State U
Southern Methodist U
Stanford U
Syracuse U
Temple U
Texas A&M U, College
Station
Texas Christian U
Texas Tech U
Troy U
Tulane U
U.S. Air Force Academy
U.S. Military Academy
U.S. Naval Academy
U at Buffalo, the State U
of New
U of Akron
U of Alabama at
Birmingham
U of Alabama, Tuscaloosa
U of Arizona
U of Arkansas, Fayetteville
U of California, Berkeley
U of California, Los Angeles
U of Central Florida
U of Cincinnati
U of Colorado, Boulder
U of Connecticut
U of Florida
U of Georgia
U of Hawaii, Manoa
U of Houston
U of Idaho
U of Illinois, Champaign
U of Iowa
U of Kansas
U of Kentucky
U of Louisiana at Lafayette
U of Louisiana at Monroe
U of Louisville
U of Maryland, College Park

U of Memphis
U of Miami (FL)
U of Michigan
U of Minnesota, Twin Cities
U of Mississippi
U of Missouri, Columbia
U of Nebraska, Lincoln
U of Nevada
U of Nevada, Las Vegas
U of New Mexico
U of North Carolina,
Chapel Hill
U of North Texas
U of Notre Dame
U of Oklahoma
U of Oregon
U of Pittsburgh
U of South Carolina,
Columbia
U of South Florida
U of Southern California
U of Southern Mississippi
U of Tennessee, Knoxville
U of Texas at Austin
U of Texas at El Paso
U of Toledo
U of Tulsa
U of Utah
U of Virginia
U of Washington
U of Wisconsin, Madison
U of Wyoming
Utah State U
Vanderbilt U
Virginia Polytechnic
Institute & State U
Wake Forest U
Washington State U
West Virginia U
Western Kentucky U
Western Michigan U

FOOTBALL
DIVISION I: FCS

Alabama A&M U
Alabama State U
Alcorn State U

Appalachian State U
Austin Peay State U
Bethune-Cookman U
Brown U
Bucknell U
Butler U
California Polytechnic
State U
California State U,
Sacramento
Campbell U
Central Connecticut State U
Charleston Southern U
The Citadel
Coastal Carolina U
Colgate U
College of the Holy Cross
College of William and Mary
Columbia U-Barnard
College
Cornell U
Dartmouth College
Davidson College
Delaware State U
Drake U
Duquesne U
Eastern Illinois U ·
Eastern Kentucky U
Eastern Washington U
Elon U
Florida A&M U
Fordham U
Furman U
Gardner-Webb U
Georgetown U
Georgia Southern U
Grambling State U
Hampton U
Harvard U
Hofstra U
Howard U
Idaho State U
Illinois State U
Indiana State U
Iona College
Jackson State U
Jacksonville State U
Jacksonville U

James Madison U
Lafayette College
Lehigh U
Liberty U
Marist College
McNeese State U
Mississippi Valley State U
Missouri State U
Monmouth U
Montana State U-Bozeman
Morehead State U
Morgan State U
Murray State U
Nicholls State U
Norfolk State U
North Carolina A&T State U
North Dakota State U
Northeastern U
Northern Arizona U
Northwestern State U
Portland State U
Prairie View A&M U
Princeton U
Robert Morris U
Sacred Heart U
Saint Francis U (PA)
Sam Houston State U
Samford U
Savannah State U
South Carolina State U
South Dakota State U
Southeast Missouri State U
Southeastern Louisiana U
Southern Illinois U at
 Carbondale
Southern U, Baton Rouge
Southern Utah U
Stephen F. Austin State U
Stony Brook U
Tennessee State U
Tennessee Technological U
Texas Southern U
Texas State U-San Marcos
Towson U
U at Albany
U of Arkansas, Pine Bluff
U of California, Davis

U of Dayton
U of Delaware
U of Maine, Orono
U of Massachusetts,
 Amherst
U of Montana
U of New Hampshire
U of Northern Colorado
U of Northern Iowa
U of Pennsylvania
U of Rhode Island
U of Richmond
U of San Diego
U of Tennessee at
 Chattanooga
U of Tennessee at Martin
Valparaiso U
Villanova U
Virginia Military Institute
Wagner College
Weber State U
Western Carolina U
Western Illinois U
Western Kentucky U
Wofford College
Yale U
Youngstown State U

FOOTBALL
DIVISION II

Abilene Christian U
Adams State College
Albany State U (GA)
American International
 College
Angelo State U
Arkansas Tech U
Ashland U
Assumption College
Augustana College (SD)
Bemidji State U
Benedict College
Bentley College
Bloomsburg U of
 Pennsylvania
Bowie State U

Brevard College
Bryant U
C.W. Post Campus/Long
 Island U
California U of
 Pennsylvania
Carson-Newman College
Catawba College
Central State U
Central Washington U
Chadron State College
Cheyney U of Pennsylvania
Chowan U
Clarion U of Pennsylvania
Clark Atlanta U
Colorado School of Mines
Colorado State U-Pueblo
Concord U
Concordia U, St. Paul
Delta State U
Dixie State College of Utah
East Central U
East Stroudsburg U of
 Pennsylvania
Eastern New Mexico U
Edinboro U of Pennsylvania
Elizabeth City State U
Emporia State U
Fairmont State U
Fayetteville State U
Ferris State U
Fort Hays State U
Fort Lewis College
Fort Valley State U
Gannon U
Glenville State College
Grand Valley State U
Harding U
Henderson State U
Hillsdale College
Humboldt State U
Indiana U of Pennsylvania
Johnson C. Smith U
Kentucky State U
Kentucky Wesleyan College
Kutztown U of
 Pennsylvania

Lane College
Lenoir-Rhyne College
Lincoln U (MO)
Livingstone College
Lock Haven U of
   Pennsylvania
Mars Hill College
Mercyhurst College
Merrimack College
Mesa State College
Michigan Technological U
Midwestern State U
Miles College
Millersville U of
   Pennsylvania
Minnesota State U
   Moorhead
Minnesota State U, Mankato
Missouri Southern State U
Missouri U of Science and
   Technology
Missouri Western State U
Morehouse College
New Mexico Highlands U
Newberry College
North Carolina Central U
North Greenville U
Northeastern State U
Northern Michigan U
Northern State U
Northwest Missouri State U
Northwood U (MI)
Oklahoma Panhandle
   State U
Ouachita Baptist U
Pace U
Pittsburg State U
Presbyterian College
Quincy U
Saginaw Valley State U
Saint Anselm College
Saint Joseph's College (IN)
Seton Hill U
Shaw U
Shepherd U
Shippensburg U of
   Pennsylvania

Slippery Rock U of
   Pennsylvania
Southeastern Oklahoma
   State U
Southern Arkansas U
Southern Connecticut
   State U
Southwest Baptist U
Southwest Minnesota
   State U
Southwestern Oklahoma
   State U
St. Augustine's College
St. Cloud State U
St. Paul's College
Stillman College
Stonehill College
Tarleton State U
Texas A&M U-Commerce
Texas A&M U-Kingsville
Tiffin U
Truman State U
Tusculum College
Tuskegee U
U of Arkansas, Monticello
U of Central Arkansas
U of Central Missouri
U of Central Oklahoma
U of Charleston (WV)
U of Findlay
U of Indianapolis
U of Mary
U of Minnesota Duluth
U of Minnesota, Crookston
U of Nebraska at Kearney
U of Nebraska at Omaha
U of North Alabama
U of North Carolina at
   Pembroke
U of North Dakota
U of South Dakota
U of West Alabama
U of West Georgia
Upper Iowa U
Valdosta State U
Virginia State U
Virginia Union U

Washburn U of Topeka
Wayne State College (NE)
Wayne State U (MI)
West Chester U of
   Pennsylvania
West Liberty State College
West Texas A&M U
West Virginia State U
West Virginia Wesleyan
   College
Western New Mexico U
Western Oregon U
Western State College of
   Colorado
Western Washington U
Wingate U
Winona State U
Winston-Salem State U

FOOTBALL
DIVISION III

Adrian College
Albion College
Albright College
Alfred U
Allegheny College
Alma College
Amherst College
Anderson U (IN)
Augsburg College
Augustana College (IL)
Aurora U
Austin College
Averett U
Baldwin-Wallace College
Bates College
Becker College
Beloit College
Benedictine U (IL)
Bethany College (WV)
Bethel U (MN)
Birmingham-Southern
   College
Blackburn College
Bluffton U
Bowdoin College

Bridgewater College (VA)
Bridgewater State College
Buena Vista U
Buffalo State College
California Lutheran U
Capital U
Carleton College
Carnegie Mellon U
Carroll U (WI)
Carthage College
Case Western Reserve U
Catholic U
Central College (IA)
Centre College
Chapman U
Christopher Newport U
Claremont McKenna-Harvey
   Mudd-Scripps Colleges
Coe College
Colby College
College of Brockport, State
   U of New York
College of Mount St. Joseph
The College of New Jersey
The College of St.
   Scholastica
College of Wooster
Colorado College
Concordia College,
   Moorhead
Concordia U (WI)
Concordia U Chicago
Cornell College
Crown College (MN)
Curry College
Defiance College
Delaware Valley College
Denison U
DePauw U
Dickinson College
Earlham College
East Texas Baptist U
Elmhurst College
Emory and Henry College
Endicott College
Eureka College
Fairleigh Dickinson U,
   Florham

Ferrum College
Fitchburg State College
Framingham State College
Franklin & Marshall College
Franklin College
Frostburg State U
Gallaudet U
Geneva College
Gettysburg College
Greensboro College
Greenville College
Grinnell College
Grove City College
Guilford College
Gustavus Adolphus College
Hamilton College
Hamline U
Hampden-Sydney College
Hanover College
Hardin-Simmons U
Hartwick College
Heidelberg College
Hiram College
Hobart College
Hope College
Howard Payne U
Huntingdon College
Husson College
Illinois College
Illinois Wesleyan U
Ithaca College
John Carroll U
Johns Hopkins U
Juniata College
Kalamazoo College
Kean U
Kenyon College
King's College (PA)
Knox College
La Grange College
Lake Erie College
Lake Forest College
Lakeland College
Lawrence U
Lebanon Valley College
Lewis & Clark College
Lincoln U (PA)
Linfield College

Loras College
Louisiana College
Luther College
Lycoming College
Macalester College
MacMurray College
Maine Maritime Academy
Manchester College
Maranatha Baptist Bible
   College
Marietta College
Martin Luther College
Maryville College (TN)
Massachusetts Institute of
   Technology
Massachusetts Maritime
   Academy
McDaniel College
McMurry U
Menlo College
Methodist U
Middlebury College
Millikin U
Millsaps College
Mississippi College
Monmouth College (IL)
Montclair State U
Moravian College
Mount Ida College
Mount Union College
Muhlenberg College
Muskingum College
Nebraska Wesleyan U
Nichols College
North Carolina Wesleyan
   College
North Central College
North Park U
Northwestern College
Norwich U
Oberlin College
Occidental College
Ohio Northern U
Ohio Wesleyan U
Olivet College
Otterbein College
Pacific Lutheran U
Plymouth State U

Pomona-Pitzer Colleges
Principia College
Randolph-Macon College
Rensselaer Polytechnic
   Institute
Rhodes College
Ripon College
Rockford College
Rose-Hulman Institute of
   Technology
Rowan U
Saint Vincent College
Salisbury U
Salve Regina U
Shenandoah U
Simpson College
Springfield College
St. John Fisher College
St. John's U (MN)
St. Lawrence U
St. Norbert College
St. Olaf College
State U College at Cortland
State U of New York at
   Morrisville
State U of New York
   Maritime College
Sul Ross State U
Susquehanna U
Texas Lutheran U
Thiel College
Thomas More College
Trine U
Trinity College (CT)
Trinity U (TX)
Tufts U
U.S. Coast Guard Academy
U.S. Merchant Marine
   Academy
Union College (NY)
U of Chicago
U of Dubuque
U of La Verne
U of Mary Hardin-Baylor
U of Massachusetts,
   Dartmouth
U of Minnesota, Morris

U of Puget Sound
U of Redlands
U of Rochester
U of St. Thomas (MN)
U of the South
U of Wisconsin, Eau Claire
U of Wisconsin, La Crosse
U of Wisconsin, Oshkosh
U of Wisconsin, Platteville
U of Wisconsin, River Falls
U of Wisconsin, Stevens
   Point
U of Wisconsin, Stout
U of Wisconsin, Whitewater
Ursinus College
Utica College
Wabash College
Wartburg College
Washington and Jefferson
   College
Washington and Lee U
Washington U (MO)
Waynesburg U
Wesley College
Wesleyan U (CT)
Western Connecticut
   State U
Western New England
   College
Westfield State College
Westminster College (MO)
Westminster College (PA)
Wheaton College (IL)
Whittier College
Whitworth U
Widener U
Wilkes U
Willamette U
William Paterson U of New
   Jersey
Williams College
Wilmington College (OH)
Wisconsin Lutheran College
Wittenberg U
Worcester Polytechnic
   Institute
Worcester State College

GOLF
DIVISION I

Alabama A&M U
Alabama State U
Alcorn State U
Appalachian State U
Arizona State U
Arkansas State U
Auburn U
Augusta State U
Austin Peay State U
Ball State U
Baylor U
Belmont U
Bethune-Cookman U
Birmingham-Southern
   College
Boise State U
Boston College
Bowling Green State U
Bradley U
Brigham Young U
Brown U
Bryant U
Bucknell U
Butler U
California Polytechnic
   State U
California State U,
   Bakersfield
California State U, Fresno
California State U,
   Northridge
California State U,
   Sacramento
Campbell U
Canisius College
Centenary College (LA)
Central Connecticut State
   U
Charleston Southern U
Chicago State U
Clemson U
Cleveland State U
Coastal Carolina U
Colgate U

College of Charleston (SC)
College of the Holy Cross
College of William and Mary
Colorado State U
Columbia U-Barnard College
Cornell U
Creighton U
Dartmouth College
Davidson College
DePaul U
Drake U
Drexel U
Duke U
Duquesne U
East Carolina U
East Tennessee State U
Eastern Illinois U
Eastern Kentucky U
Eastern Michigan U
Elon U
Fairfield U
Fairleigh Dickinson U,
    Metropolitan
Florida A&M U
Florida Atlantic U
Florida Gulf Coast U
Florida State U
Fordham U
Francis Marion U
Furman U
Gardner-Webb U
George Mason U
George Washington U
Georgetown U
Georgia Institute of
    Technology
Georgia Southern U
Georgia State U
Gonzaga U
Grambling State U
Hampton U
Harvard U
High Point U
Hofstra U
Houston Baptist U
Illinois State U
Indiana U, Bloomington

Indiana U-Purdue U at
    Indianapolis
Indiana U-Purdue U, Fort
    Wayne
Iona College
Iowa State U
Jackson State U
Jacksonville State U
Jacksonville U
James Madison U
Kansas State U
Kennesaw State U
Kent State U
La Salle U
Lafayette College
Lamar U
Lehigh U
Liberty U
Lipscomb U
Long Beach State U
Long Island U-Brooklyn
    Campus
Longwood U
Louisiana State U
Louisiana Tech U
Loyola Marymount U
Loyola U (IL)
Loyola U (MD)
Manhattan College
Marquette U
Marshall U
McNeese State U
Mercer U
Miami U (OH)
Michigan State U
Middle Tennessee State U
Mississippi State U
Mississippi Valley State U
Missouri State U
Monmouth U
Morehead State U
Mount St. Mary's U
Murray State U
New Mexico State U
Niagara U
Nicholls State U
North Carolina Central U

North Carolina State U
North Dakota State U
Northern Illinois U
Northwestern U
Oakland U
Ohio U
The Ohio State U
Oklahoma State U
Old Dominion U
Oral Roberts U
Oregon State U
Pennsylvania State U
Pepperdine U
Prairie View A&M U
Presbyterian College
Princeton U
Purdue U
Quinnipiac U
Radford U
Rice U
Rider U
Robert Morris U
Rutgers, State Univ of New
    Jersey, New Brunswick
Sacred Heart U
Saint Francis U (PA)
Saint Joseph's U
Sam Houston State U
Samford U
San Diego State U
San Jose State U
Santa Clara U
Savannah State U
Seton Hall U
Siena College
South Carolina State U
South Dakota State U
Southeastern Louisiana U
Southern Illinois U at
    Carbondale
Southern Illinois U
    Edwardsville
Southern Methodist U
Southern U, Baton Rouge
Southern Utah U
St. Bonaventure U
St. Francis College (NY)

St. John's U (NY)
St. Mary's College of
California
St. Peter's College
Stanford U
State U of New York at
Binghamton
Stephen F. Austin State U
Stetson U
Temple U
Tennessee State U
Tennessee Technological U
Texas A&M U, College
Station
Texas Christian U
Texas Southern U
Texas State U-San Marcos
Texas Tech U
Towson U
Troy U
U.S. Air Force Academy
U.S. Military Academy
U.S. Naval Academy
U of Akron
U of Alabama at
Birmingham
U of Alabama, Tuscaloosa
U of Arizona
U of Arkansas, Fayetteville
U of Arkansas, Little Rock
U of Arkansas, Pine Bluff
U of California, Berkeley
U of California, Davis
U of California, Irvine
U of California, Los Angeles
U of California, Riverside
U of California, Santa
Barbara
U of Central Arkansas
U of Central Florida
U of Cincinnati
U of Colorado, Boulder
U of Connecticut
U of Dayton
U of Delaware
U of Denver
U of Detroit Mercy

U of Evansville
U of Florida
U of Georgia
U of Hartford
U of Hawaii, Manoa
U of Houston
U of Idaho
U of Illinois, Champaign
U of Iowa
U of Kansas
U of Kentucky
U of Louisiana at Lafayette
U of Louisiana at Monroe
U of Louisville
U of Maryland, College Park
U of Memphis
U of Michigan
U of Minnesota, Twin Cities
U of Mississippi
U of Missouri, Columbia
U of Missouri, Kansas City
U of Nebraska, Lincoln
U of Nevada
U of Nevada, Las Vegas
U of New Mexico
U of New Orleans
U of North Carolina at
Greensboro
U of North Carolina,
Chapel Hill
U of North Carolina,
Charlotte
U of North Carolina,
Wilmington
U of North Dakota
U of North Florida
U of North Texas
U of Northern Colorado
U of Northern Iowa
U of Notre Dame
U of Oklahoma
U of Oregon
U of Pennsylvania
U of Portland
U of Rhode Island
U of Richmond
U of San Diego

U of San Francisco
U of South Alabama
U of South Carolina Upstate
U of South Carolina,
Columbia
U of South Dakota
U of South Florida
U of Southern California
U of Southern Mississippi
U of Tennessee at
Chattanooga
U of Tennessee at Martin
U of Tennessee, Knoxville
U of Texas at Arlington
U of Texas at Austin
U of Texas at El Paso
U of Texas at San Antonio
U of Texas, Pan American
U of the Pacific
U of Toledo
U of Tulsa
U of Utah
U of Virginia
U of Washington
U of Wisconsin, Green Bay
U of Wisconsin, Madison
U of Wyoming
Utah State U
Utah Valley U
Vanderbilt U
Villanova U
Virginia Commonwealth U
Virginia Polytechnic
Institute & State U
Wagner College
Wake Forest U
Washington State U
Weber State U
Western Carolina U
Western Illinois U
Western Kentucky U
Wichita State U
Winston-Salem State U
Winthrop U
Wofford College
Wright State U
Xavier U

Yale U
Youngstown State U

GOLF
DIVISION II

Abilene Christian U
Adelphi U
American International
   College
Anderson U (SC)
Arkansas Tech U
Armstrong Atlantic State U
Ashland U
Assumption College
Augustana College (SD)
Barry U
Barton College
Bellarmine U
Belmont Abbey College
Bemidji State U
Benedict College
Bentley College
Bluefield State College
Brevard College
Brigham Young U, Hawaii
Bryant U
Caldwell College
California State U,
   Bakersfield
California State U, Chico
California State U,
   Dominguez Hills
California State U,
   Monterey Bay
California State U, San
   Bernardino
California State U, Stanislaus
California U of
   Pennsylvania
Cameron U
Carson-Newman College
Catawba College
Central State U
Chaminade U
Chestnut Hill College
Chowan U
Christian Brothers U

Clarion U of Pennsylvania
Clayton State U
Coker College
College of Saint Rose
Colorado Christian U
Colorado School of Mines
Colorado State U-Pueblo
Columbus State U
Concord U
Concordia U, St. Paul
Dallas Baptist U
Davis and Elkins College
Delta State U
Dixie State College of Utah
Dominican College (NY)
Dowling College
Drury U
East Central U
Eckerd College
Elizabeth City State U
Erskine College
Fairmont State U
Fayetteville State U
Felician College
Ferris State U
Flagler College
Florida Gulf Coast U
Florida Institute of
   Technology
Florida Southern College
Fort Hays State U
Fort Lewis College
Franklin Pierce U
Gannon U
The Georgia College &
   State U
Georgia Southwestern
   State U
Glenville State College
Goldey-Beacom College
Grand Canyon U
Grand Valley State U
Harding U
Hawaii Pacific U
Henderson State U
Holy Family U
Indiana U of Pennsylvania
Johnson C. Smith U

Kentucky State U
Kentucky Wesleyan College
Lander U
Le Moyne College
Lees-McRae College
LeMoyne-Owen College
Lenoir-Rhyne College
Lewis U
Limestone College
Lincoln Memorial U
Lincoln U (MO)
Lynn U
Mars Hill College
Mercyhurst College
Midwestern State U
Millersville U of
   Pennsylvania
Minnesota State U, Mankato
Missouri Southern State U
Missouri Western State U
Montana State U-Billings
Morehouse College
Mount Olive College
Newberry College
Newman U
North Carolina Central U
North Greenville U
Northeastern State U
Northern Kentucky U
Northern Michigan U
Northern State U
Northwest Nazarene U
Northwood U (MI)
Notre Dame de Namur U
Nova Southeastern U
Nyack College
Oakland City U
Ohio Valley U
Oklahoma Panhandle
   State U
Ouachita Baptist U
Pace U
Paine College
Pfeiffer U
Philadelphia U
Pittsburg State U
Post U
Presbyterian College

Queens U of Charlotte
Quincy U
Regis U (CO)
Rockhurst U
Rollins College
Saginaw Valley State U
Saint Anselm College
Saint Joseph's College (IN)
Saint Leo U
Saint Michael's College
Salem International U
Seton Hill U
Shepherd U
Sonoma State U
Southeastern Oklahoma
  State U
Southern Arkansas U
Southern Illinois U
  Edwardsville
Southern New Hampshire U
Southwest Baptist U
Southwestern Oklahoma
  State U
St. Andrews Presbyterian
  College
St. Augustine's College
St. Cloud State U
St. Edward's U
St. Martin's U
St. Mary's U (TX)
St. Paul's College
St. Thomas Aquinas College
Texas A&M International U
Texas A&M U-Commerce
Tiffin U
Truman State U
Tusculum College
U of Arkansas, Monticello
U of California, San Diego
U of Central Arkansas
U of Central Missouri
U of Central Oklahoma
U of Charleston (WV)
U of Colorado, Colorado
  Springs
U of Findlay
U of Hawaii at Hilo

U of Indianapolis
U of Mary
U of Massachusetts at
  Lowell
U of Minnesota, Crookston
U of Missouri, St. Louis
U of Montevallo
U of Nebraska at Kearney
U of New Haven
U of North Alabama
U of North Carolina at
  Pembroke
U of North Dakota
U of Pittsburgh, Johnstown
U of South Carolina Aiken
U of South Carolina Upstate
U of South Dakota
U of Southern Indiana
U of Tampa
U of the Incarnate Word
U of the Sciences in
  Philadelphia
U of West Florida
U of West Georgia
U of Wisconsin, Parkside
Upper Iowa U
Valdosta State U
Virginia State U
Virginia Union U
Washburn U of Topeka
Wayne State College (NE)
Wayne State U (MI)
West Chester U of
  Pennsylvania
West Liberty State College
West Texas A&M U
West Virginia State U
West Virginia Wesleyan
  College
Western New Mexico U
Western Washington U
Wheeling Jesuit U
Wilmington U (Delaware)
Wingate U
Winona State U
Winston-Salem State U

GOLF
DIVISION III

Adrian College
Albion College
Albright College
Allegheny College
Alma College
Alvernia U
Amherst College
Anderson U (IN)
Anna Maria College
Arcadia U
Augsburg College
Augustana College (IL)
Aurora U
Averett U
Babson College
Baldwin-Wallace College
Baptist Bible College
Bates College
Becker College
Beloit College
Benedictine U (IL)
Bethany College (WV)
Bethany Lutheran College
Bethel U (MN)
Blackburn College
Bowdoin College
Brandeis U
Bridgewater College (VA)
Buena Vista U
Cabrini College
California Lutheran U
California State U, East Bay
Calvin College
Capital U
Carleton College
Carnegie Mellon U
Carroll U (WI)
Carthage College
Castleton State College
Cazenovia College
Centenary College (NJ)
Central College (IA)
Centre College
Chapman U

Christopher Newport U
Claremont McKenna-
    Harvey Mudd-Scripps
    Colleges
Clarkson U
Coe College
College of Mount St.
    Joseph
College of Wooster
Concordia College,
    Moorhead
Concordia U (WI)
Concordia U Texas
Cornell College
Crown College (MN)
Daniel Webster College
Defiance College
Delaware Valley College
Denison U
DePauw U
DeSales U
Dickinson College
D'Youville College
Eastern U
Edgewood College
Elizabethtown College
Elmhurst College
Elmira College
Elms College
Emerson College
Emory and Henry College
Emory U
Endicott College
Eureka College
Fairleigh Dickinson U,
    Florham
Ferrum College
Finlandia U
Fontbonne U
Franklin & Marshall College
Franklin College
Frostburg State U
George Fox U
Gettysburg College
Green Mountain College
Greensboro College
Grinnell College
Grove City College

Guilford College
Gustavus Adolphus College
Gwynedd-Mercy College
Hamilton College
Hampden-Sydney College
Hanover College
Hardin-Simmons U
Heidelberg College
Hendrix College
Hilbert College
Hiram College
Hobart College
Hood College
Hope College
Huntingdon College
Husson College
Illinois College
Illinois Wesleyan U
Immaculata U
John Carroll U
Johnson and Wales U
Kalamazoo College
Kenyon College
Keuka College
Keystone College
King's College (PA)
Knox College
La Grange College
La Roche College
La Sierra U
Lake Erie College
Lakeland College
Lawrence U
Lebanon Valley College
LeTourneau U
Lewis & Clark College
Linfield College
Loras College
Louisiana College
Luther College
Lycoming College
Lynchburg College
Macalester College
MacMurray College
Maine Maritime Academy
Manchester College
Manhattanville College
Marian U (WI)

Martin Luther College
Marymount U (VA)
Maryville U of Saint Louis
Massachusetts College of
    Liberal Arts
Massachusetts Institute of
    Technology
McDaniel College
McMurry U
Menlo College
Messiah College
Methodist U
Middlebury College
Millikin U
Millsaps College
Milwaukee School of
    Engineering
Misericordia U
Mississippi College
Mitchell College
Monmouth College (IL)
Moravian College
Mount Aloysius College
Mount Union College
Muhlenberg College
Muskingum College
Nazareth College
Nebraska Wesleyan U
Neumann College
New York U
Newbury College
Nichols College
North Carolina Wesleyan
    College
North Central College
North Central U
North Park U
Northwestern College
Oberlin College
Occidental College
Oglethorpe U
Ohio Northern U
Ohio Wesleyan U
Olivet College
Otterbein College
Pacific Lutheran U
Pacific U (OR)
Penn State Berks College

Penn State Harrisburg
Penn State U, Altoona
Pennsylvania State Univ.
Erie, the Behrend College
Philadelphia Biblical U
Piedmont College
Polytechnic Institute of
New York U
Pomona-Pitzer Colleges
Presentation College
Randolph-Macon College
Rensselaer Polytechnic
Institute
Rhode Island College
Rhodes College
Ripon College
Roanoke College
Rockford College
Rose-Hulman Institute of
Technology
Rutgers, The State Univ. of
New Jersey, Camden
The Sage Colleges
Saint Joseph's College (ME)
Saint Mary's U of Minnesota
Saint Vincent College
Salem State College
Schreiner U
Shenandoah U
Simpson College
Skidmore College
Southwestern U (TX)
Spalding U
Springfield College
St. John Fisher College
St. John's U (MN)
St. Joseph's College (Long
Island)
St. Lawrence U
St. Norbert College
St. Olaf College
State U of New York at
Cobleskill
State U of New York at
Farmingdale
State U of New York at
Oswego

State U of New York at
Potsdam
State U of New York
Institute of Technolo
Stevens Institute of
Technology
Stevenson U
Suffolk U
Susquehanna U
Swarthmore College
Texas Lutheran U
Thiel College
Thomas College
Thomas More College
Transylvania U
Trine U
Trinity College (CT)
Trinity U (TX)
Tufts U
U.S. Merchant Marine
Academy
U of Dallas
U of Dubuque
U of La Verne
U of Maine at Presque Isle
U of Maine, Farmington
U of Mary Hardin-Baylor
U of Massachusetts,
Dartmouth
U of Minnesota, Morris
U of New England
U of Pittsburgh, Bradford
U of Pittsburgh,
Greensburg
U of Puget Sound
U of Redlands
U of Rochester
U of Scranton
U of St. Thomas (MN)
U of Texas at Dallas
U of Texas at Tyler
U of the South
U of Wisconsin, Eau Claire
U of Wisconsin, Stout
Ursinus College
Utica College
Virginia Wesleyan College

Wabash College
Wartburg College
Washington and Jefferson
College
Washington and Lee U
Waynesburg U
Webster U
Wentworth Institute of
Technology
Wesley College
Wesleyan U (CT)
Western New England
College
Westfield State College
Westminster College (MO)
Westminster College (PA)
Wheaton College (IL)
Whitman College
Whittier College
Whitworth U
Widener U
Wilkes U
Willamette U
Williams College
Wilmington College (OH)
Wisconsin Lutheran College
Wittenberg U
Worcester State College
Yeshiva U
York College (PA)

GYMNASTICS
DIVISION I

College of William and Mary
The Ohio State U
Pennsylvania State U
Stanford U
Temple U
U.S. Air Force Academy
U.S. Military Academy
U of California, Berkeley
U of Illinois, Champaign
U of Illinois at Chicago
U of Iowa
U of Michigan
U of Minnesota, Twin Cities

U of Nebraska, Lincoln
U of Oklahoma
U.S. Naval Academy

GYMNASTICS
DIVISION III

Massachusetts Institute of
  Technology
Springfield College

ICE HOCKEY
DIVISION I

American International
  College
Bemidji State U
Bentley College
Boston College
Boston U
Bowling Green State U
Brown U
Canisius College
Clarkson U
Colgate U
College of the Holy Cross
Colorado College
Cornell U
Dartmouth College
Ferris State U
Harvard U
Lake Superior State U
Mercyhurst College
Merrimack College
Miami U (OH)
Michigan State U
Michigan Technological U
Minnesota State U, Mankato
Niagara U
Northeastern U
Northern Michigan U
The Ohio State U
Princeton U
Providence College
Quinnipiac U
Rensselaer Polytechnic
  Institute

Robert Morris U
Rochester Institute of
  Technology
Sacred Heart U
St. Cloud State U
St. Lawrence U
U.S. Air Force Academy
U.S. Military Academy
Union College (NY)
U of Alabama in Huntsville
U of Alaska Anchorage
U of Alaska Fairbanks
U of Connecticut
U of Denver
U of Maine, Orono
U of Massachusetts at
  Lowell
U of Massachusetts,
  Amherst
U of Michigan
U of Minnesota Duluth
U of Minnesota, Twin Cities
U of Nebraska at Omaha
U of New Hampshire
U of North Dakota
U of Notre Dame
U of Vermont
U of Wisconsin, Madison
Western Michigan U
Yale U

ICE HOCKEY
DIVISION II

Assumption College
Franklin Pierce U
Southern New Hampshire U
Saint Anselm College
Saint Michael's College
Stonehill College
U of Minnesota, Crookston

ICE HOCKEY
DIVISION III

Adrian College
Amherst College

Augsburg College
Babson College
Becker College
Bethel U (MN)
Bowdoin College
Buffalo State College
Castleton State College
Colby College
College of Brockport, State
  U of New York
The College of St. Scholastica
Concordia College,
  Moorhead
Concordia U (WI)
Connecticut College
Curry College
Elmira College
Finlandia U
Fitchburg State College
Framingham State College
Gustavus Adolphus College
Hamilton College
Hamline U
Hobart College
Johnson and Wales U
Lake Forest College
Lawrence U
Lebanon Valley College
Manhattanville College
Marian U (WI)
Massachusetts Institute of
  Technology
Middlebury College
Milwaukee School of
  Engineering
Neumann College
New England College
Nichols College
Northland College
Norwich U
Plattsburgh State U of
  New York
Plymouth State U
Saint Mary's U of
  Minnesota
Salem State College
Salve Regina U

Skidmore College
St. John's U (MN)
St. Norbert College
St. Olaf College
State U College at Cortland
State U College at Fredonia
State U College at Geneseo
State U of New York at
   Morrisville
State U of New York at
   Oswego
State U of New York at
   Potsdam
Suffolk U
Trinity College (CT)
Tufts U
U of Massachusetts, Boston
U of Massachusetts,
   Dartmouth
U of Scranton
U of Southern Maine
U of St. Thomas (MN)
U of Wisconsin, Eau Claire
U of Wisconsin, River Falls
U of Wisconsin, Stevens
   Point
U of Wisconsin, Stout
U of Wisconsin, Superior
Utica College
Wentworth Institute of
   Technology
Wesleyan U (CT)
Western New England
   College
Westfield State College
Williams College
Worcester State College

LACROSSE
DIVISION I

Bellarmine U
Brown U
Bryant U
Bucknell U
Canisius College
Colgate U

College of the Holy Cross
Cornell U
Dartmouth College
Drexel U
Duke U
Fairfield U
Georgetown U
Harvard U
Hobart College
Hofstra U
Johns Hopkins U
Lafayette College
Lehigh U
Loyola U (MD)
Manhattan College
Marist College
Mount St. Mary's U
The Ohio State U
Pennsylvania State U
Presbyterian College
Princeton U
Providence College
Quinnipiac U
Robert Morris U
Rutgers, State Univ of New
   Jersey, New Brunswick
Sacred Heart U
Saint Joseph's U
Siena College
St. John's U (NY)
State U of New York at
   Binghamton
Stony Brook U
Syracuse U
Towson U
U.S. Air Force Academy
U.S. Military Academy
U.S. Naval Academy
U at Albany
U of Delaware
U of Denver
U of Detroit Mercy
U of Hartford
U of Maryland, Baltimore
   County
U of Maryland, College Park
U of Massachusetts,
   Amherst

U of North Carolina,
   Chapel Hill
U of Notre Dame
U of Pennsylvania
U of Vermont
U of Virginia
Villanova U
Virginia Military Institute
Wagner College
Yale U

LACROSSE
DIVISION II

Adelphi U
American International
   College
Assumption College
Belmont Abbey College
Bentley College
Bryant U
C.W. Post Campus/Long
   Island U
Catawba College
Dominican College (NY)
Dowling College
Florida Southern College
Franklin Pierce U
Grand Canyon U
Le Moyne College
Lees-McRae College
Limestone College
Mars Hill College
Mercyhurst College
Merrimack College
Molloy College
New York Institute of
   Technology
Notre Dame de Namur U
Pace U
Pfeiffer U
Presbyterian College
Queens U of Charlotte
Rollins College
Seton Hill U
Southern New Hampshire U
St. Andrews Presbyterian
   College

Saint Anselm College
Saint Leo U
Saint Michael's College
Wheeling Jesuit U
Wingate U

LACROSSE
DIVISION III

Adrian College
Alfred U
Alvernia U
Amherst College
Anna Maria College
Babson College
Bates College
Becker College
Birmingham-Southern
   College
Bowdoin College
Cabrini College
Carthage College
Castleton State College
Catholic U
Cazenovia College
Centenary College (NJ)
Christopher Newport U
Clark U (MA)
Clarkson U
Colby College
College of Brockport, State
   U of New York
College of Mount St.
   Joseph
College of Mount St.
   Vincent
College of Wooster
Colorado College
Connecticut College
Curry College
Daniel Webster College
Denison U
DeSales U
Dickinson College
Drew U
Eastern Connecticut State U
Eastern U

Elizabethtown College
Elmira College
Emerson College
Endicott College
Fairleigh Dickinson U,
   Florham
Fontbonne U
Franklin & Marshall College
Gettysburg College
Gordon College
Goucher College
Green Mountain College
Greensboro College
Guilford College
Gwynedd-Mercy College
Hamilton College
Hampden-Sydney College
Hartwick College
Haverford College
Hendrix College
Hood College
Immaculata U
Ithaca College
Johnson State College
Kean U
Keene State College
Kenyon College
Keuka College
King's College (PA)
Lasell College
Lycoming College
Lynchburg College
Lyndon State College
Maine Maritime Academy
Manhattanville College
Marymount U (VA)
Marywood U
Massachusetts Institute of
   Technology
Massachusetts Maritime
   Academy
McDaniel College
Medaille College
Messiah College
Middlebury College
Misericordia U
Mitchell College

Montclair State U
Moravian College
Mount Ida College
Muhlenberg College
Nazareth College
Neumann College
New England College
Nichols College
Norwich U
Oberlin College
Ohio Wesleyan U
Plattsburgh State U of
   New York
Plymouth State U
Randolph-Macon College
Rensselaer Polytechnic
   Institute
Richard Stockton College
   of New Jersey
Roanoke College
Rochester Institute of
   Technology
Roger Williams U
Saint Joseph's College (ME)
Saint Vincent College
Salem State College
Salisbury U
Salve Regina U
Shenandoah U
Skidmore College
Springfield College
St. John Fisher College
St. Lawrence U
St. Mary's College of
   Maryland
State U College at
   Cortland
State U College at Geneseo
State U College at Oneonta
State U of New York at
   Cobleskill
State U of New York at
   Farmingdale
State U of New York at
   Morrisville
State U of New York at
   Oswego

State U of New York at
Potsdam
State U of New York
Maritime College
Stevens Institute of
Technology
Stevenson U
Susquehanna U
Swarthmore College
Thomas College
Trine U
Trinity College (CT)
Tufts U
U.S. Merchant Marine
Academy
Union College (NY)
U of Mary Washington
U of Massachusetts, Boston
U of Massachusetts,
Dartmouth
U of New England
U of Scranton
U of Southern Maine
U of the South
Ursinus College
Utica College
Vassar College
Virginia Wesleyan College
Washington and Jefferson
College
Washington and Lee U
Washington College (MD)
Wells College
Wentworth Institute of
Technology
Wesley College
Wesleyan U (CT)
Western Connecticut
State U
Western New England
College
Wheaton College (MA)
Whittier College
Widener U
Williams College
Wittenberg U
York College (PA)

RIFLE
DIVISION I

The Citadel
Jacksonville State U

RIFLE
DIVISION III

State U of New York
Maritime College
U.S. Coast Guard Academy

SKIING
DIVISION I

Boston College
Dartmouth College
Harvard U
Montana State U-Bozeman
U of Colorado, Boulder
U of Denver
U of Massachusetts,
Amherst
U of Nevada
U of New Hampshire
U of New Mexico
U of Utah
U of Vermont
U of Wisconsin, Green Bay

SKIING
DIVISION II

Michigan Technological U
Northern Michigan U
Saint Anselm College
Saint Michael's College
U of Alaska Anchorage
U of Alaska Fairbanks

SKIING
DIVISION III

Babson College
Bates College
Bowdoin College

Clarkson U
Colby College
Colby-Sawyer College
The College of St. Scholastica
Green Mountain College
Gustavus Adolphus College
Middlebury College
Northland College
Plymouth State U
St. John's U (MN)
St. Lawrence U
St. Olaf College
U of Maine at Presque Isle
Whitman College
Williams College

SOCCER
DIVISION I

Adelphi U
Alabama A&M U
American U
Appalachian State U
Belmont U
Birmingham-Southern
College
Boston College
Boston U
Bowling Green State U
Bradley U
Brown U
Bryant U
Bucknell U
Butler U
California Polytechnic
State U
California State U,
Bakersfield
California State U,
Fullerton
California State U,
Northridge
California State U,
Sacramento
Campbell U
Canisius College
Centenary College (LA)

Central Connecticut State U
Clemson U
Cleveland State U
Coastal Carolina U
Colgate U
College of Charleston (SC)
College of the Holy Cross
College of William and Mary
Columbia U-Barnard College
Cornell U
Creighton U
Dartmouth College
Davidson College
DePaul U
Drake U
Drexel U
Duke U
Duquesne U
East Tennessee State U
Eastern Illinois U
Elon U
Fairfield U
Fairleigh Dickinson U,
   Metropolitan
Florida Atlantic U
Florida Gulf Coast U
Florida International U
Fordham U
Furman U
Gardner-Webb U
George Mason U
George Washington U
Georgetown U
Georgia Southern U
Georgia State U
Gonzaga U
Hartwick College
Harvard U
High Point U
Hofstra U
Houston Baptist U
Howard U
Indiana U, Bloomington
Indiana U-Purdue U at
   Indianapolis
Indiana U-Purdue U, Fort
   Wayne

Iona College
Jacksonville U
James Madison U
La Salle U
Lafayette College
Lehigh U
Liberty U
Lipscomb U
Long Island U-Brooklyn
   Campus
Longwood U
Loyola Marymount U
Loyola U (IL)
Loyola U (MD)
Manhattan College
Marist College
Marquette U
Marshall U
Mercer U
Michigan State U
Missouri State U
Monmouth U
Mount St. Mary's U
New Jersey Institute of
   Technology
Niagara U
North Carolina State U
Northeastern U
Northern Illinois U
Northwestern U
Oakland U
Old Dominion U
The Ohio State U
Oral Roberts U
Oregon State U
Pennsylvania State U
Philadelphia U
Presbyterian College
Princeton U
Providence College
Quinnipiac U
Radford U
Rider U
Robert Morris U
Rutgers, State Univ of New
   Jersey, New Brunswick
Sacred Heart U

Saint Francis U (PA)
Saint Joseph's U
Saint Louis U
San Diego State U
San Jose State U
Santa Clara U
Seattle U
Seton Hall U
Siena College
Southern Illinois U
   Edwardsville
Southern Methodist U
St. Bonaventure U
St. Francis College (NY)
St. John's U (NY)
St. Mary's College of
   California
St. Peter's College
Stanford U
State U of New York at
   Binghamton
Stetson U
Stony Brook U
Syracuse U
Temple U
Towson U
U.S. Air Force Academy
U.S. Military Academy
U.S. Naval Academy
U at Albany
U at Buffalo, the State U
   of New York
U of Akron
U of Alabama at
   Birmingham
U of California, Berkeley
U of California, Davis
U of California, Irvine
U of California, Los Angeles
U of California, Riverside
U of California, Santa
   Barbara
U of Central Arkansas
U of Central Florida
U of Cincinnati
U of Connecticut
U of Dayton

U of Delaware
U of Denver
U of Detroit Mercy
U of Evansville
U of Hartford
U of Illinois at Chicago
U of Kentucky
U of Louisville
U of Maine, Orono
U of Maryland, Baltimore
County
U of Maryland, College Park
U of Massachusetts,
Amherst
U of Memphis
U of Michigan
U of Missouri, Kansas City
U of Nevada, Las Vegas
U of New Hampshire
U of New Mexico
U of North Carolina at
Greensboro
U of North Carolina,
Asheville
U of North Carolina,
Chapel Hill
U of North Carolina,
Charlotte
U of North Carolina,
Wilmington
U of North Florida
U of Notre Dame
U of Pennsylvania
U of Pittsburgh
U of Portland
U of Rhode Island
U of Richmond
U of San Diego
U of San Francisco
U of South Carolina Upstate
U of South Carolina,
Columbia
U of South Florida
U of Tulsa
U of Vermont
U of Virginia
U of Washington

U of Wisconsin, Green Bay
U of Wisconsin, Madison
U of Wisconsin, Milwaukee
Valparaiso U
Villanova U
Virginia Commonwealth U
Virginia Military Institute
Virginia Polytechnic
Institute & State U
Wake Forest U
West Virginia U
Western Illinois U
Western Michigan U
Winthrop U
Wofford College
Wright State U
Xavier U
Yale U

SOCCER
DIVISION II

Alderson-Broaddus College
American International
College
Anderson U (SC)
Ashland U
Assumption College
Barry U
Barton College
Bellarmine U
Belmont Abbey College
Bentley College
Bloomfield College
Bloomsburg U of
Pennsylvania
Brevard College
Brigham Young U, Hawaii
Bryant U
C.W. Post Campus/Long
Island U
Caldwell College
California State
Polytechnic U, Pomona
California State U,
Bakersfield
California State U, Chico

California State U,
Dominguez Hills
California State U, Los
Angeles
California State U,
Monterey Bay
California State U, San
Bernardino
California State U,
Stanislaus
California U of
Pennsylvania
Carson-Newman College
Catawba College
Chaminade U
Chestnut Hill College
Chowan U
Christian Brothers U
Clayton State U
Coker College
College of Saint Rose
Colorado Christian U
Colorado School of Mines
Colorado State U-Pueblo
Columbia Union College
Concord U
Concordia College (NY)
Davis and Elkins College
Delta State U
Dixie State College of Utah
Dominican College (NY)
Dowling College
Drury U
East Stroudsburg U of
Pennsylvania
Eastern New Mexico U
Eckerd College
Erskine College
Felician College
Flagler College
Florida Gulf Coast U
Florida Institute of
Technology
Florida Southern College
Fort Lewis College
Francis Marion U
Franklin Pierce U

Gannon U
Georgia Southwestern
  State U
Goldey-Beacom College
Grand Canyon U
Harding U
Hawaii Pacific U
Holy Family U
Humboldt State U
Kentucky Wesleyan College
Kutztown U of
  Pennsylvania
Lander U
Le Moyne College
Lees-McRae College
Lenoir-Rhyne College
Lewis U
Limestone College
Lincoln Memorial U
Lock Haven U of
  Pennsylvania
Lynn U
Mars Hill College
Mercy College
Mercyhurst College
Merrimack College
Mesa State College
Metropolitan State College
  of Denver
Midwestern State U
Millersville U of
  Pennsylvania
Missouri Southern State U
Missouri U of Science and
  Technology
Molloy College
Montana State U-Billings
Mount Olive College
New York Institute of
  Technology
Newberry College
Newman U
North Georgia College &
  State U
North Greenville U
Northeastern State U
Northern Kentucky U

Northwest Nazarene U
Northwood U (MI)
Notre Dame de Namur U
Nova Southeastern U
Nyack College
Oakland City U
Ohio Valley U
Ouachita Baptist U
Palm Beach Atlantic U
Pfeiffer U
Philadelphia U
Post U
Presbyterian College
Queens College (NY)
Queens U of Charlotte
Quincy U
Regis U (CO)
Rockhurst U
Rollins College
Saginaw Valley State U
Saint Anselm College
Saint Joseph's College (IN)
Saint Leo U
Saint Michael's College
Salem International U
San Francisco State U
Seattle Pacific U
Seattle U
Seton Hill U
Shepherd U
Shippensburg U of
  Pennsylvania
Slippery Rock U of
  Pennsylvania
Sonoma State U
Southern Connecticut
  State U
Southern Illinois U
  Edwardsville
Southern New Hampshire U
St. Andrews Presbyterian
  College
St. Edward's U
St. Martin's U
St. Mary's U (TX)
St. Thomas Aquinas College
Stonehill College

Texas A&M International U
Tiffin U
Truman State U
Tusculum College
U of Alabama in Huntsville
U of Bridgeport
U of California, San Diego
U of Central Arkansas
U of Charleston (WV)
U of Colorado, Colorado
  Springs
U of Findlay
U of Hawaii at Hilo
U of Indianapolis
U of Mary
U of Massachusetts at
  Lowell
U of Missouri, St. Louis
U of Montevallo
U of New Haven
U of North Carolina at
  Pembroke
U of North Florida
U of Pittsburgh, Johnstown
U of Puerto Rico,
  Mayaguez Campus
U of Puerto Rico, Rio
  Piedras
U of South Carolina Aiken
U of South Carolina Upstate
U of Southern Indiana
U of Tampa
U of Texas of the Permian
  Basin
U of the District of
  Columbia
U of the Incarnate Word
U of West Florida
U of Wisconsin, Parkside
Upper Iowa U
West Chester U of
  Pennsylvania
West Texas A&M U
West Virginia Wesleyan
  College
Western Washington U
Wheeling Jesuit U

Wilmington U (Delaware)
Wingate U

SOCCER
DIVISION III

Adrian College
Albertus Magnus College
Albion College
Albright College
Alfred U
Allegheny College
Alma College
Alvernia U
Amherst College
Anderson U (IN)
Anna Maria College
Arcadia U
Augsburg College
Augustana College (IL)
Aurora U
Austin College
Averett U
Babson College
Baldwin-Wallace College
Baptist Bible College
Bard College
Baruch College
Bates College
Becker College
Beloit College
Benedictine U (IL)
Bethany College (WV)
Bethany Lutheran College
Bethel U (MN)
Blackburn College
Bluffton U
Bowdoin College
Brandeis U
Bridgewater College (VA)
Bridgewater State College
Brooklyn College
Buena Vista U
Buffalo State College
Cabrini College
California Institute of
    Technology

California Lutheran U
California State U, East Bay
Calvin College
Capital U
Carleton College
Carnegie Mellon U
Carroll U (WI)
Carthage College
Case Western Reserve U
Castleton State College
Catholic U
Cazenovia College
Centenary College (NJ)
Central College (IA)
Centre College
Chapman U
Christopher Newport U
The City College of New
    York
Claremont McKenna-Harvey
    Mudd-Scripps Colleges
Clark U (MA)
Clarkson U
Coe College
Colby College
Colby-Sawyer College
College of Brockport, State
    U of New York
College of Mount St. Joseph
College of Mount St.
    Vincent
The College of New Jersey
The College of St. Scholastica
College of Staten Island
College of Wooster
Colorado College
Concordia College,
    Moorhead
Concordia U (WI)
Concordia U Chicago
Concordia U Texas
Connecticut College
Cornell College
Crown College (MN)
Curry College
Daniel Webster College
Defiance College

Delaware Valley College
Denison U
DePauw U
DeSales U
Dickinson College
Dominican U (IL)
Drew U
D'Youville College
Earlham College
East Texas Baptist U
Eastern Connecticut State U
Eastern Mennonite U
Eastern Nazarene College
Eastern U
Edgewood College
Elizabethtown College
Elmhurst College
Elmira College
Elms College
Emerson College
Emmanuel College (MA)
Emory and Henry College
Emory U
Endicott College
Eureka College
Fairleigh Dickinson U,
    Florham
Ferrum College
Finlandia U
Fitchburg State College
Fontbonne U
Framingham State College
Franciscan U of Steubenville
Franklin & Marshall College
Franklin College
Frostburg State U
Gallaudet U
Geneva College
George Fox U
Gettysburg College
Gordon College
Goucher College
Green Mountain College
Greensboro College
Greenville College
Grinnell College
Grove City College

Guilford College
Gustavus Adolphus College
Gwynedd-Mercy College
Hamilton College
Hamline U
Hampden-Sydney College
Hanover College
Hardin-Simmons U
Haverford College
Heidelberg College
Hendrix College
Hilbert College
Hiram College
Hobart College
Hood College
Hope College
Howard Payne U
Hunter College
Huntingdon College
Husson College
Illinois College
Illinois Wesleyan U
Immaculata U
Ithaca College
John Carroll U
John Jay College of
    Criminal Justice
Johns Hopkins U
Johnson and Wales U
Johnson State College
Juniata College
Kalamazoo College
Kean U
Keene State College
Kenyon College
Keuka College
Keystone College
King's College (PA)
Knox College
La Grange College
La Roche College
La Sierra U
Lake Erie College
Lake Forest College
Lakeland College
Lancaster Bible College
Lasell College

Lawrence U
Lebanon Valley College
Lesley U
LeTourneau U
Lincoln U (PA)
Linfield College
Loras College
Louisiana College
Luther College
Lycoming College
Lynchburg College
Lyndon State College
Macalester College
MacMurray College
Maine Maritime Academy
Manchester College
Manhattanville College
Maranatha Baptist Bible
    College
Marian U (WI)
Marietta College
Martin Luther College
Marymount U (VA)
Maryville College (TN)
Maryville U of Saint Louis
Marywood U
Massachusetts College of
    Liberal Arts
Massachusetts Institute of
    Technology
Massachusetts Maritime
    Academy
McDaniel College
McMurry U
Medaille College
Medgar Evers College
Menlo College
Messiah College
Methodist U
Middlebury College
Millikin U
Millsaps College
Milwaukee School of
    Engineering
Misericordia U
Mississippi College
Mitchell College

Monmouth College (IL)
Montclair State U
Moravian College
Mount Aloysius College
Mount Ida College
Mount Saint Mary College
    (NY)
Mount Union College
Muhlenberg College
Muskingum College
Nazareth College
Nebraska Wesleyan U
Neumann College
New England College
New Jersey City U
New York City College of
    Technology
New York U
Newbury College
Nichols College
North Carolina Wesleyan
    College
North Central College
North Central U
North Park U
Northland College
Northwestern College
Norwich U
Oberlin College
Occidental College
Oglethorpe U
Ohio Northern U
Ohio Wesleyan U
Olivet College
Otterbein College
Pacific Lutheran U
Pacific U (OR)
Penn State Berks College
Penn State Harrisburg
Penn State U, Altoona
Pennsylvania State Univ.
    Erie, the Behrend College
Philadelphia Biblical U
Piedmont College
Plattsburgh State U of
    New York
Plymouth State U

Polytechnic Institute of New York U
Pomona-Pitzer Colleges
Presentation College
Principia College
Purchase College, State U of New York
Ramapo College
Randolph College
Randolph-Macon College
Regis College (MA)
Rensselaer Polytechnic Institute
Rhode Island College
Rhodes College
Richard Stockton College of New Jersey
Ripon College
Rivier College
Roanoke College
Rochester Institute of Technology
Rockford College
Roger Williams U
Rose-Hulman Institute of Technology
Rowan U
Rust College
Rutgers, The State Univ. of New Jersey, Camden
Rutgers, The State Univ. of New Jersey, Newark
Saint Joseph's College (ME)
Saint Mary's U of Minnesota
Saint Vincent College
Salem State College
Salisbury U
Salve Regina U
Schreiner U
Shenandoah U
Simpson College
Skidmore College
Southern Vermont College
Southwestern U (TX)
Spalding U
Springfield College

St. John Fisher College
St. John's U (MN)
St. Joseph's College (Long Island)
St. Lawrence U
St. Mary's College of Maryland
St. Norbert College
St. Olaf College
State U College at Cortland
State U College at Fredonia
State U College at Geneseo
State U College at New Paltz
State U College at Old Westbury
State U College at Oneonta
State U of New York at Cobleskill
State U of New York at Farmingdale
State U of New York at Morrisville
State U of New York at Oswego
State U of New York at Potsdam
State U of New York Institute of Technolo
State U of New York Maritime College
Stevens Institute of Technology
Stevenson U
Suffolk U
Susquehanna U
Swarthmore College
Texas Lutheran U
Thiel College
Thomas College
Thomas More College
Transylvania U
Trine U
Trinity College (CT)
Trinity U (TX)
Tufts U
U.S. Coast Guard Academy

U.S. Merchant Marine Academy
Union College (NY)
U of California, Santa Cruz
U of Chicago
U of Dallas
U of Dubuque
U of La Verne
U of Maine at Presque Isle
U of Maine, Farmington
U of Mary Hardin-Baylor
U of Mary Washington
U of Massachusetts, Boston
U of Massachusetts, Dartmouth
U of Minnesota, Morris
U of New England
U of Pittsburgh, Bradford
U of Pittsburgh, Greensburg
U of Puget Sound
U of Redlands
U of Rochester
U of Scranton
U of Southern Maine
U of St. Thomas (MN)
U of Texas at Dallas
U of Texas at Tyler
U of the Ozarks (AR)
U of the South
U of Wisconsin, Oshkosh
U of Wisconsin, Platteville
U of Wisconsin, Superior
U of Wisconsin, Whitewater
Ursinus College
Utica College
Vassar College
Virginia Wesleyan College
Wabash College
Wartburg College
Washington and Jefferson College
Washington and Lee U
Washington College (MD)
Washington U (MO)
Waynesburg U
Webster U
Wells College

Wentworth Institute of
Technology
Wesley College
Wesleyan U (CT)
Western Connecticut
State U
Western New England
College
Westfield State College
Westminster College (MO)
Westminster College (PA)
Wheaton College (IL)
Wheaton College (MA)
Whitman College
Whittier College
Whitworth U
Widener U
Wilkes U
Willamette U
William Paterson U of New
Jersey
Williams College
Wilmington College (OH)
Wisconsin Lutheran College
Wittenberg U
Worcester Polytechnic
Institute
Worcester State College
Yeshiva U
York College (NY)
York College (PA)

SWIMMING
DIVISION I

American U
Arizona State U
Auburn U
Ball State U
Boston College
Boston U
Brigham Young U
Brown U
Bryant U
Bucknell U
California Polytechnic
State U

California State U,
Bakersfield
California State U,
Northridge
Canisius College
Centenary College (LA)
Clemson U
Cleveland State U
Colgate U
College of Charleston (SC)
College of the Holy Cross
College of William and Mary
Columbia U-Barnard College
Cornell U
Dartmouth College
Davidson College
Drexel U
Duke U
Duquesne U
East Carolina U
Eastern Illinois U
Eastern Michigan U
Fairfield U
Florida A&M U
Florida Atlantic U
Florida State U
Fordham U
Gardner-Webb U
George Mason U
George Washington U
Georgetown U
Georgia Institute of
Technology
Harvard U
Howard U
Indiana U, Bloomington
Indiana U-Purdue U at
Indianapolis
Iona College
La Salle U
Lafayette College
Lehigh U
Louisiana State U
Loyola U (MD)
Manhattan College
Marist College
Miami U (OH)

Michigan State U
Missouri State U
New Jersey Institute of
Technology
Niagara U
North Carolina State U
Northwestern U
Oakland U
The Ohio State U
Old Dominion U
Pennsylvania State U
Princeton U
Providence College
Purdue U
Rider U
Saint Louis U
Seattle U
Seton Hall U
South Dakota State U
Southern Illinois U at
Carbondale
Southern Methodist U
St. Bonaventure U
St. Francis College (NY)
St. Peter's College
Stanford U
State U of New York at
Binghamton
Stony Brook U
Syracuse U
Texas A&M U, College
Station
Texas Christian U
Towson U
U.S. Air Force Academy
U.S. Military Academy
U.S. Naval Academy
U at Buffalo, the State U
of New
U of Alabama, Tuscaloosa
U of Arizona
U of California, Berkeley
U of California, Davis
U of California, Irvine
U of California, Santa
Barbara
U of Cincinnati

U of Connecticut
U of Delaware
U of Denver
U of Evansville
U of Florida
U of Georgia
U of Hawaii, Manoa
U of Illinois at Chicago
U of Iowa
U of Kentucky
U of Louisville
U of Maine, Orono
U of Maryland, Baltimore
   County
U of Maryland, College Park
U of Massachusetts,
   Amherst
U of Miami (FL)
U of Michigan
U of Minnesota, Twin Cities
U of Missouri, Columbia
U of Nevada, Las Vegas
U of New Orleans
U of North Carolina,
   Chapel Hill
U of North Carolina,
   Wilmington
U of North Dakota
U of Notre Dame
U of Pennsylvania
U of Pittsburgh
U of South Carolina,
   Columbia
U of South Dakota
U of Southern California
U of Tennessee, Knoxville
U of Texas at Austin
U of the Pacific
U of Utah
U of Virginia
U of Washington
U of Wisconsin, Green Bay
U of Wisconsin, Madison
U of Wisconsin, Milwaukee
U of Wyoming
Valparaiso U
Villanova U

Virginia Military Institute
Virginia Polytechnic
   Institute & State U
West Virginia U
Western Illinois U
Western Kentucky U
Wright State U
Xavier U
Yale U

SWIMMING
DIVISION II

Adelphi U
Ashland U
Bentley College
Bloomsburg U of
   Pennsylvania
Bryant U
California State U,
   Bakersfield
Catawba College
Clarion U of Pennsylvania
College of Saint Rose
Colorado School of Mines
Delta State U
Drury U
Edinboro U of
   Pennsylvania
Fairmont State U
Florida Southern College
Gannon U
Grand Canyon U
Grand Valley State U
Henderson State U
Indiana U of Pennsylvania
Kutztown U of
   Pennsylvania
Le Moyne College
Lewis U
Limestone College
Mars Hill College
Minnesota State U, Mankato
Missouri U of Science and
   Technology
New Jersey Institute of
   Technology

Ouachita Baptist U
Pace U
Pfeiffer U
Queens College (NY)
Rollins College
Saint Leo U
Saint Michael's College
Salem International U
Seattle U
Shippensburg U of
   Pennsylvania
Southern Connecticut
   State U
St. Cloud State U
Truman State U
U of California, San Diego
U of Findlay
U of Indianapolis
U of North Dakota
U of Puerto Rico,
   Mayaguez Campus
U of Puerto Rico, Rio Piedras
U of South Dakota
U of Tampa
U of Texas of the Permian
   Basin
U of the Incarnate Word
Wayne State U (MI)
West Chester U of
   Pennsylvania
West Virginia Wesleyan
   College
Wheeling Jesuit U
Wingate U

SWIMMING
DIVISION III

Albion College
Albright College
Alfred U
Allegheny College
Alma College
Amherst College
Arcadia U
Augustana College (IL)
Austin College

Babson College
Baldwin-Wallace College
Baruch College
Bates College
Beloit College
Bethany College (WV)
Bowdoin College
Brandeis U
Bridgewater State College
Buffalo State College
Cabrini College
California Institute of
  Technology
California Lutheran U
Calvin College
Carleton College
Carnegie Mellon U
Carroll U (WI)
Carthage College
Case Western Reserve U
Catholic U
Cazenovia College
Centre College
Claremont McKenna-Harvey
  Mudd-Scripps Colleges
Clark U (MA)
Clarkson U
Coe College
Colby College
Colby-Sawyer College
College of Brockport, State
  U of New York
The College of New Jersey
College of Staten Island
College of Wooster
Colorado College
Connecticut College
Denison U
DePauw U
Dickinson College
Drew U
Elizabethtown College
Elms College
Emory U
Eureka College
Fairleigh Dickinson U,
  Florham

Franklin & Marshall
  College
Frostburg State U
Gallaudet U
Gettysburg College
Gordon College
Goucher College
Grinnell College
Grove City College
Gustavus Adolphus College
Hamilton College
Hamline U
Hartwick College
Hendrix College
Hiram College
Hood College
Hope College
Illinois College
Illinois Wesleyan U
Ithaca College
John Carroll U
Johns Hopkins U
Kalamazoo College
Keene State College
Kenyon College
King's College (PA)
Knox College
Lake Forest College
Lawrence U
Lebanon Valley College
Lehman College, City U of
  New York
Lewis & Clark College
Linfield College
Loras College
Luther College
Lycoming College
Macalester College
Marymount U (VA)
Massachusetts Institute of
  Technology
McDaniel College
McMurry U
Middlebury College
Millikin U
Misericordia U
Monmouth College (IL)

Montclair State U
Mount Saint Mary College
  (NY)
Mount Union College
Nazareth College
New York U
North Central College
Norwich U
Oberlin College
Occidental College
Ohio Northern U
Ohio Wesleyan U
Olivet College
Pacific Lutheran U
Pacific U (OR)
Penn State U, Altoona
Pennsylvania State Univ.
  Erie, the Behrend College
Pomona-Pitzer Colleges
Principia College
Ramapo College
Regis College (MA)
Rensselaer Polytechnic
  Institute
Rhodes College
Ripon College
Rochester Institute of
  Technology
Roger Williams U
Rose-Hulman Institute of
  Technology
Rowan U
Saint Joseph's College (ME)
Saint Mary's U of
  Minnesota
Saint Vincent College
Salisbury U
Skidmore College
Southwestern U (TX)
Springfield College
St. John's U (MN)
St. Lawrence U
St. Mary's College of
  Maryland
St. Olaf College
State U College at Cortland
State U College at Fredonia

State U College at Geneseo
State U College at New Paltz
State U College at Old
  Westbury
State U College at
  Oneonta
State U of New York at
  Cobleskill
State U of New York at
  Oswego
State U of New York at
  Potsdam
State U of New York
  Maritime College
Stevens Institute of
  Technology
Susquehanna U
Swarthmore College
Transylvania U
Trinity College (CT)
Trinity U (TX)
Tufts U
U.S. Coast Guard Academy
U.S. Merchant Marine
  Academy
Union College (NY)
U of California, Santa Cruz
U of Chicago
U of La Verne
U of Mary Washington
U of Massachusetts,
  Dartmouth
U of Pittsburgh, Bradford
U of Puget Sound
U of Redlands
U of Rochester
U of Scranton
U of St. Thomas (MN)
U of the South
U of Wisconsin, Eau Claire
U of Wisconsin, La Crosse
U of Wisconsin, Oshkosh
U of Wisconsin, River Falls
U of Wisconsin, Stevens
  Point
U of Wisconsin, Whitewater
Ursinus College

Utica College
Vassar College
Wabash College
Washington and Jefferson
  College
Washington and Lee U
Washington College (MD)
Washington U (MO)
Wells College
Wesleyan U (CT)
Westminster College (PA)
Wheaton College (IL)
Wheaton College (MA)
Whitman College
Whittier College
Whitworth U
Widener U
Willamette U
William Paterson U of New
  Jersey
Williams College
Wilmington College (OH)
Wittenberg U
Worcester Polytechnic
  Institute
York College (NY)
York College (PA)

TENNIS
DIVISION I

Alabama A&M U
Alabama State U
Alcorn State U
Appalachian State U
Auburn U
Austin Peay State U
Ball State U
Baylor U
Belmont U
Bethune-Cookman U
Birmingham-Southern
  College
Boise State U
Boston College
Boston U
Bradley U

Brigham Young U
Brown U
Bryant U
Bucknell U
Butler U
California Polytechnic
  State U
California State U, Fresno
California State U,
  Sacramento
Campbell U
Centenary College (LA)
Chicago State U
The Citadel
Clemson U
Cleveland State U
Coastal Carolina U
Colgate U
College of Charleston (SC)
College of the Holy Cross
College of William and Mary
Columbia U-Barnard
  College
Coppin State U
Cornell U
Creighton U
Dartmouth College
Davidson College
Delaware State U
DePaul U
Drake U
Drexel U
Duke U
Duquesne U
East Carolina U
East Tennessee State U
Eastern Illinois U
Eastern Kentucky U
Eastern Washington U
Elon U
Fairfield U
Fairleigh Dickinson U,
  Metropolitan
Florida A&M U
Florida Atlantic U
Florida Gulf Coast U
Florida State U

Fordham U
Furman U
Gardner-Webb U
George Mason U
George Washington U
Georgetown U
Georgia Institute of
    Technology
Georgia Southern U
Georgia State U
Gonzaga U
Grambling State U
Hampton U
Harvard U
Hofstra U
Howard U
Idaho State U
Illinois State U
Indiana State U
Indiana U, Bloomington
Indiana U-Purdue U at
    Indianapolis
Indiana U-Purdue U, Fort
    Wayne
Jackson State U
Jacksonville State U
Jacksonville U
James Madison U
Kennesaw State U
La Salle U
Lafayette College
Lamar U
Lehigh U
Liberty U
Lipscomb U
Longwood U
Louisiana State U
Loyola Marymount U
Loyola U (MD)
Marist College
Marquette U
Mercer U
Michigan State U
Middle Tennessee State U
Mississippi State U
Mississippi Valley State U
Monmouth U

Montana State U-Bozeman
Morehead State U
Morgan State U
Mount St. Mary's U
Murray State U
New Jersey Institute of
    Technology
New Mexico State U
Niagara U
Nicholls State U
Norfolk State U
North Carolina Central U
North Carolina State U
Northern Arizona U
Northern Illinois U
Northwestern U
The Ohio State U
Oklahoma State U
Old Dominion U
Oral Roberts U
Pennsylvania State U
Pepperdine U
Portland State U
Prairie View A&M U
Presbyterian College
Princeton U
Purdue U
Quinnipiac U
Radford U
Rice U
Rider U
Robert Morris U
Sacred Heart U
Saint Francis U (PA)
Saint Joseph's U
Saint Louis U
Samford U
San Diego State U
Santa Clara U
Siena College
South Carolina State U
South Dakota State U
Southeastern Louisiana U
Southern Illinois U at
    Carbondale
Southern Illinois U
    Edwardsville

Southern Methodist U
Southern U, Baton Rouge
St. Bonaventure U
St. Francis College (NY)
St. John's U (NY)
St. Mary's College of
    California
St. Peter's College
Stanford U
State U of New York at
    Binghamton
Stetson U
Stony Brook U
Temple U
Tennessee State U
Tennessee Technological U
Texas A&M U, College
    Station
Texas A&M U-Corpus Christi
Texas Christian U
Texas Tech U
Troy U
U.S. Air Force Academy
U.S. Military Academy
U.S. Naval Academy
U at Buffalo, the State U
    of New
U of Alabama at
    Birmingham
U of Alabama, Tuscaloosa
U of Arizona
U of Arkansas, Fayetteville
U of Arkansas, Pine Bluff
U of California, Berkeley
U of California, Davis
U of California, Irvine
U of California, Los
    Angeles
U of California, Riverside
U of California, Santa
    Barbara
U of Central Florida
U of Connecticut
U of Dayton
U of Delaware
U of Denver
U of Detroit Mercy

U of Florida
U of Georgia
U of Hartford
U of Hawaii, Manoa
U of Idaho
U of Illinois at Chicago
U of Illinois, Champaign
U of Iowa
U of Kentucky
U of Louisiana at Lafayette
U of Louisville
U of Maryland, Baltimore
   County
U of Maryland, College Park
U of Maryland, Eastern
   Shore
U of Memphis
U of Miami (FL)
U of Michigan
U of Minnesota, Twin Cities
U of Mississippi
U of Missouri, Kansas City
U of Montana
U of Nebraska, Lincoln
U of Nevada
U of Nevada, Las Vegas
U of New Mexico
U of New Orleans
U of North Carolina at
   Greensboro
U of North Carolina,
   Asheville
U of North Carolina,
   Chapel Hill
U of North Carolina,
   Charlotte
U of North Carolina,
   Wilmington
U of North Florida
U of Northern Colorado
U of Notre Dame
U of Oklahoma
U of Oregon
U of Pennsylvania
U of Portland
U of Richmond

U of San Diego
U of San Francisco
U of South Alabama
U of South Carolina Upstate
U of South Carolina,
   Columbia
U of South Florida
U of Southern California
U of Southern Mississippi
U of Tennessee at
   Chattanooga
U of Tennessee at Martin
U of Tennessee, Knoxville
U of Texas at Arlington
U of Texas at Austin
U of Texas at San Antonio
U of Texas, Pan American
U of the Pacific
U of Toledo
U of Tulsa
U of Utah
U of Virginia
U of Washington
U of Wisconsin, Green Bay
U of Wisconsin, Madison
Utah State U
Valparaiso U
Vanderbilt U
Villanova U
Virginia Commonwealth U
Virginia Polytechnic
   Institute & State U
Wagner College
Wake Forest U
Weber State U
Western Illinois U
Western Kentucky U
Western Michigan U
Wichita State U
Winston-Salem State U
Winthrop U
Wofford College
Wright State U
Xavier U
Yale U
Youngstown State U

TENNIS
DIVISION II

Abilene Christian U
Adelphi U
American International
   College
Anderson U (SC)
Armstrong Atlantic State U
Assumption College
Augusta State U
Augustana College (SD)
Barry U
Barton College
Bellarmine U
Benedict College
Bentley College
Bloomfield College
Bloomsburg U of
   Pennsylvania
Bluefield State College
Brevard College
Brigham Young U, Hawaii
Bryant U
Caldwell College
California State
   Polytechnic U, Pomona
Cameron U
Carson-Newman College
Catawba College
Central State U
Chestnut Hill College
Chowan U
Christian Brothers U
Coker College
Colorado Christian U
Colorado State U-Pueblo
Columbus State U
Concord U
Concordia College (NY)
Dallas Baptist U
Delta State U
Dowling College
Drury U
East Central U
East Stroudsburg U of
   Pennsylvania

Eckerd College
Emporia State U
Erskine College
Fairmont State U
Ferris State U
Flagler College
Florida Gulf Coast U
Florida Institute of
    Technology
Florida Southern College
Fort Valley State U
Francis Marion U
Franklin Pierce U
The Georgia College &
    State U
Georgia Southwestern
    State U
Grand Canyon U
Grand Valley State U
Harding U
Hawaii Pacific U
Johnson C. Smith U
Kennesaw State U
Kutztown U of
    Pennsylvania
Lake Superior State U
Lander U
Lane College
Le Moyne College
Lees-McRae College
LeMoyne-Owen College
Lenoir-Rhyne College
Lewis U
Limestone College
Lincoln Memorial U
Lynn U
Mars Hill College
Mercy College
Mercyhurst College
Merrimack College
Mesa State College
Metropolitan State College
    of Denver
Michigan Technological U
Midwestern State U
Millersville U of
    Pennsylvania

Minnesota State U, Mankato
Montana State U-Billings
Morehouse College
Mount Olive College
New Jersey Institute of
    Technology
Newberry College
Newman U
North Carolina Central U
North Georgia College &
    State U
North Greenville U
Northern Kentucky U
Northwest Missouri State U
Northwood U (MI)
Oakland City U
Ouachita Baptist U
Pace U
Palm Beach Atlantic U
Pfeiffer U
Philadelphia U
Post U
Presbyterian College
Queens College (NY)
Queens U of Charlotte
Quincy U
Rockhurst U
Rollins College
Saint Anselm College
Saint Joseph's College (IN)
Saint Leo U
Saint Michael's College
Salem International U
Seton Hill U
Shaw U
Shepherd U
Sonoma State U
Southeastern Oklahoma
    State U
Southern Illinois U
    Edwardsville
Southern New Hampshire U
Southwest Baptist U
St. Augustine's College
St. Cloud State U
St. Edward's U
St. Mary's U (TX)

St. Paul's College
St. Thomas Aquinas College
Stillman College
Stonehill College
Tiffin U
Truman State U
Tusculum College
Tuskegee U
U of Alabama in Huntsville
U of California, San Diego
U of Charleston (WV)
U of Findlay
U of Hawaii at Hilo
U of Indianapolis
U of Mary
U of Missouri, St. Louis
U of Nebraska at Kearney
U of North Alabama
U of North Florida
U of Puerto Rico, Bayamon
U of Puerto Rico, Cayey
U of Puerto Rico,
    Mayaguez Campus
U of Puerto Rico, Rio
    Piedras
U of South Carolina Aiken
U of South Carolina Upstate
U of Southern Indiana
U of the District of Columbia
U of the Incarnate Word
U of the Sciences in
    Philadelphia
U of West Alabama
U of West Florida
Valdosta State U
Virginia State U
Virginia Union U
Washburn U of Topeka
Wayne State U (MI)
West Chester U of
    Pennsylvania
West Liberty State College
West Virginia State U
West Virginia Wesleyan
    College
Western New Mexico U
Wingate U

Winona State U
Winston-Salem State U

TENNIS
DIVISION III

Adrian College
Albertus Magnus College
Albion College
Albright College
Alfred U
Allegheny College
Alma College
Alvernia U
Amherst College
Anderson U (IN)
Anna Maria College
Arcadia U
Augustana College (IL)
Aurora U
Austin College
Averett U
Babson College
Baldwin-Wallace College
Bard College
Baruch College
Bates College
Becker College
Beloit College
Bethany College (WV)
Bethany Lutheran College
Bethel U (MN)
Bluffton U
Bowdoin College
Brandeis U
Bridgewater College (VA)
Bridgewater State College
Brooklyn College
Buena Vista U
Cabrini College
California Institute of
    Technology
California Lutheran U
Calvin College
Capital U
Carleton College
Carnegie Mellon U

Carroll U (WI)
Carthage College
Case Western Reserve U
Castleton State College
Catholic U
Central College (IA)
Centre College
Chapman U
Christopher Newport U
The City College of New
    York
Claremont McKenna-Harvey
    Mudd-Scripps Colleges
Clark U (MA)
Coe College
Colby College
Colby-Sawyer College
College of Mount St. Joseph
College of Mount St.
    Vincent
The College of New Jersey
The College of St.
    Scholastica
College of Staten Island
College of Wooster
Colorado College
Concordia College,
    Moorhead
Concordia U (WI)
Concordia U Chicago
Concordia U Texas
Connecticut College
Cornell College
Curry College
Defiance College
Denison U
DePauw U
DeSales U
Dickinson College
Dominican U (IL)
Drew U
Earlham College
Eastern Nazarene College
Eastern U
Elizabethtown College
Elmhurst College
Elmira College

Emerson College
Emory and Henry College
Emory U
Endicott College
Eureka College
Fairleigh Dickinson U,
    Florham
Ferrum College
Fontbonne U
Franklin & Marshall
    College
Franklin College
Frostburg State U
George Fox U
Gettysburg College
Gordon College
Goucher College
Greensboro College
Greenville College
Grinnell College
Grove City College
Guilford College
Gustavus Adolphus College
Gwynedd-Mercy College
Hamilton College
Hamline U
Hampden-Sydney College
Hanover College
Hardin-Simmons U
Hartwick College
Haverford College
Heidelberg College
Hendrix College
Hiram College
Hobart College
Hood College
Hope College
Howard Payne U
Hunter College
Huntingdon College
Illinois College
Illinois Wesleyan U
Immaculata U
Ithaca College
John Carroll U
John Jay College of
    Criminal Justice

Johns Hopkins U
Johnson and Wales U
Johnson State College
Juniata College
Kalamazoo College
Kenyon College
Keuka College
Keystone College
King's College (PA)
Knox College
La Grange College
La Sierra U
Lake Forest College
Lakeland College
Lancaster Bible College
Lawrence U
Lebanon Valley College
Lehman College, City U of
New York
Lesley U
LeTourneau U
Lewis & Clark College
Lincoln U (PA)
Linfield College
Loras College
Louisiana College
Luther College
Lycoming College
Lynchburg College
Lyndon State College
Macalester College
Manchester College
Manhattanville College
Marian U (WI)
Marietta College
Martin Luther College
Maryville College (TN)
Maryville U of Saint Louis
Marywood U
Massachusetts Institute of
Technology
McDaniel College
McMurry U
Messiah College
Methodist U
Middlebury College
Millsaps College

Milwaukee School of
Engineering
Misericordia U
Mississippi College
Mitchell College
Monmouth College (IL)
Moravian College
Mount Saint Mary College
(NY)
Mount Union College
Muhlenberg College
Muskingum College
Nazareth College
Nebraska Wesleyan U
Neumann College
New York City College of
Technology
New York U
Newbury College
Nichols College
North Carolina Wesleyan
College
North Central College
North Central U
Northwestern College
Norwich U
Oberlin College
Occidental College
Oglethorpe U
Ohio Northern U
Ohio Wesleyan U
Otterbein College
Pacific Lutheran U
Pacific U (OR)
Penn State Berks College
Penn State Harrisburg
Penn State U, Altoona
Pennsylvania State Univ.
Erie, the Behrend College
Philadelphia Biblical U
Piedmont College
Polytechnic Institute of
New York U
Pomona-Pitzer Colleges
Principia College
Purchase College, State U
of New York

Ramapo College
Randolph College
Randolph-Macon College
Rensselaer Polytechnic
Institute
Rhode Island College
Rhodes College
Ripon College
Roanoke College
Rochester Institute of
Technology
Rockford College
Roger Williams U
Rose-Hulman Institute of
Technology
Rust College
Rutgers, The State Univ. of
New Jersey, Newark
The Sage Colleges
Saint Mary's U of
Minnesota
Saint Vincent College
Salem State College
Salisbury U
Salve Regina U
Schreiner U
Shenandoah U
Simpson College
Skidmore College
Southwestern U (TX)
Springfield College
St. John Fisher College
St. John's U (MN)
St. Joseph's College (Long
Island)
St. Joseph's College, New
York
St. Lawrence U
St. Mary's College of
Maryland
St. Norbert College
St. Olaf College
State U College at Oneonta
State U of New York at
Cobleskill
State U of New York at
Farmingdale

State U of New York at Oswego
Stevens Institute of Technology
Stevenson U
Suffolk U
Sul Ross State U
Susquehanna U
Swarthmore College
Texas Lutheran U
Thomas College
Thomas More College
Transylvania U
Trine U
Trinity College (CT)
Trinity U (TX)
Tufts U
U.S. Coast Guard Academy
U.S. Merchant Marine Academy
Union College (NY)
U of California, Santa Cruz
U of Chicago
U of Dubuque
U of La Verne
U of Mary Hardin-Baylor
U of Mary Washington
U of Massachusetts, Boston
U of Massachusetts, Dartmouth
U of Minnesota, Morris
U of Pittsburgh, Bradford
U of Pittsburgh, Greensburg
U of Puget Sound
U of Redlands
U of Rochester
U of Scranton
U of Southern Maine
U of St. Thomas (MN)
U of Texas at Dallas
U of Texas at Tyler
U of the Ozarks (AR)
U of the South
U of Wisconsin, Eau Claire
U of Wisconsin, La Crosse
U of Wisconsin, Oshkosh

U of Wisconsin, Whitewater
Ursinus College
Utica College
Vassar College
Virginia Wesleyan College
Wabash College
Wartburg College
Washington and Jefferson College
Washington and Lee U
Washington College (MD)
Washington U (MO)
Waynesburg U
Webster U
Wentworth Institute of Technology
Wesley College
Wesleyan U (CT)
Western Connecticut State U
Western New England College
Westminster College (MO)
Westminster College (PA)
Wheaton College (IL)
Wheaton College (MA)
Wheelock College
Whitman College
Whittier College
Whitworth U
Wilkes U
Willamette U
Williams College
Wilmington College (OH)
Wisconsin Lutheran College
Wittenberg U
Yeshiva U
York College (NY)
York College (PA)

TRACK, INDOOR
DIVISION I

Alabama State U
American U

Appalachian State U
Arizona State U
Arkansas State U
Auburn U
Baylor U
Belmont U
Bethune-Cookman U
Boise State U
Boston College
Boston U
Brigham Young U
Brown U
Bryant U
Bucknell U
Butler U
California State U, Bakersfield
California State U, Northridge
California State U, Sacramento
Campbell U
Central Connecticut State U
Central Michigan U
Charleston Southern U
Chicago State U
The Citadel
Clemson U
Colgate U
College of the Holy Cross
College of William and Mary
Colorado State U
Columbia U-Barnard College
Coppin State U
Cornell U
Dartmouth College
Davidson College
Delaware State U
DePaul U
Drake U
Duke U
East Carolina U
East Tennessee State U
Eastern Illinois U
Eastern Kentucky U
Eastern Michigan U

Eastern Washington U
Fairleigh Dickinson U,
  Metropolitan
Florida A&M U
Florida International U
Florida State U
Fordham U
Furman U
Gardner-Webb U
George Mason U
Georgetown U
Georgia Institute of
  Technology
Grambling State U
Hampton U
Harvard U
High Point U
Howard U
Idaho State U
Illinois State U
Indiana State U
Indiana U, Bloomington
Iona College
Iowa State U
Jackson State U
Kansas State U
Kennesaw State U
Kent State U
La Salle U
Lafayette College
Lamar U
Lehigh U
Liberty U
Lipscomb U
Long Beach State U
Long Island U-Brooklyn
  Campus
Louisiana State U
Louisiana Tech U
Loyola U (IL)
Manhattan College
Marist College
Marquette U
McNeese State U
Michigan State U
Middle Tennessee State U
Mississippi Valley State U
Monmouth U

Montana State U-Bozeman
Morgan State U
Mount St. Mary's U
New Jersey Institute of
  Technology
Norfolk State U
North Carolina A&T State U
North Carolina Central U
North Carolina State U
North Dakota State U
Northeastern U
Northern Arizona U
Northwestern State U
Oakland U
The Ohio State U
Oklahoma State U
Oral Roberts U
Pennsylvania State U
Portland State U
Prairie View A&M U
Princeton U
Providence College
Purdue U
Quinnipiac U
Radford U
Rice U
Rider U
Robert Morris U
Rutgers, State Univ of New
  Jersey, New Brunswick
Sacred Heart U
Saint Francis U (PA)
Saint Joseph's U
Saint Louis U
Sam Houston State U
Samford U
Savannah State U
Seattle U
Seton Hall U
South Carolina State U
South Dakota State U
Southeast Missouri State U
Southeastern Louisiana U
Southern Illinois U at
  Carbondale
Southern Illinois U
  Edwardsville
Southern U, Baton Rouge

Southern Utah U
St. Francis College (NY)
St. Peter's College
Stanford U
State U of New York at
  Binghamton
Stephen F. Austin State U
Stony Brook U
Syracuse U
Temple U
Tennessee State U
Texas A&M U, College
  Station
Texas A&M U-Corpus
  Christi
Texas Christian U
Texas Southern U
Texas State U-San Marcos
Texas Tech U
U.S. Air Force Academy
U.S. Military Academy
U.S. Naval Academy
U at Albany
U at Buffalo, the State U
  of New
U of Akron
U of Alabama, Tuscaloosa
U of Arizona
U of Arkansas, Fayetteville
U of Arkansas, Little Rock
U of California, Berkeley
U of California, Davis
U of California, Los Angeles
U of California, Riverside
U of Central Arkansas
U of Colorado, Boulder
U of Connecticut
U of Delaware
U of Detroit Mercy
U of Florida
U of Georgia
U of Hartford
U of Houston
U of Idaho
U of Illinois at Chicago
U of Illinois, Champaign
U of Iowa
U of Kansas

U of Kentucky
U of Louisiana at Lafayette
U of Louisiana at Monroe
U of Louisville
U of Maine, Orono
U of Maryland, Baltimore
County
U of Maryland, College Park
U of Maryland, Eastern
Shore
U of Massachusetts,
Amherst
U of Memphis
U of Miami (FL)
U of Michigan
U of Minnesota, Twin Cities
U of Mississippi
U of Missouri, Columbia
U of Missouri, Kansas City
U of Montana
U of Nebraska, Lincoln
U of New Hampshire
U of New Mexico
U of North Carolina,
Asheville
U of North Carolina,
Chapel Hill
U of North Carolina,
Charlotte
U of North Carolina,
Wilmington
U of North Dakota
U of North Florida
U of North Texas
U of Northern Colorado
U of Northern Iowa
U of Notre Dame
U of Oklahoma
U of Oregon
U of Pennsylvania
U of Pittsburgh
U of Portland
U of Rhode Island
U of Richmond
U of South Alabama
U of South Carolina Upstate
U of South Carolina,
Columbia

U of South Dakota
U of South Florida
U of Southern California
U of Southern Mississippi
U of Tennessee at
Chattanooga
U of Tennessee, Knoxville
U of Texas at Arlington
U of Texas at Austin
U of Texas at El Paso
U of Texas at San Antonio
U of Texas, Pan American
U of Tulsa
U of Vermont
U of Virginia
U of Washington
U of Wisconsin, Madison
U of Wisconsin, Milwaukee
U of Wyoming
Utah State U
Utah Valley U
Valparaiso U
Villanova U
Virginia Commonwealth U
Virginia Military Institute
Virginia Polytechnic
Institute & State U
Wagner College
Wake Forest U
Washington State U
Weber State U
Western Carolina U
Western Illinois U
Western Kentucky U
Wichita State U
Winston-Salem State U
Winthrop U
Wofford College
Xavier U
Yale U
Youngstown State U

TRACK, INDOOR
DIVISION II

Abilene Christian U
Adams State College

Adelphi U
Alderson-Broaddus College
American International
College
Anderson U (SC)
Ashland U
Assumption College
Augustana College (SD)
Bellarmine U
Bemidji State U
Bentley College
Bloomsburg U of
Pennsylvania
Bowie State U
Bryant U
C.W. Post Campus/Long
Island U
California State U,
Bakersfield
California U of
Pennsylvania
Carson-Newman College
Central State U
Central Washington U
Chadron State College
Cheyney U of Pennsylvania
Claflin U
Clayton State U
College of Saint Rose
Colorado School of Mines
Concord U
Concordia U, St. Paul
Dallas Baptist U
East Stroudsburg U of
Pennsylvania
Emporia State U
Ferris State U
Fort Hays State U
Grand Valley State U
Harding U
Hillsdale College
Indiana U of Pennsylvania
Johnson C. Smith U
Kennesaw State U
Kentucky State U
Kutztown U of
Pennsylvania
Lake Superior State U

Lees-McRae College
Lewis U
Lincoln U (MO)
Livingstone College
Lock Haven U of
   Pennsylvania
Mansfield U of
   Pennsylvania
Mercy College
Metropolitan State College
   of Denver
Millersville U of
   Pennsylvania
Minnesota State U
   Moorhead
Minnesota State U, Mankato
Missouri Southern State U
Missouri U of Science and
   Technology
Montana State U-Billings
Morehouse College
New Jersey Institute of
   Technology
North Carolina Central U
Northern Kentucky U
Northern State U
Northwest Missouri State U
Northwest Nazarene U
Northwood U (MI)
Pittsburg State U
Queens College (NY)
Queens U of Charlotte
Saginaw Valley State U
Saint Joseph's College (IN)
Seattle Pacific U
Seattle U
Shippensburg U of
   Pennsylvania
Slippery Rock U of
   Pennsylvania
Southern Connecticut
   State U
Southern Illinois U
   Edwardsville
Southwest Baptist U
St. Augustine's College
St. Cloud State U
St. Martin's U

St. Paul's College
St. Thomas Aquinas College
Stonehill College
Tiffin U
Truman State U
U of Alabama in Huntsville
U of Central Arkansas
U of Central Missouri
U of Colorado, Colorado
   Springs
U of Findlay
U of Indianapolis
U of Mary
U of Massachusetts at
   Lowell
U of Minnesota Duluth
U of Nebraska at Kearney
U of New Haven
U of North Dakota
U of North Florida
U of South Carolina Upstate
U of South Dakota
U of Southern Indiana
U of Wisconsin, Parkside
Virginia State U
Virginia Union U
Wayne State College (NE)
West Chester U of
   Pennsylvania
West Texas A&M U
West Virginia State U
Western Oregon U
Western State College of
   Colorado
Western Washington U
Wheeling Jesuit U
Winston-Salem State U

TRACK, INDOOR
DIVISION III

Adrian College
Albion College
Albright College
Alfred U
Allegheny College

Alma College
Amherst College
Anderson U (IN)
Augsburg College
Augustana College (IL)
Aurora U
Baldwin-Wallace College
Bates College
Beloit College
Benedictine U (IL)
Bethany College (WV)
Bethel U (MN)
Birmingham-Southern
   College
Bluffton U
Bowdoin College
Brandeis U
Bridgewater College (VA)
Bridgewater State College
Buena Vista U
Buffalo State College
Cabrini College
Calvin College
Capital U
Carleton College
Carnegie Mellon U
Carroll U (WI)
Carthage College
Case Western Reserve U
Catholic U
Central College (IA)
Centre College
Christopher Newport U
The City College of New
   York
Coe College
Colby College
College of Brockport, State
   U of New York
College of Mount St. Joseph
The College of New Jersey
The College of St. Scholastica
College of Wooster
Concordia College,
   Moorhead
Concordia U (WI)
Concordia U Chicago
Connecticut College

Cornell College
Defiance College
Delaware Valley College
Denison U
DePauw U
DeSales U
Dickinson College
Earlham College
Eastern Connecticut State U
Eastern Mennonite U
Edgewood College
Elizabethtown College
Elmhurst College
Emmanuel College (MA)
Emory U
Fitchburg State College
Franklin & Marshall College
Franklin College
Frostburg State U
Geneva College
Gettysburg College
Gordon College
Goucher College
Greenville College
Grinnell College
Gustavus Adolphus College
Gwynedd-Mercy College
Hamilton College
Hamline U
Hanover College
Hardin-Simmons U
Haverford College
Heidelberg College
Hiram College
Hunter College
Illinois College
Illinois Wesleyan U
Ithaca College
John Carroll U
Johns Hopkins U
Juniata College
Kean U
Keene State College
Kenyon College
Keystone College
Knox College
Lake Erie College
Lawrence U

Lebanon Valley College
Lehman College, City U of
New York
Lewis & Clark College
Lincoln U (PA)
Linfield College
Loras College
Luther College
Lynchburg College
Macalester College
Manchester College
Manhattanville College
Marietta College
Massachusetts Institute of
Technology
McDaniel College
McMurry U
Medgar Evers College
Messiah College
Methodist U
Middlebury College
Millikin U
Milwaukee School of
Engineering
Misericordia U
Mississippi College
Monmouth College (IL)
Montclair State U
Moravian College
Mount Union College
Muhlenberg College
Muskingum College
Nazareth College
Nebraska Wesleyan U
New Jersey City U
New York City College of
Technology
New York U
North Central College
North Park U
Northwestern College
Oberlin College
Occidental College
Ohio Northern U
Ohio Wesleyan U
Otterbein College
Pennsylvania State Univ.
Erie, the Behrend College

Plattsburgh State U of
New York
Polytechnic Institute of
New York U
Principia College
Ramapo College
Rensselaer Polytechnic
Institute
Rhode Island College
Rhodes College
Richard Stockton College
of New Jersey
Ripon College
Roanoke College
Rochester Institute of
Technology
Rockford College
Rose-Hulman Institute of
Technology
Rowan U
Rutgers, The State Univ. of
New Jersey, Camden
Rutgers, The State Univ. of
New Jersey, Newark
Saint Mary's U of
Minnesota
Salem State College
Salisbury U
Simpson College
Springfield College
St. John's U (MN)
St. Joseph's College (Long
Island)
St. Lawrence U
St. Norbert College
St. Olaf College
State U College at Cortland
State U College at Fredonia
State U College at Geneseo
State U College at
Oneonta
State U of New York at
Farmingdale
State U of New York at
Oswego
Stevens Institute of
Technology
Susquehanna U

Swarthmore College
Thiel College
Trine U
Trinity College (CT)
Trinity U (TX)
Tufts U
U.S. Coast Guard Academy
U.S. Merchant Marine
Academy
Union College (NY)
U of Chicago
U of Dubuque
U of La Verne
U of Mary Washington
U of Massachusetts, Boston
U of Massachusetts,
Dartmouth
U of Minnesota, Morris
U of Puget Sound
U of Rochester
U of Southern Maine
U of St. Thomas (MN)
U of the South
U of Wisconsin, Eau Claire
U of Wisconsin, La Crosse
U of Wisconsin, Oshkosh
U of Wisconsin, Platteville
U of Wisconsin, River Falls
U of Wisconsin, Stevens
Point
U of Wisconsin, Stout
U of Wisconsin, Superior
U of Wisconsin, Whitewater
Ursinus College
Virginia Wesleyan College
Wabash College
Wartburg College
Washington and Jefferson
College
Washington and Lee U
Washington U (MO)
Waynesburg U
Wesley College
Wesleyan U (CT)
Westfield State College
Westminster College (PA)
Wheaton College (IL)

Wheaton College (MA)
Whitworth U
Widener U
Willamette U
Williams College
Wilmington College (OH)
Wisconsin Lutheran College
Wittenberg U
Worcester Polytechnic
Institute
Worcester State College
York College (NY)

TRACK, OUTDOOR
DIVISION I

Alabama A&M U
Alabama State U
Alcorn State U
American U
Appalachian State U
Arizona State U
Arkansas State U
Auburn U
Baylor U
Belmont U
Bethune-Cookman U
Boise State U
Boston College
Boston U
Brigham Young U
Brown U
Bryant U
Bucknell U
Butler U
California Polytechnic
State U
California State U,
Bakersfield
California State U, Fresno
California State U,
Fullerton
California State U,
Northridge
California State U,
Sacramento

Campbell U
Central Connecticut State U
Central Michigan U
Charleston Southern U
Chicago State U
The Citadel
Clemson U
Coastal Carolina U
Colgate U
College of the Holy Cross
College of William and Mary
Colorado State U
Columbia U-Barnard
College
Coppin State U
Cornell U
Dartmouth College
Davidson College
Delaware State U
DePaul U
Drake U
Duke U
Duquesne U
East Carolina U
East Tennessee State U
Eastern Illinois U
Eastern Kentucky U
Eastern Michigan U
Eastern Washington U
Fairleigh Dickinson U,
Metropolitan
Florida A&M U
Florida International U
Florida State U
Fordham U
Furman U
Gardner-Webb U
George Mason U
Georgetown U
Georgia Institute of
Technology
Georgia State U
Gonzaga U
Grambling State U
Hampton U
Harvard U
High Point U

Houston Baptist U
Howard U
Idaho State U
Illinois State U
Indiana State U
Indiana U, Bloomington
Iona College
Iowa State U
Jackson State U
Kansas State U
Kennesaw State U
Kent State U
La Salle U
Lafayette College
Lamar U
Lehigh U
Liberty U
Lipscomb U
Long Beach State U
Long Island U-Brooklyn
  Campus
Louisiana State U
Louisiana Tech U
Loyola Marymount U
Loyola U (IL)
Manhattan College
Marist College
Marquette U
McNeese State U
Miami U (OH)
Michigan State U
Middle Tennessee State U
Mississippi State U
Mississippi Valley State U
Monmouth U
Montana State U-Bozeman
Morehead State U
Morgan State U
Mount St. Mary's U
New Jersey Institute of
  Technology
Norfolk State U
North Carolina A&T State U
North Carolina Central U
North Carolina State U
North Dakota State U
Northeastern U

Northern Arizona U
Northwestern State U
Oakland U
The Ohio State U
Oklahoma State U
Oral Roberts U
Pennsylvania State U
Pepperdine U
Portland State U
Prairie View A&M U
Princeton U
Providence College
Purdue U
Quinnipiac U
Radford U
Rice U
Rider U
Robert Morris U
Rutgers, State Univ of New
  Jersey, New Brunswick
Sacred Heart U
Saint Francis U (PA)
Saint Joseph's U
Saint Louis U
Sam Houston State U
Samford U
Santa Clara U
Savannah State U
Seattle U
Seton Hall U
South Carolina State U
South Dakota State U
Southeast Missouri State U
Southeastern Louisiana U
Southern Illinois U at
  Carbondale
Southern Illinois U
  Edwardsville
Southern U, Baton Rouge
Southern Utah U
St. Francis College (NY)
St. Peter's College
Stanford U
State U of New York at
  Binghamton
Stephen F. Austin State U
Stony Brook U

Syracuse U
Temple U
Tennessee State U
Texas A&M U, College
  Station
Texas A&M U-Corpus Christi
Texas Christian U
Texas Southern U
Texas State U-San Marcos
Texas Tech U
Troy U
Tulane U
U.S. Air Force Academy
U.S. Military Academy
U.S. Naval Academy
U at Albany
U at Buffalo, the State U
  of New
U of Akron
U of Alabama, Tuscaloosa
U of Arizona
U of Arkansas, Fayetteville
U of Arkansas, Little Rock
U of Arkansas, Pine Bluff
U of California, Berkeley
U of California, Davis
U of California, Irvine
U of California, Los Angeles
U of California, Riverside
U of California, Santa
  Barbara
U of Central Arkansas
U of Cincinnati
U of Colorado, Boulder
U of Connecticut
U of Delaware
U of Detroit Mercy
U of Florida
U of Georgia
U of Hartford
U of Houston
U of Idaho
U of Illinois at Chicago
U of Illinois, Champaign
U of Iowa
U of Kansas
U of Kentucky

U of Louisiana at Lafayette
U of Louisiana at Monroe
U of Louisville
U of Maine, Orono
U of Maryland, Baltimore County
U of Maryland, College Park
U of Maryland, Eastern Shore
U of Massachusetts, Amherst
U of Memphis
U of Miami (FL)
U of Michigan
U of Minnesota, Twin Cities
U of Mississippi
U of Missouri, Columbia
U of Missouri, Kansas City
U of Montana
U of Nebraska, Lincoln
U of New Hampshire
U of New Mexico
U of North Carolina at Greensboro
U of North Carolina, Asheville
U of North Carolina, Chapel Hill
U of North Carolina, Charlotte
U of North Carolina, Wilmington
U of North Dakota
U of North Florida
U of North Texas
U of Northern Colorado
U of Northern Iowa
U of Notre Dame
U of Oklahoma
U of Oregon
U of Pennsylvania
U of Pittsburgh
U of Portland
U of Rhode Island
U of Richmond
U of San Francisco

U of South Alabama
U of South Carolina Upstate
U of South Carolina, Columbia
U of South Dakota
U of South Florida
U of Southern California
U of Southern Mississippi
U of Tennessee at Chattanooga
U of Tennessee, Knoxville
U of Texas at Arlington
U of Texas at Austin
U of Texas at El Paso
U of Texas at San Antonio
U of Texas, Pan American
U of Tulsa
U of Vermont
U of Virginia
U of Washington
U of Wisconsin, Madison
U of Wisconsin, Milwaukee
U of Wyoming
Utah State U
Utah Valley U
Valparaiso U
Villanova U
Virginia Commonwealth U
Virginia Military Institute
Virginia Polytechnic Institute & State U
Wagner College
Wake Forest U
Washington State U
Weber State U
Western Carolina U
Western Illinois U
Western Kentucky U
Wichita State U
Winston-Salem State U
Winthrop U
Wofford College
Wright State U
Xavier U
Yale U
Youngstown State U

TRACK, OUTDOOR
DIVISION II

Abilene Christian U
Adams State College
Adelphi U
Albany State U (GA)
Alderson-Broaddus College
American International College
Anderson U (SC)
Angelo State U
Ashland U
Assumption College
Augustana College (SD)
Bellarmine U
Bemidji State U
Benedict College
Bentley College
Bloomsburg U of Pennsylvania
Bowie State U
Brevard College
Bryant U
C.W. Post Campus/Long Island U
California State Polytechnic U, Pomona
California State U, Bakersfield
California State U, Chico
California State U, Los Angeles
California State U, Stanislaus
California U of Pennsylvania
Carson-Newman College
Central State U
Central Washington U
Chadron State College
Cheyney U of Pennsylvania
Claflin U
Clark Atlanta U
Clayton State U
College of Saint Rose

Colorado School of Mines
Columbia Union College
Concord U
Concordia U, St. Paul
Dallas Baptist U
Drury U
East Stroudsburg U of
  Pennsylvania
Eastern New Mexico U
Edinboro U of
  Pennsylvania
Emporia State U
Ferris State U
Florida Southern College
Fort Hays State U
Fort Valley State U
Francis Marion U
Glenville State College
Grand Valley State U
Harding U
Hillsdale College
Humboldt State U
Indiana U of Pennsylvania
Johnson C. Smith U
Kennesaw State U
Kentucky State U
Kutztown U of
  Pennsylvania
Lake Superior State U
Lane College
Lees-McRae College
Lenoir-Rhyne College
Lewis U
Limestone College
Lincoln U (MO)
Livingstone College
Lock Haven U of
  Pennsylvania
Mansfield U of
  Pennsylvania
Mars Hill College
Mercy College
Metropolitan State College
  of Denver
Michigan Technological U
Miles College
Millersville U of
  Pennsylvania

Minnesota State U
  Moorhead
Minnesota State U, Mankato
Missouri Southern State U
Missouri U of Science and
  Technology
Montana State U-Billings
Morehouse College
Mount Olive College
New Jersey Institute of
  Technology
North Carolina Central U
Northern Kentucky U
Northern State U
Northwest Missouri State U
Northwest Nazarene U
Northwood U (MI)
Nova Southeastern U
Pace U
Paine College
Pittsburg State U
Queens College (NY)
Queens U of Charlotte
Saginaw Valley State U
Saint Joseph's College (IN)
Seattle Pacific U
Seattle U
Seton Hill U
Shaw U
Shippensburg U of
  Pennsylvania
Slippery Rock U of
  Pennsylvania
Southern Arkansas U
Southern Connecticut
  State U
Southern Illinois U
  Edwardsville
Southwest Baptist U
St. Andrews Presbyterian
  College
St. Augustine's College
St. Cloud State U
St. Martin's U
St. Paul's College
St. Thomas Aquinas College
Stillman College
Stonehill College

Tarleton State U
Texas A&M U-Commerce
Texas A&M U-Kingsville
Tiffin U
Truman State U
Tuskegee U
U of Alabama in Huntsville
U of Alaska Anchorage
U of California, San Diego
U of Central Arkansas
U of Central Missouri
U of Charleston (WV)
U of Colorado, Colorado
  Springs
U of Findlay
U of Indianapolis
U of Mary
U of Massachusetts at
  Lowell
U of Minnesota Duluth
U of Nebraska at Kearney
U of New Haven
U of North Carolina at
  Pembroke
U of North Dakota
U of North Florida
U of Puerto Rico, Bayamon
U of Puerto Rico, Cayey
U of Puerto Rico,
  Mayaguez Campus
U of Puerto Rico, Rio Piedras
U of South Carolina Upstate
U of South Dakota
U of Southern Indiana
U of Tampa
U of the Incarnate Word
U of Wisconsin, Parkside
Virginia State U
Virginia Union U
Wayne State College (NE)
West Chester U of
  Pennsylvania
West Liberty State College
West Texas A&M U
West Virginia State U
West Virginia Wesleyan
  College
Western Oregon U

Western State College of
Colorado
Western Washington U
Wheeling Jesuit U
Winston-Salem State U

TRACK, OUTDOOR
DIVISION III

Adrian College
Albion College
Albright College
Alfred U
Allegheny College
Alma College
Amherst College
Anderson U (IN)
Augsburg College
Augustana College (IL)
Aurora U
Babson College
Baldwin-Wallace College
Bard College
Bates College
Beloit College
Benedictine U (IL)
Bethany College (WV)
Bethel U (MN)
Birmingham-Southern
College
Bluffton U
Bowdoin College
Brandeis U
Bridgewater College (VA)
Bridgewater State College
Buena Vista U
Buffalo State College
Cabrini College
California Institute of
Technology
California Lutheran U
California State U, East Bay
Calvin College
Capital U
Carleton College
Carnegie Mellon U

Carroll U (WI)
Carthage College
Case Western Reserve U
Catholic U
Central College (IA)
Centre College
Christopher Newport U
The City College of New
York
Claremont McKenna-Harvey
Mudd-Scripps Colleges
Coe College
Colby College
Colby-Sawyer College
College of Brockport, State
U of New York
College of Mount St. Joseph
The College of New Jersey
The College of St. Scholastica
College of Wooster
Colorado College
Concordia College,
Moorhead
Concordia U (WI)
Concordia U Chicago
Connecticut College
Cornell College
Defiance College
Delaware Valley College
Denison U
DePauw U
DeSales U
Dickinson College
Earlham College
Eastern Connecticut State U
Eastern Mennonite U
Edgewood College
Elizabethtown College
Elmhurst College
Emmanuel College (MA)
Emory U
Eureka College
Fitchburg State College
Fontbonne U
Franciscan U of
Steubenville
Franklin & Marshall College

Franklin College
Frostburg State U
Gallaudet U
Geneva College
George Fox U
Gettysburg College
Gordon College
Goucher College
Greenville College
Grinnell College
Grove City College
Gustavus Adolphus College
Gwynedd-Mercy College
Hamilton College
Hamline U
Hanover College
Hardin-Simmons U
Haverford College
Heidelberg College
Hendrix College
Hiram College
Hood College
Hope College
Hunter College
Illinois College
Illinois Wesleyan U
Ithaca College
John Carroll U
Johns Hopkins U
Juniata College
Kean U
Keene State College
Kenyon College
Keystone College
Knox College
Lake Erie College
Lakeland College
Lawrence U
Lebanon Valley College
Lehman College, City U of
New York
Lewis & Clark College
Lincoln U (PA)
Linfield College
Loras College
Luther College
Lynchburg College

Macalester College
Manchester College
Manhattanville College
Marietta College
Martin Luther College
Massachusetts Institute of
Technology
Massachusetts Maritime
Academy
McDaniel College
McMurry U
Medgar Evers College
Messiah College
Methodist U
Middlebury College
Millikin U
Milwaukee School of
Engineering
Misericordia U
Mississippi College
Monmouth College (IL)
Montclair State U
Moravian College
Mount Union College
Muhlenberg College
Muskingum College
Nazareth College
Nebraska Wesleyan U
New Jersey City U
New York City College of
Technology
New York U
North Central College
North Central U
North Park U
Northwestern College
Oberlin College
Occidental College
Oglethorpe U
Ohio Northern U
Ohio Wesleyan U
Olivet College
Otterbein College
Pacific Lutheran U
Pacific U (OR)
Pennsylvania State Univ.
Erie, the Behrend College

Plattsburgh State U of
New York
Polytechnic Institute of
New York U
Pomona-Pitzer Colleges
Principia College
Ramapo College
Rensselaer Polytechnic
Institute
Rhode Island College
Rhodes College
Richard Stockton College
of New Jersey
Ripon College
Roanoke College
Rochester Institute of
Technology
Rockford College
Rose-Hulman Institute of
Technology
Rowan U
Rust College
Rutgers, The State Univ. of
New Jersey, Camden
Rutgers, The State Univ. of
New Jersey, Newark
Saint Mary's U of
Minnesota
Saint Vincent College
Salem State College
Salisbury U
Simpson College
Southwestern U (TX)
Springfield College
St. John's U (MN)
St. Joseph's College (Long
Island)
St. Lawrence U
St. Norbert College
St. Olaf College
State U College at Cortland
State U College at Fredonia
State U College at Geneseo
State U College at
Oneonta
State U of New York at
Cobleskill

State U of New York at
Farmingdale
State U of New York at
Oswego
Stevens Institute of
Technology
Sul Ross State U
Susquehanna U
Swarthmore College
Thiel College
Transylvania U
Trine U
Trinity College (CT)
Trinity U (TX)
Tufts U
U.S. Coast Guard Academy
U.S. Merchant Marine
Academy
Union College (NY)
U of Chicago
U of Dallas
U of Dubuque
U of La Verne
U of Mary Washington
U of Massachusetts, Boston
U of Massachusetts,
Dartmouth
U of Minnesota, Morris
U of Puget Sound
U of Redlands
U of Rochester
U of Southern Maine
U of St. Thomas (MN)
U of Texas at Tyler
U of the South
U of Wisconsin, Eau Claire
U of Wisconsin, La Crosse
U of Wisconsin, Oshkosh
U of Wisconsin, Platteville
U of Wisconsin, River Falls
U of Wisconsin, Stevens
Point
U of Wisconsin, Stout
U of Wisconsin, Superior
U of Wisconsin,
Whitewater
Ursinus College

Vassar College
Virginia Wesleyan College
Wabash College
Wartburg College
Washington and Jefferson
    College
Washington and Lee U
Washington U (MO)
Waynesburg U
Webster U
Wesley College
Wesleyan U (CT)
Westfield State College
Westminster College (PA)
Wheaton College (IL)
Wheaton College (MA)
Whittier College
Whitworth U
Widener U
Willamette U
Williams College
Wilmington College (OH)
Wisconsin Lutheran College
Wittenberg U
Worcester Polytechnic
    Institute
Worcester State College
York College (NY)
York College (PA)

VOLLEYBALL
DIVISION I

Ball State U
Brigham Young U
California State U,
    Northridge
George Mason U
Harvard U
Indiana U-Purdue U, Fort
    Wayne
Long Beach State U
Loyola U (IL)
New Jersey Institute of
    Technology
The Ohio State U
Pennsylvania State U

Pepperdine U
Princeton U
Rutgers, The State Univ. of
    New Jersey, Newark
Sacred Heart U
Saint Francis U (PA)
Stanford U
U of California, Irvine
U of California, Los
    Angeles
U of California, Santa
    Barbara
U of Hawaii, Manoa
U of Southern California
U of the Pacific

VOLLEYBALL
DIVISION II

East Stroudsburg U of
    Pennsylvania
Grand Canyon U
Lees-McRae College
Lewis U
Mount Olive College
New Jersey Institute of
    Technology
Quincy U
U of California, San Diego
U of New Haven
U of Puerto Rico, Bayamon
U of Puerto Rico, Cayey
U of Puerto Rico,
    Mayaguez Campus
U of Puerto Rico, Rio Piedras

VOLLEYBALL
DIVISION III

Bard College
Baruch College
Brooklyn College
Carthage College
The City College of New
    York
College of Mount St.
    Vincent

Daniel Webster College
D'Youville College
Eastern Mennonite U
Elms College
Emmanuel College (MA)
Endicott College
Fontbonne U
Hilbert College
Hunter College
Johnson and Wales U
Juniata College
Lancaster Bible College
Lasell College
Lehman College, City U of
    New York
Lesley U
Massachusetts Institute of
    Technology
Medaille College
Medgar Evers College
Milwaukee School of
    Engineering
Mount Ida College
Nazareth College
New Jersey City U
New York City College of
    Technology
New York U
Newbury College
Philadelphia Biblical U
Polytechnic Institute of
    New York U
Purchase College, State U
    of New York
Ramapo College
Rivier College
Southern Vermont College
Springfield College
St. Joseph's College, New
    York
State U College at New Paltz
State U of New York
    Institute of Technolo
Stevens Institute of
    Technology
Stevenson U
U of California, Santa Cruz

Vassar College
Wentworth Institute of
Technology
Yeshiva U
York College (NY)

WATER POLO
DIVISION I

Brown U
Bucknell U
Fordham U
George Washington U
Harvard U
Iona College
Long Beach State U
Loyola Marymount U
Pepperdine U
Princeton U
Santa Clara U
St. Francis College (NY)
Stanford U
U.S. Air Force Academy
U.S. Naval Academy
U of California, Berkeley
U of California, Davis
U of California, Irvine
U of California, Los Angeles
U of California, Santa
Barbara
U of Southern California
U of the Pacific

WATER POLO
DIVISION II

Gannon U
Mercyhurst College
Queens College (NY)
Salem International U
U of California, San Diego

WATER POLO
DIVISION III

California Institute of
Technology

California Lutheran U
Chapman U
Claremont McKenna-
Harvey Mudd-Scripps
Colleges
Connecticut College
Johns Hopkins U
Massachusetts Institute of
Technology
Occidental College
Pennsylvania State Univ.
Erie, the Behrend College
Pomona-Pitzer Colleges
U of California, Santa Cruz
U of La Verne
U of Redlands
Washington and Jefferson
College
Whittier College

WRESTLING
DIVISION I

American U
Appalachian State U
Arizona State U
Bloomsburg U of
Pennsylvania
Boise State U
Boston U
Brown U
Bucknell U
California Polytechnic
State U
California State U,
Bakersfield
California State U, Fullerton
Campbell U
Central Michigan U
The Citadel
Clarion U of Pennsylvania
Cleveland State U
Columbia U-Barnard
College
Cornell U
Davidson College
Delaware State U

Drexel U
Duke U
Duquesne U
East Stroudsburg U of
Pennsylvania
Eastern Michigan U
Edinboro U of
Pennsylvania
Franklin & Marshall
College
Gardner-Webb U
George Mason U
Harvard U
Hofstra U
Indiana U, Bloomington
Iowa State U
Kent State U
Lehigh U
Liberty U
Lock Haven U of
Pennsylvania
Michigan State U
Millersville U of
Pennsylvania
North Carolina State U
North Dakota State U
Northern Illinois U
Northwestern U
Ohio U
The Ohio State U
Oklahoma State U
Old Dominion U
Oregon State U
Pennsylvania State U
Portland State U
Princeton U
Purdue U
Rider U
Rutgers, State Univ of New
Jersey, New Brunswick
Sacred Heart U
South Dakota State U
Southern Illinois U
Edwardsville
Stanford U
State U of New York at
Binghamton

U.S. Air Force Academy
U.S. Military Academy
U.S. Naval Academy
U at Buffalo, the State U
of New
U of California, Davis
U of Illinois, Champaign
U of Iowa
U of Maryland, College Park
U of Michigan
U of Minnesota, Twin Cities
U of Missouri, Columbia
U of Nebraska, Lincoln
U of North Carolina at
Greensboro
U of North Carolina,
Chapel Hill
U of Northern Colorado
U of Northern Iowa
U of Oklahoma
U of Pennsylvania
U of Pittsburgh
U of Tennessee at
Chattanooga
U of Virginia
U of Wisconsin, Madison
U of Wyoming
Utah Valley U
Virginia Military Institute
Virginia Polytechnic
Institute & State U
Wagner College
West Virginia U

WRESTLING
DIVISION II

Adams State College
American International
College
Anderson U (SC)
Ashland U
Augustana College (SD)
Belmont Abbey College
Carson-Newman College
Chadron State College

Colorado School of Mines
Colorado State U-Pueblo
Fort Hays State U
Gannon U
Grand Canyon U
Kutztown U of
Pennsylvania
Limestone College
Mercyhurst College
Mesa State College
Minnesota State U
Moorhead
Minnesota State U, Mankato
New Mexico Highlands U
Newberry College
Newman U
Northern State U
San Francisco State U
Seton Hill U
Shippensburg U of
Pennsylvania
Southern Illinois U
Edwardsville
Southwest Minnesota
State U
St. Andrews Presbyterian
College
St. Cloud State U
Truman State U
U of Central Missouri
U of Central Oklahoma
U of Findlay
U of Indianapolis
U of Mary
U of Nebraska at Kearney
U of Nebraska at Omaha
U of North Carolina at
Pembroke
U of Pittsburgh, Johnstown
U of Puerto Rico,
Mayaguez Campus
U of Puerto Rico, Rio Piedras
U of Wisconsin, Parkside
Upper Iowa U
West Liberty State College
Western State College of
Colorado

WRESTLING
DIVISION III

Augsburg College
Augustana College (IL)
Baldwin-Wallace College
Bridgewater State College
Buena Vista U
Case Western Reserve U
Centenary College (NJ)
Central College (IA)
Coe College
College of Brockport, State
U of New York
College of Mount St. Joseph
The College of New Jersey
Concordia College,
Moorhead
Concordia U (WI)
Cornell College
Delaware Valley College
Elizabethtown College
Elmhurst College
Gettysburg College
Heidelberg College
Hunter College
Ithaca College
John Carroll U
Johns Hopkins U
Johnson and Wales U
King's College (PA)
Knox College
Lakeland College
Lawrence U
Loras College
Luther College
Lycoming College
Manchester College
Maranatha Baptist Bible
College
Massachusetts Institute of
Technology
McDaniel College
Menlo College
Messiah College
Milwaukee School of
Engineering

Mount Union College
Muhlenberg College
Muskingum College
New York U
North Central College
Norwich U
Ohio Northern U
Olivet College
Pacific U (OR)
Plymouth State U
Rhode Island College
Rochester Institute of
   Technology
Roger Williams U
Rose-Hulman Institute of
   Technology
Simpson College
Springfield College
St. John's U (MN)
St. Olaf College
State U College at Cortland
State U College at
   Oneonta
State U of New York at
   Morrisville
State U of New York at
   Oswego
Stevens Institute of
   Technology
Thiel College
Trine U
Trinity College (CT)
U.S. Coast Guard Academy
U.S. Merchant Marine
   Academy
U of Chicago
U of Dubuque
U of Scranton
U of Southern Maine
U of Wisconsin, Eau Claire
U of Wisconsin, La Crosse
U of Wisconsin, Oshkosh
U of Wisconsin, Platteville
U of Wisconsin, Stevens
   Point
U of Wisconsin, Whitewater
Ursinus College

Wabash College
Wartburg College
Washington and Jefferson
   College
Washington and Lee U
Waynesburg U
Wesleyan U (CT)
Western New England
   College
Wheaton College (IL)
Wilkes U
Williams College
Wilmington College (OH)
Worcester Polytechnic
   Institute
Yeshiva U
York College (PA)

Appendix 5

Mixed Sports

These lists identify institutions that offer specific sports, as well as in which division the sport competes. Go to their websites for complete information.

CROSS-COUNTRY
DIVISION I

Houston Baptist U

CROSS-COUNTRY
DIVISION II

Grand Canyon U

EQUESTRIAN
DIVISION III

Alfred U
Becker College
Bridgewater College (VA)
Colby-Sawyer College
Endicott College
Lynchburg College
Roger Williams U
U of Mary Washington
U of the South
Washington and Lee U

FENCING
DIVISION I

Lafayette College

GOLF
DIVISION III

Colby College
D'Youville College
Medaille College
U of Southern Maine
Wells College

RIFLE
DIVISION I

Mercer U
Morehead State U
Murray State U
North Carolina State U
The Ohio State U
Tennessee Technological U
U.S. Air Force Academy
U.S. Military Academy
U.S. Naval Academy
U of Akron
U of Kentucky
U of Memphis
U of Nevada
U of Tennessee at Martin
Virginia Military Institute
West Virginia U
Wofford College

RIFLE
DIVISION II

Georgia College & State U
U of Alaska Fairbanks
North
U of the Sciences in
    Philadelphia

RIFLE
DIVISION III

John Jay College of
    Criminal Justice
Massachusetts Institute of
    Technology
Massachusetts Maritime
    Academy
Rose-Hulman Institute of
    Technology
Wentworth Institute of
    Technology

SKIING
DIVISION III

Massachusetts Institute of
    Technology

SWIMMING
DIVISION II

Adelphi U

TENNIS
DIVISION III

Green Mountain College

TRACK, INDOOR
DIVISION II

Adelphi U
Holy Family U

TRACK, OUTDOOR
DIVISION II

Adelphi U
Holy Family U
North Georgia College &
    State U

About the Author

Without athletics, Dion Wheeler would never have graduated from UW–La Crosse. Growing up in an institution for dependent boys, he was an average student in high school. But a young coach inspired him to both exploit his athletic ability and to take his education seriously, as they were the foundation upon which he would "prepare for the future." And so he did.

Education and athletics have been the motivators of his time. Despite a few interruptions to experience the business world, he has taught and coached at every level: grade school, high school, and college. He has been a presenter and instructor at business, athletic, recruiting, and education seminars and has occasionally been accused of being a motivational speaker.

In addition to his recruiting experience—fourteen years at the high-school level and eleven years at the college level—he managed the recruitment of his two (now grown) children, who were both successfully recruited; one by a Division I state university, the other by a Division III private college. One was an All-American, the other's career was cut short by injury.

His ownership of a college prospect recruiting service was the experience where the final piece of the recruiting puzzle fit. There he exposed, and often negotiated for, academically and athletically qualified prospects to coaches of nearly every sport around the country. His unique grasp of the recruiting process from every angle has prepared him to write this powerful guide.

Dion is retired and lives with his wife, Dianne, in Plainfield, Illinois. He can be reached at dwheeler@ncsasports.org.